THE LONGEST STORY

THE LONGEST STORY

How Humans Have Loved, Hated and
Misunderstood Other Species

Richard Girling

ONEWORLD

A Oneworld Book

First published in Great Britain, the Republic of Ireland and
Australia by Oneworld Publications, 2021

A CIP record for this title is available from the British Library

ISBN 978-0-86154-056-3
eISBN 978-0-86154-057-0

Illustration Credits: Wolf © Education Images/Getty Images; Jackal © Pascal de Munk/
Shutterstock.com; Dolphin © Andrea Izzotti/Shutterstock.com; Lion © Brian Jackman; Red
Stag © Imagebroker/Shutterstock.com; White Rabbit © Angela Holmyard/Shutterstock.
com; Black Cat © PalSand/Shutterstock.com; Domestic Goose © Anne Richard/Shutterstock.
com; Black Rat © T. E./Shutterstock.com; Fox (Watching Us from the Undergrowth) by
Charlie Marshall licensed under CC BY 2.0; Cow © Dave McAleavy/Shutterstock.com; Dog
© Nicole Derricks/Shutterstock.com; Housefly © Gan Chaonan/Shutterstock.com; Dinosaur
© Kikujungboy/Shutterstock.com; Frog © Kurit Afshen/Shutterstock.com; Elephant © Brian
Jackman; Okapi © Jiri Hrebicek/Shutterstock.com; Heavy Horse © Nigel Baker Photography/
Shutterstock.com; Teddy Bear by thepeachpeddler is licensed under CC BY 2.0; Spider ©
Amith Nag/Shutterstock.com; Humpback Whale © Sasin Tipchai/Shutterstock.com; Battery
Hens © Cat Act Art/Shutterstock.com; Farrowing Crate © Ggamies/Shutterstock.com;
Chimpanzee © Abeselom Zerit/Shutterstock.com; Budgerigar © Ronald Wittek/Shutterstock.
com; Rhinoceros © Brian Jackman; Cod © Agencja Fotograficzna Caro/Alamy Stock Photo

Typeset by Tetragon, London
Printed and bound in Great Britain by Clays Ltd, Elcograf S.p.A.

Oneworld Publications
10 Bloomsbury Street
London WC1B 3SR
England

MIX
Paper from
responsible sources
FSC® C018072

For Caroline

Contents

Part Four: Now

Prologue

Humans' acquaintance with animals is as old as their acquaintance with each other. You would think after all this time that we would be clear in our minds about both the nature of other species and our relationships with them. Yet we are mired in confusion. To think about the attitudes of *Homo sapiens* to other species is to lose oneself in a tangle of logical and moral contradictions. How can it be that otherwise humane and caring people who 'love' animals can turn a blind eye to persistent acts of cruelty perpetrated on their behalf? How could it be that a society which cherishes the dog, or thinks it does, could treat the lives of other, equally sentient creatures as industrial processes, or would convert the world's most populous food animal, the chicken, into an honorary vegetable? Who could have believed, at any time before our own, that animal husbandry was a business best conducted indoors? What kind of people pray to baboons; make cuddly toys of man-eaters; invest their human personalities with supposedly animal characteristics; make human surrogates of frogs and guinea pigs; make fictional heroes of everything from elephants to hedgehogs while threatening the very existence of the living animals themselves? Why do so many people think that the best way to see a rare and beautiful animal is along the sights of a rifle?

For all of these, and more, there exist cogent and comprehensible explanations, but to understand them it is necessary to trace their origins deep into prehistory, and to follow their evolution over thousands of years. This is what I have set out to do: to relate the full, love–hate story of Human and Beast from first acquaintance to last. In the beginning, humans struggled to make a niche for themselves in a wilderness that favoured wolves and mammoths. In the end, wildlife is being forced out of unsurvivable man-made landscapes to forge new identities in towns and cities. It is the culmination of a process that began two or three hundred million years ago, when a branching of the phylogenetic tree first differentiated humans from apes. How that branching occurred, and the precise nature of the species it created, is a subject of controversy that still underpins arguments about sexism, racism, religious, political and economic dogma, as well as animal rights and the human propensity for violence.

Through most of historical time, from prehistory until the end of the Second World War, the book is written without benefit of hindsight. The narrative voice knows only what any reasonably educated person would have known *at the time*. The opinions and attitudes, too, are specific to each passing age. Thus we can see how and when the contradictions arose, and how, under the influence of theologians, writers, artists, farmers, hunters, warriors, empire-builders, philosophers, doctors, teachers, showmen and scientists, they have persisted, warped and magnified themselves ever since. Like evolution itself, it is a process that never ceases. Looking forward, we may anticipate a changed world in which the very nature of living organisms could be transformed by technologies more terrifying than the mythical powers of ancient gods.

Richard Girling
Norfolk, England, 2021

PART ONE

IN THE BEGINNING

Hunters, Farmers, Worshippers, Warriors

CHAPTER ONE

Sweet Reason

WE WILL WALK TOGETHER FOR AN AWFULLY LONG TIME. MAN and beast. Them and us. Best friend, worst enemy. The hunter and the hunted.

In the beginning we are inseparable. We are them, they are us; all slime from the same swamp. It will take hundreds of millions of years for anyone to understand what is now happening: organisms dividing, crystallising into species, crawling towards the random moment that we will call the Creation. Relationships develop that are variously symbiotic, parasitic or murderous. Nothing stays the same. Everything is changing into something else, sprouting fins, wings, scales and fur to prepare each one for its niche. Legs appear. Small, weasel-like animals grow and stretch, and go on stretching until they can reach up into trees. They live in the forest, where their long arms and short legs are perfect for swinging through the branches and picking fruit. We are still with them, *in* them, alive but unborn. We travel with them when they move from the forest on to the plain, and stay with them as they begin to change their posture and their shape. Arms shorten, legs lengthen, necks stretch. Upright, on two feet, we walk until we are *them* no more.

For a while we lead parallel lives, us and all the others. We gather from the same plains and forests, eat the same fruit, run from the same predators. Time passes, lots of time, perhaps a millennium or two, and we have learned to make tools out of stone. It means we can kill things and eat meat. We grow stronger, more intelligent, and see our intelligence as a mark of our superiority over all other living things. It is how we are. It is how we are meant to be. Supreme.

More centuries go by, and now we are in the north, fighting the cold in central Europe. Hunting and gathering have a different rhythm here. We do not decide what we will eat: we take only what is offered. For it is not just the ice that has to be endured. Hunger, too, is an insatiable taker of life. There is no green abundance to be gathered. Even reindeer find it hard to stay alive when scraps of grass and lichen are all that winter provides. What saves us is our brains. Our heads have swollen with the growing weight of them, and we have learned to use them well. We *think*. We *reason*. We understand that actions have consequences. We know that if we steal from another person, then he will steal from us, and that he will kill us if he has to. We know also that if we *give* to that person, then he will give to us in return. More than this. We know that if we hunt together, we will have more to eat than if we hunt alone. Our tools and weapons are sharper now, which makes us better hunters, and the meat makes our bones and brains even stronger. We do not submit to fate. If the ice swallows our land, then we migrate like reindeer towards the sun.

Always, we hunt. We share our hunting grounds with wolves, and we can see how alike we are. Like us, they follow a leader and work in packs to kill animals bigger than themselves. Like us, they kill only what they need, share it among themselves and feed their young. But our brains are bigger than theirs. We understand them in ways they do not understand us. We know how important it is not to waste anything. We have found good uses for skins and horns and sinews as well as meat. Because we live in this way, because we have *reasoned*, we know there will always be enough animals left for us to hunt, and that their fur will keep us warm.

And we have magic. By painting animals on the walls of our caves, by *creating* them from nothing, we can make new life. By carving the head of a lion on to the body of a man, we can steal the lion's power. We know there is a world of spirits that we cannot see.

*

Then the world changes. The melting of the ice is at once a good thing and a bad. The land is different now. Forests cover what were once grassy plains where the herds used to roam. The animals are much fewer, harder and further to find, and each one killed is gone for ever.

More time passes – time for our brains to grow even bigger. Unlike young animals, which have to grow up quickly and look out for themselves, our children can develop slowly and take time to learn their parents' skills. The learning is made easier and better because we have many more words with which to express our thoughts and ideas. We have memories to share, hopes to fulfil. And we have instincts that reason cannot always explain. Thus it happens one day that a man or a woman picks up a motherless wolf cub. Why do they do this? For no better reason than that it is small and helpless, big-eyed and appealing, and reminds them of a baby. The young wolf adapts easily to human life, respects the hierarchy of its new pack and faithfully follows its master.

Time is running faster now. Change is occurring over thousands of years instead of millions. Maybe two, maybe three thousand more years pass before our brains make a leap of imagination that changes the world and everything in it. We observe the faithful dog and the realisation dawns: what we have done with the wolf, we can do with others too. Even with dogs to help us, the hunt is more difficult now. Why not make it easier for ourselves by rounding up the animals and keeping them alive until they are wanted? We can convert *prey* into *livestock*. Living meat will always stay fresh, not stink like last week's kill.

But which animals to choose? Our eyes rest first on the obvious: red deer and gazelle. Both give good meat, horns and hides. Both are plentiful. Both graze on the same low ground where people live. But they are nervous, temperamental and too stupid to understand what is expected of them. They don't live like us, or like wolves. They are jealous of their ground but there is no structure to their society, no leaders that all will follow. This means they cannot do as the wolf did, and become part of the human herd.

So we move higher up the mountain and look instead at sheep. These, too, are stupid, but they are stupid in the right way. They like to bunch together, and they blindly follow their leader, who might as well be a human as a ram. Better still, being accustomed to foraging on thin ground, they live frugally. Sheep are not like deer: they are not attuned to rapid flight.

The threat to their survival does not come from predators to be outrun, but from the meanness of their environment. This is knowledge we can turn to good use. We have done it before. By following the way of the wolf, we can bring home young lambs and teach them to be human. But this needs time, and it needs patience. Some men choose instead to drive whole flocks down from the hills and to keep them behind fences. Whichever path we choose, sooner or later we will measure our rewards in meat and wool. But this is only the start of our cleverness. We know that our own children grow up to resemble their parents. So why should the same not be true of lambs? We find that by choosing which ram to couple with which ewe, we can influence the size and shape of each new generation. Over time, horns will disappear from the ewes. Fleeces become softer, woollier and less likely to be wastefully shed.

It makes us think differently about ourselves, and about our place in the world. Our superiority over other species now feels like omnipotence. As hunters we had absolute power over an animal only at the moment of its death. Now we hold entire lives in our hands. We worry that we may be trespassing upon the spheres of the gods, but we trust our holy men to appease the animals' spirits. We take seriously our responsibility to defend and care for our animals, but we do so because they are *property*, our investment for our children's future, our wealth. A man who kills a sheep now is not a hunter. He is a thief.

Our success does not satisfy us. It does not lessen our determination or slow our progress. It tells us that we have all the power we need to give new shape to the world. So we look around us. Above the wild sheep on the mountainside, leaping among the crags, are the goats. So why not these too? We see that they are hardier even than the sheep; so hardy that they do not even need grass to eat. All they need is leaves, which they rise up on their hind legs to pluck from trees. This makes them even more useful to us. Not only are their meat and their skins as good as the sheep's, but their stripping of the land helps us to clear new fields for crops, which their dung then enriches. Settlements grow around the fields, and there is harmony among neighbours.

Our tilling of the soil does not mean we turn away from the beasts. Next into the fold comes the pig. A large boar is not something lightly to be faced by a man who wants to walk away on two unbroken legs. But once again the wolf and the sheep have marked the way for us. Piglets are as weak as babies. Once they have become accustomed to human masters, they give no more trouble than our own infants do. Among trees, where they roam and feed on the forest floor, whole herds can be driven even by children. Where the land is bare they can be kept in pens. They like to huddle together, skin to skin, so they need much less space than sheep or goats. But not everybody likes them. They give plenty of meat, but many people find it less flavoursome than sheep or goat, and they give off a different kind of smell.

Our ambitions swell faster than a well-fed piglet. Now we turn our eyes even to the mighty ox. A bull is stronger than a whole family of men and faster on its hooves than any man on his feet. It can toss a person as high as a treetop, and spill his guts into the sky. A cow is a little smaller, but no milder in temper and no more willing to be handled. The men who tame these beasts are either the cleverest who ever lived, or they are the luckiest. How do they do it? *Why* do they do it? Nobody knows for certain. Sheep, goats and pigs give all the meat we need, so it is not hunger that drives us on. But still we need to possess them, to bend them to our will. What greater test of our human power could there be than to tame the fury in this murderous monster? What greater test of our reason? Oxen will not tread the path of goats and sheep. They cannot be hurried. But we know and understand their needs and their natures. They are our neighbours, and we have always hunted them. We know they can be lured by offerings of water and salt, and we know well enough how to run a spear through their sides. But we find that bringing them closer and closer to our homes is not wise. For the farmers, the ambitious grow-ers of wheat, straying cattle are worse even than the deer. They muddy the watercourses and foul them with dung and urine. They trample the crops. Reason says that they will have to be driven away again, or that we must find some other way to make them do as we want. We have many thoughts about this, and all of them call for work. The simplest way to protect the water and the corn is to keep the animals at a distance from the fields. But even the simplest way is not easy. Should even one animal break free, then the price is a ruined crop. And the animals pay a price of their own. On open ground they are easy meat for bears and wolves. There is no good answer to this. The cattle can be driven into *kraals* at night, but still many of them will be lost. There are those who think the best answer is to keep them close to the settlements and build fences to keep them off the crops. But the problems of wolves and watercourses still remain. This is why others choose to build their fences around the animals themselves.

There is danger in this. An ox inside a fence is no different from one outside it. It has the same hooves, the same horns and the same temper. Faced with these, we need good reason and a firm resolve to persist with what some people think is dangerous folly. But an ox is more than just a mountain of flesh. More than any number of goats or pigs, it shows a man's place in the world. It displays his wealth, and affords him great power in barter. If he wishes to be on good terms with his gods, then an ox is the highest form of sacrifice. Some of the gods themselves wear the heads of bulls. So we have come to this biggest moment in our time. The taming of the ox is a test of our will, of our courage and of our imagination. When the corn growers look at cattle, they do not see meat or bull gods. They see *muscle*. How much faster might they turn the soil if they had bigger ploughs? How much faster might they bring in their crops if they could pile them on carts? And what better to haul the ploughs and the carts than a pair of oxen with the strength of forty men?

But how are we to harness such monsters? We have learned much from our sheep, our goats and our pigs. We know that one ram or one boar will father many young ones with many different mothers. This is the measure of our wisdom. The men decide early which animals will make the best fathers, then all the others have their balls cut off. This has many benefits. It takes away their desire for females; it takes away their urge to fight, and the severed parts make the sweetest meat. Oxen are different from other animals only in their size. The work of the blade is the same, but the need is different. With pigs and sheep we couple the biggest sows and ewes with the biggest boars and rams, to produce the biggest piglets and lambs, so that each generation is fatter than the last. With bulls and cows we choose only the *smallest*. The clever thing is to make them small enough to handle, but still big enough to work.

We do not rest upon this great success. It does not blunt our ambition. What about the horse? This wild, prancing, fleet-footed thing looks difficult to catch, impossible to tame. And yet, after their triumph with the ox, there are men who think that no task is beyond them. They persist, and prove themselves right. In time the horse, too, is grazing peacefully in our fields. It is a job well done. The rich dark meat of a young horse is far better to eat than the sinewy flesh of an ox that has died from exhaustion. And horses bring us entertainment. Young men have taken to climbing on their backs and clinging on while the animals try to throw them off. In hard times, it makes us laugh.

Possessing more animals and planting more crops has made us even hungrier for land. Men want to own not just the sheep and the wheat but also the ground beneath their feet. Others, wise in their own way, see danger in this. They warn us that actions have consequences; that our own greed will collide with the greed of others. If men are to claim what was made by the gods, then how is it to be decided which men will have which land? It will mean fighting. It will mean weak people being driven away by the strong.

These are not the only battles we have to fight. Among the animals we have one close and constant friend, the faithful dog who serves and protects us, and who shares our lives as naturally as our own children do. We have our sheep and our goats, our pigs and our cattle and our horses, which we do not love as we love the dog but which we have good reason to keep from harm. As for all the rest, they bring only teeth, horns and claws. The red deer, which the hunters once rejoiced to see close by, is now a bitter enemy to be driven from the fields. The bear, whose spirit we once worshipped, and the wolf, once a cherished hunting companion, are now bitter enemies to be kept away from the sheep. Where we now make a god of the bull, we make a demon of the wolf. How much we forget! We used to hunt as partners across the plains. Men would fall upon deer the wolves had run to exhaustion; the wolves would fall gratefully upon the remains of our human kills. We forget how much like ourselves the wolf is; how it cherishes its young as we cherish our own. We forget that it is the mother and father of the dog. The wolf is an untameable savage that steals our children. Nobody we know has witnessed this, but we are sure it happens.

Men now begin to divide themselves more than ever into different kinds, higher and lower like the animals. There are owners of animals and land. There are thinkers, outcasts and slaves. There are the distrusted ones who do not look or speak like ourselves, and the despised ones who steal from us. There are wise men who possess all knowledge, and there are storytellers. These men come and go from distant lands, bringing stories of strange beasts that no man could imagine. They tell of an ox that walks in water, of a giant animal with spears in its mouth and tails at both ends of its body, of strange humped horses that feed on sand. They bring other stories too, which they call *tales*. In these, the animals speak with human voices and do good and bad things like people do. These stories tell us that the lion is brave, the jackal is cowardly, the fox sly, the serpent an enemy of all things alive, and that certain birds are wise. We have learned other things for ourselves: that the horse can be taught to accept the weight of a man on its back. That it can pull carts and ploughs, and bear heavy loads for long distances at great speed. We have found that the horse is better at all these things than the ox. It is as if they have crawled into each other's skins, the ox and the horse. Only those who live in lands where there are no horses, and the ones with little brain, still plough with oxen. For all the others it is the horse that draws the world along. The ox is for meat and for sacrifice, and for the milk that we have learned to steal from cows. This is the way of the world now. The ox may bring us comfort, but it is the horse that gives us power.

CHAPTER TWO

The Judgement of Jackals

PEOPLE FAR AWAY, WHO KNOW NOTHING OF EACH OTHER, ALL think the same thoughts. They sow the same crops, hunt the same animals, keep the same livestock, practise the same crafts. Some have learned faster and moved further than others, but everywhere people have become more and more alike, more knowing and more necessary to each other. It happened over great stretches of time. Small settlements grew and swallowed up their neighbours so that the strongest leaders became powerful chieftains, and the strongest chieftains became kings. Through alliances and war they took more and more land, and with the land came more and more people.

The mightiest of these lands is a country which burns in an ocean of sand. A healthy man would take a hundred days to walk from the sea to the waterfall that marks its end. It is a land made and cherished by more gods than any priest could count. A wide river cuts through the sand to the sea, where it spreads like the fingers of a hand. Along the banks, watered by floods, are ribbons of green where people have made their homes. They came from faraway places, following the river. Here they built houses of mud, sowed wheat and barley, raised sheep, pigs and cattle. At first they drank the blood of the cattle, but then they learned how to take milk and how to make cheese. They cut down trees to build boats, and used the boats to catch waterfowl and fish.

All people dreamed of living in this country. From their faraway lands they brought their different ways, their gods and their rulers. Kings traded with other kings and grew even richer. From distant parts of Africa, donkeys bore goods cherished for their beauty. They brought gold from the earth, ebony from the forest, ivory from elephants and skins from cats. To secure peace, neighbouring lands sent tributes of panther skins, tusks and living elephants. At Hierakonpolis the elephants shared a crowded menagerie with hippopotami and baboons. To men and women in this land, animals are everything. They are food, wealth, companions, gods.

Long before all this happened, there was nothing: no gods, no people, no animals or birds. More than one story is told about how the emptiness was filled. In Heliopolis, City of the Sun, people give thanks to Atum, a god so powerful that his first act was to create himself, after which he sat upon a mound amid the waters of chaos and began to make the universe. But not even Atum could manage such a labour on his own. He needed help, and this too he conjured from within himself. Some say that he ejected the god Shu with his wife and sister Tefnut by masturbating. Others believe he sneezed or spat them out. Shu, whom he appointed god of the air, and Tefnut, goddess of water, then lay together to bear the earth god Geb and the sky goddess Nut. These two in turn brought forth the deities Isis, Osiris, Nephthys and Seth. The sun itself, so it is said, hatched from a golden egg laid by the Great Honker, a goose from whose beak emerged the very first sound to be heard in the universe. All was now ready for life to begin.

When the people came, they found a land swarming with life. Fish swam, birds flew, and the Earth teemed with creatures of every kind: antelopes, gazelles and deer; ostriches and asses; elephants and giraffes; rhinoceroses, hippopotami, goats and cattle. By the water's edge, crocodiles reaped their bloody harvest. Around the desert, lions and hyenas did the same. Life for the animals was fragile and raw. For humans it was no different. As it was in every other land where people lived, they hunted and gathered plants. Like other people they learned to grow corn and to tend cattle, sheep, goats and pigs. Asses, too, they kept and turned into donkeys. Gradually they moved away from hunting and became herdsmen, fishermen and farmers.

But no land can provide for all. As the people took more and more for their farms, so less and less remained for others. Year after year the animals were driven further and further away. The elephants, the giraffes, the ostriches, the antelopes and the gazelles became at first uncommon, and then they lived only in people's memories. Only the crocodile and the hippopotamus, and other denizens of swamp and river, went on thriving as they did before. It was not a war of equals. No man on his own could kill an elephant or a lion, but against the forces of all mankind nothing could prevail. The animals were forced from the land like beaten enemies.

The heavens now teem with gods and goddesses, just as the land once teemed with gazelles. Many of these deities take the form of animals so that people find themselves kneeling before the very same creatures they have eaten for dinner. Even the mightiest gods can manifest themselves as beasts, and in the minds of the people such magic is as ordinary as the power of kings. Who could wonder that the temporal and spiritual worlds are so different? A man might pray to an animal, yet if he treats his enemy like an animal it does not mean he honours him as a god. The gods themselves are not troubled by cruelty. A man can butcher an ox without enraging the fertility goddess Hathor, who manifests as a cow. Killing a snake is no disrespect to the cobra-headed goddess of the harvest Renenutet, nor is spearing a lion any offence to the lion-headed Tefnut or Shu.

Nothing on Earth is untouched by these gods. They govern the arc of the sun, the rhythm of the seasons, the flow of the river, everything that has a beginning and an end. Life itself begins under the eye of goddesses. A divine frog and a hippopotamus watch night and day over a woman's pregnancy, her confinement and the birth of her child. The frog goddess Heqet ensures the woman's fertility, and the hippopotamus Taweret preserves mother and child from evil. And so it continues, throughout life and into eternity. There is not a breath of air, not a morsel of food, not a ray of sun or moon, not a birth or a death, not a moment of joy or of sorrow that is not given by a god. Of all their gifts, the greatest is the sun, and the greatest of the gods is Ra, who steers it across the sky. This bringer of life is seen most often wearing the head of a falcon, but there is a moment at daybreak when he becomes a humble dung-beetle. It is the job of Khepri, as Ra is called at this hour, to heave the sun out of the underworld and to push it across the sky just as a beetle heaves a dung-ball from its burrow.

When the larvae hatch and fly from the ball in glittering clouds, it reminds the people of all Ra's powers of creation and renewal.

After the sun, the greatest giver of life is the river. Its gift is the fertility of the land. Its price when the flood runs high is the homes of the people, which it turns back into mud. At the end of the day, when Ra drops the sun back into the underworld, he becomes Khnum, the ram-headed god of the river. More is owed to Khnum than just the seething waters. He gathers the clay carried down by the flood and spins it into the bodies of children. These he brings to women's wombs and commends to the care of hippopotamus and frog. Borne on these same waters come other gods to give or take from the people. The wisest of these is Thoth, creator of writing and scribe to the gods, law-maker, father of science, god of intelligence, meditation, magic and thoughtfulness, surveyor of the heavens. He wears the head of an ibis, noblest bird of the river. In his honour, millions of these beautiful creatures are hatched at Hermopolis to be sacrificed and embalmed for their flight into the afterlife. The river is home also to Sobek, an ill-tempered crocodile god who, for reasons known only to himself, might protect the weak or crush them in his jaws. Fish, too, can be touched by divinity. The tilapia preserves its young by swallowing them at moments of danger and spitting them out again when the danger passes. This is why the love goddess Hathor made it a symbol of rebirth. The Oxyrhynchus fish swallows but does not spit. Into its belly went the severed penis of the god Osiris, son of the lion twins Tefnut and Shu, which floated down to it after he was killed and cut up by his jealous brother Seth. Osiris's wife and sister, Isis, found all but one of the scattered parts and put him back together again, but the great god is condemned evermore to rule the underworld without a penis.

The meaning some people take from this is that the heavens are no place for penises, and that the purity of the gods is freedom from animal lusts. Others prefer the examples of the great masturbator Amun and the ram god Khnum, who flaunt their phalluses as instruments of power. The sexuality of the heavens, where mother, wife and sister may all be the same woman, inspires brothers and sisters on Earth to follow their example and make children together. Herdsmen and farmers have learned over time that it is not always wise for their animals to do the same.

Very little that lives and breathes is not somewhere connected to a god. Anubis, patron of death, embalming and mourning, is a jackal known for haunting graveyards. Among living animals, the most revered is the Apis bull of Memphis, which can cure disease with its breath and is reborn after death. Other gods might appear as baboons, geese, hippos, crocodiles, herons, ostriches, pigs, rams, cats or scorpions. It is of no account that the living fur and flesh lacks the virtues of the deity. In the higher regions no animal is restricted by its earthly nature. This is not always uplifting to the animal's spirit. The evil Seth is depicted as a pig, an animal once highly favoured for its flesh but now forsworn by many as unclean. Some say this is because Seth disguised himself as a black pig to attack the sky god Horus, and because Ra thereafter cursed the pig as an abomination. The Greek Herodotus in his history remarked that any man who by accident touched a pig should throw himself into the river with all his clothes on. Swineherds are not allowed in the temples, nor will any honourable man allow his daughter to marry one. For all these reasons, wise men believe the pig will never regain its place at the tables of the rich or the righteous. To eat badly is to live badly. Foreigners who come to Egypt, and who do not live as Egyptians do, are as untouchable as the pigs they eat. Swine-eating is not their only fault, or the worst. They have an incorrect way of writing, from left to right instead of right to left as Thoth has shown. Most contemptibly of all, they eat the heads of sacrificed cattle. No Egyptian will kiss a Greek, or use any knife or cooking pot that has been used by a Greek, for fear that it has been contaminated by such vileness. Only on the shoulders of Hathor is a cow's head sacred.

The priests have much more than cattle to offer to the deities. Many donkeys are needed to bring to the temples all the fowls, milk, honey, fruit, vegetables, bread and beer that are to be shared with the gods that provided them. The sharing is of great importance, for it strengthens the union between gods and those who worship them. The gods consume the *spirit* of the food; the priests and people swallow the rest. Thus it is seen that the bellies of the priests swell according to the size of the sacrifice, and that the people fatten likewise. Cattle are brought to the temples by rich citizens paying their taxes, and are butchered under the direction of priests. It is always the same. The slaughterman knots a rope around one of the animal's legs, then pulls it tight over its back until it falls. There on the ground, before an altar dripping with wine, its throat is slit. The butchers go on working with their knives until the head rolls off, when the priests call down imprecations. They pray that any evil that might befall themselves or the people of Egypt might fall instead upon the head of the butchered beast. There are but two possible destinies for such a cursed object. It might be thrown like carrion into the river, or it might be sold to Greeks. After the head is gone the butchers skin the carcass, divide the meat and the organs and roast them on the fire. It is not only in the temples that this goes on. Numerous festivals are held on special days throughout the year, when images of gods are carried through the streets or floated on barges. The festivals last for many days, and the people honour each god with gaping jaws and bursting bellies. The feasting is free, and for many ordinary Egyptians it is the only time they will ever taste meat.

Herodotus also has much to say about the cat, a creature which the Egyptians themselves brought from the wilderness into their homes. But they have not tamed it. Cats have their own goddess, Bastet, who is also protector of the pharaohs, guardian of pregnant women and a fierce defender of her father Ra. Cats are not like dogs or sheep, nor any other animals attached to the human world. The cat disdains the company of others, follows no one and lives alone in territory it marks as its own. Gifts of food might keep it close to humans, but it still hunts by itself in the dark. If the offerings cease it will not starve, nor will it submit to any master. For an Egyptian, to live with a cat is to live close to Bastet herself. Any person who kills one must pay for the crime with his life. When the gods themselves claim a cat, every person in the household will shave off their eyebrows in mourning, and the corpse will be taken to be embalmed and entombed among millions of others at Bubastis. When a dog dies, the eyebrows alone are insufficient. Every part of the head and the body must be shaved, though the dog itself may be buried among people in the city where it lived.

Horses were brought to Egypt too late to be raised up by the deities. Their place is on Earth, harnessed to chariots. Yet the gods do not ignore them. The horse is a beast of war, not a plodder in the fields, which earns it the protection of the war god Resheph and the warrior goddess Astarte. The chariot was brought to Egypt by the Hyksos people, rough invaders who took land in the delta by force. Here they stayed for more than a hundred years until they were driven out by the Theban kings Seqenenre Taa, Kamose and Ahmose. But the Egyptians understood the chariot's power, and used it to tighten their grip on the world. Mastery of a chariot, more even than skill in hunting, marks out young men of quality. In war they drive at the gallop with a man at the reins and another behind with a bow. No art is more highly esteemed than killing enemies from a chariot, which is why the pharaoh Amenhotep II is forever remembered by his people. As a boy he learned in the stables of his father, Thutmose III, and was famous as a young man for shooting arrows through copper targets while steering his chariot with reins tied around his waist. Chariots are highly prized spoils of war. Thutmose III captured eight hundred and ninety-four of them, and more than two thousand horses. In his first campaign in Syria, Amenhotep himself brought home three hundred, along with prisoners whom he hanged from the temple walls. Nobody shaves their eyebrows for slaughtered humans.

For the Egyptians themselves there is no finality in death. It is the moment of transition from one state to the next, like a port of embarkation for the heavens. But they must be fit for the journey. Before they go, they must prove to the satisfaction of Osiris, god of the underworld, that they are ready. He needs to be sure of their virtue as humans before he can allow them to go forward as spirits. In a Declaration of Innocence the soul of the deceased must swear before the god that the living person has not committed any of forty-two sins of dishonesty, violence, sexual misconduct, untruthfulness, ill-temper, blasphemy or abuse of cattle belonging to a god. The truth of the confession is tested by the jackal Anubis, who weighs the petitioner's heart against an ostrich feather. For those who balance the scales, the reward is to live on as transfigured spirits. For those who tip the scales, it is to suffer the ultimate horror of Ammit. The three most feared animals in Egypt are the lion, the hippopotamus and the crocodile. The monstrous Ammit, Eater of Hearts, is the aggregate of them all. He has the head of a crocodile, the body of a lion, the legs of a hippopotamus and the sum of all their cruelties. In his god-given task of swallowing the sinner's heart, he banishes the soul to an exile of eternal restlessness, the animals' ultimate revenge.

CHAPTER THREE

The Naming of Parts

NO EMPIRE, HOWEVER MIGHTY, LASTS FOR EVER. BIG FISH ARE swallowed by bigger fish, old lions banished by young. So it is with Egypt. The people who subdue it are called Hellenes, or Greeks. They are led by the Macedonian King Alexander III, who succeeded to the throne at the age of twenty and dedicated his life to fighting. After Egypt he conquered the Persian Empire, then the whole of the world as far as India. The people call him *Alexander the Great*, and *King of Asia*.

The Greeks are a different kind of people, lovers of wine, liberty, language and wit. Their passions are aroused by disputation, poetry, sex and the sea, and by loathing of all authority save their own. Few Greeks live more than a day's walk from the sea. A heaving deck is more comfortable to them than the rump of a horse, and they swim as naturally as they walk. They are a paradoxical people. Fear of the gods does not hinder their search for absolute truths. It is no business of the gods how a crocodile hinges its jaws, or how blood coagulates, or how a frog croaks. Greeks long ago understood that questions like these, about the structures and functions of living things, were the province of thinkers like Hippocrates and Pythagoras, far beyond the grasp of priests. The philosopher-poet Xenophanes of Colophon went so far as to insist that gods were mere projections of the human mind and that all miracles assigned to them must find their explanations on Earth. Independence of mind is as important to Greeks as independence of body, though pleasure in their own freedom does not lessen their urge to enslave others. Nor does their love of beauty blunt their swords. When no foreign enemies remain, then they fight among themselves. Wars are fought between their own city-states, Sparta and Athens, and there are bloody quarrels between democrat and tyrant.

For the Athenians, pleasure in all its many forms is as important as militarism is to the Spartans. Their minds are filled by poets, and their bellies by fishermen and farmers. Their desire for self-reliance also leads many idealistic Greeks to feed themselves from family farms. The poet Hesiod set down the priorities: a good farmer, he said, should provide himself with a house, a plough, an ox and a slave-woman to walk behind it. Animals are central to the lives of all Greeks. They hunt, breed and work them, slaughter, eat and sacrifice them to their gods. But, unlike the Egyptians, their interest extends far beyond everyday husbandry, mythology and worship. They have an insatiable need to simply *know*, with knowledge its own reward. The gods and goddesses themselves take human not animal form, though they may adopt birds and animals appropriate to their sphere of interest. Zeus, god of the sky, has his eagle. Aphrodite, goddess of love, has her dove. The huntress Artemis has her deer; Athena, goddess of wisdom, her owl. Hades, god of death, has the many-headed dog Cerberus to guard the underworld, and the sea god Poseidon has his horse.

Hunting for trade and slaves, which takes them ever further from home, instils in Greeks not just a deep understanding of the sea but also a profound dread of monsters that rise from the depths to swallow innocent sailors and their ships. It is a terror that intensifies every time a vessel fails to return to port. The sea contains friendly beings too. Glaucus, for example, was a mortal fisherman who transformed himself into a sea god, half man and half fish, by swallowing a magical herb. By some accounts it was Glaucus himself who saved the Argonauts from the storm. Real animals, too, can be saviours. For a sailor there is nothing more reassuring than the sight of dolphins dancing in the wake of his ship. Their habit of saving people from drowning began when Taras, son of Poseidon, was snatched from a shipwreck by an animal sent by his father, an event which the Greeks celebrate on their coins. The wine god Dionysus also rides a dolphin. As if to confirm their union, the animals share the Greeks' love of music, and are drawn to ships by the sound of the pipers who play to keep the rowers in unison.

Animals on land also have an ear for a tune. Stags and hinds are so mesmerised by singing and pipe-playing that they will lie down to listen, allowing hunters to slay them at their leisure. But the men are not looking for food. They hunt purely for sport and prestige. They worship the hunter goddess Artemis and the god Apollo, whose earthly love was Cyrene, a boisterous Thessalian maiden who preferred hunting to the respectable pursuits of needle and loom. When Apollo first saw her she was wrestling a lion. Wealthy Athenians like to chase boars, stags, hares, partridges, larks and quail, which their long-legged hunting dogs drive into snares or nets. There are many ways in which a bird or an animal might be killed. Hunters strike them with slings, arrows, javelins, daggers, bludgeons, even with sticks to crush the heads of hares. When the quarry is big and carnivorous, they lay branches across a steep-sided pit and bait the trap with a lamb. Some like also to fish with hook and line, though fishing is scorned as an inglorious pursuit which calls for low cunning rather than strength, and which provides no vigorous exercise. For the women of the city, the best thing about hunting and fishing is that it creates work for them making nets.

Greeks have no false notions about the lives of animals. Like herdsmen and hunters, philosophers believe that the animals' lack of reason means they are no more deserving of care than a stick, a stone or a slave. A sheep is just a weight of mutton, flesh without a soul. An elephant is no more than its ivory. The only dissenter, long ago, was Pythagoras, who forswore flesh and wine, and whose only indulgence was the honey he sometimes spread on his bread and herbs. For him it was morality, not taste, that mattered. He believed that eschewing meat was essential to ensure peace in the world. To feast on death was to lose respect for life. Hence it followed that for as long as men killed animals, they would go on killing each other. Athenians take no notice of all this nonsense, secure in the knowledge that intelligent men and women are able to distinguish between animal and human lives, and especially between animal and human flesh, which is abhorrent to them. No further thought is required.

The reality is that common Athenians eat meat only rarely. A suckling pig might be had for three drachmas, but meat from other animals is too costly for all but the wealthiest households. It is for this reason that the price of sardines and anchovies is a subject of abiding public interest.

Athenians also enjoy shellfish, squid, octopus and freshwater eels, though these, too, are expensive. This is why the fish market is one of the most crowded places in the city. Out in the fields, life is much more bountiful for the landowners, who fill their larders with pork, mutton, goat and chicken, as well as the scraps of feather and fur they bring home from the hunt. Greeks everywhere like to drink milk, especially milk from the goat, and more particularly wine, which they keep in the skins of pigs and goats. For cheese-making, cow's milk is more productive if less flavoursome than goat's. Aristotle records that nine gallons of goat's milk will produce nineteen cheeses, whereas cow's milk will make thirty. On the rare occasions that milk is obtained from a ram or a bull, or eggs are found inside a cock, the event is heavily portentous. The Oracle at Delphi reads it as a sign of future riches.

Consulting the Oracle calls for strength and stamina as well as faith. The Sybil at the sanctuary of Apollo attends only on particular days of the year, and the sanctuary itself can be reached only by a steep and rocky hillside. Even then, the priestess might have nothing to say if the signs are not propitious. If a ram does not tremble when salt is sprinkled upon it, then the Oracle stays mute. Animals, alive or dead, always have much to tell. Euripides was right to describe birds as 'the heralds of the gods'. The patterns of their flight and song tell us a great deal about what the gods have in store for us. A bird skimming downwind means the man who sees it will be successful. A bird hanging in mid-air says he will fail. It is a bad sign if an eagle flies from the left, a good sign if it comes from the right. But nothing is more eloquent than the entrails of an animal freshly killed. The divine will is revealed through the condition of the gall bladder, the liver and the vein that carries blood to it. Any abnormality of the lobes of the liver, and worst of all the absence of a lobe, is an omen fatal to any enterprise. Even the Spartans never join battle if the entrails are not propitious.

Most citizens eat meat only on feast days. The public altars on these occasions are scenes of slaughter where the people's noses are assailed by the reek of blood, smoke and roasting flesh, and their ears by the bellowing of animals facing death. At the festival of Panathenaea, held in honour of the city's goddess Athena, the feasting is preceded by gymnastic and musical contests, boat and chariot races, dancing and a magnificent procession through the streets to the altar where cattle are sacrificed by the hundred. The gift to Athena herself is the titillating aroma of burning bones and fat drifting heavenward while the roasted flesh is enjoyed by the people. Seldom is gratitude to a goddess more keenly felt.

Only philosophers understand more about animals than hunters and herdsmen do. Herdsmen know that when many cows submit to the bull, it means stormy weather is coming. They know that if a ewe or a she-goat receives a male while a north wind is blowing, then the lambs or kids will be male. If the wind is from the south, they will be female. As to colour, lambs are born white or black according to the colour of the veins beneath the tongue of the ram. The colour may also be influenced by which river the ram has drunk from: the lambs may be white or black according to the source of the water, or, in a singular case, yellow. Water is of special importance to sheep, which fatten best when they have plenty to drink. To ensure this happens, the herdsmen feed them salt.

Animals are also welcomed into people's homes. Dogs are not only popular pets and hunting companions, but they also have powers of heal-ing. The shrine of Asclepius at Epidaurus is alive with dogs and snakes that cure wounds or illnesses by licking the affected parts. Sores fade from the skin; sight returns to the blind. Cats are not as popular as dogs, and weasels are preferred for controlling mice. But not all mice are pests. Some are kept as children's pets: likewise birds, polecats, tortoises, weasels and grasshoppers. For men, animals provide sport as well as company. Dog is matched against cat, cock against cock. The birds are made to eat garlic and onions to heighten their ferocity, and their spurs lethally tipped with bronze. Much money changes hands, both in wagers and in the trading of birds. For some boys and men, their love of animals exceeds even their lust for women, and they visit sheep and goats for the same carnal purposes. The sexuality of beasts is explicit in the centaurs and the orgiastic satyrs with their horses' ears, tails and enormous phalluses. Sex, they seem to say, is where man meets beast, which he does with the blessing of the gods.

The beast in men is released in other ways too. In their treatment of slaves, enemies and inferiors they have nothing to learn from lion or crocodile. Perhaps the cruellest man who ever lived was Phalaris, a Sicilian despot whose favourite sport was roasting his enemies inside a vast bronze oven, cast in the shape of a bull. Their howls of agony, he liked to think, were the bellowings of the reawakened bull. Astrea, the virgin goddess of justice, must have smiled when his people rebelled, shut him in his own oven and made the bull bellow one last time.

The more usual place for cattle is on the sacrificial altar, shackled to a cart or plough, or trampling corn. Greater glory belongs to the horse. It serves in the cavalry, pulls a chariot or, in the guise of the winged stallion Pegasus, strikes water from mountainsides. It was through his cavalry that Alexander the Great, as drunk on power as he often was on wine, established his World Empire. It is not just their stamina, speed and agility that make horses so perfect for warfare. Being strongly hierarchical, they will unfailingly follow their leaders. The highest ranking mare leads from the front while the stallion drives the herd from behind. It is in every stallion's nature to be dominant, which is why breeders castrate all but those needed for procreation. In a cavalry charge, the stallion's position is taken by a mounted soldier but the herd's obedience is the same. It was the historian Xenophon who taught soldiers how to ride, seated on the horse's bare back or on a cloth, clinging to its flanks with their thighs. They should not perch as upon a carriage seat, but stand properly upright with their legs apart. In this position they are firmly braced to hurl a javelin or slash with a sword. So it was, astride their horses, that Alexander's men hacked their way eastwards across the world.

Yet the horse is strangely neglected by storytellers. Fabulists have long made nonsense of animals' true natures. They stand dumb creatures on their hind legs and give them human voices, vices and virtues in tales designed for moral instruction. Foxes abound in such stories. So do crows, frogs, wolves, lions, serpents, monkeys, apes and asses. There are dogs and deer, cats and mice, grasshoppers, ants and flies; but seldom a horse. Nobody is certain how or where these stories began. Many are attributed to the Greek slave Aesop; others to the mysterious Indian Vishnu Sharma. Gradually, story by story, animals take on the strengths and weaknesses of the humans they depict. Foxes are cunning, owls are wise, lions brave, wolves cruel, asses stupid, monkeys mischievous. These attributes seep from the fables into our very language. A man might be proud as a peacock, his wife stubborn as a donkey, their neighbour greedy as a pig.

It takes a person wiser than most to see the foolishness in all this, for animals are not people. But wise men and women have better things to think about than talking foxes. As happens so often with god-given phenomena, wisdom falls from the heavens in sudden showers. Within a few generations in Greece we have been blessed with Sophocles, Pericles, Euripides, Socrates, Xenophon, Plato, Herodotus and Aristotle. Which is the greatest of them? All have their advocates, but people of vision must surely answer with one voice: *Aristotle*. As tutor and mentor of Alexander the Great, he ensured the greatness not just of his pupil, but of Mother Greece herself.

Besides his own tutor Plato, Aristotle must be considered the greatest philosopher who ever lived, the very architect of our thinking. But there is more to him even than this. His mind is not engaged with just ideas and abstractions. He wants to know everything about the living world: about animals, birds, fish and insects; to understand the *what* and the *why* of everything that lives. Not even the gods know as much about such things as Aristotle describes in his great work on nature. You might call it an *Encyclopaedia of Being*, as great an accomplishment as any to be found in the Lyceum library.

In it, Aristotle examines the meat and bone, blood and sinew, birth and death of all that runs, crawls, swims or flies, including man himself, whom he investigates as dispassionately as he might inspect a goat. All animals being devoid of reason, he is unconcerned with their feelings and attaches no intrinsic value to their lives, though he allows that they may differ in their temperaments. He joins the fabulists in ascribing mischief and craftiness to the fox. The ox, he observes, is slow and even-tempered; the boar ferocious and impossible to teach. Snake and wolf are given to treachery, and the dog to fawning. Some animals are capable of receiving instruction, and some are not. The stupidest of all quadrupeds is the sheep, and the most sagacious of wild creatures is the hind. Animals vary also in the lengths of their lives. No person lives long enough to count the elephant's years. Some say it lives for one hundred and twenty; others say three hundred. A camel may reach thirty, and some dogs as much as fifteen. Dolphins which escape predation, disease and accidental death may hope to attain at least thirty. This has been proved by fishermen who nick their tails.

All this, many people of ordinary cleverness and curiosity might have seen for themselves. But Aristotle is not satisfied with appearances. He wants to look *inside* each creature, to see how it is made and how it works. He notes all the ways in which they differ, and all the ways in which they are the same. A lion when dissected looks like a dog, and an ape looks like a man, though man is alone in possessing buttocks. He makes detailed descriptions of each animal's internal organs, their uses and how they connect. He observes that the blood in some animals coagulates, while in others it does not; that the blood in man is fine and pure, while in ox and ass it is thick and black. He records the pattern of bones, sinews, fat, gristle and veins. The bones of a lion, he notes, contain little marrow but they are so hard that they spark like flints. It grieves him that the chief vein of a bloodied animal is impossible to study: it cannot be seen while the animal lives, and it collapses when it dies. For anyone who wants to look further, he advises starving an animal to the point of death, then strangling and opening it immediately. He finds there is much to be learned from an animal in the aftermath of its death or dismemberment. A chameleon after being sliced lengthwise will continue to breathe while its body turns green. The plucked-off tail of a lizard will grow again; the wing of a bee will not, though all insects will go on living when they are cut in two. He sees how the separate portions move, and notes that head or abdomen may survive if they remain connected to the thorax, but that the head alone cannot live. There is also much to beware in such observations. Variations in the natural size of animals' gall bladders, for example, may lead to mistakes in augury.

He records the size, placement and orientation of each species' sexual organs, from mollusc to elephant, and describes how they are used. He notes the disproportion in the size of some insects' sexual organs, and observes the mating of octopus and squid. Nothing to him seems unworthy of study. He records the colour, consistency, flow and volume in the semen of dog, boar, ram, bull, stallion; the intimate secretions of bitch, sow, ewe, she-goat, cow, she-mule, hind. He examines the liquids that flow from the bodies of insects alive and dead; from caterpillars, grubs and fish. Likewise from man and woman. He notes the different ages at which animals are able to breed: eight months in the pig; one year in dog, sheep and goat; two years in horse; two-and-a-half years in ass; twenty-one years in man. But he shows us that copulation is not always necessary. A female partridge, for example, will be impregnated if she only walks on the leeward side of a male. Some mullets and all eels grow spontaneously from mud, and insects spring from rotting vegetable matter. Writers who say otherwise are given short shrift. Aristotle corrects Alcmaeon's mistaken belief that goats breathe through their ears, and Herodotus's theory that vultures fly from a country yet to be discovered. He sternly reproves those who believe elephants sleep standing up, those who say that hyenas have both male and female sexual organs, and those who imagine that bees make honey from flowers. By sheer weight of evidence he reveals the truth: they distil it from morning dew.

His observations extend from the very depths of the sea right up into the heavenly sphere of eagles. He describes how a male mollusc is distinguished from a female; how and when it spawns, swims and feeds; how it discharges a thick black juice when it is alarmed. He observes sensibility in seemingly motionless sea sponges which, if tugged, will tighten their grip on the rocks. The sponges are much sought after by soldiers, who use them to line their helmets and greaves. Everything in the sea reveals its secrets to this man. He knows the habits of every fish; the pattern of its fins, gills and scales; the period of its gestation; its maladies; what it likes to eat. That fish have senses of taste and smell there can be no doubt. The fact is well understood and profitably exploited by fishermen when selecting their bait. Men also exploit the fishes' sense of hearing by making loud noises to drive them into their nets. The fish with the most highly attuned sense of hearing, Aristotle says, is the mullet.

Unlike many people who abhor them, Aristotle holds insects in high regard. No living creature is more industrious than ant, bee, hornet or wasp. He closely examines the segments and the fluid contents of their bodies, their wings, their antennae, their stings. He records the miraculous life cycle of the butterfly, and the mysterious diseases of the bee. Grasshoppers, locusts, cicadas likewise are examined piece by piece. He does not shrink even from scorpions, spiders and intestinal parasites. As it is with the insects, so it is with birds. He observes the mechanisms of flight; their breeding, nesting and feeding habits; their patterns of migration; the variations in size, colour and content of their eggs. He knows everything about their claws, their feathers, their eyelids, their particular idiosyncrasies. He notes that a clap of thunder heard while a hen is brooding means the eggs will be addled, and that hoopoes build their nests from human excrement.

Among reptiles Aristotle makes a particular study of chameleons and crocodiles, and notes that the crocodile is the only animal whose jaws hinge upwards. He admires reptiles' ability to 'slough off old age' by shedding their skins, and applauds the insatiable thirst of serpents for wine: their drunkenness makes them easier to catch. Sceptics may say that there is no purpose in all this, that such knowledge cannot be turned to profit. But this is to misunderstand the nature of the philosophical mind. It is *for its own sake* that each fact is recorded, for knowledge in its purest form is heedless of utility. This is the true landscape of the mind. Yet much in Aristotle's writing is of practical value too. He provides careful instruction on how a pig may be fattened, and warns that an over-dependence on vegetable foods will cause excessive flatulence in cattle.

Nothing in the world exceeds the magnificence of its mammals. One after another Aristotle teases them apart, organ by organ, limb by limb. He records differences in teeth, horns and tusks, and in the pattern, quality and thickness of hair. No mother knows a child better than Aristotle knows the animals: their feeding and drinking, their breeding, gestation, growth, longevity, diseases, migrations, hibernations, their temperamental dispositions, everything that separates one creature from another. Such observations are not easy. He complains, for example, that the tongue of the elephant is so small and so far back in its mouth that it is all but impossible to see. But if maladies of the tongue may be hard to diagnose, others are much easier to discover and to heal. Nothing, he finds, is more beneficial to an elephant's aching shoulder than a judicious application of roasted pork.

Aristotle gives much attention to the pig. It would not occur to many philosophers to linger so long over fat and suet, but he is pleased to discover that soups boiled from animals rich in fat, such as pig and horse, do not congeal when they cool, whereas those made from animals containing suet, such as sheep and goat, will solidify. Further, the brains of the fatty animals are found to be oily, while the suetty ones are parched and dry. It is clear to him that brains and bodies of every kind, those of insects and fish no less than birds' and mammals', need to sleep, but only mammals dream as humans do. Dolphins also snore like humans. Some of his observations, such as the general rule that male animals in red-blooded species are larger than female, are there for anyone to see. With fish and insects it is the other way about, and the single contrary mammal is the mule. Other conclusions, though seemingly simple, require long and patient recording of facts. Thus he deduces that the smallest infant, relative to the size of its parents, is the cub of a bear. By his calculation it is bigger than a full-grown mouse but smaller than a weasel. When it comes to brains, it is man's which is proportionally the largest. When it comes to *salaciousness*, it is man again who excels, being more lascivious even than the rampant horse, though it is the horse that fortifies his sexual potency. On the forehead of a newborn foal is a substance called *hippomanes*. In Aristotle's account it is broad and round, black in colour, somewhat smaller than a dried fig and highly prized for its power as an aphrodisiac.

Sexual differentiation is of enduring interest. In all animals that have a voice, and with the sole exception of cattle, that of the female is thinner and sharper than the male's. The same is true of gelded males, who sing higher for the loss of their testicles. For the benefit of herdsmen, Aristotle carefully explains when and how their animals should be castrated. He describes also the curious case of the wild boar, which suffers from itchy testicles and castrates itself by rubbing against a tree. His investigation of penises reveals that the weasel's has a bone in it and that the camel's is so elastic that it makes a perfect bowstring.

The camel itself deploys its penis with rare scruple, for it wholly shares men's abhorrence of mothers mating with their sons. Aristotle tells approvingly of a young camel that was tricked by its keeper into mounting its mother. It was so enraged that it trampled the man to death. Aristotle's observations of human bodies, lives and habits are no less particular than his observations of animals. He describes how the lines across a man's palm predict the length of his life; how men with varicose veins are less likely than others to lose their hair; how flat-footedness is a sign of roguish behaviour. Such glimpses into the nature of men might be of some use to women looking for husbands, but it is for Aristotle's scrutiny of nature that the world must be grateful to him. After Aristotle, there is no more to be understood, no question left to be asked. Who else cares how a crab shits? Or a mussel? Who would take time to notice the direction in which the hind portion of a wasp will crawl when it is separated from the rest of the body? Who would notice the differences in fauna from one place on Earth to another? Let us be glad that one man did and that we, his beneficiaries, are freed from all doubt in these matters. His conclusions are expressed with such clarity and exactitude that anyone blessed with an available supply of flesh, blood and bone could manufacture any desired animal – dog, octopus, ape, elephant, hippopotamus, goat, whale, bee, human – from his instructions. Maybe the gods, too, one day will have reason to be glad of him.

CHAPTER FOUR

Bread and Circuses

IMPERIUM. THAT IS WHAT THEY CALLED IT. *THE EMPIRE*, WHEN Rome spread across the world like fungus across a tree stump. Animals of every kind were part of our glory and now they share our disgrace. All this may become clear as we look back over the many centuries of our imperial supremacy, but there is much that would be better forgotten. Animals suffered. Men, women and children suffered with them, and in many of the same ways.

We are taught that our city began as a small village on the banks of a river, seven hundred and fifty years before the birth of the Christian prophet Jesus. We owe our thanks for it to a she-wolf that suckled Romulus and Remus, the foundling twins who were our founding fathers. Anyone sensitive to portents will know that Romulus killed his brother in a dispute over which of the city's hills should be built upon: the first and ultimate statement of Roman power. Their mother was a vestal virgin and their father the all-powerful Mars, which may be why she was spared the fate normally decreed for unchaste vestals, which was to be buried alive.

Omens, auguries and gods have always mattered. In Rome's exertion of power over its people, religion has been as mighty as the sword. As it was for the Greeks, so it is for the Romans. Every kind of animal that gives meat or milk will be sacrificed to the gods. As also with the Greeks, omens are discerned in the flight of birds and in the entrails of animals still warm after sacrifice. No issue of any importance can proceed in the face of an imperfect goat's liver; not an act of war, nor even a marriage.

Some men perusing the ancient stones have read that it was a bad sign even for an ox to shit by a shrine, though farmers welcome this life-giving magic for their soil. Of all the gods' gifts, excrement was surely the least expected.

For two hundred and fifty years Rome was ruled by kings. Then the last of the monarchs, Lucius Tarquinius Superbus, was driven into exile after his son Sextus raped the noble Lucretia, who killed herself for shame. This was not the first time sexual violence had influenced our city's history. The very lineage of the Roman people descends from the rape of women taken by Romulus's men from the Sabines. Even so, the incontinent lust of an individual, even one as high-born as Sextus, is an unusual reason for popular revolt. But thus it was. Rome on the instant declared itself a republic. Whether by coincidence or otherwise, it was in this very same year that Pliny the Elder, in his *Natural History*, recorded the existence of a speaking dog and a barking serpent.

There have been very few times when Rome has had no enemy to crush, and few were the victories that did not rest on the partnership of man with horse. But even greater terrors were inflicted by monsters from Africa. Just the smell of an elephant was enough to make horses panic, even before they saw the size of it. The war-elephants were of a race from the northern parts of Africa, smaller than others but still taller than a horse's stable. Our trouble was that our armies held no monopoly: they had to face elephants as well as deploy them. This did not always go well for us. Elephants were used against us by Pyrrhus of Ephesus and by the Carthaginian Hannibal, who marched them from Spain into Gaul, and from Gaul across the Alps into Italy. Shortly afterwards came our defeats at Trebia and Cannae, which it is said cost seventy thousand lives in an afternoon. We had to wait another fourteen years before Scipio's army put an end to Hannibal's ambitions at the Battle of Zama. This time Hannibal's elephants worked against him. When the Roman cavalry blew horns at them they stampeded through their own lines, trampling all in their path.

Within a few years there was no soil in the known world that had not felt the press of a Roman foot. Vanquished enemies were treated with the contempt they deserved, worse than dogs. Roman displeasure was feared even above the wrath of gods. The sentimental Greeks, who liked to bury friend and foe alike, were mortified to find headless bodies rotting in the battlefields. Then and now there is no finer sight for Roman victors than carnivores feasting on the dead. What better use for enemy eyes than to nourish a bird? What better use for enemy flesh than to fatten a jackal? Nor did we grant any honour to those we took alive. Diodorus complained that Perseus, the beaten king of Macedonia and his children, were cruelly crushed with condemned men into a dungeon where they stank like goats. Diodorus may be a favourite historian of the Greeks, but he is maidenlike in his misunderstanding of Rome. This is the way those disgraced by defeat must always be treated. *Like animals.*

After the sack of Corinth our victory was complete, our farms and flocks worked by the many thousands of captives now bound to us as slaves. We had achieved a miracle of nature. Slaves tending sheep: one kind of animal caring for another.

As Rome underwent its metamorphosis from Republic to Empire, the city itself was a stew of contrasting lives. Julius Caesar was murdered. Antony and Cleopatra killed themselves after losing to Octavian at Actium, and Octavian himself became Augustus. In the streets of our city, the stink of bodies, human and animal, is more repulsive than any farm or pig-pen beyond the *urbs*. This is why the *urbs* are shunned by the poets. 'Let my delight be the country', wrote Virgil, 'and the running streams amid the dells – may I love the waters and the woods'. But there is no Virgil of the *urbs*. Oxen shit in the streets. Mules shit in the streets. Men shit in the streets, or tip their ordure from their windows. Rubbish mounts up in stinking heaps. Rotting food, human waste, all things broken or unwanted, the corpses of cats and dogs: all these, and worse, accumulate in streaming mountains of filth. There is *life* here too. Though live animals are seldom tossed so carelessly to the rats, no such scruple attaches to babies. Weak, deformed or unwanted girls are cast upon the heaps to be scavenged by men looking for slaves to raise, or even for infant brides. Some women guard against pregnancy with worms taken from the heads of certain spiders.

Flies everywhere abound, among the living and the dead, and everywhere bring torment. It is said that the Emperor Domitian entertained himself by stabbing flies with his pen, which was an adroit piece of skill if the story is true. Worse luck befell his elder brother Titus, whose nose was invaded by a gnat that ate his brain. Or so it is said.

The animals in the streets are themselves a kind of plague. Carters and muleteers, meeting in thoroughfares too narrow for them to pass, berate each other with rude words and cracks of the whip until one of them backs off. Sometimes one might even meet a loaded camel, though wiser men prefer mules. A camel is a foul-tempered, foul-breathing thing that spits at all it sees and is as likely as an elephant to frighten the horses. In such a stew, and at a time when politics is argued at knife-point, violence is never far away. This is why Caesar, during his brief rule as *Dictator perpetuo*, decreed that the traffic must cease at night, and that some respect must be shown to those who need to sleep.

Rome is a city of extravagant wealth and direst poverty, where richest and poorest live within sight and sound of each other. The wealthy have their villas, their servants and their long nights of feasting. The poor must live in mean tenements called *insulae*, which grow meaner floor by floor as they rise. The very poorest build rough shelters against better men's walls. As for the destitute, they sleep in rich men's tombs, or in the streets when they are driven out. Many people throughout the Empire live no better than Greeks, and worse than foreign slaves. There is a law which says that the owners of rampaging animals must pay for the damage they cause, or otherwise surrender the offending animal to the person who has suffered. As is right and proper, the statute is intended to be of benefit only to those able to afford a lawyer. As is also proper, it is unavailable to those who live beyond the margins of civility. This is why no action was taken against the owner of an ox which escaped from the market, fled up the stairs of an *insula* and leaped to its death from the third storey. The only regrets were expressed by those who failed to witness it.

A Senator at dinner will vomit more food than a poor man eats in a month. There is no shame in this. A pauper by his nature is less than a tradesman, and a tradesman less than a gentleman. A rich man lives by the profit of his lands. He owes no charity to those who are obliged to trade or toil.

For men of taste, gastronomy is an art superior even to the poems of Virgil. No man ever spoke emptier words than Marcus Porcius Cato, who said that a healthy diet should include nothing but greens, duck and pigeon. He might as well have told the lion to spare the lamb. For the true glories of the table, we should listen rather to the *Epigrams* of the poet Marcus Valerius Martialis. Who would not drool at his homage to the suckling pig? 'Let the rich man place before me the nursling of a sluggish mother, fattened upon milk alone, and he may feed off an Aetolian boar himself.' There is no part of a pig that cannot please him. 'You would hardly imagine that you were eating cooked sows' teats, so abundantly do they flow and swell with living milk.' He delights in thrushes, turtle doves, gammons, goose livers, dormice, partridges, pheasants, flamingos' tongues, turbots, oysters, sturgeons. He extols the thrush as the most delicate of birds, and the hare as the most succulent animal. Of others he is more circumspect. In a duck, the only parts worthy of a gentleman's table are the breast and the neck. 'Return the rest to the cook', he says. Likewise, the only part of a char worth eating is the liver. He quarrels with those willing to eat the chitterlings of a virgin pig. 'I prefer them from a pregnant sow.' Some creatures he eschews entirely. To eat a peacock would be an insult to its beauty, and wood-pigeons an affront to one's wife. 'They make sluggish and blunt the manly powers. He who wishes to be a lover should not eat of this bird.'

Tradesmen may feed their families on sea hedgehogs, mullets, chickens and eggs, while the poor have to rely on street vendors or squalid bar counters, and the poorest of all must scavenge. Rome is one city but many different worlds. A man who wants for a scrap of cheese cannot know what it is to eat a fat dormouse rolled in honey and poppy seeds. These little animals are the very symbols of wealth and indulgence. Marcus Terentius Varro tells us how they should be raised for the table. First they must be nurtured in gardens full of nut trees, and then lavished with acorns and chestnuts when the trees are empty. To be made fit for eating, they should be fattened inside jars of nuts and kept in the dark. Pliny tells us that our Senators in one of their maddest moments once attempted to prohibit these subtle delicacies, for the absurd reason that such emblems of inequality were anathema to sensitive men. Sensible men took no notice.

The rearing of any animal requires both knowledge and skill. Nature provides the raw material: men hone it to perfection. The great Columella, our highest authority on all things agricultural, notes, for example, the need to castrate young boars to keep them from fighting, and to spay females to make them fat. He is particular also about farm dogs, which he says should be of ample size with a loud and sonorous bark. They must also be of a single colour. Sheepdogs should be white, so that they are distinguishable from wolves, and yard dogs black to frighten thieves. An animal of mixed colour is good for nothing.

For knowledge of the natural world no one surpasses Pliny, whose work builds upon that of his revered predecessor Aristotle. In his *Natural History* may be found all the prevailing notions of the universe, the Earth, the sun, the moon, the stars, the wind, the rain and the thunder. Beyond this he provides us with a history of man and of all the creatures with which our world is shared. He deplores the example of the Greeks, who have turned animals into deities, and of others whose gods embrace 'certain obscene things, which are not to be spoken of'. Most absorbing are his revelations of how animals influence the living world, and how in their turn they are influenced by it. He notes, for example, that it is the breath of animals that draws down wind and rain. The moon, too, is of great importance. Oysters, whelks and shellfish of all kinds swell and shrink under its influence. More strikingly even than this, the entrails of the field-mouse correspond in number to the age of the moon, the ant always rests at changes of the moon, and diseases in the eyes of beasts of burden increase or diminish according to its phases. Man himself, Pliny observes, is the only animal that is not always killed when lightning strikes without thunder at night, 'all other animals being killed instantly'.

His great encyclopaedia of species begins with the elephant. Though it is the dog that lives most amenably with man, it is the elephant that is closest to us in wit and learning. An elephant will understand the language of its homeland and do whatever it is told to do. Some say it possesses also a religious sensibility. In a quite different way, Pliny admires the dragons of India and Ethiopia, which grow to twenty cubits in length and have magical powers of navigation. They are the cleverest and most enduring of swimmers. At the seashore, four or five of them will bind themselves together, then broach the waves with their heads held high like sails on a raft. In this way, riding wind and tide, they find their way to greener pastures in Arabia.

Even stranger sights are met during droughts in Africa, when thirsty animals congregate at each small trickle of water. There is a proverb passed down from the Greeks: 'That Africa evermore bringeth forth some new strange thing or other.' And here by the shrinking waters we see the evidence. Various males leap upon females of every sort, whose subsequent offspring, Pliny explains, comprise 'many strange shaped beasts, of a mixed and mongrel kind'. He does not say from which clay the serpent *Amphisbaena* was wrought, but notes its singularity in having two heads, one at each end, 'as if she were not hurtful enough to cast her poison at one mouth only'.

Pliny tells how sick or wounded animals cure themselves with herbs, and how a porcupine, by stretching its skin, can launch its spines like arrows at bothersome hounds. Even the lion faces mortal danger from a tiny animal called *Leontophonos*, whose flesh is so poisonous that a lion will die at the merest lick of it. The lion's answer is to crush it with his paws, 'and so killeth him without setting tooth to his body'. The Leontophone for his own part is ready to drench the lion with urine, 'knowing right well that his piss is a very poison to him'.

When it comes to mad dogs, Pliny advises that the surest remedy for their bite is the root of a wild rose, and that there are ways to save the dog itself from madness. Here he agrees with Columella: 'that when a whelp is just forty days old, if his tail be bitten off at the nethermost joint, and the sinew or string that cometh after, be likewise taken away, neither the tail will grow any more, nor the dog fall ever to be mad'. No less than Aristotle, Pliny is contemptuous of superstition. 'That men may be transformed into wolves, and restored again to their former shapes, we must confidently believe to be a lie.'

One by one he proceeds through the lives and habits of all the creatures of the wild: panther and tiger, camel and crocodile, rhinoceros and water horse, hart and stag, hyena, bear, rat, hedgehog, hare, ass, ape and monkey.

He tells us everything that anyone could ever know about the more familiar animals of field and hearth. Like Marcus Valerius Martialis, he holds the hare in such esteem that cooks, too, may benefit from his words. 'There is a most dainty dish served up at the table made of leverets or rabbits, either cut out of the dams' bellies or taken from them when they be suckers.' Reading this, who could restrain an urge to rush directly to the table?

The Romans' fascination with animals does not end with their natural history or usefulness in the kitchen. The fables of Aesop are as popular with the Romans as they were with the Greeks, though they have been refined by the Roman fabulist Gaius Julius Phaedrus to rid them of sentimentality. Rome is not Greece. The weak here do not conquer the strong. A frog or a sheep might dare to confront an eagle or a wolf, but it will suffer for its insolence.

The Colosseum in Rome is the most beautiful building in the world. It is made of the finest travertine stone, hauled during the reign of Vespasian from the quarries at Albulae, and its four storeys reach nearly one hundred and thirty cubits into the sky. The columns on the first storey are of Doric design. On the second they are Ionic and on the third Corinthian. The fourth is made into walled compartments with windows that look down into the arena. Below them is seating enough for forty-five thousand Romans and standing-room for five thousand more. On many occasions these numbers are greatly exceeded. It is said that the common populace, unruly at best, has been kept in line by the double promise of the corn dole and regular entertainments: *bread and circuses*, in the scornful language of the poet Juvenal. It seems unlikely, however, that in a city of a million people, the fifty thousand who have time and money to spend in the Colosseum are those of inadequate means. The good behaviour of such people cannot be guaranteed. There are some who say that the elegance of the Colosseum is alien to its function. Perhaps they have spent too much time with that ancient fool Pythagoras, for they are wrong. Their ungracious words are a grave insult to Vespasian and the emperors who followed him, and a slur upon the memory of those brave gladiators who, even as they face death, pledge their loyalty. 'Hail Caesar', they cry. 'Those about to die salute you!'

The gladiatorial contests and wild beast hunts are the ultimate expression of our contempt for death. Towns in the provinces also have arenas, where the traders who buy and sell gladiators, the *lanistae*, provide men to fight. Each *Familia gladiatorum* has fighters of various kinds: slaves bought and trained by a *lanista*, men found starving in the streets; even the sons of good families who have lost their fortunes. But things are done differently in Rome. Here it is the city's financial officers, the *Procuratores*, who bear responsibility, and the gladiators are condemned criminals and prisoners of war.

Animals for the contests are brought from every corner of the Empire and kept at the Emperor's *vivarium* by the Praenestine gate. Into this vast space are crammed every kind of exotic beast from ostrich to elephant. Here, too, visitors come to stare at these rare creatures before they are taken to the arena. The fights between men are made more interesting by their armament. Some have a sword and a full war-shield. Some have a dagger and a tiny round shield, called a *buckler*, strapped to their forearm. Some have only a net and a trident. With these they thrust and feint until only one of a pair remains standing. Sometimes when a fallen man has fought bravely, the Emperor signals to the victor to let him live. More often he is killed. Those wounded in combat are tended by physicians who owe much of their learning to a Greek, the famed pioneer of surgery Galen of Pergamon, who earned his commission from the High Priest of Asia by cutting open a live animal and proving that urine was made in its kidneys. This he did by strangulation of the kidneys and penis, which caused many of those present to be glad that they were not beasts.

Animals, too, vary in their armoury. They may have teeth, tusks, claws, beaks, speed, strength, agility, size, cunning. Like the gladiators they must fight to the death, though the crowd will be outraged if mercy is denied to one who deserves it. There was fury at one Games when elephants were killed by African hunters after they had knelt and begged for mercy. So great is the variety and number of the combatants that you could believe the pages of Pliny had come alive. From Africa come lions, elephants, leopards, hyenas, hippopotami, rhinoceroses, giraffes, ostriches. Europe sends bulls, bison, bears and boars. Tigers are brought from India. Sometimes the animals fight each other. Sometimes they face the *bestiarii*. These unluckiest of gladiators have only leather tunics to protect them. Their usual weapon is the hunting spear, though sometimes they carry firebrands or bows. It happens sometimes that arrows are shot by spectators from their seats, but this cowardly act is deplored by those who understand there is no glory without courage. Not all the spectacles end in death. To amuse the crowd, elephants may be taught to dance or kneel to the Emperor, tigers may lick their keepers' hands, panthers may be harnessed to chariots. Some even say that lions can be taught to catch live hares and then obediently release them from their jaws, though few have seen this happen.

In all the years since the Emperor Titus held the first Games, more animals have died here than there are stars in the sky. Nine thousand were killed in Titus's Games, and eleven thousand in the celebrations that followed Trajan's victory over the Dacians. More money has been won and lost in wagers than would keep an army in the field for a year. The rich stake their fortunes, and the poor their last *denarii*. Events proceed always in the same order. The day begins with animal entertainments and concludes with gladiators in the afternoon. In between these two great spectacles, condemned criminals are brought to be executed *ad bestias*, which is to say torn to death by animals. This is not the only way criminals provide entertainment with their deaths. When a drama calls for a death on stage, it is common for a condemned man to be sacrificed for the sake of authenticity. This had an unfortunate parallel when Crassus was beaten by the Parthians at Carrhae. As if defeat were not ignominy enough, his severed head was used in a play performed in celebration of a wedding.

A man can walk from the Colosseum to the Circus Maximus in less time than it takes a gladiator to slaughter a pig. Inside the circus, two hundred and fifty thousand Romans crowd in to bet on the horse and chariot races. The chariots are favourite. During the reign of Augustus, it was usual for twelve races to be run every day in Games that might last fifteen days. Since Caligula, the number of races each day has been increased to twenty-four, each one seven circuits of the track, which is a great distance for a dozen vehicles charging at full speed while jostling for space. The circuit measures six hundred paces in length and two hundred in width, with turning posts at each end. The horses most often are harnessed in teams of four, though sometimes it might be two and sometimes as many as ten. The animals are specially bred in Italy, Greece, Africa and Spain. They are trained from the age of three, and begin racing two years later. As victories accumulate, so does an animal's fame. Names such as *Tuscus* and *Victor* are cheered throughout the Empire. *Tuscus* has three hundred and eighty-six prizes to his name, and the immortal *Victor* four hundred and twenty-nine. Dressed for the occasion, beribboned in the colours of their *factions*, sparkling with bejewelled manes and breastplates, horses like these exude pride in their very sweat.

The charioteers are skilled, courageous and clad like the horses in the colours of their *factions*. For the race, they stand with the reins tied around their bodies, whip in hand and dagger ready to cut themselves from a wreck. When the race begins, the roar of the crowd can be heard far beyond the city. The excitement increases as the racers approach the turning posts, for it is here that the dangers are greatest. Even the smallest deviation in speed or direction, or an overly aggressive manoeuvre, can be fatal. A crash is a sight both pitiful and thrilling, feared and longed for by the crowd. Some men and horses never rise again, while others rise and fall, over and over until they too lie still. Surviving horses freed from the reins career wildly around the circus, threatening injury to themselves and to others. The horror is worst, or best, when a charioteer still attached by the reins is dragged behind a bolting horse, dying by degrees.

It is *judgement* that separates bravery from recklessness, so that the best men win race after race. The most exalted are the elite *miliarii*, men who have won a thousand times. Who does not know the name of Pompeius Musclosus, whose victories numbered three thousand five hundred and fifty-nine, or Flavius Scorpus, two thousand and forty-eight? Such men, who were born slaves, are rewarded with wealth and celebrity. But even the best of them have no answer to the randomness of fortune. Many of them, when forsaken by luck, die in the wreckage of their chariots, their spirits borne aloft on the roar of the crowd.

Do they die in vain? No. Circus and Colosseum boldly display the Roman indifference to pain and death. Here too the whole world can see that our Emperor commands nature as certainly as he rules his client kings.

When Augustus asked for four hundred and twenty African leopards, then Africa made sure he had them. It is the same with elephants. The demands of the arena are more than equalled by the desire for ivory, which the wealthiest Romans use to craft their furniture. By ship and by mule, tusks are brought from the forests of India as well as from the shores of Africa. In the nearest part of that great continent, the tenacity of its greatest animal at last has been exhausted. The demands of Rome caused it first to become depleted and then to be eradicated altogether, so that not a single one remains of its kind. Such is the unanswerable might of our Empire.

Out in the streets one may hear it said that it is not lion or elephant, nor even the horse, that keeps the economy turning: it is the miraculous mule. *Miraculous* because this indispensable beast, necessary for the transport of people and goods, for working the land and for mobilising the army, is no mere accident of nature but a creation of man himself. A mule is made by the joining of a male donkey with a female horse. If the parentage is the other way about, female donkey with male horse, then the outcome is a *hinny*, a useful beast but smaller than a mule. A mule may never excite the Circus Maximus but it greatly exceeds the horse in its sureness of foot, its fitness for long journeys and its capacity for loads. What would break the back of a horse is light work for a mule.

This is a subject on which Columella has much wisdom to impart. If Aristotle and Pliny were the greatest *accumulators* of knowledge, then Columella is the greatest *employer* of it. He tells us that any donkey foal which is to be used for breeding mules should be taken from its mother at birth and given to a suckling mare. It must grow up among horses, for it needs to learn their behaviour and respond like a stallion to a mare in oestrus. Nature now puts an obstacle in its path. A mare is so much taller than a donkey that, no matter how aroused the suitor might be, congress is impossible. To overcome this disadvantage, the mare must be held within a special cage in which the donkey may approach her on a slope. The act of procreation then can be accomplished with ease. After the birth, says Columella, the infant should be left with its mother for a year, then taken to the mountains to harden its hooves.

Columella also has much to say about the many varieties of cattle, and how animals of different kinds can be blended to produce yet more variety in size and form. Animals in this way can be adapted to thrive in one sort of country or another, or to plough soils of different kinds. Such is the genius of man.

Animals are beloved also as friends. Any animal small enough to share a house may be suitable for adoption as a pet. We keep apes and monkeys, mice, ferrets, snakes, birds of every kind from geese to quail, and in some houses even fish such as turbot from the sea. Ravens, magpies and parrots are among the many birds that can be taught to speak like humans. The banishment of the cat is in great part explained by its antagonism to such birds and other small creatures it regards as prey. The ferret by contrast is kept precisely because of its ferocity. According to the geographer Strabo, this half-trained cousin of the polecat was first brought to Rome from the northern shores of Africa, though the truth of this distant event is impossible to know. The sharpness of its teeth disqualifies it from the human embrace but suits it ideally to the hunting of rabbits, and for controlling mice and rats.

Above all animals, we Romans reserve our highest esteem for the dog. To say *the* dog is badly to mislead, for dogs show greater variety in size and form than even we humans do. There are long-legged hunting dogs and the deep-chested Molossians which guard our houses and our flocks. Many an argument has been cut short by the appearance of one of these slavering monsters, and many a thief sent upon his way. Among women, the favourites are the tiny white Maltese lapdogs. Pliny rather haughtily writes of these 'pretty little dogs that our dainty dames make so much of, called Melitaei, if they be ever and anon kept close unto the stomach, they ease the pain thereof'. Juvenal in the sixth of his Satires, *The Ways of Women*, asserts that a woman's infatuation with her pet may be such that she would 'fain let the husband die to save a lap-dog'. To the unfortunate husband falls the unfeminine duty of carrying the animal outside, in whatever weather, to void its bowels. This is all too much for Plutarch, who recalls how the sight 'of wealthy strangers carrying up and down with them in their arms and bosoms young puppy dogs and monkeys, embracing them and making much of them' had provoked Julius Caesar into wondering whether such women were capable of childbirth. Caesar's meaning is clear, that doting upon a pet is a poor substitute for human intercourse. This is an opinion shared by many men of high birth and power, but it is in the nature of such men that they connect more easily with each other than with the common people.

Caesar perhaps may be forgiven his ignorance. How could he have known any other kind of man than Senator, slave or soldier? But one might have expected a thinker such as Plutarch to be more aware of the common mind, and to understand that the happiest pets are to be found in the happiest households. As Jupiter weeps, and as the new religion tugs at the very roots of our Empire, it may be that now is the time to reflect upon what it is that makes us Romans. It is an irony that would bring smiles to the faces of Aristotle, Pliny and Plutarch. Whether it is in the Colosseum, or in the Circus Maximus, or in the laps of our wives and mothers, it is through our animals that we know ourselves as people.

CHAPTER FIVE

Dominion

AND SO THE PRAYERS WERE ANSWERED. THE ROMAN EMPIRE stumbled like a tripped bully, then crumpled and died. This was a victory that took determination, defiance and pain, for Christians had more to endure than just the crucifixion of their saviour. People of faith had been mocked by the Greeks and tortured by the Romans, yet their persecution only strengthened their belief. The more they suffered the louder they prayed, and faith spread like a fever. One by one the old gods sank into a pagan past and people everywhere rejoiced.

None of this happened without bloodshed. Nothing in history ever does. Jesus of Nazareth was born during the reign of Caesar Augustus into a violent world in which a man's life was worth no more than a dog's. Caesar himself was a brute. There was nothing soft about the sandalled feet of his marching armies, which brought more and worse destruction than any biblical plague. For the unhappy people of Gaul it was a mortal sin merely to occupy the land through which they passed. Caesar's reward when he died was not the vilification he deserved. It was to be declared *Divus Julius*, an immortal god. Many centuries passed before it was safe to laugh at what happened next. Caesar's last breath was barely out of his body before a comet flashed across the sky. *See!* said the faithful. Behold the spirit of Caesar rising up to heaven! It followed that all his many successors were worshipped as living gods. Beasts were sacrificed to them as if to Jupiter or Apollo. Did any creatures ever die more vainly than these?

The persecutions that followed the crucifixion are a stain on all humanity. Justice was so slow in coming that faith was strained like a sail in a tempest. There was no miracle; no sudden visitation by the dove of peace; no increment in the value of human life. The Roman populace, including many Christians, enjoyed their bloodbaths in the Colosseum for *four hundred years* after the crucifixion. It was not until Constantine finally declared Christianity to be the one true faith that the Emperor put an end to executions *ad bestias*, and even then not before he had disposed of two Frankish kings in the amphitheatre at Treves.

Nothing has mattered more to civilised society than the Holy Bible. It is in Genesis, the first and most ancient of its texts, that we are told the full extent of the Lord's gift to his people. In the twenty-seventh and twenty-eighth verses of the First Chapter we read:

27 So God created man in his own image, in the image of God created he him; male and female created he them.

28 And God blessed them, and God said unto them, Be fruitful and multiply, and replenish the earth, and subdue it; and have Dominion over the fish of the sea, and over the fowl of the air, and over every living thing that moveth upon the earth.

The words are few but their import is vast. Their full meaning was explained by St Augustine of Hippo in his *City of God*, where he points us to the thirteenth verse of the twentieth chapter of Exodus:

13 Thou shalt not kill.

The Commandment contains these four words only. As Augustine says, there is 'no limitation added nor any exception made'. Thou shalt not kill. That is the entirety of it. Some scholars have taken this to mean that the stricture is boundless; that it must extend 'even to beasts and cattle, as if it forbade us to take life from any creature'. Well, says Augustine: if that be so, then why not include also plants? 'For though this class of creatures have no sensation, yet they also are said to live, and consequently they can die; and therefore, if violence be done them, can be killed.' Do we therefore offend the Creator when we pluck a daisy?

Augustine puts the point concisely. 'When we say, Thou shalt not kill, we do not understand this of the plants, since they have no sensation. But then the same must be said of the irrational animals that fly, swim, walk, or creep, since they are dissociated from us by their want of reason.' They feel nothing; they know nothing. Therefore, as Genesis says, they are 'by the just appointment of the Creator subjected to us to kill or keep alive for our own uses'. The meaning of the Commandment is as clear as a mountain stream: *Thou shalt not kill man*, but to other animals we may do whatever we please.

Our education is completed by St Thomas Aquinas with his two great works *Summa contra Gentiles* and *Summa Theologica*. In the first of these he agrees that a living animal is a *sentient soul*. But it is not an *immortal* soul. It lacks reason and therefore must perish with the body. It cannot pass into the afterlife because a dead animal consists of *nothing*. The sentient soul in a man is altogether different, for it has 'intellectual power'. 'Hence', says Aquinas, 'the very substance of this soul must be raised above the bodily order both in being and in activity; and therefore it is neither generated by the generation of the body, nor perishes by its destruction.' It is immortal. Thus a virtuous man and his family may ascend into heaven but they must leave their animals behind. This is of great comfort to hunters and butchers, who will not be confronted in the afterlife by those they have killed. During their time on Earth they may with God's blessing let fly their arrows and wield their knives without fear. Aquinas does counsel against the most painful methods of slaughter, but this is not through any feeling for the animals themselves. Rather it is to encourage men 'to be less inclined to be cruel to other men, through being used to be kind to beasts'. Some see in this an echo of Pythagoras, but the comparison is false. Pythagoras was writing many hundreds of years before the Bible. Without its guidance, he took a deviant view of man's sacred right to consume flesh.

What is reassuring to butchers is much less welcome to soldiers. What if they are killed and their bodies eaten by vultures or hyenas? What then becomes of their souls if the animals cannot bring them into heaven? Once again Augustine has the answer. The faithful, he says, need have no fear, for 'assurance has been given that not a hair of their head shall perish, and that, therefore, though they even be devoured by beasts, their blessed resurrection will not hereby be hindered'. The belly of a hyena may be a strange route into heaven, but it is as good as any other.

Another mistake is to suppose that animals may be happy or sad. One might as well attribute happiness to a turnip. Absence of reason means absence of feeling. It is as simple as that. As Aquinas says in *Summa contra Gentiles*:

> *Happiness is a good proper to man: dumb animals cannot be called happy except by an abuse of language.*

*

By the same token a hunted animal cannot be unhappy. Men exist. Animals exist. It is in the nature of God's Earth that the one should chase the other, as beasts do among themselves. Hunting is not butchery. It is the job of butchers to slit the throats of animals bred and kept for the purpose. Wild beasts have no master save the Lord. Some men imagine that by chasing deer they reawaken some part of themselves which is as natural and instinctive as the animals' urge to flee. Yet the very wilderness is shrinking around us. Our northern lands are not like the ones subdued by Julius Caesar. In Caesar's time they were deep, dark and savage places haunted by wolves, goblins and the worst of men. Now civilisation has turned them into a new kind of Eden. By clearing the forests and tilling the soil we have tamed the wilderness, filled our bellies and multiplied ourselves in number. All this is as the Bible ordained. We have *Dominion*. It follows also that men of rank must have dominion over lesser men. What is granted to a baron is not given to a peasant. A poor man may chase a rabbit or a hare, but deer are for the nobility alone. A poor man if he trespasses can expect no mercy. He may die like an animal, stitched inside the skin of a stag and fed to the hounds. He may be pegged down, blinded, castrated or frozen to death according to the nobleman's whim. The only certainty is death.

Though they differ in other ways, Frenchmen, Germans and Englishmen all share a passion for sport. This is how it has been in England since 1066 when the conquerors brought their *venérie* from France. Yet all is not as it seems. Deer are stolen by more than just desperate individuals with families to feed. There are places where bands of thieves work together like armies, which could not happen unless they had men of high rank to command them. This they do entirely for profit. There is a hungry market for stolen meat not just among commoners but also among the nobility themselves, and in religious houses where monks are forbidden all meat not obtained by hunting. Deceit is a favourite sauce at the monastery table. Such is the monks' love of pork that they have devised a clever answer to the proscription of butcher's meat. Instead of slaughtering their hogs in the usual way, they set them free and run them down with hounds.

The barons observe two seasons for deer: from the twenty-fourth day of June to the fourteenth of September, and from November the eleventh to February the second. The first is the best, for this is when the stags and bucks may be taken. These are fatter, meatier and far more succulent than the skinny does and hinds which are hunted in winter. In prudent households much of the flesh is salted down for the larder, where it will keep throughout the year. For charity, any forest carrion is given to the poor and the sick.

It is not just with hounds that men like to hunt. The art of falconry was practised long before the birth of Christ, and was brought to Europe by the Goths. Nothing makes a man happier than to feel the weight of a hawk or a falcon on his wrist. A good gyrfalcon is worth its weight in silver. Henry II paid eleven marks for a pair of these, and ten more to have them trained. Words matter in falconry as much as they do in venery. The true *hawk* is the female bird, and the male is the *tiercel*. He is smaller and less ferocious than her, and thus cheaper for a poor man to buy. The highest authority on the sport is high indeed, no less than the Holy Roman Emperor, Frederick the Second of Hohenstaufen, whose *De arte venandi cum avibus*, or *On the Art of Hunting with Birds*, tells us more about birds than was known even to Aristotle. All the ranks of society are reflected in falconry's order of precedence. Only the noblest are allowed a peregrine. A yeoman might have a goshawk, and a priest if he is lucky might aspire to a sparrowhawk.

Even archbishops take such matters seriously. The young Thomas Becket spent more time hunting with hounds and hawks than he did with his books. At home he amused himself with monkeys and parrots.

Some have read this as a sign of weakness. To possess hounds or livestock is right and proper; but monkeys and lapdogs are of no interest to sober minds. This is why pets are so abhorred by people of faith, and why at Narbonne in 1260 the Franciscans forbade religious houses in their Order to keep any animals but cats and *certain birds* for killing vermin. Yet they might as well have ordered pigeons out of the trees. In one unruly convent the Archbishop of Rouen found nuns cosseting dogs, squirrels and birds. It was the same in England, where William of Wykeham raged against the sisters of Romsey Abbey, 'who bring with them to church birds, rabbits, hounds and such like frivolous creatures, to which they give more heed than to the offices of the church'. It has been explained to *les religieuses* that the prohibition is for their own peace of mind. They pray to a God who will not allow their beloved pets into heaven. With what sense of grief, then, must these sad women contemplate the afterlife?

Genesis, Augustine and Aquinas all say the same: that treating an animal like a human is heresy. Nuns ignore this at peril to their mortal souls. Yet the lesson goes unheeded by noble ladies whose attachment to dogs seems only to increase as the animals themselves grow smaller. By clasping these tiny pellets of fur close to their bosoms and, most disgustingly, by kissing them on the lips and feeding them from their own plates, they offend all canons of decency and faith.

There is no such problem with the horse. Though it has in many places supplanted the ox at plough and cart, its true calling lies in the service of knights. The *tourney*, or *tournament*, is another gift from the French, whose tournaments remain the best in the world. Knights ride across Europe to take part in them. Each *tourney* begins with a *melee*, in which opposing bodies of horsemen try to force each other to retreat. It has been called a *mock battle*, though an observer might struggle to see much in the way of *mock*. Some knights strut from the field with lances aloft. Others slink away in shame. An unlucky few lie where they fell. The animals, too, may pay for their courage with broken legs, which truly means *with their lives*. Later in the day come the *jousts*, when knights charge at each other with quivering lances. Here the worst damage is to the loser's dignity, and to the pride of his squire. It might also be said that no man quite catches a damsel's eye as well as a victorious knight fluttering his pennant. How ladies do glory in men's animal natures!

Though animals are given for our *use*, a philosopher might say that we need also to *understand* them. The best way to do this is by reading the *Bestiaries*. These wise and wonderful books contain every fact about every creature on Earth. In the remotest regions live animals that most men know only through words and pictures: the lion, for example, the tiger and the leopard, which we are told is the bastard offspring of a lioness and a *pard*. We are taught how to catch a unicorn. If a maiden ventures alone into the woods, then the animal will soon enough leap mild as a lamb into her lap. As to the lynx, it is famous chiefly for its piss, which hardens into a precious stone called *Lyngurium*. This is not quite the bounty it may seem, for the animal does all it can to ensure that the stones are never found. This it does by burying its piss in sand.

Yet dissent is as necessary to philosophy as breath is to the living body. Every opinion spawns its opposite. Some say that the elephant is the biggest animal in the world; others say it is the dragon. With fish, however, there can be no argument. The biggest is the whale. This is so very large that sailors sometimes mistake it for an island, upon which they land and light their fires. It is a fatal error. As soon as the great fish feels the heat he plunges into the deep, taking ship and sailors with him.

Some animals are known for their cunning. The hyena, for example, lures people out at night by mimicking the sounds of speech and vomiting. The bison in Asia cheats hunters by emitting a fart so fierce that it squirts out the entire contents of its bowels, enough to cover three acres of ground. Its pursuers then cover their noses and flee. Tiny animals, too, richly reward our interest. The liver of the mouse mirrors the ocean by swelling at full moon. As to the weasel, some greybeards say it conceives through its ear and gives birth through its mouth. Others say it is the other way about. What we should understand from all this is that the ordinary creatures of field and forest are as marvellous and as mysterious as the lion and the crocodile. A sick stag will cure himself by eating venomous snakes which he sucks like water from their holes. Is that not miraculous? A female bear will use her paws like chisels to carve her formless foetus into a cub. Cleverest of all is the beaver, which eludes pursuers by biting off its testicles. As these are such efficacious medicines, the hunters stop to gather them while the animal scampers off to safety.

Of course there are dissenters. No bison could expel that much shit, they say. Who has ever seen a beaver bite off its testicles? *Give us the name of any virgin who has found a unicorn in her lap.* All should be ignored. St Augustine has said *it does not matter* whether any particular animal exists or not: all that counts is what it signifies. What does the elephant do when he desires to father a child? He turns eastward and heads with his wife towards Paradise, where the *Mandragora* plant grows. The wife first eats from the root of the plant, then feeds some to her husband. Now comes the miracle! It is upon that very instant that she conceives, which she does as chastely as the mother of Jesus, for the idea of copulation is revolting to her husband. The significance of this blameless couple is as plain as an apple on a tree. *They are Adam and Eve.* Consider also the lion. For three days after his wife gives birth he keeps a distance from his family, through all of which time the cubs lie utterly dead. They come alive only on the Third Day when they feel the breath of their Father. 'Just so did our own Father raise Our Lord Jesus Christ from the dead on the Third Day.' Think of the panther, who sleeps for three whole days after he has eaten. On the Third Day he wakes, and with a violent belch releases a scent of allspice so sweet that it commands all others to follow him. Only the dragon when he hears the belch becomes fearful and flees into his cave, where he sinks into endless torpor. Thus did the one true Panther, Our Lord Jesus Christ, rise up on the Third Day and banish the Devil!

The *Antalops*, too, is a living parable. God gave it two great horns with which to clear away obstacles. Even the tallest trees tumble before it. But when the animal is careless, these very same horns are its downfall. They become trapped in thorns, where the animal is easy meat for hunters. Again the meaning is clear. Our own two great horns are the Testaments of the Bible. Armed with these, and proceeding with care, we may free ourselves from the thickets of sin. We fail only when we snare ourselves in the thorns of temptation and fall prey to the lurking Devil. For temptation is the Devil's favourite tool. Why do wolves' eyes shine in the dark? As the Bestiaries say, it is because the Devil intends his works to seem 'beautiful and salubrious' in the eyes of 'darkened and fatuous' men and women. Like the wolf, he circles the flock and seeks out vulnerable souls.

The Devil is helped by those who deny the truth. Never forget the vulture or what it teaches us. Like the elephant it conceives without coition. The Devil's disciples say that our faith hangs on a falsehood: that no woman without a man can conceive and give birth to a son. By their own mouths are they condemned! Do they really suppose that the Mother of God cannot do what a vulture does?

PART TWO

NEXT

Artists and Thinkers

CHAPTER SIX

Darkness into Light

THIS IS A TIME THAT HISTORY WILL NEVER FORGET. IT WILL BE remembered as a time of change. A time of rebirth. A time for humans to rejoice in their own special genius, for we know now that the world is not just as God made it for us. It is how we have made it for ourselves. The people who say these things are not irreligious. They do not deny Christ. They say only that dogma should not be the enemy of reason.

The father of this new movement was Francesco Petrarch, a wise and brave man who restored the classical texts of the Greeks and the Romans. These were the very alpha and omega of civilisation. They contained the sum of all knowledge, and it was their loss after the fall of Rome that began the Age of Darkness. Through all the centuries that followed, knowledge was a forbidden fruit in an orchard of serpents. The Church guarded our thinking as jealously as barons protected their right to hunt. Civilisation froze like a horse at a cliff. Now, thanks to Petrarch and Boccaccio, our minds have been unlocked. 'After the darkness has been dispelled,' says Petrarch, 'our grandsons will be able to walk back into the pure radiance of the past.' At last we can praise man's achievements in art and philosophy as devoutly as we thank God for his works. Plump men in holy vestments may mutter *blasphemy*, but the rest of us cry *freedom*.

It is much easier now to ask important questions. What is a human? What is an animal? Aside from our immortal souls, what is it that separates one from the other? In many ways we are exactly alike. We eat and shit as they do. We multiply through fornication as they do, and like them we do this more through lust than desire for children. The Church rightly abhors such instincts, but signals its abhorrence by condemning adultery not just in men but also *in beasts*. Yes! It seems that even these are capable of mortal sin, though they have no immortal souls. There is a shred of logic in this. Where there are righteous animals there must also be sinful ones, for righteousness cannot exist without its opposite. Thus the pure-bred horse and all the fishes are praised for breeding only with their own kind, and the mule is excoriated because it is the *bastard offspring* of horse and donkey. This, the holy men say, is *contrary to nature*. Yet even this is not the worst of sins. There is a deed so heinous that we struggle even to give it a name. It is an act often committed but seldom confessed: *the fornication of a man or a woman with a beast*. The unasked question is: why should this matter? A person might not choose to indulge in this peculiar pleasure for himself, but there are some who can see no harm in it for others. What is less easy for honest sinners to forgive is the hypocrisy of moralising bishops who linger too long at the nunneries. Sin is sin, no matter whose fur is fluffed.

Yet it is not our likeness to beasts that should concern us. It is, rather, what *separates* us from them. One such thing is cleanliness. Clothing our bodies is another. So is cooking our food. Filth, nakedness and raw bones are negations of civility. All people can agree at least on this. We may agree also that culture stands to nature as soul stands to body, as heaven stands to Earth and as man stands to beast. Just as domestication is necessary for an animal to achieve its full potential, so is culture necessary to man. Culture is *domestication of the self*. For the dawning of this truth we have to thank first Petrarch but then also the Medici family of Florence, whose sponsorship has made that city the beating heart of the new movement. The critics are right to say that not all the city's artists and philosophers are scrupulous observers of the Ten Commandments. There are murderers, adulterers and sodomites among them. But so there are also among the pious.

Florence loves pageantry as well as it loves art. The very grandest of its many grand celebrations is the *Procession of the Magi*, which is held each year at the Feast of the Epiphany. Behind this glorious spectacle stands the *Compagnia de' Magi*, a brotherhood ruled by the Medici family. It is to the Medici patriarchs Cosimo, Piero and Lorenzo that we owe the works of Donatello, Michelangelo, Botticelli, Leonardo, Raphael and Gozzoli. The city's gratitude for these is demonstrated by cheering throngs on the day of the feast. What a scene it is! You could believe Noah himself had moored his Ark at the Medici Palace and that its living cargo now marched in line behind the First Family. Those who doubted the existence of *camels* are confounded by their own eyes. Behind them come buffaloes, deer, monkeys, eagles, cheetahs, leopards. The people feel the warmth of their bodies as they pass, and the fierce heat of their breath. They hear the strange growls and grunts, and smell the musky scents of foreign dung.

Like Romans at the Colosseum, the people are reminded of their supreme authority. Brute obeys man; it is never the other way about. But Florence is not Rome. It does not amuse itself by slaying animals. It would rather turn them into art; to *create*, not to destroy. On the walls of the Medici Chapel, Benozzo Gozzoli has painted the most glorious vista of the procession itself. In Gozzoli's vision the animals represent only their own alien beauty and their subjugation to human masters. Other painters are more artful. In their hands an animal may provide insights into our very souls. The dog is a fine example. His presence in a portrait might be flattering to the sitter, for a well-bred dog denotes a well-bred owner. On the other hand it might be a sly comment on a moral degenerate. The animal itself is as perplexing to philosophers as it is useful to artists, for feelings towards it are complex. A favourite hound or lapdog may be cherished like a child, yet the very same animal might symbolise depravity. What do you call a man who steals your silver, defiles your wife or reeks of shit? It is not pig or goat, nor hyena or crocodile, nor even rat. The heinous sinner is a *dog*. Men *die like dogs*. For condemned souls with swords at their throats, it may be the last word they hear on Earth. This is why dogs in art provoke so much debate.

In Florence and Venice animals are painted with such accuracy that one could reach out and stroke them. But the question in every case is: *why is it there?* Does it suggest a noble lady's place in society, or her loyalty to her husband? Does it suggest the impetuous lusts of 'a bitch on heat'? Or is it a portent of evil? Does the painter intend a benediction or a fart in the face? Husbands have drawn blood over such things. The only certainty is that animals in art have *meaning*. No good artist will take so much trouble to paint a creature simply for its own sake, or to record the mere fact of its existence. In kennel as in villa there is a hierarchy. A fine hunting dog might represent its owner's wealth and virility, but there is no place for working dogs of humbler kinds. We do not see them at the turnspit, or hauling a cart, or herding sheep. Nor do we see them bite the hands of their masters, nor even the arses of thieves.

Other animals similarly have their place. The rabbit's ability to conceive without fornication makes it the perfect symbol of a maiden's chastity. Rabbits in art are always white, though the ordinary drab kind has a rare significance of its own which no artist has yet explored. Because baby rabbits are not thought *proper meat*, it follows that monks can eat them during fasts as innocently as they swallow water. Artists are also fond of the rabbit's mortal enemy the stoat, which they like to paint when its brown coat turns in winter to snow. As is well known, a stoat in ermine will die at once if its pelt is soiled, so it too is a symbol of virtue. Yet symbolism is an awkward thing which can twist this way or that. A stoat in a picture might just as well imply virtue's *absence*. In one such portrait of a lady, the snow-white ermine at her breast is nought but the painter's ferret. What we understand by this is that *appearances are deceptive*. Other creatures useful to portraitists include serpents, which for obvious reason represent evil, temptation and the Fall. An ape with an apple in its hand means the same, and a shackled monkey stands for poor imperfect man crippled by mortal lusts. Less obviously, the tiny goldfinch signifies healing and redemption. Scholars remind us that when a bird flew down to pluck at the crown of thorns, a drop of Christ's blood coloured its face and breast. The same is often said of the robin. As to the glorious peacock, 'whose flesh will never decay', what more perfect symbol could there be for the immortality of the soul?

Does the Bible permit us to torment and kill animals without mercy? Yes, say the greybeards. That is what Genesis intends. But the disciples of St Francis do not agree. Their vision is set down by a nameless Franciscan friar in a lengthy treatise on the Ten Commandments. The book is written in English and takes the form of a dialogue between a rich man called *Dives* and a poor friar called *Pauper*. Orthodox theologians dismiss it as heretical, yet the ideas have a powerful appeal to sentiment. Men love their hounds, so why should they not love creatures of other kinds? To kill an animal, the treatise says, is no sin if there is a reason for it. 'It is granted to man to slay beasts when it is profitable to him for meat or clothing, or to avoid the nuisance of beasts which are tiresome to man'. Pauper's authority for this is the ninth book of Genesis, verses one to four:

1 And God blessed Noah and his sons, and said unto them, Be fruitful, and multiply, and replenish the earth.

2 And the fear of you and the dread of you shall be upon every beast of the earth, and upon every fowl of the air, upon all that moveth upon the earth, and upon all the fishes of the sea; into your hands are they delivered.

3 Every moving thing that liveth shall be meat for you; even as the green herb have I given you all things.

4 But flesh with the life thereof, which is the blood thereof, shall ye not eat.

Our friar turns next to the twelfth book of Deuteronomy, verses twenty-three to twenty-five:

23 Only be sure that thou eat not the blood: for the blood is the life; and thou mayest not eat the life with the flesh.

24 Thou shalt not eat it; thou shalt pour it upon the earth as water.

25 Thou shalt not eat it, that it may go well with thee, and with thy children after thee, when thou shalt do that which is right in the sight of the Lord.

From this he deduces that 'God allowed man to slay beasts, fish and fowl, to profit him but not to kill out of cruelty or self-aggrandisement or wilfulness, and so when He forbade man to eat meat with blood He forbade him to kill cruelly'. Man should show pity to animals, and 'rejoice that they are God's creatures'. It follows that to kill cruelly or without just cause is a sin, and that God's vengeance will fall upon those who offend. This is a doctrine which delights the poor of the world but is anathema to the rich. For any man who enjoys the hunt, Pauper's words are as sour as green apples. The proscription of bloody meat, he will say, is a concocted argument aimed maliciously at hunters. Many churchmen agree. So do military men who depend on the hunt to prepare horses and men for war. Also they say: if hunting is wrong, then why does Pauper not condemn also butchery? Among common people, butchers are slandered more often than hunters for their 'lust for blood and want of mercy'. Apparently there are some who believe like Pythagoras that it is wrong to kill any animal even for food. Leonardo da Vinci has been mentioned as one of these, though this most unlikely assertion is not supported by evidence.

It is important to remember that Pauper is a Franciscan and that the founder of his Order was that great slave to impoverishment Francis of Assisi. Francis was not poor by chance. Like Dives he was born rich. Most men would thank God for their good fortune and welcome all they were given. But not Francis! He was so ashamed of his wealth that he hid himself away in huts and caves, wandered as a beggar and devoted himself to poverty. Above all, he was famous for feeding birds and for taming a wolf, which his disciples say was proof of his love for all creatures. It is in this same spirit that Pauper preaches to Dives. There is much here for philosophers to chew upon, but not all men are philosophers. Many are simpletons who are too easily misled. This is especially true in England, which is a backward sort of place haunted by wizards and women who talk to cats. The people there go in thrall to *Arthur*, a king who was taught by a wizard to speak the language of badgers and owls. Yes, indeed! The English are princes of idiocy. Not even Francis imagined he could *converse* with beasts, for how can such a thing be? Animals have no *reasoning*, and without reasoning there is nothing to be spoken of. According to legend, one of King Arthur's knights was led by a white hart into a forest, where a holy man told him that the brute was Christ himself. Such are the perils of warped imaginations!

For men of sound mind the lessons are plain. They must be sceptical of all they read and hear. They should know how to separate falsehood from truth. But they should understand that such judgements are not straightforward. What is virtue to a Franciscan may be ingratitude to others. What would God prefer? For all his gifts to be gratefully received?

Or for them to be haughtily declined? Sanctimony is soggy ground. You could say that a saint flaunting his goodness is as vain as a baron flaunting his wealth. In the real world, where men rule everything that lives, *Dives and Pauper* stands with the ancient follies of Pythagoras. A wise man will go no further down Pauper's road than Genesis and Deuteronomy allow. So says the Church, and so say the thinkers of Florence.

And what would Pauper say about horses ridden into battle? Is this not cruelty? Should we not release them to enjoy the freedom of the forest? Is it not time for us to settle our differences without violence? No! The world does not work in that way. It never has. No people know this better than we Florentines. It was just thirty miles from here, at San Romano, that four thousand of our cavalry crushed the threat from Siena. The glory of that victory is shown in three great paintings by Paolo Uccello in which it is the *animals*, not the men, that are bathed in glory. Many fine horses died on that day, but Florence slept more soundly for their courage. Who could say that this was not the will of God? Without the horse there is no victory. Without victory there is no future for the state or for the Church, and men have no identity. The road travelled by Pauper leads only to chaos and disgrace.

There is another good question for the friars to ponder. Johannes Gutenberg's printing press has spread the Bible to more people than have known it in all man's time on Earth. Scholars say that the entire structure of society will be changed by the printed word, and many of them fear the consequences. Knowledge in the wrong hands, they say, will be misused. But we should dismiss such backward thinking and open our arms to progress. Yet we might also ask: what is the value of such a gift when it is weighed in so much blood? The number of Bibles printed by Gutenberg in 1456 was thirty. Each of these was impressed upon vellum made from the skins of half-grown calves. How many of these infant cattle died to make thirty copies of the Bible? Thirty? Fifty? One hundred?

No, my friends. The number was five thousand, nine hundred and fifty.

CHAPTER SEVEN

Dying for a Cat

THE CHURCH HAS BEEN SMOULDERING LIKE A HAYSTACK, AND now we feel the flames. The reasons for it are the heretic Luther with his *Ninety-five Theses*, and the sordid business of Henry VIII with Catherine of Aragon. No Pope could let these pass unpunished. Hence the Council of Trent has cracked down upon dissenters of every kind: the so-called *Protestants* with their joyless visions of God and the world, and the supposed 'rationalists' of Florence, Venice and Urbino. To deny the tenets of the Church, says the Ecumenical Council, is a heresy punishable by death. This why the Inquisitors stoke their fires and human flesh crackles like pork.

It is not just through art and philosophy that the ground has shifted. The world itself has a new size and shape. Brave men have sailed over the horizon and brought back news of whole new continents. Beyond the ocean they came across sandy islands and then lands, vast beyond imagining, where they found animals and birds that no one had ever seen before, and new kinds of people. Nothing there is familiar. There is no regular livestock; no cattle, no sheep, no goats. Instead, the people in the southern parts raise guinea pigs. Some of these are roasted for the table. Others are used in sacred rituals and embalmed like pharaohs. Further north the people hunt a kind of aurochs called *bison* or *buffaloes* which drift in great herds across oceans of grass. Before the Spanish came with their horses, the hunting here was crude and wasteful. Yelling tribesmen would drive entire herds over a cliff, or trap them in ravines. Now they hunt from horseback with bows and arrows, and kill no more than they can eat.

The conquistadores carried with them also mules, donkeys and proper livestock. Back to Europe they brought llama and alpaca, guinea pig, Muscovy duck and turkey. The man who introduced the turkey to England, an explorer called William Strickland, was honoured with a seat in Parliament and a turkey on his coat of arms. England is forever strange in its thinking about birds and animals. What can you say about a country where a heron perching on a church is an omen of the plague? Or a country whose queen calls her courtiers by the names of animals! Her Lord Chancellor Sir Christopher Hatton was *Sheep*; the Earl of Oxford *Boar*; Elizabeth's suitor Robert Dudley *Robin*. Perhaps this was why a tender redbreast was one of her favourite dishes.

But not everyone is so distracted. As Petrarch said, the world has waited a very long time for an heir to Aristotle and Pliny, and now it has one. Conrad Gessner, a physician from Zurich, has published three great tomes of such immense scholarship that we can scarcely believe they are the work of a single mind. First came the *Bibliotheca universalis*, a compendium of all the books in the world. Then *Pandectarum sive Partitionum universalium Conradi Gesneri*, which contains all the world's knowledge. And then *Historiae animalium*, which describes all the animals and everything that has ever been written about them. It is more than four thousand pages long, with descriptions and engravings of every animal, bird, amphibian and fish that is known anywhere to exist. Many of these are familiar: the unicorn, the dragon, the basilisk, the jumart, the griffin, the whales and the sea-monsters swallowing ships. But there are many others so outlandish that no ordinary person could ever have suspected their existence: the porcupine, the sloth, the *walrus*, which is like a mermaid cursed by the Devil.

It takes a while for new ways of thinking to change old ways of doing. Even some priests and philosophers believe the ancient *Bestiaries* and *Fables* hold more truth than the *Historiae animalium*. Why did God create the beasts? Simple, they say. It was to teach us the difference between right and wrong, sacred and profane, beautiful and ugly. The English of course disagree. They say that no animal designed for its purpose can be called ugly. Toad, slug, weevil, serpent: all are as charming as a basket of kittens. Have they never heard of the elephant? A beast so hideous that it muddies the water to spare itself the sight of its own reflection?

What flows from all this is *sentimentality*. Some women seem to think that a lap without a dog is like a breast without a chemise. In England, too, they believe that a pet is better than any herbalist at treating illness. If a sick woman hugs her dog to her breast, then it will soak up her illness like a rag soaks up water. Wherever there is space for an animal, there will *be* an animal. Bishops rant against pets in church, yet fences are still needed to keep dogs from pissing on the altars. A devoted animal may subdue even the fear of death. After the execution of Mary, Queen of Scots, her blood-smeared 'little dogge' was found beneath her gown and resisted every attempt to extract it. The English make menageries of their houses with creatures of every kind. Monkeys, tortoises, even otters, squirrels and rabbits pass for amenable company, and parlours twitter with canaries. There is money in it, too.

Despite all this, the English still claim to know the will of God. Puritans in their obsession with the Fall of Man believe that the proper condition for a beast is misery. For any wild creature the line between blessing and curse is thin indeed. What was it that drove Ivan the Terrible to send his army into Siberia? What value could such a frozen waste have for the people of Russia? The question is answered by the Church. What God provides for animals must be free for men to take for themselves. If fur warms creatures in an icy waste, then it will do the same for humans. But is it not remarkable that an animal's pelt should be worth so much more than its flesh? So much, indeed, that it can drive one country to invade another? On the other hand, how strange it is that some of the most disagreeable creatures have neither flesh nor fur to give! They take, they destroy, they give nothing back. A new kind of rat, brown not black, has come from the east. These voracious pests are so busy at night that the ground in certain places seems to ripple in the dark. Those who know them say that these brown insurgents are bigger and fiercer than the black; that they are better at digging, swifter to breed and have yet to find anything they will not eat. Though their affection is not reciprocated, they enjoy the company of humans, so that they have swarmed into the cities and driven their unfortunate black cousins back to the ports.

It is observations such as these that confuse the philosophers. Montaigne and others now say that man's sovereignty over the rest of Creation is illusory, and that God cares for the rat as much as He cares for His people. Yet they affirm also that animals lack reason and free will. How, then, can rat and man be equal? The very idea of it maddens the Church and makes hunters laugh. In England, only one dictum of Montaigne's is taken to heart: that to hunt without killing is like 'swiving without orgasm'. This way of thinking fits the English like a codpiece. For them the courtship of the hunt counts for nothing without the climax of a slaughter. Fat Henry hunted as incontinently as he wed. Sport for him was rape, not seduction. It meant rounding up deer by the hundred, then letting loose his dogs. It was the conquest that counted, not the pursuit.

Queen Elizabeth was more promiscuous even than her father. A London mercer describes her visit to Kenilworth in the summer of 1575. By this account the entertainments began on a hot Monday evening when hounds drove a hart into water. What a prospect! The excited queen high on her horse, horns echoing, hounds baying, footmen scurrying like beetles. The mercer paints a colourful picture: the deer's head 'lyke the sail of a ship' as it swam in vain for its life and the waters darkening around it. The rest of the week was filled with music and dancing, gentle promenades and chasing deer. One poor animal, the mercer tells us, was spared its life at the expense of its ears. One must wonder: what use does a queen have for such things? Is not the animal's need so much greater than hers? It was on the Thursday of that week, the fourteenth day of July, that the festival reached its height. The queen clapped her hands, the gates to the Inner Court were thrown open and a mob of bears rushed in to face a pack of mastiffs. It is clear from his words that the mercer was as thrilled as his monarch by all the *tossing and tumbling* that ensued: dogs snapping at the throats of bears; bears ripping the scalps and skins of the dogs. At the end, as the broken bodies were dragged away, there was such an 'expense of blood and leather' that a whole month's licking would not make them whole again. Even in her dotage the queen did not forswear her sport. Her favourite recreation was to sit comfortably in a bower, listening to music while she shot at captive deer with a crossbow.

The royal example impressed itself upon the people. In London a story is told of some lawyers on St Stephen's Day who summoned a huntsman to their Great Hall at the Inner Temple. As the gentlemen hallooed, blew their horns and drained their cups, the huntsman opened a sack, tipped out a fox and a cat and loosed his hounds in front of the fire. In the interests of legal exactitude, the word 'hunt' here was stripped to its bones. *To kill in comfort and without risk*: that is the proper meaning of it, a simple issue of man asserting a God-given right. It can be no coincidence that in their *venery* the French and the English use the very same word to mean both lusting after women and chasing deer.

Montaigne is not the only one who deplores such thinking. Thomas More in *Utopia* writes that pleasure in killing is proof of corrupted minds. Yet his opinion counts for little. It is only among the most effete of city folk that we find a bookish minority who share his feeling. Even these ardent sentimentalists have their limits. None can perceive any sensibility in a *fish*; nor do they care very much for the feelings of horse or pig. They understand that the purpose of a horse is to work, and that it is in the nature of things for it to fall down when it is spent. Sensible men know also that this is a boon to hungry dogs.

Some deplore even the keeping of fowls, though this has nothing to do with sentiment. It is all about the quality of the meat. Thomas Moffet, a respected Doctor of Physick, has much to say about this. Though he is both English and a Puritan, it should not be assumed that he is wrong. No reasonable man can doubt his assertion that lean meat is unfit to eat, and that animals and birds need to be fattened for the table. Unfattened meat is good only for hawks and vultures. He does agree that hens squashed without light into narrow spaces can do nothing more than sit and sleep, and that this in itself encourages plumpness. But then he puts the question: 'whether this penning up of Birds, and depriving them of Light, and cramming them so often with strange Meat, makes not their Flesh unwholesome to us as well as fat?'

To this he answers: 'that to cram Capons, or any Birds, and to deprive them of all Light, is ill for them and us too: For tho' their Body be puffed up, yet their Flesh is not natural and wholesome; witness their small discoloured and rotten livers; whereas Hens and Capons feeding themselves in an open and clean Place with good Corn, have large, ruddy and firm Livers.' With this the philosophers agree, as they agree also with his insistence that nature should not be taxed beyond its strength. In a closed and darkened space the air and the birds themselves all stink of dung, whereas in a clean and spacious house all will be pure and sweet.

It follows that what is right for birds is right for beasts. Only if they have space to walk and feed will they grow wholesome as well as fat. Yet what is wisdom for, if not to be ignored? Pigs are crammed in so tightly that they must lie unmoving on their bellies. It is only when they are taken for slaughter that they can see what another pig looks like standing up. There is another question asked by cooks. What should be done with animals toughened by age? How can they be made tender? The remedy has been known since ancient times. It is *terror*. By showing a lion to a bull before he slaughtered it, a Greek butcher could render its flesh as tender as a steer's. This is why even those who decry hunting cannot object to bull-baiting. The Spanish derive the same benefit from their *corridas*, where men fight bulls to the death. Before a *corrida*, when the animals are driven from the fields, headstrong young men run through the streets ahead of them in a race against their horns. In some places this bull-running is a sport in its own right, without any *corrida*. In Pamplona it is held in honour of St Fermin, who was martyred by being dragged along by a charging bull. People should salute his memory whenever they enjoy a tender dish of beef.

The English have neither saint nor *corrida*, though they have a way of bull-running that is peculiar to themselves. The town of Stamford is famous for the run it holds every year after Martinmas. But Stamford is not Pamplona. *There is only one bull.* Even this sad animal is not preceded by brave young men risking their backsides but instead is riotously pursued by every man, woman and child who can lay hands on a stick, and by all the town's dogs. The point of the chase is to drive the animal off a bridge and into the River Welland. This may be better exercise than hunting a fox in a hall, but it is no more dignified. Before the chase, the animal's tail and horns are cut off so that the people can enjoy their sport without risk. In another town, called Tutbury, the objective is to cut off a piece of the animal's skin or a tuft of its hair before it crosses the River Dove. No wonder the Spanish look askance! Such undignified affairs are less bull-running than bull-baiting on the hoof.

Bull-baiting of the ordinary kind is as common in England as the *corrida* is in Spain. Not everyone who enjoys these events can afford the animal's flesh, but all can enjoy the sight of it being tormented into tenderness. The usual way is to tie the bull to a stake, goad it with pepper, then set dogs on it one by one. The bull-dogs are no ordinary curs. They are specially bred with powerful jaws which, once they are closed, are impossible to prise apart. How marvellous it is that man can create animals *to his own design*: pigs to give more meat, cows to give more milk, horses to provide more labour, dogs to bite more bulls. And what a mystery it is that we have not practised such alchemy on ourselves! The job of this man-made dog is to clamp his teeth into the bull's nose. The job of the bull is to toss the dog back into the crowd. On rare occasions a bull will break loose, whereupon it is not just dogs that fly through the air. Bears are treated in exactly the same way. In towns and cities they are baited in special places called *bear-gardens*. In other countries, too, baiting is done for the amusement of the common people, and much money is wagered on the outcome. It is the same at dog and cock-fights. For those without money to gamble, there are games to play with cats. These may be stuck on spits, roasted on bonfires, boiled alive or tossed from the roofs of houses. Thus there is sport for people of all kinds and classes.

Everywhere now the Inquisition is doing its duty. Bonfires are lit, witches turned to ash. We now know what before we could only suspect: that dying animals, failed crops and milkless cows, barren wives, deaths and diseases, owls that suck blood from infants, are all the work of witches and warlocks. We know, too, how to recognise such people. Sinning with beasts is proof of guilt. Men who couple with sows, cows and she-asses are burned with their paramours. So are women who lie with dogs. Thanks to the Inquisition, we know that those who practise bestiality and sodomy are child-eaters who would sooner lick the arse of a donkey than kiss the Papal ring. All this we have on the authority of the German Inquisitor Heinrich Kramer, whose *Malleus Maleficarum* has been read more times than any other book except the Holy Bible. He lays bare the error of those who say witches do not exist, or who doubt their evil powers. As Kramer says, *there have always been witches*, and they have wrought incalculable harm. They are agents of the Devil as surely as the Pope is agent of the

Lord. Times without number they are seen in wild places, naked to the waist, writhing on their backs as they receive the seed of an *incubus*. Men, too, are bewitched. They may imagine themselves turned into animals or robbed of their penises. The penises themselves are scooped up and kept in birds' nests, where the witches fatten them on corn. Kramer describes a woman at Holy Communion who, on receiving the Body of Our Lord, spat it into her handkerchief and buried it with a toad. On that occasion the crime was discovered before any harm could be done, but this was a rare piece of luck. In the mountains and in the meadows, malevolent women kill each other's cattle by drying up their milk. By burying serpents under stable doors they kill horses. By sacrificing black cock-birds they bring down hail and lightning. By changing themselves into animals, they flit wherever they will. Such deceits have their risks, however, and revenge can be sudden. There was great joy in Berne when a wizard was stamped to death after he turned himself into a mouse.

The only answer is to burn witches until none remain alive. Yet the Inquisitors proceed with caution, for they will not convict a woman unless she confesses. This she always does when pressed. In one town alone, forty-eight women confessed and were burned in five years. In another place forty-one did so in a single year. As Kramer says, there is no village too small to harbour a witch. It often happens that such a woman will have her memory refreshed by questioning. Her mind may become clearer when she is hung by her thumbs, or feels red hot iron or boiling water. These are infallible tests. By withstanding torture she shows her immunity to pain, which in itself is proof of witchcraft. The proof is reinforced if her shaven body reveals irregular marks. At the end, no matter how piteous and detestable her cries at the stake, we must remember the words of Exodus: 'Thou shalt not suffer a witch to live.'

In perfidious England, dissent and heresy are only to be expected. A Member of the English Parliament, one Reginald Scot, has published a treatise called *The Discoverie of Witchcraft* in which he dares to defame Kramer. This work is utterly misnamed, for its subject is not the *discovery* of witchcraft but the *denial* of it. Scot rejects even the value of confession. He says witches cannot change men into animals, cause harm to children and cattle, couple with incubi, ride through the air, steal men's genitals or create monsters. All these to him are gross absurdities and an 'offence against nature'. Yet his opinion is an offence against philosophy. Witchcraft is a corruption of nature as surely as it is a corruption of the spirit, which is why it is punished by death. Without shame or apology, Scot denies countless well-attested observations by men of impeccable character. Worst of all he derides the authority of the Church. For all these reasons, Scot's heretical book should be burned along with all the witches he says do not exist. But we should not exaggerate his influence. He is widely ignored even by the Justices of the Peace who preside over the English courts. More women in that merciless country are burned than in any other. This is not to say that witchcraft in England is like witchcraft anywhere else, or that its hags work as others do. In England it is not the spawn of an incubus that gives rise most often to suspicion; it is a cat.

The peculiar nature of this animal is proven by its prowling in the dark and its blood-curdling cries when it fights or copulates. This is important, for the difference between English and other witches needs to be understood. Elsewhere in Europe witches change themselves and others into animals, and use serpents, toads and suchlike to wreak their spells. In England the hag herself does not become an animal. Instead she takes an animal as her *familiar*, a servant-devil that does her bidding. The demon may be a dog or a toad, but most often it is a cat, which the witch suckles with her own blood through a secret teat.

These are not the only differences. In Europe it is the Inquisition that bears down upon these women. In England it is the common people. Always when disease breaks out they see the work of a witch. The search for an old woman with a cat does not take long. The arbiter of justice then is a lake or a pond into which the hag is thrown. If she drowns she is innocent. If she swims, guilty.

If the woman is given instead to the Justices, then the very possession of a cat will testify to her guilt and it will be for the witch herself to prove her innocence. Her examination begins with the shaving of her body, particular attention being given to her private parts. As it is in other countries, this is done in order to find *marks of the Devil*, which may be any kind of blemish that fails to bleed when pricked. In England such marks are said to be the teats from which familiars suck. If other proofs are needed, then the interrogation may proceed to thumbscrews, the rack and *strappado*, when the witch's wrists are tied behind her back and she is hoisted by a rope. After the confession comes the burning. In some lesser cases the witch might be kept in jail and brought out from time to time to be mocked in the pillory. The guilty cat is burned on the fire.

What more is there to be said? How much mightier is the power of God, revealed through man, than the power of the Devil revealed through beast?

CHAPTER EIGHT

Ugly Truths

CLEVER MEN SUCH AS ARISTOTLE AND GALEN USED TO THINK that the best way to learn about animals was to cut them up and watch them die. All this ended in the Age of Darkness. The Church proclaimed that experimentation was a pointless diversion that put philosophers at risk of their mortal souls. To seek such knowledge was to seek to know the mind of God! What greater heresy could there be than that?

Yet philosophers cannot freeze their minds. They think even while they sleep, and they crave *enlightenment.* It was at the height of the Florentine movement that a Flemish man called Andreas Vesalius looked back over time, liked what he saw and was hailed as Aristotle reborn. He took philosophy all the way back to a time before Christ and began again where Aristotle and Galen had left off. Ignoring the Church, he cut up cadavers both human and animal, and then did the same with living animals. His operations were performed with theatrical flourishes before adoring audiences whose excitement mounted with every flash of his blade. The climax of his performance, when he cut open a pregnant bitch, would be rewarded with wild applause. But this was more than just showmanship. Vesalius's notes from these operations were the material for his famous work *De humani corporis fabrica*, which men of intelligence now accept as the last word on human anatomy, even though most of his subjects were pigs and sheep.

Others are so revolted by such spectacles that they defy the Church in other ways. Contrary to doctrine, they argue that animals suffer as humans do, and that they should be treated likewise with sympathy and care. For what do shepherds and cowherds tell us? *That animals are as aware as any child of what is being done to them.* If dog or horse did not feel the whip, then how could they be taught to obey? And how could anyone who has witnessed the agonies of a wounded animal pretend it feels no pain? What were Vesalius's audiences applauding if not the agonies of sentient beings?

For those who think like this, the Devil incarnate is the Frenchman René Descartes, a man of warty physiognomy whose ugliness extends deep into his soul. Descartes is called a philosopher, though his reasoning is brittle. *Cogito ergo sum!* This, he says, is the only fact of which he can be certain: he *thinks*, therefore he *is*. Upon this elfin pinnacle he balances an entire pyramid of conclusions. These persuade him to believe that there exist in the world two different kinds of material: *mind* and *body*. Man with his intelligence and immortal soul is composed equally of both, but birds and beasts are body alone. He quarrels with those who say that animals' powers of reason are inferior to humans'. They are wrong, he says, because animals have *no reason at all*. The cleverest beast is closer to a block of stone than it is to the lowest human. Animals, he says, have no thoughts and thus no sensations. It must follow therefore that they are unable to suffer, and that they may be regarded as insensible objects composed of meat. For all these reasons it is to Descartes that the disciples of Galen, Aristotle and Vesalius now look, and who pursue their work in the certain knowledge that the shrieking of a wounded animal is the mindless reaction of a machine, as senseless as a clock.

So what does it mean to be an animal in the seventeenth century? If it is large, meaty and fleet of foot it will be hunted. If it is small, plentiful and nourishing to dogs it will be handled as carelessly as a lump of dough. If it is a pigeon, its legs and wings may be torn off for the convenience of a hawk. If it is a hare, its feet may be severed so that young hounds can more easily learn how to kill it. Cruelty is one issue on which Catholics and Protestants can agree. In England the Catholic Earl of Shrewsbury encouraged his tenants to kill deer with their bare hands, but Cromwell's men were no kinder. Cats were stuffed inside burning effigies of the Pope so that the hated Antichrist could be heard screaming in agony. At Ely Cathedral a dissenter named William Smith showed his loathing of the liturgy by roasting a cat on a spit.

Strangely, though, the Puritans were not entirely lacking in kindness. They did try to end cruel sports, though this might have had as much to do with their loathing of popular entertainments as any sympathy for the animals. Their efforts in any case were fruitless. With the Restoration of the Monarchy in 1660 came the restoration of cock-fighting, bear-baiting and all the rest. Sport is essential to the education of any son of an English gentleman. It begins at school with *cock-throwing*. No game could be simpler. A bird is tied to a post and weighted sticks are thrown at it until it dies of its injuries. From their fathers, boys learn how to set dogs on to ducks, feed hens to pike, bait badgers and bite off the heads of songbirds, which is a favourite game at fairs. The English do not have this bloody field all to themselves. *Goose-pulling* is a popular test of horsemanship throughout the civilised world. Again the rules are swift to learn. The head of a goose is smeared with grease and the bird hung by its feet from a scaffold. The prize goes to the first man who gallops underneath and plucks off the head. In the sport's defence, it can be said that it is no crueller to geese than regular husbandry, and at least the end is swift. Birds intended for the table enjoy no such comfort. To ensure tenderness they are immobilised by having their legs cut off, or their feet nailed to the floor. This gentle work is done usually by women.

With dogs, it is a strange fact that kindness *decreases* as the animal grows in usefulness. At the top of the pyramid a lapdog will eat more meat in its lifetime than any peasant, and will be coddled on tasselled cushions until it dies of idleness. Next in order of privilege come the hounds, which are better fed than the servants who feed them and are more likely to be remembered by name. None of this goes unnoticed by the reformers. 'From whence observe', writes John Bunyan,

> that the ungodly world do love their dogs better than the children of God …
> As for instance, how many pounds do some men spend on their dogs, when
> in the mean while the poor saints of God may starve for hunger? They will
> build houses for their dogs, when the saints must be glad to wander and

lodge in dens, and caves of the earth … Again, some men cannot go half a
mile from home but they must have a dog at their heels; but they can very
willingly go half a score miles without the society of a Christian.

This may well be so, though any man might prefer a hound to the company
of a preacher. After the hounds come the guard dogs, which roam their
owners' properties looking for people to bite. Their ferocity is guaranteed
by irregular feeding, regular thrashings and careful breeding. Many a visitor
has had cause to regret a nocturnal visit to the privy, and many a villager
has been mauled by animals that have jumped the fence. To a dog, children
are of no more account than a weasel, a cat, or anything else with a throat
to rip out. Remorse in these cases is as scant as alms at a bullfight. Dogs
bite: that is their nature. Children should mind where they go.

Lower still are the working dogs, which are kept outside and fed only
for as long as they are fit for work. Hanging or drowning then terminates
their employment, after which their final service will be to render their
fat in an oven.

Right at the bottom are the animals kept for blood sports. For gamblers,
the appeal of these contests is their very unpredictability. A dog may survive, or it may be torn apart by a bull, a bear or a badger or even another
dog. At the court of King James dogs faced worse odds even than these.
In 1610 three of them were put into a cage with a lion. Two were killed
outright and one fatally wounded. In the English Parliament a motion was
lost because so many of its members had gone to witness a fight between
dogs and tigers.

Elsewhere, dogs continue to suffer for science. The new Professor of
Anatomy at Padua, Matteo Realdo Colombo, sees pain as the very key to
enlightenment. How strong is a mother's love for her pups? To measure this
he cut open a pregnant bitch, removed her puppies and tortured them in
front of her. Churchmen were deeply moved by the way she dragged herself
across the floor to comfort them. *Aaaah!* What could be more uplifting?
If a mere animal could behave with such nobility, then how much more
might be expected from a human!

Out in the streets, no animal fares worse than the horse. Who has not
seen some poor broken-down nag whipped into one last effort before it

goes to the dogs? Who has not seen a spirited young animal broken by hot irons? Some believe such cruelties are rarer now. If they are, then the reason is self-interest rather than sympathy. Even a common work-horse is worth a lot of money, and one of the new racing animals bred from Arab stallions and English mares is a fortune on the hoof. What sensible person would treat such an investment carelessly? This is such obviously good sense that in the American colonies it has been enshrined in law. The Massachusetts Body of Liberties, enacted in 1641, decrees that:

> No man shall exercise any Tirranny or Crueltie towards any bruite Creature which are usuallie kept for man's use.
>
> If any man shall have occasion to leade or drive Cattel from place to place that is far of, so that they be weary, or hungry, or fall sick, or lambe, It shall be lawful to rest or refresh them, for competant time, in any open place that is not Corne, meadow, or inclosed for some peculiar use.

The words that matter here are 'which are usuallie kept for man's use'. This suggests that no concern should be wasted on animals that cannot be turned to profit. The English poet Gervase Markham, best known for his knowledge of women, says the same. His vast compendium *The English Huswife, Containing the Inward and Outward Virtues Which Ought to Be in a Complete Woman*, provides instruction in every feminine skill from physic and surgery to the extraction of oils, seating of banquets and choice of wines, cloth-making, brewing, baking and *other things belonging to a household*, whatever those might be. To prepare himself for his study of the female sex, Markham first considered the horse. In *Cavelarice, or the English Horseman*, he records such a catalogue of barbarity that any sensitive reader would hasten to turn the page. He deplores in particular the way horses' mouths are re-fashioned to fit the bit, rather than the bit made to fit the mouth. Seldom has cruelty scored a greater victory over common sense. The animals' teeth are pulled, their mouths enlarged with knives and the wounds sealed with hot irons. Even this is not the worst of it. Some horses poke out their tongues, a fault corrected by cutting off the portion that protrudes. Markham protests against 'this tyrannical martyring of poor horses', and argues that 'if either your horse's teeth stand too straight, or his mouth be too shallow, that you make the proportion of the bit less, and fit with the work of nature'. Unluckily for the animals, hunters and racers persist in their belief that nature is a flawed enterprise that needs human genius to put it right.

Others go even further. In 1635 the Parliament of Ireland introduced an Act against Plowing by the Tayle, and pulling the Wooll off living Sheep. This not only gave precedence to a horse's welfare over its owner's pocket but extended its protection to sheep. One might be astonished that such an Act was necessary. Why would a man pluck a living sheep as he would a dead hen? Answer: to save the cost of shears. It is the same with the plough: tying it to a horse's tail saves the expense of a harness. According to travellers, some countries on the far side of the world protect their animals even at cost to themselves. In Japan, where a god called Buddha is worshipped, we are assured that the eating of meat is *prohibited by law*. Not even Pythagoras could have foreseen that.

Though the name of Edward Topsell does not rank with Aristotle, Pliny or Pythagoras, he does bear comparison to Conrad Gessner. In his *Historie of Foure-Footed Beasts*, Topsell faithfully follows Gessner's *Historiae animalium* in his description of species. But he is moved by a higher purpose. Unlike Gessner he is not a physician but a devout minister of the church. Unlike Gessner, too, his mission is not merely to *identify* animals. He wants to assign to each of them its proper place in the chronicle of good and evil. Which are man's friends, and which his enemies? Which should we eat, and which should we dread? The Holy Scriptures, he says, tell us that beasts have but three divine uses. These are 'in sacrifice, in visions', and in the 'reproof and instruction of man'. It is in this last category that Topsell puts down his marker. He asks: What can we learn from storks and woodpeckers? And he answers: 'Care of the young for the old.' Or from ants, bees, fieldmice and squirrels? 'The rewards of hard work.' The intractable nature of the lion teaches us not to submit to the Devil. From the dog we learn love and faithfulness, and from bears the evils of lust. Bears, he says, have a habit of seizing innocent maidens and ravishing them in their caves. No beast is more sinful than that. By contrast he extols the camel, which copulates discreetly in private and which shares our horror of incest.

Topsell has little good to say about the cat, a 'dangerous beast' that is good for nothing but murdering mice. He does nevertheless admire the modesty of the female. Her urge to copulate, he says, is driven solely by love of young, which all Christians should take as their example. His favourite animal is the elephant. No other creature, he says, is 'so great and ample demonstration of the power and wisdom of the Almighty'. It is a 'living mountain' and yet so amenable that it can be managed as easily as a dog. It is also chaste, loyal, intolerant of adultery and murder, and a devout worshipper of sun, moon and stars. He draws a sharp contrast with the treacherous hyena, the malign and crafty fox, the deceitful panther and many more. Serpents have a whole book to themselves. In effect he entwines the rational observations of Aristotle and Gessner with the mythologies of Bestiary and Fable. This brings Topsell to his point. To understand the difference between right and wrong, he says, all we need do is study the world around us. Nature is a living sermon.

Yet it leaves open the question of justice. If the usefulness of a dog or a horse cannot ensure its safety, then how do we show gratitude to the wild ox? Since time began it has supplied us with meat, milk, leather and hard work. No animal has given more, and yet we persecute it so mercilessly that none remain in the whole of Europe. Likewise England has rid itself of the wild boar, though people there drool over fat bacon and every yard has a pig in it. Why is it that such useful animals have been so thoroughly extirpated when pestilential creatures such as the rat multiply even as they are slaughtered? Like the boar, the wolf has disappeared from places like England where forests have been turned into fields. But like the boar it still flourishes in European forests where its eyes glow at night like the lamps of the Devil. The conquistadores met a plague of them on the plains of America, where they follow the herds of bison. For those who have seen only cattle in the fields, the bison is a shock, more like something from a Bestiary than a common milk-cow. It is a monstrous thing. A cow to a bison is like a lapdog to a mastiff. A bull can kill another with a single stab of its horns. It will charge at anything that annoys it, and it is faster than a horse. Except for the very young, the old, the sick and the dying, the wolf is no more dangerous to it than a rat is to a man. This is why natives who hunt the bison disguise themselves in wolf-skins.

Yet the colonists continue to hate the wolf as deeply as the Inquisitor hates the heretic. It is a hatred they share with the native peoples whose lands they invade, and which helps them settle their conflicts. The natives are placated, and inspired to kill more wolves, with gifts of blankets and beads. Cows are given to those who kill the most.

Perhaps it is because the slaughter of wolves is not called *sport* that the Puritans do not condemn it. Yet even in the bear-garden or cockpit it is not the bloodshed that seems to offend them so much as the drunken disorder of the gamblers. They decry horse-racing for the same reason. But even here they lack consistency. During the short life of Cromwell's Protectorate, it was not the rich man's hunting or racing that were forbidden but only the cock-throwing and cock-fighting of the common man. We are sunk in a mire of illogic. Why do people not eat horse when they have such a liking for cow? Why do we not eat caged birds when we have such a liking for wild? Why do dogs work turnspits but never grace the spits themselves? Why do we not harvest rats? We are inconsistent even in our inconsistencies. People in some parts of Europe, especially those where French is spoken, do enjoy a plate of horse, as do those anywhere in the world who face starvation. Better a horse than a dog, a rat or a person, though dogs and cats are eaten *in extremis*.

It is through such gaps in our reasoning that myths, fears and omens fly in like vampires through a cave. On the accession of James in 1603 every copy of Reginald Scot's *The Discoverie of Witchcraft* was seized and burned, so that cat-loving old ladies could resume their procession to the stake. People saw omens in crows, ravens, foxes, hares, hedgehogs, rats, beetles. Everything that walks or flies is seen in some part of the world as a harbinger. It is not just the poor and uneducated who are prey to such nonsense. On the thirty-first day of May 1604, while Sir John Bennett was addressing the English Parliament, a jackdaw flew into the House. The appearance of a crocodile could not have induced greater panic. The members saw this small, inoffensive bird as such an ill omen that they declared *Malus Omen*, abandoned the debate and fled from the chamber. Even plants are accorded special powers. Some people believe, for example, that the moonwort fern will open any door when pushed into the key-hole, and that it will loosen the shoes of any horse that treads on it. This was what happened to the Earl of Essex, Captain-General of the Roundheads, whose cavalry all shed their shoes when they gathered near Tiverton in Devonshire. Many of the horses were newly shod, and no other explanation could be found than the carpet of moonwort beneath their feet. As the same fern is supposed to promote honesty, it follows that Essex's account is seldom questioned. Perhaps it was this very misfortune that explained his rout at the Battle of Lostwithiel. Or maybe his path was crossed by a hare, or the enemy met a goat. By such petty accidents, we are asked to believe, wars are won and lost.

All this is in defiance of religion. But is the Puritans' belief that animals should be rested on the Sabbath so very different from such drivel? There is no indication that any amount of rational thought or patient observation will persuade the Church to disobey the Bible. The case of Galileo Galilei is the foremost example. Irrespective of its truth or falsity, his theory of *heliocentrism* was declared by the Inquisition to be a *formally heretical* contradiction of the Scriptures, for which he was kept under house-arrest until he died. Galileo's view was *outward* from the world by way of his telescope. Now we are able to look *inward* by way of the microscope, which allows us to see the unseeable: fragments of life so tiny that their existence could never have been suspected. Imagine what Aristotle might have done with such a thing! And imagine how he would applaud the enterprising Dutchmen Antonie Philips van Leeuwenhoek and Jan Swammerdam. It was Leeuwenhoek who discovered the tiny organisms called *animalcules*, and Swammerdam who showed that the egg, larva, pupa and imago of an insect are all different stages of *the same creature*. Using the same instrument, the Italians Marcello Malpighi and Francesco Redi have discovered the composition of human blood, and have disproved the old belief, held by Aristotle himself, that worms and flies generate from mud and rotting vegetation. From this of course arises a difficulty. Philosophers find it as hard to gainsay Aristotle as the Pope to gainsay the Gospels. Even the great natural philosopher Jan Baptist van Helmont cannot let go of his belief in spontaneous generation. This he proved by storing a stale shirt with a handful of wheat. After a gestation of twenty-one days, the shirt gave birth to a family of mice.

For a rational thinker there is nothing more difficult than to forswear Aristotle and Pliny, yet scepticism is the soil from which all philosophy grows. Every theory, even Aristotle's, must withstand scrutiny. The two great obstacles that stand in our way are the unbending dogmas of the Church and the mischief of its loyal servant René Descartes. Those who speak for the innocent now call him *the worst man in the world*.

CHAPTER NINE

The Worst Man
in the World

UNLIKE PHILOSOPHERS, CHURCHMEN HAVE NO CAUSE TO QUES-
tion the mind of God. They know it better than they know their own. *What
God wants. What God says. What God intends.* All these are understood
with crystal clarity. It is a plain fact that God created animals for the use
of man, and that man was created for *himself.* This is why the nostrums of
Descartes met so little opposition, and why he was able to devise a whole
new way of thinking, called 'mechanistic philosophy', without offending
the Church.

Descartes believed that the entire universe is a machine bound by the
laws of mathematics. The same is true of animals and people. They too
are machines obedient to the same laws, so that their responses to pain
and emotion are the foreseeable outcomes of mechanical interactions. In
humans there is but one difference, which is the possession of an *immaterial
mind* which endows us with reason, language and knowledge of our creator.

This way of thinking had two principal effects. It encouraged natural
scientists to persist with their experiments, and it gave rational endorse-
ment to the Church's faith in God's gift. Yet there is a puzzle. The sheer
boundlessness of the gift begs some awkward questions. We may be grateful for a cow or a horse, but what use to us is a toad or a crocodile? Men
travelling abroad are finding new animals of every size, shape and habit.
So far from being useful, many of these are so hostile to humans that they

will kill and even eat us. It is clear also that there must exist in deserts and forests creatures which nobody has ever seen. What purpose could God have intended for any of these?

The Puritan preacher Jeremiah Burroughs asks us to remember the Fall of Man. It was 'through our own sin', he says, that we forfeited so much of our dominion. Therefore:

> When you see any creature rebel against you, call to mind your rebellion against God. It is true, God maintains, in some measure, man's dominion over the creatures still, that the world, and human society, may see a little child driving before him a hundred oxen, this way or that, as he pleases, showing that God has continued somewhat of man's dominion over them. But a great part is lost by our sin. If we, who are the servants of God, rebel against him, it is just with God that the creatures, which were subjected to us, should rebel against us.

A man bitten by a dog therefore should understand that his festering toothmarks are the wages of sin. He should understand also that he can punish the dog as harshly as he likes. There is no reason to doubt God's goodness when he allows harm to be done to an animal, for 'there is no suffering'. This was the genius of Descartes: to make his credo fit so snugly with the Faith that nobody could see the join. For every question there is an answer. Where lies the soul? Descartes locates it precisely, in a tiny gland deep inside the brain. Sceptics wonder how something the size of a grain of rice could control a machine as large and complex as a human body. Others point out that this same gland, the *pineal*, exists in animals which have no souls and thus no need of a box to keep them in. But back again comes the answer, tight as a tinker's purse. God is all powerful. If he so chose, he could give the power of speech to a rock. Only a heretic would doubt his ability to find space in a tiny gland for a soul.

Though Descartes expunges all *moral* objection to the dissection of live animals, there remains a question of efficacy. Sceptics say that studying animals tells us nothing about humans because their bodies are so different. A sheep does not walk on two legs and recite the Gospels. A man does not bleat and grow wool. The dissectors reply that the similarities are greater than the differences, and they find an influential supporter in the English philosopher Francis Bacon, whose turn it is to be celebrated as the finest thinker since Aristotle. Bacon recalls the Greek philosopher Celsus, who opposed the dissection of living humans many hundreds of years before the Church. Few now quarrel with this, though it means students of the human body are gravely limited in what they can see. This matters because rational science will accept nothing that cannot be shown by observation. No conclusions can be drawn without evidence. That is the very foundation of inductive reasoning, and the ground on which Bacon has devised the new methods of investigation which he sets out in his *Novum Organum*.

Although he endorses Celsus's condemnation of *anatomia vivorum* in humans, he says nothing against the dissection of animals. This is entirely consistent with the teachings of the Anglican Church. Philosophers have a right and a duty to work with what God has provided. Specifically, says Bacon, this means applying themselves to 'the dissection of beasts alive, which notwithstanding the dissimilitude of their parts may sufficiently satisfy this inquiry'.

Another name now enters the story. William Harvey is a man who has dismembered more animals even than Descartes but who has not been so utterly vilified. Some think it is Harvey's modesty that makes him less objectionable. Others say it is because his methods are justified by his achievements. Harvey and Descartes are contemporaries, yet they are as different as milk from water. Descartes, being of the sickly type, was taught by Jesuits in France. Harvey, being robust, studied at the University of Padua, where Vesalius had been Professor of Anatomy. They are yet more dissimilar in their ways of working. Descartes examined more dead animals than living ones, and did so only to confirm what he had already deduced through his theory of mechanics. He believed that metaphysical and philosophical reflections revealed absolute truths that were invisible to the human eye. Harvey believed the opposite. For him, nothing existed that was not worth looking at. He would cut open any living thing he could lay hands on. Importantly, too, he was as interested in the animals themselves as he was in their likeness to humans. Unlike Descartes he did not seek just to confirm what he had already decided but rather to make entirely new discoveries. His stated intention was to 'learn and teach anatomy not from books but from dissection, not from the tenets of Philosophers but from the fabric of Nature'. It was in this way, after years of labour and corpses beyond number, that he famously discovered the mechanism of the heart and the circulation of the blood. A pragmatist would say that such a discovery is its own justification. A compassionate man might ask: is it so important to know such things that no amount of suffering is too much?

And so it goes on: knives stab and slice, blood gushes like rain. Delving into a pulsing body with all its strange textures, colours and smells can turn a man's stomach but it will not prick his conscience. In England, one of Charles II's first actions after his restoration in 1660 was to grant a royal charter to a group of philosophers who now call themselves the Royal Society. Among its members was the alchemist Robert Boyle, a man who seems to have been shy of seething innards yet who did not hesitate to use living creatures when it suited him. For him, knowledge was its own reward regardless of utility. With his friend Robert Hooke he built a pump that would seal a captive animal in a vacuum. In this way, they reasoned, they could test the animals' need for air. The first creature to die in this apparatus, which its creators did not think of trying first on themselves, was a lark.

Yet opposition to cruelty is gathering force. The diarist John Evelyn spoke for many when he deplored the suffering of a dog whose thorax and diaphragm were cut away to allow a clearer view of its beating heart. He was also a ferocious critic of cruel sports, and wrote despairingly of a horse he saw being baited. This 'very gallant' animal fought for its life so fiercely that no dog could get a grip on it 'till the men run him through with their swords'. The bear-garden disgusted him. On 16 June 1670, he recalls, 'one of the bulls tossed a dog full into a lady's lap as she sat in one of the boxes at a considerable height from the arena. Two poor dogs were killed, and so all ended with the ape on horseback, and I most heartily weary of the rude and dirty pastime'.

Hunting, too, is being critically reappraised, though not by the hunters themselves. For them the issue could not be simpler: ownership of land confers all the rights and privileges won through the blood of their ancestors. That is the will of God. Any peasant who steals game anywhere in Europe knows what to expect. Into this ocean of injustice the churches have dipped scarcely a toe. The Archbishop of York deplored the waste of corn and of human life that hunters caused, yet he would not condemn hunting outright. For all their high tone, the clergy themselves chase animals as blithely as they fish for carp. The Puritans are little different. If they feel any concern, then it is for the oppression of the common man denied entry to the forest. There is an ancient conceit that the true value of the hunt lies in preparing young men for war, with deer standing for the enemy. Those of inferior birth have always smiled at this. They know very well the characters of their lords and masters.

The contempt is mutual. Many in the landed classes believe that men lacking money or education are closer to animals than they are to gentlemen. Labels such as *cur, mongrel, hyena, sheep, vermin, pig, goat, rat, serpent, mule, shrew* are attached to people without homes or work, people with disturbed minds, people who live simple lives in faraway lands, people with black or yellow skins, disagreeable women. A pregnant wife may be called a *sow*, and any woman a *cow* or *silly goose*. Many churchmen so despise women that they deny them even the possession of souls, and compare them to the *brute beasts* of the Bible. But there are good animals as well as bad. Many a man lives contentedly with his cherished *hen* or *duck* and dotes upon their beloved *cubs, puppies* or *kids*. For good or ill, the whole of humankind is a menagerie. A busy person is a *bee*, a brave one a *lion*, a handsome one a *swan*, a strong one an *ox*. English streets are lined with variously coloured Swans, Lions, Boars and Harts as well as the Dogs and Ducks and Horses and Hounds that receive the thirsty hunters. As it is with inns, so it is with the theatre. William Shakespeare's playhouse in Southwark was The Swan, and the bard himself the Swan of Avon. Every ambitious young person sooner or later will *spread his wings*.

Some churchmen are more unsettled by pets even than they are by women. They say pet-owning is heretical because pampering an animal means treating it as a human. Most people take no more notice of this than they do of a fluttering moth. No period of history has been more infested with dogs, or more in love with them. It is often said that loving an animal is a mark of low intelligence, though there is little evidence for this. Samuel Pepys confessed to weeping over *a canary*. Cats, too, have multiplied, though this may have more to do with controlling mice than with any capacity for affection. There remains, too, the animal's unfortunate association with witchcraft. During the English Civil War a man calling himself the Witchfinder General followed pets to their homes and ensured the torture and execution of women by the hundred. Justice was doubly denied. This dreadful man, whose name was Matthew Hopkins, survived to die of natural causes and not by the hanging he deserved.

In 1665, not twenty years after Hopkins's death, it was the animals themselves that faced execution when an outbreak of the plague raced through the city and cut down Londoners like corn. 'God preserve us all', said Pepys as house after house fell dark. 'The towne grows very sickly,' he wrote on 15 June, 'and people to be afeard of it.' The terror was justified. Week after week Pepys consulted the Bills of Mortality, which showed the numbers of deaths climbing from hundreds into thousands. By the end of that year, 68,596 bodies had been laid in the London clay. The City Corporation in its panic ordered the destruction of all dogs and cats, which it believed were spreading the disease. Pigeons, ponies and pigs also fell under suspicion and negligent owners were hauled before the courts. It is not known whether these measures had the desired effect. What is certain is that, freed from the attention of cats, the rats multiplied like maggots on a corpse.

It is clear and obvious that love for an animal is not always reciprocated. Nor does the evidence give much support to those who argue, like Pythagoras, that kindness to animals makes people kinder to each other. In his *Historie of Foure-Footed Beasts* Edward Topsell states the opposite: 'They which love beasts in a high measure', he says, 'have so much less charity to men'. But this in turn is dismissed by reformers. To be a *moral* being, they say, one must first be *humane*, which means allowing that animals suffer. A pamphlet called *Examen Legum Angliae: or the Laws of England examined by Scripture, Antiquity and Reason*, printed in London in 1656, denounces gambling as an 'abomination' and declares that bear-baiting, cock-fighting and horse-racing are 'unlawful before God, and yet not condemned by our Law. Those who indulge in such practices are unrighteous men, of hard hearts, bloody and cruel minds, having no mercy, nor sense of sin'. Thus, say the reformers, this leads directly to cruel and excessive punishment of men and women. That anyone should lose his life for any minor theft or felony 'is a Law against the Law of God'. Not even a traitor should face the gross inhumanity of being hanged by the neck, then cut down alive, his entrails and genitals cut off and burned before his eyes, his head lopped off and body divided into quarters. Would any humane person do this to a dog?

But the reformers are a small faction who lack influence. The gentry might share their dislike of bull-baiting and cock-throwing, but not their objection to hunting. The churches, too, speak in a babble of tongues. During the English Civil War a party of dissenters called the *Levellers* argued that all people should be equal before the law and that they should tolerate conflicting beliefs. The pamphleteer Richard Overton attacked the Church with the head-down ferocity of a bull. In *Man Wholly Mortal* he dismissed the immortal soul as a *ridiculous invention* which Christians had copied from heathens. Men and beasts are like plants, he said. They endure for one lifetime only. From this it follows that there are only two states of being: *living* and *dead.* It could be argued, therefore, that animals are due more kindness in their lifetimes, or that humans are entitled to less. Others accept the moral equivalence of human and animal lives but turn Overton's reasoning on its head. What it means, they say, is not that men and animals die into nothingness, but that *all* are resurrected after death. While orthodox churchmen continue to insist that only humans can look forward to the life everlasting, a few prevaricate and say the truth has yet to be revealed. All this drips into the well of confusion. Does man have a right to treat animals as he chooses, or does he not? What is an ordinary person to make of such a stew?

The confusions extend right across the world. There are *Hindus*, to whom cattle are sacred and who teach that no living thing should be harmed. In the same part of the world are *Jains*, who sweep the ground to preserve the lives of worms and beetles. There are *Buddhists*, who say that no animal should be harmed and who yet believe that sinful humans will be reborn as beasts. Man and beast are first made equal but then not equal at all! It is said also that a Turkish woman was raised up to heaven for giving a dog her own piss to drink. Would the Levellers preach tolerance of all these?

In Europe, while philosophers, hunters, bishops and butchers speak of *necessary physical cruelty*, men and donkeys, women and dogs, are burned for *unnecessary physical love*. This has a bearing on the way we understand human relationships too. Some say that the hierarchies in animal societies show the importance of rank. This means that a man of high birth who beds a scullery maid commits an offence very like bestiality. Just as animals are arranged from high to low, so too are humans.

Despite all these skeins and snarls, people are tending towards the belief that the world was not created for us alone. If it makes sense to accept that the sheep was created for man to eat, then it must follow that man himself was made food for lions. A bigger question even than this: if animals were condemned by the Sin of Adam to live in the wilderness, then why should man punish them for what he himself has brought upon them? This is why the Puritans say that taking pleasure in the suffering of an animal is contrary to Christian values. But it is not just Puritans who align themselves with nature. The poet Margaret Cavendish, Duchess of Newcastle, is a firm believer in the old faith, yet in a case of man versus sparrow her sympathies lie with the bird:

> The *Sparrow* said, were our *Condition* such,
> But *Men* do strive with *Nets* us for to catch:
> With *Guns*, and *Bowes* they shoot us from the *Trees*,
> And by small *shot*, we oft our *Lifes* do leese,
> Because we pick a *Cherry* here, and there,
> When, *God* he knowes, we eate them in great feare.
> But *Men* will eat, untill their *Belly* burst,
> And *surfets* take: if we eat, we are *curst*.
> Yet we by *Nature* are revenged still,
> For eating over-much themselves they kill.

She in turn is chastised by Thomas Hobbes in *The Elements of Law Natural and Politic*. All animals, he says, exist in a state of mutual hostility, and so are entitled to do whatever is necessary for their own well-being. Man in this respect is no different, so it must follow that 'nothing is unlawful to any man that tendeth to his own safety or commodity'. Such is the law of nature. Man is 'master of the irrational creatures', which he may preserve or destroy for his own purposes. It would be 'a hard condition of mankind' if a savage beast had the right to kill a man, and the man no right to kill the beast. And, we might infer, a hard condition if sparrows were allowed to steal fruit we have grown for ourselves.

Most people accept at least the usefulness of Hobbes's argument. Even if we believe our dominion over nature is a myth, we must accept that our culture and economy depend upon it. Otherwise we would have no crops, no industry, no meat or milk, no towns and villages and little understanding of our own bodies. It might not be moral, but it is expedient.

The weight of learned opinion may be shifting, but it makes little difference to the animals. Descartes' countryman Nicolas Malebranche continues to insist that dismembering live animals is only *apparently* harmful to them, so there is no reason to stop the experiments. The Dutchman Baruch Spinoza on the other hand argues that they do have feelings but agrees with Hobbes that this does not affect our right to use them.

The most influential enemy of Descartes is the philosopher-physician John Locke, who believes that the suffering of a wounded animal is as painful as the same injury to a human. His treatise *Some Thoughts Concerning Education* has been translated into every language in the civilised world and holds out the hope that the next generation will be kinder than the last. The answer, he says, lies in education, to cure children of their feline instinct for cruelty. 'When they have got possession of any poor creature, they are apt to use it ill. They often torment and treat very roughly, young birds, butterflies, and such other poor animals which fall into their hands'. This, he says, should be corrected by their parents and teachers. Though he makes no mention of Pythagoras, his reasoning is the same:

> For the Custom of tormenting and killing of Beasts, will, by Degrees, harden their Minds even towards Men; and they who delight in the Suffering and Destruction of inferior Creatures, will not be apt to be very compassionate or benign to those of their own kind.

What a pity it is that Descartes was not alive to hear him.

CHAPTER TEN

Mother Goose

HOW HIGH CAN TWO PEOPLE TOSS A FOX? HEIGHTS BEYOND twenty-four feet have been claimed though never proved. The only certainty is that the record must belong to a royal court. Intemperance is how kings and princes show their wealth and power. Everything is done to excess: consumption of food and wine, costume, cruelty, compassion, expenditure of lesser lives. What value to such prodigals is the life of a fox? Or indeed the life of anything? On a single day at Dresden the King of Poland, Augustus II, with his courtiers and guests tossed away the lives of 647 foxes, 533 hares, 34 badgers and 21 wildcats. Augustus himself was a monument to vanity who liked to be called 'Augustus the Strong'. His favourite trick when tossing a fox was to use *just one finger*. This he hooked into one end of the sling while a pair of courtiers took the other. *Wheee!* Up it goes! Higher than a willow tree!

Augustus's delight in animal-tossing was passed on to his son, though Augustus III's best score was a disappointing 414 foxes, 281 hares, 32 badgers and 6 wildcats, a long way short of his father's. The small number of cats had nothing to do with scarcity but everything to do with savagery. A wildcat should be the first choice of any man who desires his arms, face and legs to be torn to shreds. The animal is nothing but claws and teeth. But the question is: why is any of this worth noticing? What new is there to say about such games when they have been played for centuries? The answer lies in the question. Those hundreds of years have brought prodigious changes in science and understanding. We know now that animals are not just insensible machines. So why do we persevere with such cruelty? Dresden is far from the worst. Other courts have looked all the way back to Imperial Rome, forcing lions, bears, wolves and bulls to fight each other as if nothing has changed since the Colosseum.

Now as then, common people ape their masters. They entertain themselves in all the old familiar ways: dog-fights, cock-fights, goose-pulling, baiting anything that will fight a dog. Those who can't lay their hands on a dog, a cock or a goose can set fire to a cat, or stuff one into a bag and hammer it to pieces. Or they might visit an inn, where sport and ale go together as naturally as bread and cheese. Some establishments in England call themselves Dog and Duck after the sport of the same name. This is the simplest game of all. Ducks are tipped into a pond with a dog and a splendid contest then ensues. The birds duck and dive while the dog lunges at them when they rise for air. When all is done, the gamblers return to their trades, carter, coachman or post rider, and get on with the regular business of driving their horses to death.

On the hunting field, kings and emperors vie to establish themselves as the champion slaughterers of the eighteenth century. To improve their scores, some will claim every kill made by any person anywhere on their land. What other explanation could there be for Louis XV, the so-called 'Louis the Beloved' of France, claiming to have killed ten thousand red deer on his royal estates? Even this preposterous boast falls short of Prince Johann Georg II of Saxony, who claimed 111,141 deer in twenty-four years, which is *thirteen a day*. It would be easier to believe in the charity of bishops.

Considering this mountain of corpses, what need is there to ask how hunting has fallen into such ill repute? In his *Les Moeurs des Israelites*, or *The Manners of the Ancient Israelites*, the church historian Abbé Claude Fleury convicts them not just of cruelty but of blind stupidity:

> This relic of ancient barbarism is continued among us in full vigour; and without any kind of reason to vindicate the practice. By it our gothic ances-tors provided for their sustenance: but their descendants use it as a species of pleasure, without being impelled to it by any kind of necessity. Often the peaceable inhabitants of a whole country are thrown into confusion by vast numbers of dogs and horsemen, breaking through their enclosures,

and destroying the hopes of their agricultural toil. And all this to run a poor timid helpless animal out of breath! Is not such a practice as this as disgraceful to humanity as it is to common sense?

Samuel Johnson, as much a man of the field as a man of letters, writes of his own experience. According to a Mr Hamilton, who met him one day near Brighton, he 'rides as well, for aught I see, as the most illiterate fellow in England'. 'I have now learned by hunting', says Johnson himself, 'to perceive, that it is no diversion at all, nor ever takes a man out of himself for a moment: the dogs have less sagacity than I could have prevailed on myself to suppose; and the gentlemen often call to me not to ride over them. It is very strange, and very melancholy, that the paucity of human pleasures should persuade us ever to call hunting one of them.' It appears nonetheless that the melancholy was not too oppressive for the great man to bear.

Venison to the nobility is like ambrosia to the ancients, and just as much of a myth. The only way it surpasses other meats is in its price. On the plate it is no better than mutton, pork or beef. Many would say it is worse. This has not happened by accident. Stockmen for centuries have worked to improve their animals. Through careful selection they have made them bigger, meatier and easier to handle. Pigs and cattle now exist in breeds which are as different from each other as black men from white.

To better understand animal husbandry we should turn first to John Laurence, Prebendary of Salisbury Cathedral, whose *A New System of Agriculture*, published in 1726, was dedicated to the Princess of Wales. Laurence previously had written three substantial works about his passion for gardening. In his garden, he wrote, 'a Man may converse with himself and consider, that … his garden is his Paradise'. This vision of Eden, however, did not extend to the pig, which he deemed an unavoidable evil. 'Altho Hogs are the most hurtful, spoiling and ravenous Beasts, and are in themselves great Evils, yet they are almost necessary Ones to the Husbandman, who otherwise could make very little Profit of the Refuse of his House and Garden.' He notes that they are great lovers of lettuce, and of all other greens except turnip, and that they fatten nicely on carrots, sweet whey and milk. He is equally clear about what they should *not* be allowed to eat. 'Let not your Hogs eat man's Dung, not Pidgeon's or Poultry's Dung, which generally brings the Meazles. And if you suffer them much to eat Carrion, Flesh, or Garbage, it will but teach them to devour the poultry, or at least to be ravenous after young Chickens, Turkies and Ducks.'

He is more generous to cattle, though he disapproves of some who trade in them. 'In London, when calves are kill'd, the Butchers blow them; and some, when flay'd, lay them whole in Water, or wet Clothes, for several Hours, or whole Nights. The Blowing makes them look fat and large, the Watering white.' Neither wolf nor lion can exceed man's appetite for meat. 'It has been computed, that in the City of London, upwards of One Hundred Thousand Beeves, as many Calves, and Six Hundred Thousand Muttons, are killed and consumed in a year.' If all these were drawn up nose to tail, the procession would stretch for more than 950 miles.

According to Laurence, English sheep are the best in the world. They give the finest mutton and the finest wool. Yet they are awkward animals with a weakness for *the rot*, a kind of dropsy which may occur in two different forms. The lesser of these is *ascites*, in which the animal's belly 'is very much swell'd with Water, gotten out of the Vessels, Guts, Veins, Arteries &c'. In the other form, *anasarca*, 'the whole Body is swelled with water, gotten out everywhere, which makes all the flesh affected to be watery and flabby'. Avoiding these catastrophes, says Laurence, calls for an attentive shepherd. In wet seasons he must drive his flock to the driest place he can find, or otherwise on to a saltmarsh, 'which purges away the over-great Moisture as it comes, and so leaves them in a tolerable Tightness'. For added protection in the north of the country, between Michaelmas and Christmas the sheep should be greased with tar, butter and salt. A good greaser, Laurence says, can treat twelve sheep in a day. If this is not done, 'they will not live three Years, but will die of the Rot', and the wool will fall from their backs. In deep winter on the Romney Marsh in Kent the frosts can be so hard that the sheep struggle even to stand. When this happens, says Laurence, the shepherd should rub tar on their legs to restore the feeling.

At table, Laurence's favourite is rabbit stew, which he believes is the perfect bargain with nature: free meat available to all. The rabbit is not like other animals. It is a wild creature that was caught and domesticated, but then escaped and became wild again. People say it was the Romans who brought it to Europe, and the Normans who carried it from France into England. Laurence himself does not recount the animal's history, but he admires the way it has seized its chance:

> Where then it so happens that there are any large Wastes, Heath Ground, or Barren Plains, (especially if the Mounds and Fences are not made with Ivy Hedges), there nothing turns to the Farmer's greater Profit, than to stock such Ground with Wild Rabbits, which of all other Creatures useful in Life, are the greatest Increasers and Breeders.

Of the havoc wrought by the animals on crops and gardens he says nothing at all.

But if the rabbit is strange, man is even stranger. Look at him in one way and you see brutal disregard for other lives. Look again and you see a mess of sentimentality. Even the warmonger Frederick the Great asked to be buried with his dogs. It was always supposed that pet-keeping was an indulgence peculiar to civilised societies in Europe. But we now learn that this is incorrect. Sailors have found islands in the southern ocean where dogs far outnumber humans, and where some people keep even bats and lizards. Women in Hawaii have been seen to clasp a puppy to one breast while suckling their infant at the other. Though this may strike some people as an abomination, it has made philosophers think again about animals of every kind. They have begun to speak of animal *welfare* and to see wild animals as objects of interest, not just vermin or lethal enemies. Men of intellect now talk of *studying nature*. A Swedish physician called Carl Linnaeus has made a list of every known plant and animal in the world. In his *Systema Naturae* of 1735 he gives new names in Latin to every creature according to its *kingdom* and *order*, so that each one has a lineage like a duke. These names are the new language of science, and the new way in which the Creation is to be spoken of.

But this ordered view is not welcomed by all. It is inimical to the Romantics, who are devoted to the impenetrable mystery of savage beasts and wild places. They prefer to worship nature, not understand it; to be awed by the sublime, not informed by science. Roaming abroad, they are drawn to the wildest, most inhospitable places where they *commune with nature*. This strikes many people as contrary to the very powers of reason that distinguish man from beast. Stupider still are those who fall prey to superstition. Not even the evidence of their own eyes can persuade some people to doubt that a dead cat built into a wall will rid a house of mice and rats.

The only rule of history is that one thing leads to another. As learned people begin to think more sympathetically about their animals, so they are moved to think even more carefully about their children. What is an infant, they wonder, but a savage beast lacking in coherent thought? A savage beast driven by primitive instincts to scream for its own survival. How is such a creature to be civilised? John Locke compared children's minds to blank slates. It was the parents' duty, he said, to make sure that only sound ideas were chalked there. Others have expanded on his thinking. Jean-Jacques Rousseau in France and Johann Bernhard Basedow in Germany have done perhaps more even than Locke himself to guide parents along the narrow pathway from *nature* to *nurture*. The scale of the task is made clear in the very first line of Rousseau's great work of 1762, *Emile, or On Education*:

> Everything is good as it leaves the hands of the Author of things; everything degenerates in the hands of man.

Men and women by nature are coarse and selfish beings who think only of themselves. It is only through education that they are moulded into citizens, and the process begins in infancy. For Basedow the purpose of education is to encourage children in the two great essentials: happiness and usefulness. Nothing is worth teaching that does not contribute to one of these, and the *way* of teaching matters as much as what is taught. Children learn best by observing the world and playing together, not by reciting Latin nouns. Like Francis Bacon, Basedow believes that seeing and touching are more important than reading and listening. This is why his book of instruction, *Elementarwerk*, contains so many beautiful pictures of people and animals, engaging to the eye as well as to the mind.

Animals are as important as chalk and slate. Writers and storytellers conjure whole new worlds with rhymes and stories that are as different from the fables of antiquity as they are from the hellfire sermons of the Puritans. The animals in these stories speak with human voices and walk on two feet. Some wear boots or disguise themselves as grandmothers. They feel human emotions and are loved or hated for their virtues or sins. Foremost among these writers is the Frenchman Charles Perrault, who in 1695 published a collection of tales called *Contes de ma Mère l'Oye*. The unfortunate English would have to wait another thirty-four years before they could read *Tales of My Mother Goose* in a language their children could understand. Who now does not know 'Puss in Boots', 'Little Red Riding Hood' or 'Diamonds and Toads', in which vipers and toads spew from the mouth of a selfish daughter? In the latter half of the eighteenth century there appeared a whole new body of rhymes called *Mother Goose's Melody, or Sonnets for the Cradle*. It is said that some of these were the work of the playwright Oliver Goldsmith. But it does not matter who composed them. What counts is that they help educate our children. If Jean-Jacques Rousseau heard them before his death in 1778, then he would have died with a smile on his lips. In the rhyme of 'The Black Sheep', a boy is punished for his constant whining:

> Bah, bah, black sheep
> Have you any wool?
> Yes, marry have I,
> Three bags full;
> One for my master,
> One for my dame,
> But none for the little boy
> Who cries in the lane.

Other creatures have to suffer in silence:

> Ding dong bell,
> The cat is in the well.
> Who put her in?
> Little Johnny Green.
> What a naughty boy was that.
> To drown poor Pussy cat,
> Who never did any harm,
> And kill'd the mice in his father's barn.

Many of the rhymes are written to show the virtues of kindness and mercy:

> One, two, three,
> Four and five,
> I caught a hare alive;
> Six, seven, eight,
> Nine and ten,
> I let him go again.

In others, it is the animals themselves that dispense justice:

> Tell tale tit,
> Your tongue shall split,
> And all the dogs in our town
> Shall have a bit.

In prose, too, tiny protagonists have lessons to impart. This is an entirely new sort of literature: books written for children with as much care and intelligence as any work intended for their parents. These are improving works, but they are not *tracts*, and they have a realism very different from the whimsies of Mother Goose. They are packed with adventures in which good and bad resolve themselves without recourse to magic or any whiff of the pulpit. Some of the very best are the work of the English writer Dorothy Kilner, whose *The Life and Perambulations of a Mouse* is narrated by a young mouse called Nimble. When Nimble conducts his three brothers on a tour of the house they were born in, their eyes are soon opened to the realities of the wider world. At first it seems much kinder than they expected:

> The apartment which we entered was spacious and elegant; at least, differed so greatly from anything we had seen, that we imagined it the finest place upon earth. It was covered all over with a carpet of various colours, that not only concealed some bird-seeds which we came to devour, but also for some time prevented our being discovered; as we were of much the same hue with many of the flowers on the carpet. At last a little girl, who was at work in the room, by the side of her mamma, shrieked out as if violently hurt. Her mamma begged to know the cause of her sudden alarm. Upon which she called out, 'A mouse! A mouse! I saw one under the chair!' 'And if you did, my dear,' replied her mother, 'is that any reason for your behaving so ridiculously? If there were twenty mice, what harm could they possibly do? You may easily hurt and destroy them; but, poor little things! They cannot, if they would, hurt you.' 'What, could they not bite me?' inquired the child. 'They may, indeed, be able to do that; but you may be very sure that they have no such inclination,' rejoined the mother.

But the little adventurers soon learn that not all in the human universe is as welcoming. Defying their mother, they return time and again to the cupboard where the plum-cake is kept. It is here that Nimble's brother Softdown suddenly sniffs a most enticing aroma:

> 'Come along,' said he, 'here is some nice cheese, it smells most delightfully good!' Just as he spoke these words, before any of us came up to him, a little wooden door dropped down, and hid him and the cheese from our sight.

The unconcealed intention of these authors is to teach children to treat animals, and hence each other, with the same kindness they would want for themselves. Is it not strange, however, that by making ourselves more like these virtuous animals we desire to cure ourselves of *beastliness*?

CHAPTER ELEVEN

Tainted Meat and Healing Teats

ANYONE COUNTING EUROPEAN WARS IN THE EIGHTEENTH CEN-
tury will need more than their fingers and toes. It would be easier to
count the countries that have *not* sent men and horses to die on foreign
fields. Lithuanians, Russians, Spaniards, Greeks, Swiss, Englishmen, Scots,
Austrians, Swedes, Germans, Dutchmen, Poles, Frenchmen, Irishmen and
Turks: all were absorbed into the blackened earth. Europe's belligerence
stretched even to India and America, where the colonists struggled to
free themselves from Britain's grasp. Dead humans were counted in the
millions. Nobody counted the horses. The men in the saddle were heroes:
the animals beneath them were spoilt equipment.

We reveal our attitudes to animals by the labels we attach to them.
Cavalry horses are *property*; the scavengers feasting on them are *vermin*.
This word has a long history. Its parent is the Latin *vermis*, meaning that
lowest of things the *worm*. Two things may be understood from this. First,
that worms are held in deep contempt. Second, that we regard most other
creatures in the same hierarchical way. Worm, fox, tiger, badger: what
are they but *vermes*? We might say the same about humans. What do we
mean when we compare a man to an animal, or when we treat him like
one? It is no different. Hatred for the one means hatred for the other. If
the animal is vermin, then so too is the man. In every part of the world
where Europeans have set foot, those we call *natives* are displaced like black

rats driven away by brown. Only when such primitives learn to be useful do they progress from vermin to beast. Our name for them then is *slave*, and we buy and sell them like cattle. Every empire in history has done the same. Conquered peoples are *property*.

It is by means of such property that the East India Company intends to rule the east. It is upon such property that the thirteen States of America depend for their prosperity. Why did God make skins of different colour if not as badges of entitlement? In *Robinson Crusoe* it is by his enslavement of another human that Daniel Defoe's shipwrecked hero proves his worth as a white man. Slaves differ from horses in one respect only: when they die they are not sold for cats' meat. So the question is this: if it is so difficult for us to feel compassion for members of our own species, then how can we feel it for others?

History at last is writing its answer. Among the white races at least, oppressed peoples are turning against those who oppress them. Peasants' uprisings in Germany, and against the French occupiers of Flanders and Luxembourg, have been brutally put down, but the French Revolution shows that no people will remain subservient for ever. Even among the privileged classes there is growing distaste for needless cruelty. As the century draws to its close, a movement for the abolition of slavery is spreading rapidly from the English Quakers.

What is good news for humans is good also for other species. Those who fight for the liberty of human souls are the same who care most deeply for animals. A new word is being used to describe what happens in laboratories. Those who believe that the organs of an animal have no more feeling than the cogwheels in a machine, speak soothingly of science. Those who realise that screams of pain mean exactly what they say, speak of *vivisection*.

Some are so disgusted by such cruelty that they turn away from the religion that allows it to happen. The French cleric Jean Meslier now describes himself as an atheist. The philosophy of Monsieur Descartes, he says, is 'a ridiculous opinion, a pernicious principle, and a detestable doctrine, because it clearly tends to stifle in the hearts of men all feelings of kindness, of gentleness, and of humanity'. Other thinkers have come to God's rescue, or so they imagine. A just and benevolent Creator, they say, would *not allow* innocent creatures to suffer. Therefore it must follow that

they do not suffer and that René Descartes was right. The dominion over
all things granted in the book of Genesis is nothing but a plain statement
of fact. By God's design, beasts are dumb, insensible, and beyond the scope
of moral concern.

Others reject this as nonsense. The poet Alexander Pope argues that
the more thoroughly 'the inferior creation' falls under human power, 'the
more answerable we should seem for our mismanagement of it'. The very
fact that animals cannot expect any reward or recompense in the afterlife
means that we should treat them with kindness in the present. Who sets
the better example? Man or beast? Pope has no doubt:

> It is observable of those noxious animals, which have qualities most pow-
> erful to injure us, that they naturally avoid mankind, and never hurt us
> unless provoked or necessitated by hunger. Man, on the other hand, seeks
> out and pursues even the most inoffensive animals on purpose to persecute
> and destroy them.

The strongest advocate is the English philosopher Jeremy Bentham, who
is revolted equally by the maltreatment of animals and cruelty to slaves.

> The day has been, I grieve to say in many places it is not yet past, in which
> the greater part of the species, under the denomination of slaves, have been
> treated by the law exactly upon the same footing as, in England for example,
> the inferior races of animals are still. The day may come when the rest of
> the animal creation may acquire those rights which never could have been
> withholden from them but by the hand of tyranny. The French have already
> discovered that the blackness of the skin is no reason why a human being
> should be abandoned without redress to the caprice of a tormentor. It may
> come one day to be recognized, that the number of legs, the villosity of the
> skin, or the termination of the os sacrum, are reasons equally insufficient
> for abandoning a sensitive being to the same fate. What else is it that should
> trace the insuperable line? Is it the faculty of reason, or, perhaps, the faculty
> of discourse? But a full-grown horse, or dog, is beyond comparison a more
> rational, as well as a more conversible animal, than an infant of a day, or
> a week, or even a month old. But suppose the case were otherwise, what

would it avail if the question is not, Can they reason? Nor, can they talk?
but, Can they suffer?

To the consternation of Old Testament dogmatists, some thinkers now
openly quarrel with man's assumption of supremacy. 'The lives of men
depend upon the same laws as the lives of all other animals', writes the
Scottish philosopher David Hume, 'and these are subjected to the general
laws of matter and motion. The fall of a tower, or the infusion of a poison,
will destroy a man equally with the meanest creature. An inundation
sweeps away every thing without distinction that comes within the reach
of its fury.' The life of a man, he says, 'is of no greater importance to the
universe than that of an oyster'. Logic therefore insists that if a man is no
more significant than an oyster, then an oyster is no less significant than
a man. If none but a savage would eat a human, then by what right does
he put an oyster on his plate? Or a rabbit, a hare, a sheep, a pig or an ox?

Many people have been persuaded by writers such as the Anabaptist
Thomas Tryon to renounce meat altogether. Tryon himself seems an
improbable champion: it cannot have been what his parents, simple village
folk, expected of him. He was put to work, carding and spinning wool, at
the age of six, but it was not until he was twelve, while working at tiling and
plastering with his father, that he gave any hint of things to come. Somehow,
in the crumbs of time left over from his labours, he taught himself to read
and write. His next enterprise was to keep a few sheep which, at the age
of seventeen, he sold to raise the three pounds he needed to move from
Gloucestershire to London. There, as so many had done before him, he
expected to make his fortune. But fortune struck in a most improbable
way. His employer, a Fleet Street castor-maker, was a strict Anabaptist who
swiftly converted the young apprentice to his stern and sober creed. Tryon
thereafter devoted himself to scholarship, avoiding the company of other
young men in favour of long nights of study and contemplation. By the age
of twenty-six he had eschewed all meat and adopted a Pythagorean diet
of water, fruit, bread, butter and cheese. There were echoes of Pythagoras
in his writing too. If Christians would only desist from killing and eating
animals, he said, then 'in a short time, human murders and devilish feuds
and cruelties amongst each other would abate'.

He excoriated the wealthy for their greed, and implored them to share his disgust at their 'ungodly paunches', their 'bellies swollen up to their chins', and the 'begored gobbets' with which they stuffed their mouths. In his most influential work, *The Way to Health and Long Life*, his poor opinion of the meat trade swelled into revulsion:

> Is there any comparison to be made between an Herb-Market, and a Flesh-Market? In one there is a thousand pieces of the dead Carkasses of various Creatures lie stinking, the Chanels running with Blood, and all the Places full of Excrements, Ordure, Garbage, Grease, and Filthiness, sending forth dismal, poysonous Scents, enough to corrupt the very Air: In the other, you have delicate Fruits of most excellent Tastes, wholesome Medicinal Herbs, savoury Grains, and most beautiful, fragrant Flowers, whose various Scents, Colours, &c. make at once a Banquet to all the Senses, and nourish the purer Spirits, and refresh the very Souls of such who pass through them, and perfume all the circumambient Air with redolent Exhalations. This was the Place, and Food ordained for Mankind in the beginning: The Lord planted a Garden for him, replenish'd with all manner of ravishing Fruits and Herbs: There was no *Flesh-Markets* nor *Shambles* talk'd of in the primitive times; *But every green Herb, Fruit, and Seed shall be for Food to Man*, saith the Creator. Which if it had been still observed, Man had not contracted so many Diseases in his Body, and cruel Vices in his Soul, by making his Throat an open Sepulchre, wherein to entomb the dead Bodies of Beasts; nor should the Noble Image of the Deity have been thus shamefully defiled with Brutalities.

Alexander Pope agreed with him. Our gluttony, he said, is even more destructive than our sports: 'lobsters roasted alive, pigs whipt to death, fowls sew'd up, are testimonies of our outrageous luxury'. Like Tryon he believed flesh-eaters paid for their sins with their health. 'Those who divide their lives betwixt an anxious conscience and a nauseated stomach, have a just reward of their gluttony in the diseases it brings with it.' Tryon's book was published in 1691 but has had its greatest effect in the eighteenth century. One of those influenced by it was the future American statesman and scientist Benjamin Franklin, who read it in 1722 at the age of sixteen. In his autobiography Franklin recorded the multiple advantages of restricting his dinner to 'a Bisket or a Slice of Bread, a Handful of Raisins or a Tart from the Pastry Cook's, and a Glass of Water'. By this 'light repast' he could save a great deal of money and time which he could better use for study. It also improved the quality of his work, 'in which I made the greater Progress from that greater Clearness of Head & quicker Apprehension which usually attend Temperance in Eating & Drinking'.

Unlike Tryon, however, Franklin framed his argument in practical rather than ethical terms. He gave up flesh-eating because it helped him, not because he cared about suffering animals. This left open the door to temptation, which duly arrived at sea:

> I believe I have omitted mentioning that in my first Voyage from Boston, being becalm'd off Block Island, our People set about catching Cod & hawl'd up a great many. Hitherto I had stuck to my Resolution of not eating animal Food; and on this Occasion, I consider'd with my Master Tryon, the taking every Fish as a kind of unprovoked Murder, since none of them had or ever could do us any Injury that might justify the Slaughter. All this seem'd very reasonable. But I had formerly been a great Lover of Fish, & when this came hot out of the Frying Pan, it smelt admirably well. I balanc'd some time between Principle & inclination: till I recollected, that when the Fish were opened, I saw smaller Fish taken out of their Stomachs: Then, thought I, if you eat one another, I don't see why we mayn't eat you. So I din'd upon Cod very heartily and continu'd to eat with other People, returning only now & then occasionally to a vegetable Diet. So convenient a thing it is to be a reasonable Creature, since it enables one to find or make a Reason for every thing one has a mind to do.

Franklin was not the only one whose moral certainties were undone by the aromas of the kitchen. When the scents of frying or roasting reach the nostrils, the question is not Can they reason? or Can they talk?, but How do they taste? Even Bentham concluded that meat-eating could be justified if the animals died painlessly:

> If the being eaten were all, there is very good reason why we should be suffered to eat such of them as we like to eat: we are the better for it, and

they are none the worse. They have none of those long-protracted antici-
pations of future misery which we have. The death they suffer in our hands
commonly is, and always may be, speedier, and by that means a less painful
one, than that which would await them in the inevitable course of nature.

The same applied to vermin:

If the being killed were all, there is very good reason why we should be
suffered to kill such as molest us: we should be the worse for their living,
and they are never the worse for being dead.

*

Nor was any animal worse for being dead when the vivisectors had finished
with it. Anyone can cut open a live animal. All you need is a knife and a
strong stomach. In England one of the bloodiest pairs of hands belonged to
a clergyman. When he was not ministering to the needs of his Teddington
parishioners, the Reverend Stephen Hales was up to his elbows in a dog or
a horse. Despite this strange hobby he managed to earn the friendship of
Alexander Pope, who nevertheless was appalled by Hales's 'hands imbued
with blood'. Another clergyman, Thomas Twining, rector of All Saints,
Fordham, in Essex, wrote a satirical poem, *The Boat*, which included a
verse about his fellow man of God:

> Green Teddington's serene retreat
> For Philosophic studies meet,
> Where the good Pastor Stephen Hales
> Weighed moisture in a pair of scales,
> To lingering death put Mares and Dogs,
> And stripped the Skins from living Frogs,
> Nature, he loved, her Works intent
> To search or sometimes to torment.

The problem for Pope and Twining was that their opinion was not widely
shared. Far from being shunned for his blood-letting, Hales was admitted

to the Royal Society. Contrary to Twining's satire, he was not randomly poking about inside his terrified subjects. He was inserting flexible tubes into their arteries, connecting these to glass tubes and measuring how high the column of blood rose inside them. Up and down went the mark with each heartbeat; and up it went again when the animal was stressed. Hales's achievement in being the first man to measure blood pressure made him famous not only in England but throughout Europe. France admitted him to the Royal Academy of Sciences in Paris. Italy elected him to the Academy of Sciences in Bologna.

The Swiss physiologist Albrecht von Haller, Professor of Medicine at Göttingen, was a more orthodox sort of experimenter. It is easy to understand why the abolitionists hated him. He spent the middle years of the century cutting open dogs and testing the 'irritability' of their tissues. This he did by lacerating or burning them, or by applying acids and other stimuli which he knew would cause pain. He then extended his investigations to other species, upon which the same experiments were endlessly repeated. By Haller's own admission, a hundred and ninety animals of various kinds perished in this way. He argued that the comparison of one animal with another, and the remorseless replication of the same procedures, was the only pathway to the truth.

But *what* truth? Many would say that comparing dog with horse, or horse with pig, tells us nothing about the human body. To learn about that, you would have to cut up *people*. Human vivisection might have been acceptable to the ancients, but it cannot pass in the eighteenth century. Now it is not the learned professors who instruct us, but rather the handed-down wisdom of ordinary folk. For colic in children, the most efficacious treatment is fried pigeon's dung applied to the navel, followed by an enema of hot cow's milk. Excrement is also important in treating cancer of the breast, which is cured by an ointment of rose petals, sage, bay and chamomile which has been left to mature for eight days in a dunghill. For the falling sickness, the remedy is the leg bone of a deer, cooked and ground with the hair of a healthy young man, to be swallowed two days in advance of a new moon. The correct dose is the amount that can be held on a silver groat. Cures for smallpox include mixtures of tar water and sheep's dung, though the best answer is to be a dairyman or a milkmaid living with cattle.

Though cancer and falling sickness are terrible for those afflicted by them, it is smallpox that kills the most. For as long as people have lived on Earth, smallpox has been looking to sweep them off it. No person, high or low, is beyond its reach. History itself twists in its grip. It was the death from smallpox of Queen Mary II that led to the replacement of Stuarts by German-speaking Hanoverians on the English throne. It was smallpox that killed Louis XV of France. Not everyone who catches it dies: perhaps eighty out of every hundred adults, and sixty children will be spared, but the price of survival is disfigurement and blindness. No war has ever taken such a toll. Some say that the cost to Europe during this century alone has been 400,000 deaths and millions more ruined lives. Few people of normal intelligence imagine that tar water and sheep's dung will save a sick person's life. Three facts only have been verified by observation: that dairymaids succumb less often than scullery maids, that some cases are more survivable than others, and that those who survive seldom catch it a second time. In the early years of the century, these last two facts had a profound effect on the way people behaved. It was a desperate calculation, like bargaining with the Devil. Parents deliberately infected their children by putting them to bed with mildly suffering relatives. Sometimes they would even offer money for a sufferer's scabs. By contracting a mild and survivable form of the disease, it was hoped, the child would gain lifelong immunity.

It was at this exact point that science and folklore linked hands. In the second decade of the century, reports reached London of a kind of inoculation, or *variolation*, being practised in Constantinople. This was far more daring than the usual method of contracting smallpox by consorting with a sufferer. It involved deliberately milking the disease from sick people, transferring pus from a sore and passing it to the healthy. The method was best described by Lady Mary Wortley Montagu, wife of the British Ambassador to Turkey, in a letter written to a friend in 1717:

> A propos of distempers, I am going to tell you a thing, that will make you wish yourself here. The small-pox, so fatal, and so general amongst us, is here entirely harmless, by the invention of engrafting, which is the term they give it. There is a set of old women, who make it their business to perform the operation, every autumn, in the month of September, when the great

heat is abated. People send to one another to know if any of their family has a mind to have the small-pox; they make parties for this purpose, and when they are met (commonly fifteen or sixteen together) the old woman comes with a nut-shell full of the matter of the best sort of small-pox, and asks what vein you please to have opened. She immediately rips open that you offer to her, with a large needle (which gives you no more pain than a common scratch) and puts into the vein as much matter as can lie upon the head of her needle, and after that, binds up the little wound with a hollow bit of shell, and in this manner opens four or five veins ...

The children or young patients play together all the rest of the day, and are in perfect health to the eighth. Then the fever begins to seize them, and they keep their beds two days, very seldom three. They have very rarely above twenty or thirty in their faces, which never mark, and in eight days' time they are as well as before their illness.

Variolation at first was regarded by physicians in Europe with a mixture of fascination and horror. They were in a quandary. Even if the efficacy of the method could be proved, it still might not justify the ethically dubious practice of implanting a potentially fatal disease into a healthy person. Then Lady Montagu took the decisive step. She persuaded the British Embassy's surgeon in Constantinople, Charles Maitland, to inoculate her own young son. Back in London she became an enthusiastic proponent of the Turkish method, and was angered by physicians who scorned it as a foreign folk remedy. Then fate intervened. London in 1721 was struck by yet another smallpox epidemic and Lady Montagu asked Maitland to inoculate her three-year-old daughter Mary. This was the first time the procedure had been used in Britain, and the child became a subject of intense scrutiny. The result was a triumph for Lady Montagu over the sceptics. Young Mary developed mild symptoms but then made a swift and complete recovery while others suffered and died. For many anxious parents, this was enough to persuade them. Variolation was a gamble, but surely a lesser one than facing an epidemic with no defence at all.

Though physicians were impressed, they still wanted proof of cause and effect. The inadequacy of animal experiments now became clear. The only subjects who could demonstrate the effects of variolation in humans were *people*. As no one could be expected to volunteer their own bodies to be experimented upon, what the physicians needed was a class of people who could be treated like animals without troubling the consciences of the experimenters. This was why, under the direction of the King's surgeon Sir Hans Sloane, six condemned prisoners at Newgate prison were offered a bargain. In the presence of an audience they would submit themselves like dogs to the knife in return for their liberty if they survived. Skins were duly cut, pus inserted, symptoms recorded. To the great satisfaction of Lady Mary Wortley Montagu, all six walked free.

Although many physicians were now persuaded that the process was safe, and although the Prince and Princess of Wales set an example by having their daughters Amelia and Caroline inoculated in 1722, the controversy continued. In America the issue was more a war of words than an informed debate, with both sides summoning God as their witness. The front line was in Boston, Massachusetts, which in 1721 suffered its sixth smallpox epidemic since the city's foundation in 1630. Inoculation was championed there by two Puritan clergymen, Cotton Mather and Benjamin Colman, who faced opposition from anti-inoculists led by William Douglass, physician and founder of the *New England Courant*. It was in the columns of that newspaper that the argument raged back and forth. Mather, Colman and others of the Puritan clergy argued in letters to the editor that inoculation saved lives:

> The Operation within these four Months past has been undergone by more than Threescore Persons, Among which there have been Old & Young, Strong &Weak, Male & Female, White & Black, Many Serious and virtuous People, some the Children of Eminent Persons among us.
>
> Of all the number that have passed under the Operation, there has Not so much as One miscarried [died]. It has done well in all, and even beyond Expectation in most of them.

Malign rumours were furiously denied:

> The stories about the peculiar *Stench* attending these Persons are malicious Inventions. There is not a *Syllable* of truth in them.

The Formidable Stories we have had about their *Sores* are Egregious
Fictions and Falsehoods ...

The prevention of death, they said, was not only lawful: it was a *duty*. 'Those
who don't use Inoculation are in bad Terms with the sixth Commandment
[Thou shalt not kill]. They who call Inoculation the *Work of the Devil, &c.*,
are guilty of blasphemy.' But nobody in Boston stands on the wrong side
of God. The real blasphemy, said the sceptics, was to interfere with the
will of the Lord, who alone had the power to cause or to cure disease and
who was the sole arbiter of who would live and who would die. Making
healthy people sick was a sin, doubly so because they could then infect their
neighbours. And so, on both sides of the Atlantic, the arguments raged:
dogma against dogma, sceptics against the converted.

The one thing that cannot be disputed is *numbers*. Whether they come
from God or the Devil, numbers are *facts*. And the facts, as the Secretary
of the Royal Society James Jurin concluded from records in London and
Boston, were that the death rate among inoculated people during an
epidemic was one in sixty. For the rest it was one in five or six. From this
it seemed clear which side of the argument God was on. Among those
persuaded by the evidence was Catherine the Great of Russia, who had
herself inoculated by the English physician Thomas Dinsdale. What finally
settled the issue, however, was folklore and cows' teats. Folklore said that
dairymaids enjoyed some magical protection against the pox, and it was
known that the teats could be infected by a common disease called cowpox.
It was an English country doctor, Edward Jenner, who made the connection.
Milkmaids often developed a mild version of the bovine disease. A few
pustules would flare briefly on the skin, then the girls quickly recovered.
Jenner postulated that this was what conferred their fabled immunity to
smallpox. The process was easily explained. Pus from infected teats could
enter the bloodstream through any small opening in a girl's skin, when it
would have exactly the same effect as inoculation. Jenner then proceeded
to put theory into practice.

He began with an infected cow and a milkmaid called Sarah Nelmes
who had caught cowpox from it. Pus from Sarah's arm was scratched
into the arm of an eight-year-old boy, James Phipps, who then suffered

a typically mild case of cowpox exactly as Sarah had done. This was just what Jenner had expected. *Quod erat demonstrandum*: it proved the connection between ulcerated teat and ulcerated arm. But the life-and-death question still remained. Could this new process of *vaccination* really confer immunity to smallpox? Two months later, in July 1796, Jenner variolated young James in both arms with pus from smallpox sores. Then he did it again, and again.

It is a rare thing for the desired outcome of an experiment to be that nothing happens. The only blemishes on the boy's skin were the tiny marks left by the inoculation. Of fever and pocks there was not a sign.

Where in Genesis do we find any suggestion of the cow as saviour of human life? Where in the world do we hear any expression of gratitude to animals for the comforts they provide? Philosophers come and go, but they leave the Earth largely unmoved. The German Immanuel Kant is another who ploughs the well-worn furrow. 'He who is cruel to animals', he writes, 'becomes hard also in his dealings with men. We can judge the heart of a man by his treatment of animals.' Laid out before him when he wrote this was *The Four Stages of Cruelty*, a sequence of engravings by William Hogarth which shows the moral disintegration of a coachman. The man begins his criminal career by torturing dogs, proceeds by way of beating horses to murdering his pregnant lover, and ends up being taken down from the gallows and dissected before an audience in a theatre. But Kant's concern for non-human life goes no deeper than this: that cruelty like cowpox is a contagion that passes from beast to man. In every other respect he remains sunk to his haunches in the Old Testament. 'The fact that the human being can have the representation "I" raises him infinitely above all the other beings on earth. By this he is a person … that is, a being altogether different in rank and dignity from things, such as irrational animals, with which one may deal and dispose at one's discretion.'

Everything changes. Everything stays the same.

PART THREE

LATER

Saviours and Slaughterers

CHAPTER TWELVE

Mercy

OPINIONS VARIED ABOUT THE MEMBER OF PARLIAMENT FOR Shrewsbury, Sir William Pulteney. Some said he was the richest man in Britain; others that he was only one of the richest. By common consent he was one of the scruffiest. None of this detracted from his reputation as an assured and sensible speaker, certain of his facts, who was usually heard with respect. The one recorded exception occurred on 18 April 1800, when he introduced a bill to abolish 'the savage custom of bull-baiting'. If he had called for the abolition of moonbeams, his proposal could scarcely have been greeted more derisively. Was the man out of his mind?

In reality he was only marginally ahead of his time, and perhaps more in tune with public opinion than many of his colleagues. His death in 1805 came just too soon for him to witness the worldwide uprising against animal cruelty. The next attempt to change the law came in 1809, when Lord Erskine in the House of Lords introduced an Act to Prevent Malicious and Wanton Cruelty to Animals. He described a scene he had witnessed in a London street:

There was a cart, loaded with greens to a most unmerciful extent, drawn by one horse. The poor animal was in such a state that its skin alone covered its bones; and, what was more shocking upon nearer observation I perceived there was no cart-saddle to prevent the chain from cutting through the skin of the animal's back; and, upon still nearer inspection, I saw the blood and matter descending its side. Besides this, the fetlock-joint was dislocated, the skin broken, and, upon every exertion of this wretched creature, the bone was visible to the eye.

Erskine put an end to the animal's suffering by chasing the owner down the street and buying it from him. But this only brought into sharper focus the crux of the problem: the status of animals as *property*, and the right of owners to treat them as they pleased. Erskine's answer to this was the same as it was to slavery. He did not support the abolition of the slave trade, but he did think slaves should be treated kindly. Animals, he told the House, 'are created, indeed, for our use but not for our abuse'. Judges and juries, he said, saw no difficulty in distinguishing between appropriate treatment of slaves and wanton cruelty, and the same should apply to animals. This was an issue of supreme importance not just to Britain but to people and animals everywhere. 'The bill I propose to you, if it shall receive the sanction of Parliament, will not only be an honour to the country, but an era in the history of the world.' The sense of history, however, did not proceed beyond their lordships. Though the House of Lords approved Erskine's bill, the Commons, in fear of its animal-owning electorate, threw it out. Its most scornful opponent was William Windham, Minister for War. When soldiers were being whipped, and men and women sent to the gallows, he wondered, why should Parliament have any care for a baited bull?

One of those who supported Pulteney's and Erskine's bills was Colonel Richard Martin, the Irish MP for Galway, who was a determined opponent of bull-baiting, dog-fighting and cruelty to cattle. In 1822 he finally succeeded where Pulteney and Erskine had failed. With the support of the anti-slavery campaigner William Wilberforce and numerous public petitions he persuaded the House of Commons to approve his Ill Treatment of Cattle Bill by a margin of twenty-nine votes to eighteen. The Act, popularly known as Martin's Act, was specific to farm animals but strangely omitted bulls. These, along with dogs and cats, were added to later drafts. The Act in its original form declared that any person wantonly and cruelly beating, abusing or ill-treating 'any Horse, Mare, Gelding, Mule, Ass, Ox, Cow, Heifer, Steer, Sheep, or other Cattle ... shall forfeit and pay any Sum not exceeding Five Pounds, not less than Ten Shillings ... and if the person or persons so convicted shall refuse or not be able forthwith to pay the Sum forfeited, every such Offender shall … be committed to the House of Correction or some other Prison … for any Time not exceeding Three Months'. Martin was rewarded with a fond nickname by King George IV, who called him 'Humanity Dick', and by sarcastic cartoons which depicted him with asses' ears. 'The Terrible Paragraph!! Or Dickey Donkey's Dream is "all my Eye and Betty Martin"', said the rubric beneath one of them. The drawing showed him on a sofa recoiling in horror from three visions of himself being violently threatened by a coachman, a drover and a coster-monger. 'My eyes, how he Lies!' said the coachman as he booted Martin in the backside. The cartoonist's message was that caring for animals was not just unmanly, as Windham and his kind seemed to believe: it was *inhuman*. Who but an ass would mind about asses?

The House of Commons, too, showed little sympathy. On 15 June 1824 it rejected Martin's Slaughtering of Horses Bill, which would have obliged slaughterhouses to record the amount of feed given to each animal and imposed fines on anyone caught hauling a cart with a disabled horse. But Martin was not discouraged. Public opinion was moving in his direction and was being helped along by a large body of English clergymen. One of these was the Reverend Arthur Broome, curate of St Mary's Church, Bromley St Leonard's, who had been ordained by the Bishop of London, Beilby Porteus, a radical churchman who was the first Anglican of high rank to campaign against slavery. Broome's ambition, following the mixed fortunes of legislation in Parliament, was to establish a society dedicated to the welfare of animals. He made his first attempt in 1822 but, despite all his best efforts, the idea failed to take hold.

Martin's Act meanwhile was attracting as much scorn from welfare campaigners as it did from Windham and the bull-baiters. In 1823 the anti-slavery campaigner Elizabeth Heyrick redirected her attention from suffering humans to persecuted animals. Her pamphlet *Cursory Remarks on the Evil Tendency of Unrestrained Cruelty, particularly on that practised in Smithfield Market* was twenty-four pages of sustained outrage. Nobody was spared. Martin's Act, she said, 'will do as much towards diminishing the propensity or restraining the infliction of cruelty, as the current of a mighty river would be diminished by extracting from it drops of water'.

Anyone who doubted it could see for themselves on any Monday morning at Smithfield Market:

> Let them take their station at an upper window … and, from this field of observation, they will acquire a deeper insight into human nature – into the extremes of depravity into which it may be sunk, than they could easily obtain from any other quarter.

She described sheep and cattle bleeding from goads driven repeatedly into their bodies, and being bludgeoned about their heads as they collapsed with exhaustion after being made to stand, night and day, waiting for the sale. The brutal drover, she wrote:

> goads the patient animal in the most tender parts of his body: he strikes it upon the head and the horns, not because he hopes it does <u>not</u> [feel pain], but because he knows it does feel it acutely.

She was at one with Pythagoras in her opinion of where this must lead. Cruel treatment of a beast led directly to cruel treatment of our own species. 'The cruel man must, in every relation of society, be a bad man: a bad husband, a bad father, a bad son, a bad citizen.' She observed for herself this coarsening effect when she passed close to an animal that had been stunned by violent blows to the head. She did not remonstrate with the drover, being aware that it would be 'extreme folly' to do so. But the look in her eye was enough:

> The remonstrance conveyed in the pleading of my countenance caught the eye of the drover … who instantly lifted his weapon against me with such a savage, vindictive menace, as if he would, had he dared, have felled me to the ground.

But her low opinion of Martin and his followers was misplaced. They were not standing idly by. Broome himself had paid for some private prosecutions, and had paid an inspector to keep watch at Smithfield Market. Neither had he given up hope of establishing a society for the protection of animals. On 16 June 1824, at Old Slaughter's Coffee House in St Martin's Lane, he convened a meeting under the chairmanship of Sir Thomas Fowell Buxton, the socially reforming Member of Parliament for Weymouth and Melcombe Regis. Among those present were William Wilberforce, 'Humanity Dick' Martin, Lewis Gompertz and various other clergymen, lawyers and Members of Parliament. Together they resolved to form the Society for the Prevention of Cruelty to Animals, with Broome as honorary secretary. Martin's celebrity as author of the Cruel Treatment of Cattle Act meant that many people assumed he was the driving force behind the new society, but he modestly gave the credit to Broome. Credit was certainly due. Broome established an office in Regent Street and produced a stream of books and pamphlets intended to persuade or shame people into recalibrating their moral compasses. His many like-minded friends in the Church responded with fiery sermons. Broome's great misfortune was that his enthusiasm ran away with him like a driverless cart. And like a driverless cart he ended with a crash. The cause of it was his own tireless activity, which resulted in the society's expenditure far exceeding its income. This might not have mattered so much had the evangelical Broome not personally guaranteed its losses. The law being no respecter of good intentions, in 1826 he found himself among rogues, ne'er-do-wells and fellow unfortunates in a debtors' prison. His friends and colleagues Richard Martin and Lewis Gompertz hastened to his rescue. But though they successfully raised enough money to settle the society's debts and secure Broome's release, his reduced circumstances meant that he had to surrender his position as secretary. He was replaced in 1828 by Gompertz.

Here was a man whose zealotry made even Broome look half-hearted, and whose vegetarianism was more extreme even than Thomas Tryon's. Not only did he refuse to eat meat: he would not sit in any vehicle drawn by a horse and would not wear wool, leather, silk or anything else derived from animals alive or dead. In 1821, to improve the speed of horseless transport he had invented a new and improved kind of velocipede, though few people had the strength of leg to travel very far on one. The extreme and unyielding nature of Gompertz's views was an irritation to the society's committee, meat-eaters who wanted to campaign for the *welfare* of animals bred for slaughter, not for the abolition of the trade. His Jewishness also counted against him when these men of the pulpit resolved that membership of the society should be for Christians only. In 1833 he was forced to resign.

Two years later the SPCA helped achieve another success in Parliament. Martin's Act in its time had been a hard-fought victory, but it had enshrined a glaring inconsistency. Why should we care so much more about farm animals than we did about dogs and bears? In 1835, to great rejoicing among the SPCA but rather less among the wider populace, Parliament finally honoured the memory of Sir William Pulteney. The Act was duly amended to prohibit cock-fighting and the baiting or fighting of bulls, bears, badgers and dogs.

But Gompertz had raised and left hanging another issue of great concern to a small but growing minority. Twenty years earlier, the poet Percy Bysshe Shelley had published a pamphlet, *A Vindication of Natural Diet*, in which he identified meat-eating as the root of all humanity's ills and vegetable-eating as the only remedy. As befits a Romantic, his language was passionate. 'The supereminence of man', he wrote, 'is like Satan's, a supereminence of pain.' To understand the folly of eating meat, one had only to consider the structure of the human body, which was 'fitted to a pure vegetable diet, in every essential particular':

> Comparative anatomy teaches us that man resembles frugivorous animals in every thing, and carnivorous in nothing; he has neither claws wherewith to seize his prey, nor distinct and pointed teeth to tear the living fibre. A Mandarin of the first class, with nails two inches long, would probably find them alone inefficient to hold even a hare … Let the advocate of animal food, force himself to a decisive experiment on its fitness, and as Plutarch recommends, tear a living lamb with his teeth, and plunging his head into its vitals, slake his thirst with the steaming blood; when fresh from the deed of horror let him revert to the irresistible instincts of nature that would rise in judgment against it, and say, Nature formed me for such work as this. Then, and then only, would he be consistent.

Anyone who wanted to enjoy a long and healthy life, he said, need only observe two simple rules. 'Never take any substance into the stomach that once had life. Drink no liquid but water restored to its original purity by distillation'. The reward for this simple way of life would be to 'invigorate the body, by rendering its juices bland and consentaneous, and to restore to the mind that cheerfulness and elasticity, which not one in fifty possess on the present system'. This he could prove by mathematics. In the following year, he said, the results would be revealed of a study of sixty people who had lived for more than three years on his recommended diet. The study already was in its third year and all its subjects were in perfect health. No such example, Shelley asserted, could be found in any sixty people taken at random from the meat-eating majority. Another group of seventeen had lived for seven years on the same diet, without a death or any but the mildest ailment. 'Surely when we consider that some of these were infants, and one a martyr to asthma now nearly subdued, we may challenge any seventeen persons taken at random in this city to exhibit a parallel case'. There was no disease of mind or body, he said, that could not be mitigated by vegetables and purified water. Our only malady then would be the effects of old age. Even the Napoleonic wars might have been prevented if Napoleon had resisted the lure of meat:

> Surely the bile-suffused cheek of Buonaparte, his wrinkled brow, and yellow eye, the ceaseless inquietude of his nervous system, speak no less plainly the character of his unresting ambition than his murders and his victories. It is impossible, had Buonaparte descended from a race of vegetable feeders, that he could have had either the inclination or the power to ascend the throne of the Bourbons.

Animal husbandry was harmful in other ways too. Pasturage in particular was a waste of land which, if planted with vegetables, would allow people to feed themselves more efficiently. Better still, the country would no longer be economically dependent on exports of wool and thus would be freed from 'the caprices of foreign rulers'. There would be no need for costly imports and the 'avarice of commercial monopoly' would be weakened. 'Let it ever be remembered', he said, 'that it is the direct influence of commerce to make the interval between the richest and the poorest man wider and more unconquerable.' Only by renouncing animal flesh and fermented liquors could a society work for the 'liberty, security and

comfort of the many' and not 'the avarice and ambition of the few'. And
for any who doubted the benefits of what some people were beginning to
call *vegetarianism*, he added a final word:

> It may be here remarked, that the author and his wife have lived on vegeta-
> bles for eight months. The improvements of health and temper here stated
> is the result of his own experience.

One of those who influenced Shelley was the English physician William
Lambe. In 1815, two years after Shelley wrote his tract, Lambe himself
published a book of 250 pages whose very title, *Water and Vegetable Diet
in Consumption, Scrofula, Cancer, Asthma and Other Chronic Diseases*,
testified to the enormity of his claims. In 1850, to great acclaim, the book
was published in America. Vegetable diets by this time, though still uncon-
ventional, were no longer quite so inimical to popular opinion. Britain in
1847 and America in 1850 had both established vegetarian societies, and
many Americans, fearful of cholera and other epidemic diseases, adopted
a diet devised by a firebrand Presbyterian minister, Sylvester Graham, who
extolled the virtues of home-made bread. Graham's exalted reputation,
however, did not long survive his death in 1851, when it was revealed that
he had undergone a deathbed reversion and eaten meat in a desperate
attempt to save his own life.

Outside the vegetarian brotherhood, few people took much interest in
any of this. Those committed to animal welfare shared the SPCA's belief
that what really mattered was cruelty, and that the most blatant cause of
avoidable suffering was vivisection. Experiments on live animals were
especially common in France, where they were promoted and practised
in medical schools, and it was a French surgeon, François Magendie, who
had become the principal target of the abolitionists' rage. 'Humanity Dick'
Martin denounced him as 'a disgrace to society' for his work on dogs, which
Martin described in shocking detail to his fellow MPs. The experiments, he
said, were 'so atrocious as almost to shock belief'. During a demonstration
in London, Magendie compounded his notoriety by telling a wriggling dog
to keep still, *Soyez tranquille*, while it was being vivisected. His attempt
at humour – *Il serait plus tranquille s'il entendait français* (he would be

calmer if he understood French) – served only to enhance his reputation for callousness. His reputation in England, that is, for in France he was lauded as a scientist of worldwide importance. The same applied to his even more distinguished pupil Claude Bernard, who in 1851 succeeded him as Professor of Physiology at the Collège de France. Bernard could not accept that medicine was a proper science. Nothing, he said, could be learned about the workings of the body from the observation of the sick while alive, or from their dissection when dead. Only vivisection could provide the necessary insights. 'We shall succeed in learning the laws and properties of living matter', he wrote in his *Introduction to the Study of Experimental Medicine* in 1865, 'only by displacing living organs in order to get into their inner environments. To learn how men and animals live, we cannot avoid seeing great numbers of them die, because the mechanisms of life can be unveiled and proved only by knowledge of the mechanisms of death.' His one regret was that the laboratories in France were so greatly inferior to those in Germany. Even so, he managed to cleave his way through such a vast number of dogs, many of them strays that he rounded up and took home to his cellar, that his wife and daughters were moved, or perhaps shamed, into establishing a shelter for strays.

Opposition to vivisection in Britain meanwhile had grown into a powerful political movement that had impressed even Queen Victoria. In 1840 she raised the SPCA to the rank of *Royal* Society for the Prevention of Cruelty to Animals. The introduction of ether in 1849 did little to quieten the storm, for its effect was to *calm* the animals rather than to spare them pain. Sixteen years later Bernard made scant mention of it in his *Introduction*. In 1861 the RSPCA sent a delegation to Emperor Napoleon III, begging him to ban vivisection in medical schools – a petition angrily denounced by the French Academy of Medicine. But not all opponents of vivisection were moved by high-minded concerns for animal welfare. What many people objected to was the arrogance of the vivisectors themselves, which they regarded as symptomatic of the abusive power exercised by rich and influential elites over the poor. In 1857 the RSPCA launched a campaign to take live animals out of the laboratories, and had some success twenty years later when Parliament approved the Cruelty to Animals Act of 1876, the first such law anywhere in the world. The Act did not ban vivisection outright, but it did impose restrictions and penalties for trans-gressors. Most importantly it decreed that any experiment involving a live animal must be intended to advance our understanding of physiology, or of knowledge likely to be useful in saving or prolonging life, or alleviating suffering, and the experimenter must hold a licence issued by a Secretary of State. Any scientist causing pain for any other purpose could be fined up to fifty pounds for a first offence, and one hundred pounds or three months' imprisonment for any subsequent offence. Though this largely reflected the public mood, it did not altogether succeed in increasing the popularity of the RSPCA. If people disliked and distrusted the arrogance of doctors, then they disliked even more the arrogance of clergy, MPs and other men of privilege who had campaigned against bull-baiting and dog-fights while having nothing to say about hunting. There was a perceived discrepancy, too, in their attitudes to horses flogged by impoverished carters and those whipped by hunters and jockeys.

The SPCA, or RSPCA as it became, was the first animal protection society anywhere in the world. But the rest of the world was watching, and none more closely than the Americans. No matter how quickly an organisation might grow, it must always start small and depend upon the enterprise of a committed individual. In Britain that individual was Richard Martin. In America it was Henry Bergh, a former diplomat born in New York who had inherited a fortune from his shipbuilding German father. He had served as secretary and acting vice consul to the American legation in St Petersburg before resigning in 1864, unable to face another Russian winter. During a wide-ranging tour of Europe he had witnessed all the same cruelties that had so disgusted Richard Martin. The crucial event was a meeting with the president of the RSPCA, Lord Harrowby. Whatever Harrowby said to him had far-reaching consequences. In 1866 Bergh founded and became first president of the American Society for the Prevention of Cruelty to Animals, resolved to oppose vivisectors, slaughterers, carters, shooters, cruel sportsmen and abusers of every kind. Their early successes included a horse ambulance in New York, the jailing of a man for beating a cat to death, and the substitution of clays for live birds at pigeon-shoots. Like Elizabeth Heyrick and others throughout history, Bergh believed that humanity was indivisible: cruelty to animals and cruelty to humans arose from the same malign instincts. 'Mercy to animals means mercy to mankind', he said. 'Men will be just to men when they are kind to animals.' But where Heyrick extended her concern from people to animals, Bergh's journey was in the opposite direction. In 1875, nine years after creating the ASPCA, he helped found the New York Society for the Prevention of Cruelty to Children. He died in 1888, by which time only one of the thirty-eight states in the union did not have laws against animal cruelty.

The good fortune of animals in Britain and America was to live in countries ruled by non-conformists. In Britain many of the early members of the SPCA were Anglicans who took their message into the pulpit. Similarly in America, Episcopalian ministers vigorously preached against cruelty. Those in Catholic countries were not so lucky. The RSPCA in England was misled by the Cardinal Archbishop of Westminster, Henry Edward Manning, who declared that vivisection was 'the certain infraction of the first laws of mercy and humanity'. They wrongly supposed that this reflected the views of the Pope. It did no such thing. Pius IX, a connoisseur of theological error, ruled against the establishment of an animal protection society in Rome because, as the Bible made clear, it was a mistake to suppose that humans bore any responsibility for the welfare of soulless animals. That was the business of God alone.

CHAPTER THIRTEEN

Pictures, Poems and Parks

THE PROTECTION SOCIETIES CONCENTRATED THEIR EFFORTS ON the creatures that were easiest to protect: pets, working animals and livestock. But people were beginning to worry about wild animals too. A wealthy Frenchman bequeathed $100,000 to the ASPCA on condition that it would extend its concern to 'the wild things of forest and plain'. Churchmen meanwhile continued to wrestle with the conundrum of a supposedly benevolent Creator and the unstoppable cruelties of nature. It was not easy to discern God's mercy when he had sent so many predators and parasites to cause so much pain, death and disease to innocent others. The utilitarian philosopher and atheist John Stuart Mill pressed the point in his *Nature and Utility of Religion*:

> In sober truth, nearly all the things which men are hanged or imprisoned for doing to one another are nature's everyday performances. Killing, the most criminal act recognized by human laws, nature does once to every being that lives, and in a large proportion of cases after protracted tortures such as only the greatest monsters whom we read about ever purposely inflicted on their living fellow creatures.

The best reply on God's behalf was William Paley's *Natural Theology, or Evidences of the Existence and Attributes of the Deity collected from the appearances of nature*, published in 1802. Paley was an English clergyman and philosopher whose self-appointed mission was to demonstrate that everything in the living world was essential to God's purpose. The predatory system, he wrote, was 'a spring of motion and activity in both the hunters and the hunted':

> The pursuit of its prey forms the employment, and appears to constitute the pleasure, of a considerable part of the animal creation. Using the means of defence, flight, or precaution forms the business of another part. And even of this latter tribe – the prey – we have no reason to suppose that their happiness is much damaged by their fears … Contemplating the insecurity of their condition with anxiety and dread would require a degree of reflection which (happily for themselves) they do not possess. Despite the number of its dangers and its enemies, the hare is as playful an animal as any other.

God's purpose, he said, is to maintain a happy balance, and the key to this is *superfecundity*. Put simply, the losses to predators are offset by overproduction of prey so that both populations remain constant. By this reasoning you would expect the smallest and most vulnerable animals to produce more young than larger ones with fewer enemies, which is exactly what happens. This explains why a single codfish in one season spawns more eggs than there are people in England.

> An elephant produces only one calf; a butterfly lays six hundred eggs. Birds of prey seldom produce more than two eggs; sparrows and ducks frequently sit on a dozen. In the rivers we meet with a thousand minnows for one pike; in the sea, a million of herrings for a single shark. Compensation obtains throughout. Defencelessness and devastation are repaired by fecundity.

Wherever a species multiplied beyond the capacity of nature to sustain it, said Paley, it was the predators' job to cut it down to size. Without this controlling mechanism, 'there may be no species of terrestrial animals that would not overrun the earth if it were permitted to multiply in perfect safety; or species of fish that would not fill the ocean if it were left to its natural increase without disturbance or restraint'. We should accept therefore that nothing is without purpose, and not complain about exorbitant numbers of bothersome insects. Without the happy industry of gnats, he said, vast tracts of North American forest would be 'nearly lost to sensitive existence'. Without the swarms of mice which north-eastern Europeans find so distressing, the plains of Siberia would be lifeless. As it is, 'the Caspian deserts are converted by their presence into crowded warrens.' But the natural world, like the human, is never static. When the forests are cleared and the swamps are drained, the gnats will make way for others. When the population of Europe spreads north and eastwards, then the mice will give way to herds and flocks. Humans, too, have their part to play:

> When old countries become exceedingly corrupt, simpler modes of life, purer morals and better institutions may rise up in new countries, where fresh soils reward the cultivator with more plentiful crops. In this way different portions of the globe come into use successively as the residence of man; and in his absence entertain other guests which fill the chasm by their sudden multiplication.

*

Others were looking at wild animals and places in very different ways and for very different reasons. What the Romantics loved was the wildness itself. This was not always easy for the rest of us to understand. They protested their love principally through art and poetry, so that their philosophy could seem more rhyme than reason. Brotherhood appears to have been at the heart of it, bound into a skein of mysticism that included rocks, torrents, trees, animals, humans and God. Woods were temples where devotees communed with nature. To experience true wildness in such places was a journey of the spirit. 'For everything that lives is holy', wrote William Blake, 'life delights in life.' His own delight, expressed in a poem called 'The Fly', embraced even William Paley's bothersome insects:

> Little Fly
> Thy summer's play,
> My thoughtless hand
> Has brush'd away.
> Am not I

A fly like thee?
Or art not thou
A man like me?

For Samuel Taylor Coleridge, the soulmate was an ass:

How *askingly* its footsteps hither bend?
It seems to say, 'And have I then one friend?'
Innocent foal! Thou poor despis'd forlorn!
I hail thee BROTHER – spite of the fool's scorn!
And fain would take thee with me, in the Dell
Of Peace and Equality to dwell.

Both of these were written in 1794. William Wordsworth later addressed the cuckoo – 'O blithe-new-comer!' – and the nightingale, 'Ethereal minstrel! pilgrim of the sky!' If it was natural, or 'red in tooth and claw' as Tennyson put it, then it was sublime. The most hated enemies of Romanticism were landscape 'improvers' such as William Kent, Lancelot 'Capability' Brown and Humphry Repton who thought nature needed a helping hand. To Romantic eyes their ha-has, carriage drives, artfully clumped trees and serpentine lakes were poison in nature's veins. John Constable created his own masterpieces by steadfastly looking the other way. 'A gentleman's park', he said, 'is my aversion. It is not beauty because it is not nature.'

It was not just in landscape that artists took a Romantic view of the world. Animals, too, were painted in all their natural savagery. No one dipped his brush in more blood than the Frenchman Eugène Delacroix. There was no room in his pictures for well-bred dogs or shiny horses. His *Tiger Attacking a Wild Horse* is as raw as nature itself. There is nobility in the way he presents a lion standing protectively over his lioness; sublime cruelty in his picture of a lion devouring a goat. Pain and death fill every frame. A tiger confronts a snake; another toys with a tortoise. A lion seizes a lizard. Such naturalistic depictions are as far from the idealised visions of the Renaissance as an eagle from a canary. An animal to Delacroix is not just tooth, fur and claw: it is a body pierced by experience and animated by a soul. Britain's great master of animal art was Sir Edwin

Landseer, a favourite of Queen Victoria whose gaze seemed to pass clean through the skin of the beast to the terrors within. Viewers of his work are forced to share the animals' suffering. An orphaned fawn sucks desperately at the teats of a mother shot by hunters. A speared otter is held aloft as hounds slaver and lunge; a terrified stag is beset by hounds in a mountain torrent; a petrified fox awaits its bloody fate. But not all is terror and pain. The Romantic vision was of the unquenchable spirit of the wild. Landseer most famously caught this in his monumental portrait of a Highland stag, *Monarch of the Glen*, and in the four bronze lions that were ranged around Nelson's Column in 1867. These were critically scrutinised by the Superintendent of London Zoo, Abraham Dee Bartlett, and his friend the eccentric naturalist and Inspector of Fisheries Frank Buckland. When they had finished measuring and making notes, they rushed back to Regent's Park to check them against real animals in the zoo. The only fault they could find was the forgivable absence of whiskers. 'The complicated flexures of the opening nostril', Buckland noted, 'are true to the eighth of an inch'.

All this has had a powerful influence on the way people think about animals. Delacroix, Landseer and Gustave Courbet simultaneously intensified public opposition to hunting and stimulated new interest in all things wild and exotic. Not only the paintings but the animals themselves became popular exhibits. Zoos at first were conceived as closed institutions reserved for scientific study. London was the first, opening at Regent's Park on 27 April 1828, followed by Dublin in 1831 and Downs' Zoological Gardens, Nova Scotia, in 1847. By the end of 1827, well before its opening to non-members in the following year, London already provided 'suitable dens, aviaries and paddocks' for some two hundred animals including 'two beautiful llamas, a leopard, kangaroos, a Russian bear, ratel, ichneumons, &c., &c., besides a pair of emus, cranes, gulls, gannets, corvorants, various gallinaceous birds, and many others'. One of these others was a griffon vulture named 'Dr Brookes', after the anatomist Joshua Brookes, who had helped establish the zoo's scientific credentials with a lecture on the dissection of an ostrich. A report from the zoo to the offices of the Zoological Society of London in February 1828 reveals an ambitious institution soberly dedicated to good order and progress.

MENAGERIE. – Received eleven wild ducks from the Lake, caught
for the purpose of pinioning, and then to be returned.

Received six silver-haired rabbits from Mr Blake.

Otter died, in consequence of a diseased tail.

Emu laid her fourth egg on the 24th.

All animals and birds well.

WORKS. – Pit for bear, house for llamas in progress.

Boundary wall for supporting the bank next to the Bear's pit begun.

SERVANTS. – All on duty.

NO. OF VISITORS. – Four.

PARTICULAR VISITOR. – Lord Auckland.

The zoo opened to non-members in 1828 but it was not an invitation to
the common horde. Only a select few were welcome. The Society's declared
intention was 'to prevent the contamination of the Zoological Garden by
the admission of the poorer classes of Society'. Visitors were admitted only
on the written authority of a member, and for a fee of one shilling. It was
not until 1847 that the *hoi polloi* were finally let in. London's example was
followed by public zoos in Melbourne and Central Park, New York, both in
1860. Nowhere in the world was zoo-keeping a suitable calling for anyone
lacking ingenuity, humour or courage. Imagination rather than common
sense was the essential requirement for anyone needing to corral a dis-
oriented bear, an angry rhinoceros or some unidentifiable species that he
had never seen before. The greatest of all nineteenth-century zoo-keepers
was London's Abraham Dee Bartlett, a taxidermist who in 1858 had taken
delivery of London's first gorilla. Following the heroic precedents of Lords
Nelson and Byron, it arrived pickled in a barrel of spirits. Bartlett seldom
knew what would happen next. The unpredictability of wild animals
extended far beyond the imaginations of poets and painters. Bartlett
described a confrontation between two boa constrictors that both wanted
the same pigeon. The eleven-foot-long victor, having a two-foot advantage
over its rival, lost all interest in the pigeon and swallowed the other snake
instead. In the process, it distended itself so grossly that it became as stiff
as a flagpole. At least Bartlett could be certain of what a boa would eat,
which was pretty much anything it could stretch its jaws around. Other

creatures could be kept alive only by a risky process of trial and error. The animals that were brought to his door were not captive-bred specimens with well-known needs and habits. They were wild-caught exotics which often arrived in bad health and with no record of their natural diets. One day in 1869 he received what he was able eventually to identify as the zoo's first panda. Its condition greatly distressed him:

> I found the animal in a very exhausted condition, not able to stand, and so weak that it could with difficulty crawl from one end of its long cage to the other. It was suffering from frequent discharges of frothy, slimy faecal matter. This filth had so completely covered and matted its fur that its appearance and smell was most offensive.

He correctly identified it as a red panda, *Ailurus fulgens*, but this was no help to him in deciding how to care for it. What on earth did red pandas eat?

> The instructions I received with reference to its food were that it should have about a quart of milk per day, with a little boiled rice and grass. It was evident that this food, the change of climate, the sea voyage, or the treatment on board ship had reduced the poor beast to this pitiable condition.

His first offering, raw and cooked chicken and rabbit, was furiously rejected, but he did persuade the animal to swallow a little arrowroot mixed with egg-yolk, sugar and boiled milk. After this came strong beef tea, well sweetened and thickened with pea-flour, Indian-corn flour and 'other farinaceous food, varying the mixture daily'. The animal thanked him with ill temper and bared claws.

> When offended, it would rush at me and strike with both feet, not, like a cat, sideways or downwards, but forward, and the body raised like a bear, the claws protruding, but not hooked or brought down like the claws of a cat ...

Only when it had recovered sufficiently to be released into the gardens was the animal's ingratitude fully explained. It paused briefly to take stock, then ran straight to a tree, *Pyrus vestita*, which, like the panda itself, was a native of China. Moments later it was contentedly feasting on leaves and berries. Bartlett had been trying to force meat on a vegetarian. Time after time with new arrivals, this was how it went. Zoo-keepers were not mere custodians, they were naturalists learning through experience what their animals needed. Some problems could be solved only at mortal risk to the handlers. Bartlett described the hazardous process of extracting a broken tooth from a hippopotamus. This involved a pair of forceps more than two feet long which Bartlett wielded from behind a fence. The task in the end was facilitated by the hippo's own rage. Its great jaws, wide enough to bite a canoe in half, gave him the chance he needed to grasp, pull and twist the 'coveted morsel' from its mouth. 'One of the most remarkable things', he noted, 'appeared to me to be the enormous force of the air when blown from the dilated nostrils of this great beast while enraged. It came against me with a force that quite surprised me.' Transporting and handling wild creatures could be just as hazardous to the animals themselves, and none more so than the giraffes. Their enormous height, long necks and gangling limbs made them particularly difficult to load and unload from ships, and their accidental deaths were often dramatic. Some tumbled from dockside cranes; two burned to death in a fire at London Zoo, and three more broke their necks against a wall at Hamburg. From Africa and across the world, the capture, transport and sale of wild animals was building into a profitable international trade that would cause as much suffering to local peoples as it did to elephants, rhinoceroses, lions and tigers.

The pantheistic spirituality of the Romantics, who saw nature as a kind of stairway to the heavens, was translated in the popular mind into a new fascination with wild places and the animals that lived in them. From this grew a desire to protect and preserve them. It is a moot point whether this burgeoning concern arose out of compassion for species critically endangered by encroaching humans, or out of the self-interested belief that there was some benefit to humans in communing with them. Nowhere was the pace of change faster than in America. By the early 1870s, in the words of the US Army commander at Fort Dodge, the air in Kansas 'was foul with a sickening stench', and the vast plain a 'dead, putrid desert'. Three hundred

years earlier the conquistadores had stared open-mouthed at herds of buffaloes that stretched from one horizon to the next. One expedition-leader
described them parting like the Red Sea, just long enough to let his men
pass through before closing behind them. The animals were uncountable,
though some people reckoned there were thirty million. Buffaloes outnumbered humans like flies now outnumbered carcasses. According to the first
official census, the population of the United States in 1790 was less than four
million, though it would reach more than seventy-five million by the end of
the nineteenth century. The consequence for the buffalo, and for the native
tribes erroneously called 'Indians', was catastrophic. White settlers seeking
land and fortune surged west on a tide of hope and destruction, some two
million of them in the 1870s alone. With them came guns. Never have so
many trigger fingers twitched with such devastating effect. The Romantic
notions of Blake, Coleridge and Wordsworth counted for nothing here.
Where the Indians had killed to feed and clothe themselves, the newcomers
just killed. Professional hunters swarmed like hyenas, though with none
of that animal's hatred of waste. Hence the stink of carcasses stripped of
their hides. Hence the prairies and plains devoid of all movement save
that of men with their wagons, horses, cattle and railways. Libbie Custer,
whose husband General George Armstrong Custer died at the Battle of
the Little Bighorn, complained of passengers firing through the windows
of moving trains:

> When the sharp shrieks of the train whistle announced a herd of buffaloes
> the rifles were snatched, and in the struggle to twist around for a good aim
> out of the narrow window the barrel of the muzzle of the firearm passed
> dangerously near the ear of any scared woman who had the temerity to
> travel in those tempestuous days.

It was, she said, 'the greatest wonder' that more people were not killed.
But there was no such miracle for the buffaloes. They might have survived
the random fire of amateur shooters jostling at the windows of the Santa
Fe Railroad, but the professionals attacked with cool precision and wild
ferocity, as if the sight of a living buffalo were an affront to their manhood.
One-shot kills were the mark of an expert, though the animals' natural

instincts, or 'stupidity' as the hunters interpreted it, greatly simplified the task. When the leader of a herd was shot, the others would circle around it, as easy to pick off as ducks on a pond. One hunter boasted of collecting two hundred and sixty-nine hides at the expense of three hundred cartridges. Others made even more extravagant claims. The army scout-turned-showman William 'Buffalo Bill' Cody was said to have killed four thousand, two hundred and eighty buffaloes in the space of eighteen months between 1867 and 1868. In the first three months of its existence in 1871, the new settlement at Dodge City shipped forty-three thousand and twenty-nine hides and one-and-a-half million pounds of meat. There were a few men in Congress who apparently welcomed this slaughter as a means of 'civilising' and controlling the Indians by destroying their source of food. But this was hardly necessary. The ceaseless influx of homesteaders meant that by the late 1870s the Indians were outnumbered, forty to one, by the whites, and the plains had been ploughed, railroaded and taken over by cattle. Even allowing for exaggeration, the numbers of dead were so shocking that public opinion began to turn against the killers. But it was too late. The buffaloes were gone. A bill introduced by Congressman Greenbury Fort 'to prevent the useless slaughter of buffaloes within the Territories of the United States' passed both houses of Congress but never became law because President Ulysses S. Grant could see no point in signing it.

Yet the Romantics had not written or painted in vain. The wider public might not have understood their mysticism, but it was inspired to feel new respect for wilderness and a love of pristine beauty. Travellers now went out of their way to visit remote and frightening landscapes and to feel themselves, however briefly, reconnected with the awesome power of nature. What the transformation of the American West also made clear was that such places were defenceless against human incursion and that, inexorably one by one, they would be lost unless something was done to save them. This obviously could not happen without changes in the law. This time Ulysses S. Grant did not withhold his signature. On the first day of March 1872, he signed into law a Congressional bill establishing Yellowstone, a vast tract of land straddling parts of Wyoming, Montana and Idaho, as the world's first national park. The site was well chosen. Yellowstone's rugged mix of mountains, canyons, lakes, rivers and a volcano gave refuge to grizzly bears, elk, wolves, buffaloes, coyotes, deer, mountain goats, bighorn sheep, lynx, cougars, as wild as any place could be. But it was also the ancestral home and hunting ground of Indians who did not warm to the idea of being redefined as trespassers. For this and other reasons Yellowstone in its early years was not quite the haven its founders intended. Victims included several tourists killed or wounded by angry Indians, and thousands of elk and buffaloes shot by poachers. Visitors at first were slow to arrive: only three hundred in 1872, and by 1883 had still reached only a modest five thousand. For the animals if not the Indians, matters improved when the army took control in 1886. The buffalo population was reinvigorated by animals from a private herd and the number of visitors rapidly increased. The success of Yellowstone led to the establishment of three more American parks before the end of the century: Sequoia and Yosemite, both in 1890, and Mount Rainier in 1899. All this we owe to the Romantics. Though we may forget their brotherhoods of flies and asses, we may be eternally grateful for what they have handed down to us.

Not just pictures and poems but parks and people, bears and buffaloes, the haunted silences of the truly wild.

CHAPTER FOURTEEN

Old Bones, New Ideas

CRUELTY IN THE NINETEENTH CENTURY MEANS DIFFERENT things to different people. A clerk in the city does not think of animals as a herdsman does. Men who enjoy dog-fights have little in common with those who hunt foxes. Those who shoot birds are not like those who keep them in cages. A man who takes a dog for a walk is no friend of the one who might cut up his pet in a laboratory. Right and wrong circle each other like wrestlers.

The hard truth is that society is a mirror held up to nature. When power meets weakness, power wins. A big boa will always swallow a smaller one; a rich man will always swallow a pauper. That is how nature works. Thus abolitionists who interrupt a foxhunt risk the wrath of the magistrates. For working men at the cockpit it is the law itself that comes calling. To them, the RSPCA represents an upper-class conspiracy against ordinary people.

Sympathy for animals in these circumstances can seem indulgent. Those wealthy enough to travel abroad are often disturbed by what they see. In southern Europe, where Papal authority is strongest, visitors from the north are appalled not just by the *corrida* but even more by the sight of domestic animals being maltreated and songbirds shot for the table. Back in England they direct their anger at their social inferiors, cab-drivers, bargees and other hard-pressed tradesmen who flog their horses to the very last gasp. The tradesmen themselves see this hard treatment as economic good sense. Horses do not come cheap, and you cannot afford to let one go without squeezing every last ounce of work from it. Putting a tired animal out to grass is all very well if you are rich, but unaffordable if you are not. The welfare campaigners' faith in the Cruelty to Animals Act of 1835 was to a degree fanciful. Bringing the Act into law was easy. All it took was a few fine words and a vote in Parliament. Imposing it was rather more difficult. A prudent carter might now look over his shoulder before reaching for the lash, but few animals will notice any difference in their workload. Those determined to continue cock-fighting, badger-baiting or dog-fighting similarly find little trouble in evading the law.

The legislators intended the Act to have wider benefits than just the protection of animals. Just as importantly, it would prevent 'the demoralization of the people'. The only people actually demoralised were the few, almost all from the lower classes, who found themselves in court. It was this very inequality in the law that prompted John Stuart Mill in 1868 to decline the vice-presidency of the RSPCA. A year later the influential Oxford historian A.E. Freeman published an outspoken article on 'The Morality of Field Sports' in the *Fortnightly Review*. Freeman recalled Lord Erskine's failed attempt to introduce an Act to Prevent Malicious and Wanton Cruelty to Animals in 1809, when the opposition was led by the Whig Minister for War William Windham. It was central to Windham's case that it would be hypocritical to abolish bull-baiting while foxhunting, shooting and fishing continued with the full blessing of the law, and it went without saying that Parliament had no intention of prohibiting any of these. Freeman turned this argument back on itself:

> From the admitted right to torture a fox, Windham inferred the right to torture the bull. From the admitted sin of torturing the bull I infer the sin of torturing the fox.

He argued, as others had done, that killing for pleasure could not be morally justified. This was difficult to refute and won support from more than just the disaffected lower classes. Many middle-class professionals in towns and cities were unconvinced by the landowners' argument that foxhunting was essential preparation for military service, or that it rid the country of vermin. But their concern was selective. Opponents of cruelty generally were moved by animals' shrieks of pain. While this aroused compassion for horse, dog, deer and fox, it was of no benefit to fish. Their perpetual silence and supposed numbness to pain meant they found few champions even among the elders of the RSPCA or the Church. Clergymen who had argued so vehemently against cruel sports happily dangled their hooks for carp and barbel. One who did speak up for the fish, though he was an ardent fisherman himself, was Her Majesty's Inspector of Salmon Fisheries, Frank Buckland:

> If we listen to a lecture from a learned professor upon the brains of animals, he will point out the human brain as being at the highest end of the scale, the brain of the fish at the lowest. Holding up the brain of a fish, beautifully prepared in spirits of wine, he will say: 'There, gentlemen, is an example of a badly-developed brain. The creature to which it belonged is proverbially dull and stupid.' Yet the next day, if we look over Richmond-bridge, we may behold the same learned but sportless professor puzzling his well-developed brain to catch the creature which but yesterday he was asserting had so little brains. The brain of the fish is quite sufficient to keep him off the professor's hook, angle he never so wisely.

The poet Byron, in Canto XIII of *Don Juan*, had no doubt that fish could feel pain, and was contemptuous of those who inflicted it:

> Boats when 'twas water, skating when 'twas ice,
> And the hard frost destroy'd the scented days:
> And angling too, that solitary vice,
> Whatever Izaak Walton sings or says:
> The quaint, old, cruel coxcomb, in his gullet
> Should have a hook, and a small trout to pull it.

Few shared Byron's sensitivity. The real argument was less about the sensibility of fish than rights of ownership. On biblical authority, Christians believed fish were given by God for all to enjoy, and that wild creatures could not be private property. Some were moved by this to argue that even the game laws were an affront to God, and many more were ready to claim the freedom of lake and river. The writer and wood-engraver Thomas Bewick spoke up for the landless majority:

> No reasonable plea can ever be set up to show that the fish of rivers ought to be the private property of any one. Can it be pretended that because a river or a rivulet, passes through an estate, whether the owner of it will or not, that the fish which breed in it, or which live in it, ought to be his? They are not like the game, which are all fed by the farmer, for fish cost nobody anything; therefore, in common justice, they ought to belong to the public.

Bewick, who was a practised observer of nature widely celebrated for his *History of British Birds*, passed rather swiftly over the question of whether or not fish had sensation. He satisfied himself that they 'had little sense and scarcely any feeling', and definitely less of either than any land animal. Like William Paley he sought justification in the innate cruelty of the wild: 'We see through all nature that one kind of animal seems destined to prey upon another, and fishes are the most voracious of all.'

The author of *Rural Rides*, William Cobbett, was one of many who believed we could not properly respect our fellow humans if we did not show respect for animals. All country women and girls, he said, should learn to milk and make butter. This would teach them, 'from their infancy, *to set a just value upon dumb animals*' and to 'grow up in the *habit* of treating them with gentleness and feeding them with care'. Cruelties such as nailing down geese were abhorrent:

> He who can deliberately inflict torture upon an animal, in order to heighten the pleasure his palate is to receive in eating it, is an abuser of the authority which God has given him, and is, indeed, a tyrant in his heart. Who would think himself safe, if at the mercy of such a man?

Much has changed since Cobbett wrote those words in 1821. The world at the end of the nineteenth century is very different from the world at the beginning of it. The oneness with nature and intimacy with animals that

Cobbett extolled are no longer the common experience. Steam engines, not horses, drive the new industries, and people in towns and cities, middle and lower classes alike, have but a blurred sense of where their food comes from. Not one in a thousand could milk a cow. The rosy-cheeked milkmaid is no longer the girl next door, but a goddess-like figment of poetic imagination.

> Now give me your milking-stool awhile,
> To carry it down to yonder stile;
> I'm wishing every step a mile,
> And myself your only sweetheart.
> When the morning sun is shining low,
> And the cocks in every farmyard crow,
> I'll carry your pail,
> O'er hill and dale,
> And I'll go with you a-milking.

So wrote the Irish poet William Allingham in his ballad *The Milkmaid*, evoking a romantic vision far removed from the pale-skinned millworkers and factory girls who were the future wives of most ordinary young men. When they looked out of their windows it was not meadows they saw, but walls and chimneys. The shift in public attitudes was gradual but profound. For common people throughout most of history, kindness to animals was unaffordable. In poor Victorian households struggling against hunger, even kindness to children was a luxury. If there was a mouth to feed, then it had to earn its keep. Children were sent down coalmines, up chimneys and into factories, laundries and shipyards. *In extremis* they were put to pickpocketing or prostitution. In matters of welfare or discipline they were to be treated as *human animals*, a notion made explicit in 1809 when Lord Erskine introduced his ultimately unsuccessful Bill for Preventing Malicious and Wanton Cruelty to Animals. How, he asked, were magistrates to distinguish between 'the justifiable labours of the animal, which from Man's necessities is often most fatiguing,' and pitiless maltreatment? 'How are they to distinguish between the blows which are necessary, when beasts of labour are lazy or refractory, or even blows of sudden passion and temper, from deliberate, cold-blooded, ferocious cruelty...?' His answer was simple.

What was cruel to an apprentice was cruel to an animal, and this was the principle that magistrates should apply when considering their verdicts. Of course this could cut both ways. Men who were kind to apprentices might be kind also to horses. Men who abused their apprentices might be cruel also to their animals. For 'apprentices', the common people understood 'children'. The only animals met by most townsfolk now are their pets. Infatuation with dog, cat and canary encourages more and more people to think of themselves as 'animal-lovers' and to pass judgement on those who put animals to work. The Victorians also had an excessive concern for decency. The docking of horses' tails was deemed cruel by some, and indecorous by the more fastidious members of society who took offence at the naked exposure of the animal's hind parts. One of these was Thomas Bewick in his *General History of Quadrupeds*:

> A strong, bony, and active kind of Horse is now used in our carriages, instead of the old black Coach-Horse, which is almost universally laid aside. The docked tail, offensive both to humanity and decency, is rarely to be seen: propriety and good sense have at length prevailed over a custom replete with absurdity; and our Horses are permitted to retain a member both useful and ornamental. But we have still to regret, that the cruel practice of forming the tail, by cutting and nicking it on the underside, is yet continued.

Not everyone was impressed by pet-lovers' assertions of moral superiority. The incarceration of undomesticated wild species or the isolation of tame social ones seemed hardly less cruel than beating a horse. But history is on the side of pets, and the scales weighted heavily in their favour. Wherever they ventured in the world, explorers saw pets being treated very differently to working animals. Australian Aborigines seemed to take better care of their breast-fed dingos than they did of their children. Miniature dogs were prized more highly among the Comanche nation in the American West than the horses upon which their lives depended. A relationship with a dog is *personal*. A relationship with a horse is an unsentimental contract of food in exchange for labour. There are differences even in livestock. Cows are dignified like pets with personal names but sheep and pigs are condemned to lifelong anonymity. Perhaps this is another legacy of the milkmaid. Pressing her cheek to the warm flank of a favourite cow, she would develop a relationship far more intimate than anything experienced by a shepherd or a swineherd.

The case against pets was made most powerfully by Arthur Schopenhauer, the German philosopher whose ideas underpin the work of many of the nineteenth century's greatest thinkers. In *Parerga und Paralipomena*, written in 1851, he begins by explaining the essential differences between people and animals. Man, he says, is burdened with a consciousness and an intellectual horizon that embraces the whole of life and beyond. This makes us prey to fear and anxiety. Animals bear no such burden. Their consciousness is confined to the present moment, and it is this very limitation that allows them the one advantage they enjoy over humans. The animal, Schopenhauer says, 'is the embodiment of the present; the obvious peace of mind which it thus shares frequently puts us to shame with our often restless and dissatisfied state that comes from thoughts and cares'. It is this very absorption in the present, peculiar to animals, which contributes so much to the pleasure we derive from them. 'They are the present moment personified and, to a certain extent, make us feel the value of every unburdened and unclouded hour, whereas with our thoughts we usually pass it over and leave it unheeded.' But it does not follow from this that the benefit to its owner can excuse ill-treatment of a pet.

The above-mentioned capacity of animals to be more satisfied than we by mere existence is abused by egotistic and heartless man, and is often exploited to such an extent that he allows them absolutely nothing but bare existence. For example, the bird that is organized to roam through half the world, is confined to a cubic foot of space where it slowly pines to death and cries; and the highly intelligent dog, man's truest and most faithful friend, is put on a chain by him! Never do I see such a dog without feelings of the deepest sympathy for him and of profound indignation against his master. I think with satisfaction of a case, reported some years ago in The Times, where Lord — kept a large dog on a chain. One day as he was walking through the yard, he took it into his head to go and pat the dog, whereupon the animal tore his arm open from top to bottom, and quite right too! What he meant by this was: 'You are not my master, but my devil who makes a hell of my brief existence!'

May this happen to all who chain up dogs.

It was not just atheists like Schopenhauer who were attacking Christian orthodoxy. The new science of geology was wreaking havoc with conventional notions of the Creation and stirring panic among biblical fundamentalists. The problem was that the men responsible for this outrage were not heathens or infidels but devout churchmen who knelt before the same God as they did. Membership of the Church of England was a compulsory requirement for entry to Oxford University, and academicians had to be ordained. Foremost among these holy irritants was William Buckland, father of Frank, Canon of Christchurch and Oxford's first Professor of Geology. The heresy of men like Buckland was to cast doubt on the Flood, and to suggest that there had been life on Earth before Adam. It was one more battle in a long war of faith against reason. The difficulty for the one, and advantage to the other, was the accumulation of evidence. The discovery of fossils proved to all but the most implacable anti-scientists that entire species had existed and died out long before man trod the earth. William Buckland's personal experience was a perfect encapsulation of the wider turbulence in science and religion. In the book that established his reputation, *Reliquiae Diluvianae*, published in 1823, he argued from geological evidence that the biblical Flood was real. The entire world had indeed been covered in water. He had seen the proof of this in a cave in Yorkshire which, before the flood, had been a hyena's den. There he had found the remains of twenty-three other species including tiger, bear, wolf, elephant, rhinoceros and hippopotamus, all now extinct in Britain. He looked also at the muddle of soils and rocks that overlay the bedrock, and saw in this, as well as in the sculpting of the valleys, irrefutable evidence of a landscape scoured by water. If only temporarily, this served to assuage some of the concern that churchmen were feeling. But the evidence was not irrefutable, and one of those who refuted it was William Buckland himself. In his *Bridgewater Treatise* of

1836 he performed an elegant *volte face*. He now accepted that there was no convincing evidence for a flood and that the true architect of the landscape was ice.

New words entered the language of science. In 1824 Buckland wrote the very first description of a fossil dinosaur, *Megalosaurus*, 'the great lizard', and identified stones found inside fossilised skeletons as the animals' faeces, to which he gave the name *coprolites*. His examination of these undigested remnants of ancient prey brought him into close alignment with William Paley, for it proved the 'general law of Nature, which bids all to eat and be eaten in their turn'. Carnivores throughout time had fulfilled their ordained purpose, 'to check excess in the progress of life, and maintain the balance of creation'. Even earlier than this, in his inaugural address to the university in 1818, he had done his best to close the gap between religion and science. There was no real inconsistency, he said, between scriptural belief that the world was only thousands of years old, and the scientists' belief that it was millions. *In the beginning*, said the first verse of the first chapter of Genesis, *God created the heaven and the earth*. Well so he did, said Buckland, but he did so not in six days but in a continuing process spanning the millennia, a complex catalogue of creation, extinction and development which, species by species, had made the world as we know it. By this means had God completed his grand design.

This might have acquitted Buckland of atheism, but it did not silence the elders. The Prussian Ambassador Baron Bunsen observed in a letter to his wife that 'Buckland is persecuted by bigots'. When Buckland travelled abroad in 1852, the pious Dean of Christchurch, Thomas Gaisford, exulted: 'Buckland has gone to Italy, and we shall hear no more, thank God, of geology!' In the English West Country, a local rector asked Buckland to agree with him that the 'Father of English Geology', William 'Strata' Smith, was *an ignorant old humbug*. Another told him: ''Tis all very well for you to humbug those fellows at Oxford with such nonsense, but we know better at Mugbury!' In fact many of the fellows at Oxford were well pleased when Buckland left the university to succeed 'Soapy Sam' Wilberforce as Dean of Westminster. Not even the geologists themselves were all of the same mind. Adam Sedgwick, priest and Woodwardian Professor of Geology at Cambridge, took aim at the evolutionists in an angry letter to Charles Lyell.

If their theory was right, he said, then 'the labours of sober induction are in vain; religion is a lie; human law is a mass of folly, and a base injustice; morality is moonshine; our labours for the black people of Africa were works of madmen; and man and woman are only better beasts!' But his priestly fury only underlined the crisis of faith that academicians now had to face. Geology was wrapping its claws around Genesis as painfully as a goshawk grips a pigeon. Worse was to follow.

In 1858 the British naturalist and geographer Alfred Russel Wallace visited the island of Ternate in the Indian Ocean. A difficult question was on his mind. William Paley's theory of superfecundity made sense as far as it went, but it could not explain the processes inscribed in the fossil record. It was in Ternate that Wallace finally came up with the answer: *evolution by natural selection*. He realised that species changed over time because the fittest animals would select the fittest mates and bear offspring that would pass on their superior characteristics. Wallace wrote immediately to Charles Darwin, who had been working for several years on the same idea but had been shy of publishing it. Darwin's conclusion had rested initially on his observations of Galapagos finches, which he deduced had evolved from a single common ancestor into thirteen distinct species which, through natural selection, had adapted themselves to the varying environments on the islands where they lived. Some had become strong-beaked seed-eaters; others were expert at catching insects. Darwin tested and confirmed his theory by selectively breeding pigeons to enhance or exaggerate particular characteristics. From all this he concluded that changes to a population over time could be so profound that it would become a whole new species. In 1859, emboldened by Wallace, Darwin decided to delay no longer. On 24 November of that year he published *On the Origin of Species*. If geology had loosed a volley of grapeshot on Christian faith, then Darwin delivered a cannonade that even now, as the century nears its end, continues to reverberate. Many believe the smoke will never clear.

The counter-attack was immediate. Adam Sedgwick, who had taught Darwin at Cambridge, wrote to his former pupil:

If I did not think you a good tempered & truth loving man I should not tell you that … I have read your book with more pain than pleasure. Parts of it I admired greatly; parts I laughed at till my sides were almost sore; other parts I read with absolute sorrow; because I think them utterly false & grievously mischievous – You have deserted – after a start in that tram-road of all solid physical truth – the true method of induction – & started up a machinery as wild I think as Bishop Wilkins's locomotive that was to sail with us to the Moon. Many of your wide conclusions are based upon assumptions which can neither be proved nor disproved. Why then express them in the language & arrangements of philosophical induction?

On the other side, Darwin received an equally trenchant letter from the biologist Thomas Henry Huxley, who declared himself 'prepared to go to the stake' for his theory:

I trust you will not allow yourself to be in any way disgusted or annoyed by the considerable abuse and misrepresentation which, unless I greatly mistake, is in store for you. Depend upon it you have earned the lasting gratitude of all thoughtful men. And as to the curs which will bark and yelp, you must recollect that some of your friends, at any rate, are endowed with an amount of combativeness which (though you have often and justly rebuked it) may stand you in good stead. I am sharpening up my claws and beak in readiness.

Huxley was as good as his word. His claws and beak were widely deployed, and never more savagely than during his debate with 'Soapy Sam' Wilberforce, William Buckland's predecessor as Dean of Westminster and now Bishop of Oxford, during their famous debate at the Oxford University Museum on 30 June 1860. Wilberforce's error was to imagine that he could wound his opponent with scorn. Was it through his mother's or his father's side, he wondered, that Huxley had descended from a monkey? Claws and beak at full stretch, Huxley pounced. He would 'not be ashamed to have a monkey for his ancestor', he said, but he would be 'ashamed to be connected with a man who used his great gifts to obscure the truth'. Wilberforce might have been crushed, but the debate was far from over. It was not at all coincidental that the man who prepared the bishop for the debate was the biologist Sir Richard Owen, a fierce controversialist and outspoken critic of Darwin. It was in that same year, 1860, that the British Museum decided to separate the works of man from the works of God. Books, manuscripts and antiquities would stay at the museum in Bloomsbury but the natural history collection would have a new home in Kensington. When the new Natural History Museum opened in 1881, its first superintendent was that same Richard Owen, a man who had derided *Origin of Species* as an 'abuse of science'. To the great dismay of Huxley and others, his plan for the museum was less an exposition of natural science than a reverent celebration of God's holy works.

This was, nevertheless, the anti-Darwinians' last hurrah. In 1884 Owen was replaced by one of his sternest critics, William Henry Flower, a close ally of Huxley, student of monkey brains and a committed Darwinian. No person hoping to understand the world would ever look at a chimpanzee, or at himself or any other living thing in the same way again. But this hard-fought revolution in scientific thought would be kinder to some than to others. Evolution has no destination or good intentions, and ideas, like finches, can evolve in unpredictable ways. Darwinism was a step into the future that would have very different implications for the stuffed specimens of the Natural History Museum than it would for the forests, plains and peoples of Africa.

CHAPTER FIFTEEN

Has a Frog a Soul?

DOGS ARE CHERISHED FOR THEIR VERSATILITY. THEY HAVE hauled carts, turned spits, herded sheep, defended property. Under the knives of vivisectionists they have revealed the workings of their bodies. Aside from their innards, however, nobody ever cared much about what they looked like. A sheepdog had no more need than a shepherd to please the eye. All that mattered was speed, strength and obedience. But that is history. In these more cultivated times, no civilised person can be satisfied with utility alone. A dog in the nineteenth century needs to be as refined in its looks as a rich man's mistress. Even the simple word 'dog' is no longer an adequate expression of an animal's identity. Why promenade with a mere hound when you could be seen with a King Charles Spaniel?

Of course dogs have always been bred to type, from long-legged hunters to the dwarfs on ladies' laps. But never did anyone imagine there could be a right or a wrong way for them to look. On 28 June 1859, five months before Charles Darwin published his theory of natural selection, a cattle show at Newcastle-upon-Tyne in north-east England included for the first time a class for dogs that would award prizes for *un*natural selection. This was the idea of a correspondent to *The Field* magazine, a gamekeeper called Richard Brailsford who believed that dogs had degenerated into a sorry pack of 'weeds, wastrils and mongrels' which urgently needed improvement through selective breeding. The best way to encourage this, he suggested, would be to hold competitive dog shows. But Brailsford used the word 'dog' in a very particular way. He did not mean bulldogs, household pets and other canine riff-raff whose lower-class owners would turn the show into a bear-garden. He meant only gun-dogs, such as setters and pointers, which were as well-bred as their masters. The Newcastle show duly proceeded on this narrow prescription, with guns awarded to the lucky winners. Of other breeds there was not a whisker to be seen. In a nation packed from top to bottom with dog-lovers this looked like yet another case of prejudice against the lower classes. The line could not hold. Though hunters threatened to avoid any event that failed to meet their sporting ideals, it was only a matter of months before shows were thrown open to dogs of every size, shape and pedigree. Competition was intense, and furious owners of bulldogs, spaniels and terriers were soon following the example of the sportsmen in lodging bitter complaints about biased or incompetent judging.

Controversy was no bar to popularity. In 1863 a show in the Cremorne pleasure gardens, beside the Thames at Chelsea in west London, was graced on its opening day by the Prince of Wales and Princess Alice, and attracted 100,000 visitors in a week. *The Field* was unable to contain its rage. It complained that too many dogs had been crammed into too small a space with no access to water, and that two-thirds of them were not of the sporting kind. 'A large mass of wretched brutes collected from the highways and byways,' it said, had been misidentified, put into the wrong categories and judged by ignoramuses. None of this, however, could deter owners from entering the shows or the public from going to see them. In 1872, fifty dog shows were held across the length and breadth of Britain. A year later the Kennel Club set itself up as the supreme arbiter of each breed's looks and temperament. These imposed strict standards for such important issues as shape and size of head, shoulder-height and length and shape of leg. This looking-glass vanity, however, did not always work to practical advantage. For a gun-dog, the relationship between comeliness and ability in the field was no easier to perceive than the connection between a woman's looks and her skill in the kitchen. By now dog shows were beginning to look like a profitable business, attracting the notice of even the American showman and connoisseur of freaks P.T. Barnum. Makers of dog biscuits, too, were quick to recognise a commercial opportunity. In 1878, to the dismay of the Kennel Club, which sensed unworthy motives, the general manager of Spratt's Patent Company, Charles Cruft, organised his first show in Paris. Where dogs led, cats soon followed. At Crystal Palace in July 1871 the first properly organised cat show attracted 170 entries from all classes of society and included every sort of cat from Siamese and Persians to a Scottish wildcat.

All this has had consequences. Intimate acquaintance with their pets, and pride in their pedigrees, encourages owners to treat their favourites as small furry humans, sagacious, sympathetic and loyal. The name given by scientists to this sentimental humanising of non-human species is *anthropomorphism*, an aberration that confuses instinct with reason. In 1894 the British ethologist Conwy Lloyd Morgan published what has become known as 'Morgan's Canon', now widely accepted by the scientific community, in which he decreed:

> In no case may we interpret an action as the outcome of a higher psychical faculty, if it can be interpreted as the outcome of the exercise of one that stands lower in the psychological scale.

In other words we should not rush to explain animals' behaviour in terms of human mores when it is better explained by natural instincts or reflexes. Three years after Lloyd Morgan published his canon, the Russian physiologist Ivan Pavlov showed how dogs could be 'conditioned' to drool by the ringing of a bell. Anyone who has ever set eyes on a dog knows that it will salivate as soon as it catches sight of its dinner. It does not have to learn this: the reflex is innate. But Pavlov noticed something else: that dogs in his laboratory would drool at the very sound of his assistants' *feet* even before they had scent or sight of the food they brought. He was then able to transfer this reaction from the tramp of feet to the chime of a bell, which he rang every day before dinner. This, he said, was a *conditioned response*. The English naturalist Frank Buckland many years earlier had noticed something similar in his cats, which at half past one every day would run downstairs when they heard the cry of the cats' meat man. But scientists insist that animals' responses to such stimuli should not be confused with *reasoning*. A stimulus may be innate or it may be learned, but it is a stimulus all the same and the response to it is involuntary. It may be that many other examples of animals' apparently human behaviour can be explained in the same way, thus showing that anthropomorphism has more to do with nursery stories than it does with rational thinking.

But Darwin here throws up a difficulty. If it is true that animals and men evolved from common ancestors, then should we not then *expect* them to display similarities? 'Most of the more complex emotions', he wrote in *The Descent of Man, and Selection in Relation to Sex,* 'are common to the higher animals and ourselves.'

> Every one has seen how jealous a dog is of his master's affection, if lavished on any other creature; and I have observed the same fact with monkeys. This shews that animals not only love, but have desire to be loved. Animals manifestly feel emulation. They love approbation or praise; and a dog carrying a basket for his master exhibits in a high degree self-complacency or pride. There can, I think, be no doubt that a dog feels shame, as distinct from fear, and something very like modesty when begging too often for food. A great dog scorns the snarling of a little dog, and this may be called magnanimity. Several observers have stated that monkeys certainly dislike being laughed at …

Much thought has been given to monkeys. An English physician, Louis Robinson, discovered that infants only a few weeks old could hang by their fingers from a bar for as long as two minutes, far in excess of anything they needed as human babies but precisely similar to the clinging power of young monkeys. The psychology of monkeys themselves was the subject of a study by the Canadian biologist and Zoological Secretary of the Linnean Society of London, George Romanes. Prompted by his great hero Charles Darwin, Romanes borrowed a young brown capuchin monkey from London Zoo and entrusted it to his sister Charlotte, who kept it chained to a wash-stand in her invalid mother's bedroom. Every day from the moment of its arrival on 18 December 1880, to the moment of its departure at the end of the following February, Charlotte wrote down her observations. What soon became obvious was that the monkey was capable of both deep affection and fierce jealousy. 'He has taken a fancy to my mother, and (she holding his chain) he plays with her in a gentle and affectionate manner in her bed, but flies angrily at any of the servants who come near.'

It also became clear that the monkey was both adept and imaginative in its use of tools. A dish made a serviceable hammer for cracking walnuts, but only for as long as the monkey could find nothing better. When offered a real hammer, 'he uses it in a proper manner for that purpose'. He understood how to create leverage with a fulcrum: 'He breaks a stick by passing it down between a heavy object and the wall, and then hanging on to the end, thus breaking it across the heavy object.' He adapted a piece of wire netting to press the juice from an orange, and worked out how to screw and unscrew the handle of a hearth-brush. He understood how a key could be used to unlock a trunk, learned to open and close folding shutters, and carefully dismantled anything he could get hold of, including a bell-handle beside the mantelpiece which involved the removal of three screws. Charlotte was astonished by his persistence:

> One remarkable thing is that he should take so much trouble to do that which is no material benefit to him. The desire to accomplish a chosen task seems a sufficient inducement to lead him to take any amount of trouble. This seems a very human feeling, such as is not shown, I believe, by any other animal. It is not the desire of praise, as he never notices people looking on; it is simply the desire to achieve an object for the sake of achieving an object, and he never rests nor allows his attention to be distracted until it is done.

One thing the monkey could *not* do was recognise his own reflection. 'Strange to say', noted Charlotte, 'he appeared to mistake the sex of the image, and began in the most indescribably ludicrous manner to pay to it the addresses of courtship.' But this psychological mis-step did nothing to curb the Romanes' excitement at what they had witnessed, nor did it shake their belief in its significance. 'I confess', wrote George in reviewing Charlotte's diary, 'I should not have believed what I saw unless I had repeatedly seen it with my own eyes. As my sister once observed, while we were watching him conducting some of his researches, in oblivion to his food and all his other surroundings – "when a monkey behaves like this, it is no wonder that man is a scientific animal!"'

In *Animal Intelligence*, Romanes argued that even microscopic protozoans such as amoebae possessed some mental capacity. 'No one can have watched the movements of certain Infusoria without feeling it difficult to believe that these little animals are not actuated by some amount of

intelligence.' Few people, he asserted, were 'sceptical enough' to doubt that
the expressions of affection, sympathy, jealousy and rage shown by a dog or
a monkey were 'analogous to those in man of which these expressions are
the outward and visible signs'. And what was true for dog or monkey must
surely hold good for others, regardless of how different they might appear:

> That is to say, if we observe an ant or a bee apparently exhibiting sympathy
> or rage, we must either conclude that some psychological state resembling
> that of sympathy or rage is present, or else refuse to think about the subject
> at all; from the observable facts there is no other inference open.

Above all, Romanes' observations led him to believe that animals possessed
intelligence and reasoning. When the little monkey began to unscrew the
hearth-brush, it did so in full knowledge of what it was trying to achieve.

> Reason or intelligence is the faculty which is concerned in the intentional
> adaptation of means to ends. It therefore implies the conscious knowledge
> of the relation between means employed and ends attained, and may be
> exercised in adaptation to circumstances novel alike to the experience of
> the individual and to that of the species.

Conscious knowledge! Intentional adaptation of means to ends! These are
very different from conditioned responses, and far beyond the hardening
consensus among evolutionary theorists that mammals alone experience
any degree of consciousness. The idea that an animal, even a monkey, might
also possess anything that could be called 'intelligence', 'reason' or 'morality' is as alien to cautious minds as belief in mermaids. The conditioned
response of dog-owners nevertheless is to trust Romanes. They believe
they are united with their pets in a special bond that involves love, respect
and mutual understanding. Indeed, says Darwin in *The Expression of the
Emotions in Man and Animals*, in displaying these emotions the dog is not
so much man's equal as his superior. A human 'cannot express love and
humility by external signs, so plainly as does a dog, when with drooping
ears, hanging lips, flexious body, and wagging tail, he meets his beloved
master'. Who therefore would quarrel with Frederick of Prussia's assertion

in 1789 that the dog is 'man's best friend'? And how, the dog-lover might ask, is friendship possible without intelligence?

This special place in human affections means that the dog is the one animal above all that enrages the anti-vivisectionists. The scientists themselves have shown some understanding of this. As early as 1831, one of the most vilified vivisectors of the day, Marshall Hall, proposed that experimenters should take care to inflict only minimum pain, which meant preferring 'lower' animals such as fish and frogs to 'higher' ones such as dogs and apes. At the end of the century the controversy remains unresolved. Despite repeated outcries, the animal laboratory has become the most important school of learning for the life sciences, which its practitioners argue should be accorded the same high status as physics. But their hubris only stokes the abolitionists' rage. Between the two entrenched positions there is neither compromise nor willingness to listen. The protectionists condemn the scientists as arrogant and inhuman. The scientists deride their opponents as ignorant, sentimental, enemies of science and an obstacle to the betterment of human health.

The most effective campaigner for abolition is the Irish writer and suffragist Frances Power Cobbe, whose tireless efforts persuaded the British government to appoint the Royal Commission that led to the Cruelty to Animals Act of 1876. But this fine-sounding piece of legislation turned out to be not quite the victory that the protectionists had supposed. For Cobbe, who in 1875 founded the Victoria Street Society for the Protection of Animals Liable to Vivisection, the first organisation dedicated exclusively to the removal of live animals from laboratories, it was a betrayal. The Act did lay down some conditions, and it did impose fines for those who caused excessive suffering, but it contained a fatal weakness. It was the *scientists themselves*, not the protectionists, who were to decide what was justifiable and what was not. Nor was there much comfort to be taken from the widespread adoption of anaesthesia. It was often inexpertly administered, so that subjects woke up during the experiment, and it encouraged researchers to expend animal lives with ever greater profligacy. This prompted George Hoggan, a reformed vivisector and founder member of the Victoria Street Society, to remark: 'I am inclined to look upon anaesthetics as the *greatest curse* to vivisectible animals.'

As Hoggan died in 1891 we cannot now ask him which 'vivisectible animals' he had in mind, but it is no slur on his memory to suggest it would not have been frogs. Lacking fur, warm blood and an affectionate demeanour, the unlucky frog, though as sensitive to pain as any other, is regarded by those on both sides of the argument as a species of vegetable, to be sliced and diced in whatever way the experimenter pleases. Its sufferings were expertly summarised by St George Mivart, Lecturer in Comparative Anatomy at St Mary's Hospital, London, in his natural history of the species, *The Common Frog*, in 1874:

> The Frog is a never-failing resource for the physiological experimenter. It would take long indeed to tell the sufferings of much-enduring Frogs in the cause of Science! What Frogs can do without their heads? What their legs can do without their bodies? What their arms can do without either head or trunk? What is the effect of the removal of their brains? How they can manage without their eyes and without their ears? What effect results from all kinds of local irritations, from chokings, from poisonings, from mutilations the most varied? These are questions again and again addressed to the little animal which, perhaps more than any other, deserves the title of 'the Martyr of Science'.

This was written four years after Thomas Henry Huxley presented to the Metaphysical Society in London a paper entitled *Has a Frog a Soul?* Even its secondary title, *and of What Nature Is That Soul, Supposing It to Exist?*, gave little indication of the outlandish disquisition that was to follow. The issue had long divided physiologists into two irreconcilable camps. One believed with Descartes that the motions of an animal's body were no more than mechanistic responses to external stimuli. The other, as Huxley phrased it, held that 'all the rationally condapted movements of the body have been referred to the operation of a soul, which they conceive to work the machinery of the body as a musician may play upon an organ or other instrument'. What made the frog such an ideal subject was precisely the kind of procedure that St George Mivart would later describe. Huxley himself reflected upon the consequences of cutting off a frog's leg, or of severing various portions of its brain. How would a frog's component parts behave in isolation from each other? What if you cut off the head and then dropped acid on to a thigh? Answer: the Martyr of Science would try to wipe it off with its foot. What if you then cut off the foot? Answer: it would try again with its footless leg before transferring the effort to its other foot. As the behaviour of the severed or separated parts of a frog always seemed perfectly rational, then it must be imagined that the soul, *Supposing It to Exist*, must dwell separately in each part of the body, or be spread throughout the whole. If we accept the hypothesis that a frog does have a soul, Huxley argued, then the actions performed by a severed head and trunk 'will be equally purposive, and equally show that there is a something in each half which possesses the power of adapting means to ends in a manner which is as deserving as the epithet "rational" in the one case as in the other. The separated head and trunk may be sent a hundred miles in opposite directions, and at the end of the journey each will be as purposive in its actions as before.' It is not known whether this last experiment was ever carried out. What *is* certain is that no learned gentleman would ever present to the Metaphysical Society of London a paper that envisaged such treatment of a dog.

This dichotomy derives in part from the special relationship of man with his 'best friend', but also from the idea that some animals are 'higher' than others. The frog is low, the dog is high and man is highest of all. Darwin rejected this idea, or at least this way of talking about it. Evolutionary theory says that each species adapts over time to fit the environment in which it lives, so that 'high' and 'low' have no useful meaning. No man can outsoar an eagle. As Frank Buckland observed, the vast learning of the professors dangling their hooks off Richmond Bridge was of no more use to them than their top hats and waistcoats. In the aquatic environment it was the fish, not they, that stood higher in sense and understanding. And what of the dog? Its senses of smell, hearing and anticipation are vastly more acute than the muffled senses of the rationally thinking human. So what do 'high' and 'low' really mean? There is also a question for evolutionists who doubt that animals have souls. At what point in their progression from the soulless ape were souls inserted into humans? The problem with all such musings is that they ignore common experience. One might make an intellectual case against the concepts of 'high' and 'low', but it would be a hard task to convince the common man, or even the educated one, that a chimpanzee is not higher than a snail and a man not higher than a chimpanzee.

This might be called 'common sense'. Yet common sense cannot account for the favouritism that elevates some animals as friends and condemns others as vermin. It cannot explain why we eat the flesh of some but clutch our throats at the prospect of others. In some cases this is a consequence of religious faith. Jews and Mohammedans may not eat pig. The Hindus of India consider cows sacred. But religion has no bearing on the attitudes of the British, who will eat beef at any hour of the day but would rather starve than roast a horse. This has nothing to do with the quality of the meat. Frank Buckland was one who tried to change the public mind. He convinced himself of the succulence of horse at a lunch he shared with the Superintendent of London Zoo, Abraham Dee Bartlett, at which they sampled 'two exceedingly fine hot steaks'. One of these was 'rump-steak proper', and the other a slice of horse, but they were not told which was which. When they compared notes, they found they both preferred the horse. 'Uncommon good', said Buckland.

The lesson is obvious. It would be highly beneficial for the British to eat horse, as indeed many other peoples of Europe happily do. What better way to feed the hungry? Nobody in England, or anywhere else, can walk for more than a few minutes without seeing some kind of horse. It may be a pit pony, a cart-horse, hunter, riding hack, post-horse, donkey or giant of the plough. How shameful it is that their flesh when they die is wasted or fed to pets! How much better it would be to make them into steaks and stews affordable even to poor families whose tables so rarely see meat. The argument had intelligence on its side but not sentiment. On 6 February 1868, an excited throng of London's intellectual elite gathered at the Langham Hotel to set an example to the public with a grand banquet of horseflesh. Buckland dolefully recorded the diners' reaction:

> Many … reminded me of the attitude of a person about to take a pill and draught; not a rush at the food, but a 'one, two, three!' expression about them, coupled not infrequently by calling in the aid of olfactory powers, reminding one of the short and doubtful sniff, that a domestic puss not over-hungry takes of a bit of bread and butter. The bolder experimenters gulped down the meat, and instantly followed it with a draught of champagne, then came another mouthful and then, as we say, *fiat haustus ut antea.*

So great was the revulsion that Buckland only half-jokingly prescribed horseflesh as an antidote to crime. All that was needed to keep men honest, he said, was to serve horsemeat in jail. 'Be assured these fellows who would garrote you, murder your wives and children, or commit the most fearful crimes, would shudder at the thought of dining upon horse-flesh.' Buckland, who was honorary surgeon to London Zoo as well as Her Majesty's Inspector of Fisheries, was an eccentric with a purpose. He wanted to feed the people, and he wanted them to eat meat. Chief among his eccentricities was cooking and eating animals that died in the zoo. Panther chops, elephant trunk, roasted giraffe neck, fried viper, wombat, any body-part of any species left over from a *post mortem*: how could he know how something tasted unless he sampled it? Nor did he keep these exotic meats all to himself. In 1874 four hundred people paid 10s 6d each to travel by special train from London to hear him give a lecture at Brighton Aquarium. The first they knew that London Zoo's old rhinoceros had died was when Buckland served it to them baked in a pie. But this was neither joke nor madness. He had set out his thinking several years earlier in an address to the Society of Arts, in which he pointed out what seemed to him a glaring anachronism. Scientists by this time had catalogued 140,000 species of animal, yet only forty-three regularly saw the inside of an oven. Could anything be more wasteful?

In another lecture Buckland led his audience on an imaginary tour of London Zoo, visiting every edible species of bird or animal that had been bred there. *Quod erat demonstrandum!* If it could be done in the zoo, then why not in field or farmyard? The French, unencumbered by the British reserve in matters of horse and frog, had already had the same idea. In 1854 a Société d'Acclimatation was established in Paris with the express purpose of identifying new species to breed for the table. It enjoyed royal patronage and its more than two thousand members had a thirty-three-acre garden in which to test their theories. Buckland was impressed, and quickly founded an Acclimatisation Society of his own. This assembled for the first time on 26 June 1860, and two years later gathered for a celebratory dinner at a fashionable London club. The feast began with soups made from birds' nests and a kind of Chinese sea slug called *bêche-de-mer*. These unsightly items took a day of soaking and a night of rapid boiling to reduce them from the consistency of horses' hooves to something more like ordinary garden slugs. According to Buckland the flavour fell somewhere between a calf's head and the glue pot. Next came a stew made from 'choice portions' of kangaroo, only slightly marred by the fact that the meat had travelled from Australia in a tin with an ill-fitting lid and had begun to decompose. It certainly did nothing to weaken Buckland's conviction that the kangaroo was an ideal species for English parks. Later in the meal came hams of kangaroo and wild boar, spiced sweetbreads, Syrian pig, Canadian goose, Australian meat biscuits and three new birds from South America. The most successful, and literally fought-over, dish was a 'Pepper Pot' of spiced West Indian meats which tasted so good that Buckland had to protect it from the waiters ('I was obliged to tap their fingers with a spoon').

By the time of its first annual report, the society could list among its patrons three dukes, three marquises, eight earls, seven viscounts, three knights, the Chief Justice and the president of the Royal College of Surgeons. Its first president was the Marquis of Breadalbane, later succeeded by the Duke of Newcastle and the Prince of Wales. Its achievements, however, were modest. There was some success with Canadian quail and some exotic vegetables (Chinese yams and African peas and beans). Buckland himself had bought a flock of Chinese sheep ('very useful and curious') and imported from Prussia a stock of a freshwater fish called zander, a kind of perch that looked like a pike. There had been talk, but talk only, of eland, capybara and beaver. The Admiralty played its part by instructing ships' captains to bring back other species from around the world, but so far there was nothing on the menu that had not been there for centuries, and no sign of affordable meat for the urban poor. Buckland himself would be enthused by the Duke of Marlborough's emu and kangaroo paddocks at Blenheim Palace, but these were never more than amusing curiosities. The Acclimatisation Society was easily, and perhaps deservedly, mocked. The livestock industries in Britain and across Europe never seriously strayed from their narrow commitment to cattle, sheep, pigs and poultry, and Buckland had to refocus his attention on fish.

*

Though the public may not have cared much for exotics in their ovens, they flocked to see them in menageries, zoos and circuses. In Europe and America, fascination with wild animals earned fortunes for showmen such as Phineas T. Barnum and the Ringling Brothers. In Britain, one of the most popular attractions was Wombwell's Royal Menagerie, a travelling zoo that kept three separate shows permanently on the road. In 1858 Frank Buckland met one of these at Windsor, where he was shocked by the 'startling roar of a lion thundering down the avenues of the Long Walk'. The show included fifteen vans hauled by forty-five horses, with a staff of thirty or forty keepers who slept with their animals in the vans. At the showground the caravanserai was drawn up in two lines with the ticket office at one end and a pair of elephants at the other. These were the only animals not to ride in the vans, though they were never fully open to public view. Moving between showgrounds they had to walk, ten miles a day inside a twenty-seven-foot bottomless van that revealed only their feet. If you wanted to see a whole elephant, then you needed the price of a ticket. For this you could also marvel at lions and their cubs, a hyena, a bear, an Indian rhinoceros and 'war camels from the Crimea' which Wombwell had bought to replace a dead giraffe.

One of the most prized exhibits was a tiger Wombwell had bought from a London dealer called Charles Jamrach, famed for being able to supply anything from a canary to a rhinoceros. The tiger was a particular attraction because of its notorious past. Somehow it had escaped from Jamrach's shop and fled with a young boy in its jaws. The German-born Jamrach himself earned lasting celebrity by chasing after the animal, prising open its jaws and freeing the fortunately uneaten victim. In the world of zoos and circuses, Jamrach was an important provider of exotic birds and animals. He and his agents haunted docksides across Britain and Europe, ready with pocketfuls of cash to reward any sailors who managed to bring back a rarity. In zoological circles Jamrach's was not so much a business as an institution. P.T. Barnum was among his customers, and Frank Buckland counted him a friend. But lions, elephants, giraffes and rhinoceroses are no ordinary commodities. Selling them is easy. Tracking them, catching them and bringing them back alive is a different matter altogether.

CHAPTER SIXTEEN

Beings Akin to Ourselves

THERE WAS ONE NAME IN THE ANIMAL TRADE THAT STOOD above even Charles Jamrach's. This was a German fishmonger's son, Carl Hagenbeck of Hamburg, whose cargoes from Africa made Noah's two-by-two look like a failure of ambition. In twenty years he shipped seven hundred leopards, a thousand lions, four hundred tigers, a thousand bears, eight hundred hyenas, three hundred elephants, seventy rhinoceroses, three hundred camels, a hundred and fifty giraffes, six hundred antelopes, tens of thousands of crocodiles, boas and pythons, and more than a hundred thousand birds. To this bountiful harvest must be added all the combined efforts of Jamrach and countless others who traded in wildlife. For the European colonists in Africa, this was not just one more way of exploiting the continent's natural resources or of exerting power over native peoples. To capture or kill a wild animal was the ultimate test of manhood.

But this burnishing of their virility had its price. Live animals could be caught only at the cost of many more dead, for not even the bravest of hunters could trap a full-grown elephant or rhinoceros. They concentrated on the young, which meant they first had to kill the adults that protected them and thus badly depleted the breeding stock. Suffering was unavoidable. Sometimes an elephant would be cleanly shot. Just as often it would be maimed and left to die. Giraffes and antelopes were easier. The hunters had only to put a herd to flight, then wait for the calves to exhaust themselves and fall behind. Hyenas, cats and baboons were more easily caught in pits and traps, though the challenge here was to reach them before the lions did. When the trophy was an adult baboon the test was less to get it *into* the trap than to get it out again. Carl Hagenbeck explained how this was done:

> First their jaws are muzzled with strong cord, made of palm strips; then hands and feet are tied; and lastly, to make assurance doubly sure, the animal's whole body is wrapped up in cloth, so that the captive has the appearance of a great smoked sausage! The parcel is then suspended from a pole carried by two persons, and conveyed triumphantly to the station.

A half-ton baby hippo, too, could be difficult to handle. 'When these creatures are agitated,' Hagenbeck explained, 'they break into profuse perspiration, which causes them to become so slimy and slippery that it is difficult to make the noose hold.' The trick was to pass a rope over the animal's forelegs and neck. 'As soon as the noose is fixed in position the animal is hoisted a few inches off the ground, by the combined efforts of about twenty men pulling on the rope. Half a dozen others jump into the pit, and bind together the forelegs and the hindlegs, as also the jaws; for the animals are obstinate and malicious, and it does not do to run any risks with them.' This was the kind of expert knowledge that Hagenbeck felt entitled him to describe himself as 'a naturalist first and a trader afterwards'.

The question of 'reasonable suffering' might have arisen in the mind of a true naturalist, but the realities of the trade precluded sentiment. Wherever there was a conflict of interest, the issue was settled with a bullet. No opportunity was wasted. Young hippopotami too large for the pit were not just left on the plains. Nor were the even more dangerous crocodiles. Against these, the weapon of choice was the harpoon. Sometimes the animal would be killed outright, in which case it was left where it fell. Sometimes it was merely incapacitated, in which case it would be hauled away in the hope that it would heal over time and the hunter would have a live, if imperfect, animal to deliver to a customer. Hagenbeck affirmed that 'no less than three-quarters of the hippopotami formerly brought to Europe used to be caught in this fashion'. But this apparently straightforward assertion conceals an important fact. Most of the animals that embarked on the journey were dead before they reached port.

Journeys from Africa were always attritional. Hagenbeck himself described a caravan setting out across the desert from north-eastern Sudan towards the Red Sea. This ambulant menagerie included young elephants, giraffes, hippopotami, buffaloes and cages full of cats, pigs and baboons. For meat and haulage they were accompanied by a hundred and fifty head of cattle, hundreds of sheep and goats, and more than a hundred camels. The caravan moved only at night, but still had to endure heat not far below the daytime temperature of 113 degrees Fahrenheit. Two men on foot were needed to drive each antelope, three for each giraffe and as many as four for an elephant. The lions, leopards, baboons, pigs, birds and other small animals travelled in cages lashed to the backs of camels. At the very heart of the caravan, pairs of camels were harnessed with poles across their saddles. From each of these hung a baby hippo in a cage, and each was followed by another six or eight camels carrying the water needed to keep the hippo alive. It wanted more than just enough to satisfy its enormous thirst. For the sake of their hides, hippos needed also to wallow, which they did every day in ox-hide baths. With waterholes as far as sixty miles apart, progress was agonisingly, and often fatally, slow. It would take six weeks for the survivors to reach the sea. Hagenbeck did not make light of this:

> However carefully we organise our expedition, it is inevitable that many of our captives should succumb before we reach our journey's end. The terrible heat kills even those animals whose natural home is in the country. The powerful male baboons are very liable to sunstroke, which kills them in half an hour; and any weak point in their constitution is sure to become aggravated during the journey. Whether this is due to the terror and strain which they underwent at their capture, or to being confined in cramped cages, I cannot say. But the fact remains that not more than half of them arrive safely at their destination, despite our utmost care.

By 'destination' he meant only the seaport. The greater part of the journey still lay ahead. A caravan, or what remained of it, would be ferried by steamer to Suez, whence it would proceed to Europe either by sea or train by way of Alexandria and Trieste to Genoa or Marseilles. Not even the luxury of a rail ticket could guarantee an animal's survival. Hagenbeck lost three elephants in a single journey, all killed by rats gnawing their feet. Yet the sea voyage was incomparably worse. Seasick animals in tiny cages buffeted and drenched by rough seas had only the slimmest chance of survival. Big cats became so frantic that they were blinded or bled to death by the raking of their own claws. The agonies were acute and prolonged. From start to finish, Hagenbeck's caravan from the Sudan took three months and ended as it had begun. The giraffes and elephants bound for London Zoo, though weakened by the journey, still had to walk another eight miles from the docks to Regent's Park. Journeys from other parts of the world were even worse. A consignment of wild foals took eleven months to reach Hamburg from Mongolia, by which time only twenty-eight of the original fifty-two were still alive. Wild sheep fared even worse. More than sixty of them embarked on the same journey and not a single one survived.

The humane instincts and good intentions of reputable dealers such as Hagenbeck and Jamrach were laudable in theory but small comfort in practice. Frank Buckland described how Jamrach sent his son to India to collect a pair of rhinos with a market value of £1,600. The journey back to London began well enough. A gang of forty coolies walked the animals two hundred miles to Calcutta, where they were taken aboard the *Persian Empire*. On board with them went enough fodder to keep them alive for a hundred and twenty days. It seemed plenty, but it made no allowance for the unpredictability of the seas. The ship was delayed, weeks passed and the animals starved. 'The poor things were reduced to such extremities that they ate sawdust and gnawed great holes in a spare mast.' Animals from south-east Asia always fared badly. An administrator at London Zoo reckoned that the price of one live orang-utan was four killed in the wild. Yet this was better than most. Overall, the best estimate was that ten animals were sacrificed for every one delivered alive. But even that is an understatement, for few animals caught in the wild would survive long in a zoo. None of this deterred the traders. The losses only inflated the demand for replacements and lured more and more entrepreneurs into a market where prices went up daily. In 1870 an American dealer paid Hagenbeck £1,000 for three African elephants, which he thought was a fine piece of business. 'But it seems I was wrong. For my American friend took the animals to his own country and sold them for £1,700, £1,600 and £1,500 respectively.'

Zoo animals may have suffered, but their pains were as nothing compared to the agonies of those sold to the circus. Their needs and natures counted for nothing when the sole priority was obedience, and where the only inducements were whips and hot irons. With great revulsion Hagenbeck recalled seeing four 'trained' lions, sold at auction in London, whose whiskers had been scorched off and who were 'frightfully burned about their mouths'. To give Hagenbeck his due, he led by example. 'My enthusiasm for my own calling', he said, 'originated more, if I may say so, in a love for all living creatures than in any mere commercial instincts.' Though this might be swallowed with a pinch of salt, nobody could deny that the zoological park he founded at Hamburg was a model for others to follow. Unlike earlier zoos it allowed space for animals to roam in enclosures that bore at least some resemblance to their natural habitats. 'I desired above all things', said Hagenbeck, 'to give the animals the maximum of liberty.'

> I wished to exhibit them not as captives, confined within narrow spaces, and
> looked at between bars, but as free to wander from place to place within as
> large limits as possible, and with no bars to obstruct the view and serve as
> a reminder of their captivity.

Artificial mountains were built for chamois and ibex, 'wide commons' were laid out for animals of the plains and secluded glens for the carnivores. Instead of bars there were trenches to separate the humans from the exhibits. On the question of animal intelligence, Hagenbeck was firmly on the side of George Romanes. 'Brutes', he affirmed, 'are beings akin to ourselves. Their minds are formed on the same plan as our minds; the differences are differences of degree, not of kind. They will repay cruelty with hatred, and kindness with trust.' This was why he condemned barbaric methods of training for the ring. At his own circus in Hamburg he proved to the world that rewards were far more effective than punishments in persuading an animal to obey. He was not a man to downplay the significance of his own achievements: 'There is probably no sphere in which the growth of humanitarian sentiment has been more striking than in the treatment and training of performing animals.'

The setting aside of whips and irons, however, was no guarantee of good health. Hagenbeck himself ran a performing troupe of lions, tigers, cheetahs and bears that he wanted to perform at the Great Exhibition at Chicago in 1893. The plan foundered in 1891 when, after months of preparation, the troupe made its debut at the Crystal Palace in London. All the animals fell ill and died later in Germany of the glanders, for which Hagenbeck blamed 'the bad meat which was supplied by the unscrupulous contractor in England'. In 1892 his menagerie was hit again; this time by cholera which then spread from the animals to the unfortunate people of Hamburg. Even this disaster, however, had educational value. 'How true it is', he said, 'that cholera is spread through the agency of foul drinking water, was clearly demonstrated by the fact that after the veterinary surgeon had ordered the animals to be given boiled water only, no more of them were attacked by the disease.' The moral was plain to see. When animals suffer, humans suffer. What is good for animals is good for humans too.

Zoos and circuses are not the only destinations for wild animals. Above all, the nineteenth century has been an age of discovery. In the cause of science, multitudes of known and unknown species have poured into private collections and museums all over the world. Soon after the British Museum began its system of registering new specimens in 1837, it was receiving more than a thousand mammals a year. Though the scientists were striving for clarity, everywhere they struggled with confusion. Identical species might be given different names by different scientists, or similar names with different spellings, and multiple species might be recorded under a single name. The crucial difference between zoos and museums, however, was not between commerce and learning. It was between life and death. Men like Hagenbeck and Abraham Dee Bartlett needed their animals alive. The cataloguers and taxidermists of the Natural History Museum in London, and other such institutions throughout the world, needed them dead, and they needed them in quantity. The men who supplied that need became heroes of almost mythical standing. Principal among these, and the one whose rifle did more than any other to stock the Natural History Museum in London, was Frederick Courteney Selous, the tireless hunter who was the real-life inspiration for Rider Haggard's fictional adventurer Allan Quatermain in *King Solomon's Mines*. His trigger finger supplied the museum with jackals, hunting dogs, hyenas, lions, leopards, cheetahs, buffaloes, antelopes, gazelles, wildebeest, reedbucks, waterbucks, bushbucks, kudus, elands, elephants, giraffes, warthogs, hippos, zebras, rhinos and elephants. Others from around the world provided wolves, otters, lynx, bison, goats, chamois, deer, moose and reindeer. Tigers in India were particularly prized, but it was in Africa that the killing rose to its orgiastic climax. What better demonstration of manhood could there be than to stand over the carcass of a ferocious animal bigger than yourself? One of the most shameless braggarts was Roualeyn Gordon-Cumming, the Old Etonian son of a Scottish baronet who liked to be known as 'the lion hunter'. In 1850 he recorded his exploits in a self-glorifying book, *Five Years of a Hunter's Life in the Far Interior of South Africa*. In London, *The Times* newspaper of 19 September 1850 was breathless in its admiration for this 'prince of hunters, conqueror and autocrat of all the beasts':

> We are conscious of our great audacity in venturing even to quote the achievements of a hero, now for the first time in his life weeping because there are no more animals left to vanquish … What can the feeble quill say of a gentleman who quitted Great Britain that he might take part in a war against savages …

For Gordon-Cumming it was war indeed: war against everything with a beating heart. Not even Rider Haggard could have imagined such feats. How, for example, was our hero to extract a wounded hippopotamus from a waterhole? Not a problem! Gordon-Cumming plunged into the water with a knife and made slits in the animal's hide. Through these he threaded a thong which his men then hauled upon to bring the beast ashore. It has to be allowed, however, that Gordon-Cumming was not the idle fantasist some people took him for. No less an authority than David Livingstone attested that, for all its braggadocio, the book conveyed a 'truthful idea' of the hunter's life, which in Gordon-Cumming's case meant sleeping in bothies roofed with elephants' ears and lurching around southern Africa in an overloaded wagon train. The persistent attentions of tsetse flies meant that this unwieldy transport, when it was not bogged down or shedding its wheels in a river, needed frequent changes of oxen. His men, too, were vulnerable to disease, buffaloes and lions. Gordon-Cumming awoke one morning to find the only trace of his chief wagon-driver was a leg bitten off below the knee but still wearing its shoe. In the course of four expeditions he recorded the loss of forty-five horses, seventy cattle and seventy dogs. Gordon-Cumming himself was enfeebled by rheumatic fever and too much rhinoceros meat, but nothing could keep him from the slaughter. When the barrel of his favourite gun burst and he had no ammunition for its replacement, he made bullets by melting down his snuffers, spoons, candlesticks, teapots and cups. He then put them to excellent use:

> I was loading and firing as fast as I could, sometimes at the head and sometimes behind the shoulder, until my elephant's forequarters were a mass of gore, notwithstanding which he continued to hold stoutly on, leaving the grass and branches of the forest scarlet in his wake.
>
> Having fired thirty-five rounds with my two-grooved rifle, I opened fire upon him with the Dutch six-pounder; and when forty bullets had perforated his hide, he began for the first time to evince signs of a dilapidated constitution.

Gordon-Cumming bagged elephants as lesser men trapped rats. His personal score rose to fifty, then to a hundred. Few were clean kills, but involved what Gordon-Cumming liked to call 'fights', in which the animal received bullet after bullet from the hunter on his horse, while being all the time harried by his dogs. One of these noble contests lasted from half past eleven in the morning until after sundown, by which time the 'venerable monarch of the forest' was heavier by the weight of fifty-seven bullets. Taking his pick of five old bull elephants, he found, was 'so overpoweringly exciting that it almost takes a man's breath away'. Inconveniently, however, not all the animals died where he could find them. Gordon-Cumming was time and again mortified by wounded beasts dragging themselves away, leaving only trails of bloody footprints into the bush. He declared himself to be 'very much annoyed at wounding and losing in the last week no less than ten first-rate old bull elephants'. This had nothing to do with sympathy for the suffering animals, but everything to do with the loss of two hundred pounds' worth of ivory. It was 'vexing' for him 'to think that many, if not all of them, were lying rotting in the surrounding forest'. Another day, when tusks were 'stolen' from an elephant he had shot, he rushed to the nearest village and threatened to shoot the chief.

The immense profits to be had from ivory attracted many others to the harvest. Bullets were discharged by the ton, and the plains and forests strewn with carcasses missing nothing but their tusks. Vultures of every kind enjoyed the feast. But it could not last. No population of any animal could survive an assault that killed them faster than they could breed. In Natal, exports of ivory collapsed from nineteen tons, the product of 950 elephants, to sixty-six pounds in 1895. In the Eastern Cape, none have been seen for seventy years.

Though elephants were the most profitable, they were not the only species in Gordon-Cumming's sights. Antelopes, rhinoceroses, hippos, giraffes, lions, wildebeest, buffaloes, zebras, kudus, elands, wild boars and crocodiles all crumpled before him. He found as much or more beauty in death as in life. 'I was struck with admiration at the magnificence of the noble black buck, and I vowed in my heart to slay him'. He was unable to find words adequate to his feeling when a wounded lion crawled off to die. 'No description could give a correct idea of the surpassing beauty of this most majestic animal, as he lay still warm before me.' His trophies caused a sensation when they were displayed at the Great Exhibition in 1851. In all, the collection weighed nearly twenty-seven-and-a-quarter tons. But this was not the weight of animals he had killed, nor any indication of their number. The trophies that thrilled the crowds at the Crystal Palace were only heads, horns, tusks and skins. The rest of the flayed or headless carcasses had been left where they fell. On one occasion Gordon-Cumming chased and shot 'the finest bull' in a herd of giraffes and took nothing from it but the tail.

There was only one animal in the whole of Africa that he never shot. By 1799, twenty-one years before he was born, the very last bluebuck, remembered by scientists as *Hippotragus leucophaeus*, was killed in South Africa. The quagga, another South African species that in appearance was half horse and half zebra, and which was hunted by Dutch settlers for meat and skins, clung on for a few decades more but was extinct in the wild by 1878. The last captive specimen died in Amsterdam five years later. The wonder is that other species somehow managed to survive. In 1866 a single company in the Orange Free State exported the skins of 152,000 blesbok and wildebeest. In 1873, 62,000 wildebeest and zebra went the same way. No reasonable observer of all this could doubt that further extinctions were likely. The first to act on these fears were not scientists or theologians fearful for the survival of the Creation, but English gentlemen fearful for the future of their sport. They needed animals to exist in sufficient numbers for them to shoot. This was a matter of sufficient importance for members of the British government and aristocracy to sign a letter to the Governor-General of Sudan, Lord Cromer, protesting at the loss of a nature reserve north of the Sobat River. As the signatories also included the Secretary of the Zoological Society of London and the Director of the Natural History Museum, they could credibly assert that they were motivated by a simple love of nature.

In Romantic minds there was no contradiction. The hunter himself was a child of nature, communing with his gun as eloquently as a poet communes with his pen. Others could see only a vicious oaf incapable of empathy or respect for life. But these were very much in the minority. For readers of adventure stories, the Great White Hunter was a hero like no other. Whether through factual accounts such as Gordon-Cumming's, or in fantastical fictions such as Rider Haggard's *King Solomon's Mines* or R.M. Ballantyne's *The Gorilla Hunters*, Africa fed the imaginations of young and old alike. In *The Gorilla Hunters* of 1861, three young friends, Jack, Ralph and Peterkin, set sail from England with the intention of shooting as much African wildlife as they can find, and in particular the great man-monkey of the book's title, only recently discovered in West Africa. It is the only animal on Earth that the pugnacious Jack has never shot, an omission he is determined to correct. Peterkin likewise is eager to shoot a gorilla, or to prove 'the enormous puggy' to be a myth. 'And so, reader,' writes the narrator Ralph, 'it was ultimately settled, and in the course of two weeks more we three were on our way to the land of the slave, the black savage, and the gorilla.' No adventure was ever more glorious than the slaughter that now ensues. Beasts of every kind are stalked, and their deaths so bloodily recorded that one might suppose Ballantyne to have been inspired by his fellow Scot, Gordon-Cumming. Ralph describes the three friends being 'brought to a stand' by a tremendous roar.

> Immediately after, a large male lion bounded from among the bushes, and with one stroke of his enormous paw struck down a negro who stood not twenty yards from us. The terrible brute stood for an instant or two, lashing his sides with his tail and glaring defiance. It chanced that I happened to be nearest to him, and that the position of the tangled underwood prevented my companions from taking good aim; so without waiting for them, being anxious to save, if possible, the life of the prostrate negro, I fired both barrels into the lion's side. Giving utterance to another terrible roar, he bounded away into the bush, scattering the negroes who came in his way, and made his escape, to our great disappointment. We found, to our horror, on going up to the fallen hunter, that he was quite dead. His skull had been literally smashed in, as if it had received a blow from a sledge-hammer.

Ralph professes himself unable to describe his feelings 'on beholding thus, for the first time, the king of beasts in all the savage majesty of strength and freedom, coupled with the terrible death of a human being'. But he has no time to linger over his grief. Almost immediately two elephants come 'crashing out of the bushes', diverting all his attention and firepower. But the three companions bring enlightenment as well as death to the Dark Continent, and divide their time between hunting and missionary work. They are encouraged by a trader who warns them that the natives' customary joviality will be set aside when they fall 'under the influence of their abominable superstitions. Then they become incarnate fiends, and commit deeds of cruelty that make one's blood run cold to think of.' And then, at last, comes a gorilla. 'I can compare it to nothing,' says Ralph, 'for nothing I ever heard was like it. If the reader can conceive a human fiend endued with a voice far louder than that of the lion, yet retaining a little of the intonation both of the man's voice and of what we should suppose a fiend's voice to be, he may form some slight idea of what that roar was.'

It is here that we find Charles Darwin lurking at the corner of the page. For what *was* the gorilla? Where in the natural order did it stand? The

Romantic view of nature had no more chance than the Creation of surviving the onslaught of Darwinism. Strength was all. Ballantyne of course
had no notion of this, but his characters are good indications of where
the world was heading. As the nations of Europe scoured the world for
new territories to colonise, verse twenty-six of the first chapter of Genesis
began to take on new shades of meaning. Dominion over the beasts had
been stretched to include dominion over the 'black savage'. Just as white
Europeans had exerted their superiority over animals, they now did the
same with people they saw as beast-like specimens of their own species.
Those who made a study of human societies declared that black men were
related more closely to orangs than to white people. In *The Descent of Man*,
Darwin himself compared them to monkeys:

> He who has seen a savage in his native land will not feel much shame, if
> forced to acknowledge that the blood of some more humble creature flows
> in his veins. For my own part I would as soon be descended from that heroic
> little monkey who braved his dreadful enemy in order to save the life of his
> keeper ... as from a savage who delights to torture his enemies, offers up
> bloody sacrifices, practises infanticide without remorse, treats his wives like
> his slaves, knows no decency, and is haunted by the grossest superstition.

Cruelty to native peoples was nothing new. The conditions in which slaves
were shipped to America were, if anything, worse than those endured by
Hagenbeck's beasts. A captive human was worth so much less than a rhinoceros. For the white men driving dark-skinned people from their lands,
Darwin now supplied a justification in science. Those who had evolved
to be strong were designed, by no less an authority than nature itself, to
exercise power over those who had evolved to be weak. Just as the princes
and barons had once appointed themselves masters of the European forests,
Great White Hunters now appointed themselves masters of the African
plains. Their baggage was carried for them not by white peasants but by
enslaved black men who subsisted on animal fodder. The final step was
taken by Carl Hagenbeck. His conviction that animals were 'beings akin to
ourselves' led him directly to a 'brilliant idea'. He reasoned that if animals
were akin to humans, then we equally must be akin to them, and in the

diversity of our own species we should find as much to amaze us as in the novelties of the jungle. Therefore, along with the animals in his zoo and travelling shows, he would exhibit exotic *people*. He began with a family of Lapps, whom he shipped to Hamburg with their reindeer in 1874.

> The first glance sufficed to convince me that the experiment would prove a success ... On deck three little men dressed in skins were walking about among the deer, and down below we found to our great delight a mother with a tiny infant in her arms and a dainty little maiden about four years old, standing shyly by her side. Our guests, it is true, would not have shone in a beauty show, but they were so wholly unsophisticated and so totally unspoiled by civilisation that they seemed like beings from another world. I felt sure that the little strangers would arouse great interest in Germany.

He was right. 'All Hamburg comes to see this genuine "Lapland in miniature"', which he set up behind his house in Neuer Pferdemarkt. Its success was assured because the exhibits themselves had 'no conception of the commercial side of the venture', so it did not occur to them 'to alter their own primitive habits of life. The result was that they behaved just as though they were in their own native land, and the interest and value of the exhibition was greatly enhanced.' Just as his audience had accepted the exploitation of animals from Africa, so it now accepted the exploitation of humans. Hagenbeck himself had no doubt. 'My experience with the Laplanders taught me that ethnographic exhibitions would prove lucrative; and no sooner had my little friends departed than I followed up their visit by that of other wild men.' First came Nubians and then Greenland Eskimos, who were displayed in Paris, Berlin and Dresden as well as in Hamburg. Then came 'Somalis, Indians, Kalmucks, Cingalese, Patagonians, Hottentots and so forth'. They were soon worth more to Hagenbeck even than his elephants. 'Towards the end of the seventies, especially in 1879, the animal trade itself was in an exceedingly bad way, so that the anthropological side of my business became more and more important.' His ultimate triumph was the great Cingalese exhibition of 1884, when a caravan of sixty-seven men, women and children with twenty-five elephants and many different breeds of cattle caused 'a great sensation' in

Europe. 'I travelled about with this show all over Germany and Austria, and made a very good thing out of it.'

Great sensations were happening elsewhere too. In England in 1883 a statistician called Francis Galton, who was greatly influenced by his cousin Charles Darwin, invented the word *eugenics* to describe his idea for improving the human race. His theory was in a way obvious and in other ways shocking. As Darwin and thousands of years of husbandry had clearly shown, selective breeding could produce animals vastly superior to their forebears. So why not do the same with humans? This could be achieved, said Galton, by encouraging only people with 'desirable traits' to breed and raise children, while preventing lesser mortals from doing the same. The appeal to racial purists was irresistible.

Four years later the German philosopher Friedrich Nietzsche published *On the Genealogy of Morals*, in which he, too, gave some thought to what it meant to be an acceptable human, and in which he, too, turned his attention to nature. He was perhaps only half-joking when he said you should 'never trust a thought that occurs to you indoors'. For him, civilisation was a sickness brought on by man's 'cooping up of his animal nature' and suppression of his animal instincts. Giving free rein to those instincts must necessarily involve suffering and cruelty, without which humans must lose their vitality. The consequences were plain to see in the 'mad paroxysms of nonsense' that burst from man 'the moment he is prevented ever so little from being a beast of action'. Man needed above all to rediscover his nature, to uncivilise himself. 'I want to state very clearly', he said, 'that in that period when human beings had not yet become ashamed of their cruelty, life on earth was happier than it is today.'

> Watching suffering is good for people, making someone suffer is even better – that is a harsh principle, but an old, powerful, and human, all-too-human major principle, which, by the way, even the apes might agree with. For people say that, in thinking up bizarre cruelties, the apes already anticipate a great many human actions and, as it were, 'act them out'. Without cruelty there is no celebration: that's what the oldest and longest era of human history teaches us – and with punishment, too, there is so much celebration!

To ensure good mental health, he said, we must 'revert to the innocence of wild animals', for deep within us 'lurks the beast of prey, bent on spoil and conquest'. To insure against madness, the hidden urge must be satisfied from time to time, and 'the beast let loose in the wilderness'. There were many in the hunting fraternity, the poets of the gun, who rejoiced at this espousal of their cause; but there were many, too, who felt a sudden clutch of unease.

PART FOUR

NOW

Fakers, Factories and Geneticists

CHAPTER SEVENTEEN

Nature Fakers

ON 13 MARCH 1910, A CURIOUS HEADLINE APPEARED IN THE *New York Times*:

BATTERSEA LOSES
FAMOUS DOG STATUE

Erected as Protest Against Vivisection,
It Was Constant Source of Trouble.

POLICE HAD TO GUARD IT

Medical Students Resented What They Thought Was
an Insult to the Profession – Case Now in Court

The story behind this strange turn of events – a lost statue, rioting medical students – had begun in London seven years earlier, on 1 May 1903. The occasion was the annual meeting of the National Anti-Vivisection Society, when its Honorary Secretary, Stephen Coleridge, nephew of the poet Samuel Taylor Coleridge, delivered what would turn out to be a momentous speech. Much of it was the kind of stuff that might be expected from any opponent of live animal experimentation, which he routinely condemned as 'cowardly, immoral and detestable'. But then, as *The Times* reported on 4 May, he moved swiftly from the general to the particular:

At the University College in London there was a laboratory licensed for vivisection, and into its dark portals passed a never-ending procession of helpless dumb creatures – dogs, lost or stolen from their homes, followed one another down that Via Dolorosa into a scene of nameless horror, where man degraded his race and his manhood, and brought upon that University a smirch that time itself would never erase.

Coleridge then read out a statement from a witness who had been present on 2 February during an experiment conducted by a Dr W. M. Bayliss. The subject of the procedure was a brown terrier dog which was brought into the lecture room with its legs fixed to a board, its head clamped, and its jaws so tightly muzzled that it was 'deprived of every power to give audible expression to its pain'.

In the skin of the abdomen there were several scarcely healed scars and wounds; in one of them, that seemed to be rather fresh, there were left a pair of clamping forceps. The neck was opened widely for the stimulation by electricity of a certain gland. The dog struggled forcibly during the whole experiment, and seemed to suffer extremely during the stimulation. No anaesthetic was administered in his presence. He believed that if the public knew what went on in those dens of infamy, they would not wait for supine legislation or for the second or third readings of Bills in Parliament, but would go in their thousands and set free the victims from their cages, would smash to atoms the horrible instruments of torture, and would leave every laboratory in the kingdom a heap of ruins.

At this the audience clapped and cheered. Coleridge's account of the brown-dog experiment included two flagrant breaches of the Cruelty to Animals Act of 1876. Contrary to law, no anaesthetic had been administered, and the dog had been vivisected more than once. The Act clearly specified that only one procedure should be performed on an animal, after which it must be killed. Offenders faced a fifty-pound fine for a first offence, rising to one hundred pounds or three months' imprisonment for subsequent offences. This left the experimenter, Dr William Maddock Bayliss, FRS, Assistant Professor of Physiology at University College, with little choice. He sued for libel. The case opened at the Old Bailey on 12 November, when his counsel, Rufus Isaacs, argued that the witness had been wrong on every point. The dog had been properly anaesthetised, and it bore no previous scars. Coleridge's witness, he said, was 'a lady from Sweden, and a member of an anti-vivisection society' who took an erroneous view of what took place. 'The person who wrote the libel', he went on, 'must have been the most ignorant person that ever entered a lecture room for medical students, or been influenced by animus.' A rather different story emerged during cross-examination. The dog had indeed undergone an earlier procedure, an examination of its pancreas, by Professor Ernest Starling who, instead of killing it as the law required, had passed it on to Bayliss. The entire medical profession in Britain was on the edge of its seat, fearing the worst, while its two professional journals, *The Lancet* and the *British Medical Journal*, followed the proceedings line by line. In the end the case turned on a fine piece of reasoning by Dr Bayliss, who was asked by Coleridge's counsel, Lawson Walton, whether he believed Professor Starling had been under any legal obligation to destroy the dog once he had finished with it:

> ANSWER: The dog was being destroyed: the experiment was made on the dog during the process of its destruction.
> QUESTION: Then do you say you may kill a dog by inches?
> ANSWER: The animal was to all intents and purposes dead from the time the anaesthetic was given to it.
> QUESTION: You say you are entitled to put an end to the dog by opening it out for further experiment and for further demonstration?
> ANSWER: Yes.

That was enough for the jury. It retired at twenty minutes to five in the afternoon and returned twenty-five minutes later to return a unanimous verdict in favour of the plaintiff and to award him £2,000 in damages. 'The result was received with a considerable amount of applause amongst the public in court,' reported the *British Medical Journal* in its jubilant account of the affair. The Home Secretary, Aretas Akers-Douglas, also seemed satisfied that justice had been done. When asked in Parliament by Sir Arthur Osmond Williams, the member for Merionethshire, whether he proposed to take any action over Starling's breach of the Act, he replied that 'having considered most carefully all the facts of this case', he 'came to the conclusion that I was not called upon to take action'. The wider public, however, was not so easily persuaded, and sections of the press were outraged. The *Daily News*, whose founder and first editor had been Charles Dickens, opened a subscription fund for Coleridge that raised the enormous sum of £5,735. The International Anti-Vivisection Council was also busying itself with fundraising, determined that the little brown dog should live on as an eternal rebuke to vivisectors everywhere. It raised £130 for a permanent memorial, which it decided should take the form of a drinking fountain surmounted by a bronze statue of the dog and bearing a challenging inscription:

> In Memory of the Brown Terrier Dog done to Death in the Laboratories of University College in February 1903, after having endured Vivisection extending over more than two months and having been handed from one Vivisector to another till Death came to his Release. Also in Memory of the 232 dogs vivisected at the same place during the year 1902. Men and Women of England, how long shall these things be?

The International Anti-Vivisection Council applied first to the London Council for permission to erect the fountain in Battersea Park, just south of the River Thames. When this was refused, it made a gift of the fountain to Battersea Borough Council which, being threatened with writs of libel, accepted it only on condition that the Anti-Vivisection Council would indemnify it. On the afternoon of Saturday 15 September 1906, the Mayor of Battersea, William Rines, proudly unveiled the new fountain at the Latchmere Recreation Ground. According to *The Times*, 'he said the gift was accepted despite threats of all sorts of pains and penalties. In the interests of humanity the council were prepared to take whatever consequences might come to them'. These were bold words indeed.

What followed was a sensation that aroused excitement even on the other side of the Atlantic. Riots, marches, attacks on the fountain with sledge-hammer and paint-pot, all testified to the fact that passions ran high on both sides. Who were the greater enemies of society? Those who burrowed through the entrails of sentient beings? Or those who obstructed the cause of medicine? There was a brief, uneasy peace while University College considered whether or not it had grounds to sue the little brown dog, then the medical students took matters into their own hands. They marched, they rioted, and the statue itself was saved from destruction only by a twenty-four-hour guard by the Metropolitan Police. Arrests and fines handed down at London's police courts only inflamed the students' passions. On 10 November 1907, *The Times* reported that ten students from the Middlesex and University Hospitals, who had attacked the dog with a sledge-hammer and tried to wrench off its legs, were fined five pounds each at the South-Western police court. On 27 November it described what happened afterwards. A crowd of students marched in procession back to University Hospital, where they burned an effigy of the learned magistrate, Mr Paul Taylor. Three days later, the paper reported, a mob of young students from schools and colleges across London 'went to the UCH and made some efforts to induce the students there to come out and promenade along the streets. The hospital students did not come out, but those who had gone there marched through several streets arm in arm, 13 or 14 in a row, hustling the pedestrians off the pavements, and creating a serious obstruction to vehicular traffic.' In Great Russell Street the demonstrators defied Inspector Sewell's instruction to disperse, then were scattered by mounted policemen. Rioters also attacked the Anti-Vivisection Hospital in Prince of Wales Drive, and fought for many hours with police in Trafalgar Square, making it another busy day for the Bow Street magistrates.

In Battersea itself, the invasion by middle-class troublemakers did not go down well with the local youth, who ran out to defend the little brown dog, and their own turf, with their fists. The students themselves, ranks swelled by supporters from other universities, then moved on to take violent issue not just with anti-vivisectionists but also with any other group it thought guilty of non-establishment thinking: socialists, trade unionists, even suffragettes, who saw a parallel between the victimisation of women and cruelty to animals. A meeting called by the President of the National Union of Women's Suffrage Societies, Millicent Fawcett, was literally broken up in a litter of smashed chairs and tables. This proud victory for science over sentiment was reported by the *Daily Express* under the headline

'Medical Students' Gallant Fight With Women'. The Brown Dog Riots, as they became known, persisted until the early hours of 10 March 1910, when Battersea Borough Council, by now in Conservative rather than Liberal hands, sent four workers with a protective cordon of one hundred and twenty policemen to tear the statue down. Despite twenty-thousand signatures on a petition to save it, and a congregation of three thousand anti-vivisectionists in Trafalgar Square, the little brown dog was melted down by the council's blacksmith.

All this served to deepen the doubts and divisions in the public mind. Newspapers, too, were divided. Some, like the *Daily News*, supported the protectionists. Others, like the *Daily Express*, sided with the vivisectors and accused their opponents of whipping up false sentiment with hysterical language. The divisions spread slowly across the rest of Europe but more quickly in America, where the American Anti-Vivisection Society modelled itself on Frances Power Cobbe's Victoria Street Society. One of the society's two founder-members, Caroline Earle White, took advice from Cobbe before launching the AAVS in 1883. The prevalence of women in the anti-vivisection movement was no coincidence, for feminists saw the animal laboratory, and the pleasure that scientists and students evidently took from it, as yet another demonstration of masculine dominance and power of the strong over the weak. There was a real fear that what started with live animals would end with live humans. Frances Power Cobbe made this explicit in one of her many books, *Vivisection in America*, published in 1890:

> There is another phase of the subject as yet but little thought of. There is no argument in favour of Vivisection which does not apply more completely, more forcibly, to men than to animals. If the inferior is justly sacrificed to the higher, the legality of the surrender to scientific torture of idiots, criminals, those incurably diseased, and, indeed, all ignorant and brutalized men, including vivisectors, is beyond question. The lives of these are valueless to society, when they are not, as they usually are, noxious to it. At present vivisectors are timid and hypocritical. They sigh that the 'rat or two' that they ask in their love for humanity is grudgingly bestowed; but they do not mention so freely the hundreds of experiments in which

they keep animals skinned, with nerves laid bare, irritated with electricity and in every possible way, cut open their living bodies, roast, crucify, boil, subject them to experiments causing the most excruciating agony in the most sensitive nerves – and the greater the suffering the greater the 'joyful excitement' with which they inflict it. They already say among themselves that no true results can be reached *without human subjects*.

Men were almost always outnumbered by women at anti-vivisection meetings, sometimes by as many as three to one. This could not entirely be explained by feminine sensitivity. It was in large part political. The practice of medicine, feminists believed, was an exclusively male domain in which women and animals were cast as victims. Even among women of spotless virtue, it rankled that the United Kingdom's Contagious Diseases Acts of 1864, which was designed to rid the armed forces of venereal disease, subjected prostitutes, but not their clients, to arrest, humiliating medical examinations and incarceration. A British election pamphlet of 1880 urged all liberal-minded voters to favour candidates opposed to vivisection. Then, 'you may be tolerably sure that in other questions he will support the cause of the weak against the strong, of religion against materialism, and of the right against might'. By the end of the nineteenth century, however, even within the protectionist movement, opinion was moving away from the total abolition of vivisection towards the more attainable goal of tighter regulation. For Frances Power Cobbe, who in 1898 was expelled from the presidency of the Victoria Street Society, it was no less a betrayal than the 1876 Act itself. She died in 1904.

Another powerful opponent of the vivisectors was George Bernard Shaw, whose play *The Doctor's Dilemma*, written in 1906, dripped scorn on to every kind of scientific fad, including germ theory and vaccination as well as vivisection. 'As a matter of fact,' he declared in his preface to the play, 'the rank and file of doctors are no more scientific than their tailors … The distinction between a quack doctor and a qualified one is mainly that only the qualified one is authorized to sign death certificates, for which both sorts seem to have about equal occasion.' People who claimed to cure disease, he concluded, should be regarded in the same way as fortune tellers – or, perhaps, the augurs of ancient Rome who could read portents in the entrails of goats. But Shaw's scepticism was not directed at the medical profession alone. In the preface to *Back to Methuselah: A Metabiological Pentateuch*, a collection of five plays published in 1921, it was the turn of the evolutionists to feel the lash of his pen. The very title of the preface, 'The Infidel Half Century', gave due warning of what was to follow. It was as if wit had been poured into the mould of a medieval pope:

> The Darwinian process may be described as a chapter of accidents. As such, it seems simple, because you do not at first realize all that it involves. But when its whole significance dawns on you, your heart sinks into a heap of sand within you … To call this Natural Selection is a blasphemy, possible to many for whom Nature is nothing but a casual aggregation of inert and dead matter, but eternally impossible to the spirits and souls of the righteous. If it be no blasphemy, but a truth of science, then the stars of heaven, the showers and dew, the winter and summer, the fire and heat, the mountains and hills, may no longer be called to exalt the Lord with us by praise; their work is to modify all things by blindly starving and murdering everything that is not lucky enough to survive in the universal struggle for hogwash.

*

In other spheres of business, hogwash was a seam of gold. Vast were the fortunes made from fairground freaks, none more so than the notorious 'Feejee Mermaid', which tripled the takings of P.T. Barnum's American Museum in New York in 1842. The exposure of this fraud, created by a Japanese fisherman who stitched the tail of a fish to the body of a monkey, cautioned scientists to be wary of all 'new' species. An earlier victim of their scepticism was the platypus. The first recorded specimen of this improbable creature was sent to London in 1798 by the Governor of New South Wales, Admiral John Hunter. Though this distinguished naval officer was a most unlikely hoaxer, no one would risk being fooled. Who could possibly believe that a beaver with a duck-bill stuck on to it was not a sailor's prank? The eminent naturalist George Shaw, Fellow of the Royal Society, co-founder of the Linnean Society and a future Keeper of Natural History at the British Museum, would eventually write the first scientific description of *Ornithorhynchus anatinus*, but not before he had snipped at Hunter's specimen in search of the hoaxer's stitches. A century later came the okapi, which resembled a chestnut-coloured horse with the legs and rump of a zebra. Who could accept such an aberration, or believe that it had existed, unknown and unsuspected, in the high-canopy forests of Central Africa? A painting of the animal by the explorer-naturalist Sir Harry Johnston was laughed to scorn and denounced as a hoax by the director of the Natural History Museum, Professor Ray Lankester. Not until 1901, when skin and skulls were shown to a crowded meeting of the Zoological Society of London, was the species recognised as genuine. By way of apology it was named in its discoverer's honour, *Okapia johnstoni*.

Back in Africa, more attention was being given to the plight of familiar species than to the discovery of new ones. Foremost among those expressing fear were the very same English gentlemen who had complained to the Governor-General about the loss of their hunting ground in Sudan. Their letter to Lord Cromer was no ordinary public petition. Among its signatories were the Duke and Duchess of Bedford, the future foreign secretary Sir Edward Grey, Philip Lutley Sclater who served for forty-two years as Secretary of the Zoological Society of London, the explorer Sir Harry Johnston and his recent antagonist Professor Lankester, and the zoologist Oldfield Thomas, who had described and catalogued some two thousand new mammals for the Natural History Museum. Also lending his name was the museum's hunter-in-chief, Frederick Courteney Selous, a man above all others who could recognise a dearth of things to shoot. This was the group that would become the driving force behind the world's very first international environmental organisation, the Society for the Preservation of the Wild Fauna of the Empire, founded in 1903. The SPWFE grew rapidly into one of the most exclusive institutions in the English-speaking world. Its vice-presidents included Lord Cromer; Lord Milner, Governor of the Cape Colony and High Commissioner for Southern Africa; Lord Curzon, Viceroy of India; and Lord Minto, Governor-General of Canada. President Theodore Roosevelt, himself a keen big-game hunter, was an honorary member, as were Lord Kitchener and Alfred Lyttelton, Britain's Secretary of State for the Colonies. But their interest was highly selective. By 'Wild Fauna of the Empire' they did not mean mice or moles or anything else too small to be shot at. What they wanted was a guaranteed supply of species big enough to hunt, a clearly self-interested aspiration that earned them the sobriquet 'penitent butchers'. Their description of themselves as 'a modest and unpretentious group of gentlemen' similarly invited derision, but any kind of protection for wild animals was better than none. In urging the protection 'from appalling destruction' of wild animals throughout the British Empire, the SPWFE spread its considerable influence across fully a quarter of the globe.

But hunting was not the only threat to wild species. A book that many of the SPWFE's founders would have read was the sadly prophetic *Man and Nature; or Physical Geography as Modified by Human Action*, published nearly fifty years earlier by the American diplomat and philologist George Perkins Marsh. This early environmental masterwork began with a quotation from Horace Bushnell's *Sermon on the Power of an Endless Life*, written in 1858:

> Not all the winds, and storms, and earthquakes, and seas, and seasons of the world, have done so much to revolutionise the earth as MAN, the power of an endless life, has done since the day he came forth upon it, and received dominion over it.

Marsh was one of the nineteenth century's greatest polymaths. In his book he cites references from two hundred and ten different publications, written in a babble of tongues including French, Italian, German, Dutch and Norwegian. Like all good natural scientists he understood the importance of observation. 'Sight is a faculty', he wrote. 'Seeing, an art. The eye is a physical, but not a self-acting apparatus, and in general it sees only what it seeks.' What his own eye saw was a world knocked off balance by human interference. With his frock coat, top hat and Old Testament beard he was a man of forbidding appearance, contemptuous of vice. 'I wish I could believe', he wrote, 'that America is not alone responsible for the introduction of the filthy weed, tobacco, the use of which is the most vulgar and pernicious habit engrafted by the semi-barbarism of modern civilization upon the less multifarious sensualism of ancient life'. Like the church elder he closely resembled, he saw ancient wisdom as the only remedy for contemporary ills. The Roman Empire, he noted, had enjoyed 'a productiveness of soil of which we at present discover but slender traces'. The vast and hungry armies of Persians and Tartars, for example, were able to feed themselves on long marches from the produce of lands which now 'would scarcely afford forage for a single regiment'. Wherever he looked, he saw evidence of 'man's ignorant disregard of the laws of nature' and of his 'treacherous warfare on his natural allies'. He saw crops and wild plants shrivel as a result of the misguided slaughter of insectivorous birds. He saw good soil turned to dust by deforestation:

> When the forest is gone, the great reservoir of moisture stored up in its vegetable mould is evaporated, and returns only in deluges of rain to wash away the parched dust into which that mould has been created. The well-wooded and humid hills are turned to ridges of dry rock, which encumbers the low grounds and chokes the watercourses with its debris ... The whole earth, unless rescued by human art from the physical degradation to which it tends, becomes an assemblage of bald mountains, of barren, turfless hills, and of swampy malarious plains.

Human improvidence, he concluded, could reduce the Earth 'to such a condition of impoverished productiveness, of shattered surface, of climatic excess, as to threaten the depravation, barbarism, and perhaps even extinction of the species'. God's work, he contended, was in all cases superior to the works of man:

> Not only is the wild plant much hardier than the domesticated vegetable, but the same law prevails in animated brute and even human life. The beasts of the chase are more capable of endurance and privation and more tenacious of life, than the domesticated animals which most nearly resemble them. The savage fights on, after he has received half a dozen mortal wounds, the least of which would have instantly paralyzed the strength of his civilized enemy, and, like the wild boar, he has been known to press forward along the shaft of the spear which was transpiercing his vitals, and to deal a deathblow on the soldier who wielded it.

There was no better example of man's 'terrible destructiveness', Marsh said, than killing animals and birds for those tiny portions of their bodies that were of commercial value. In South America, wild cattle had been 'slaughtered by the millions for their hides and horns'. The North American buffalo had been purged for its skin or tongue; the elephant, walrus and narwhal for their tusks; whales for their oil and whalebone; the ostrich for its feathers. Already one big marine mammal, Steller's sea cow, *Hydrodamalis gigas*, had been driven to extinction for the sake of its oil, fat and fur, and more were bound to follow. Seals, walruses and sea otters were in rapid decline, and the most saleable fish had been 'immensely reduced in numbers'. The single piece of good news was a change in fashion for top hats:

> When a Parisian manufacturer invented the silk hat, which soon came into almost universal use, the demand for beavers' fur fell off, and this animal – whose habits, as we have seen, are an important agency in the formation of bogs and other modifications of forest nature – immediately began to increase, reappeared in haunts which he had long abandoned, and can no longer be regarded as rare enough to be in immediate danger of extirpation. Thus the convenience or the caprice of Parisian fashion has unconsciously exercised an influence which may sensibly affect the physical geography of a distant continent.

Unfortunately for distant continents, Marsh's warnings did not penetrate the minds of his most influential fellow countrymen. Theodore Roosevelt, elected President of the United States in 1901, liked to describe himself as a 'naturalist' with an unsentimental, clear-sighted view of the realities of the wild. One of these realities was the Great White Hunter. Roosevelt himself was a prolific slaughterer of African wildlife who regarded hunting as both the best expression of the American pioneering spirit and the dominance of white men over black. The Great White Hunter, he believed, was 'the archetype of freedom' and the finest embodiment of 'the stern, manly qualities that are invaluable to a nation'. Winston Churchill was a kindred spirit. In 1907, as Parliamentary Under-Secretary for the Colonies, he visited East Africa ostensibly to inspect the new Uganda railway, but in fact spent more time shooting his way across Kenya than he did on official duties. Two years later, just weeks after leaving office and supported by the Smithsonian Institute, Roosevelt embarked on an epic specimen-collecting expedition to East and Central Africa. This was guided from time to time by no less a figure than Frederick Courteney Selous and required the employment of two hundred native porters. Even for a continent accustomed to the likes of Roualeyn Gordon-Cumming, the carnage was spectacular – on the evidence of Roosevelt's own account, far more than was needed to satisfy the Smithsonian's need for specimens. The frontispiece of his book of the expedition, *African Game Trails*, shows a photograph of him, taken by his son Kermit, standing over the corpse of a lion, one of seventeen (nine to father, eight to son) that the pair of them shot during the safari. At the end of the book Roosevelt records their final scores. For Theodore, a grand total of two hundred and ninety-six trophies. For Kermit, two hundred and sixteen. Seventy-five different species went into the bag, ranging from elephant (eleven shot between them) to dikdik and porcupine (two each). They counted twenty rhinoceroses, eight hippos, nine giraffes, three baboons, nine hyenas, twenty-nine zebras and vast numbers of antelopes, gazelles, monkeys and birds. The official record of the Smithsonian Institute reveals that the expedition as a whole 'enriched' the biological collections of the United States National Museum and National Zoological Park with portions of 11,400 animals including the skins of one thousand large mammals.

Even this was not the whole of it. Readers of *African Game Trails* may come away with the impression that Selous alone could stand comparison with the author as a crack shot. The truth was rather different. Roosevelt was overweight, short-sighted and as likely to wound an animal as to kill it. No count was made of the creatures that dragged themselves away to die in the bush. An animal's suffering might even be prolonged for the sake of a photograph. Roosevelt describes how Kermit, taking aim at an old lioness, 'crumpled her up' with his first shot. 'He then put another bullet into her, and as she seemed disabled walked up within fifty yards and took some photos.' When the lioness eventually managed to gather herself for a charge, 'he stopped her with another bullet, and killed her outright with a fourth'. Was any word ever more mendaciously misapplied than that 'outright'? At the end of it all, to pre-empt his critics, Roosevelt adds an exculpatory note commending his own restraint:

Kermit and I kept about a dozen trophies for ourselves; otherwise we shot nothing that was not used either as a museum specimen or for meat – usually for both purposes. We were in hunting grounds practically as good as any that have ever existed; but we did not kill a tenth, nor a hundredth, part of what we might have killed had we been willing.

This restraint should not be mistaken for sentimentality. Two years earlier, while he was still President of the United States, Theodore 'Teddy' Roosevelt played a decisive part in what became known as the 'nature-fakers controversy'. This was all about the way animals were portrayed in contemporary literature. On one side stood John Burroughs, venerable American conservationist, nature writer and strict Darwinian, who despised the mysticism, sentimentality and scientific ignorance of the Romantics. Even more abhorrent to him were the anthropomorphic distortions of a new generation of nature writers such as the Reverend William J. Long, Charles G.D. Roberts and Ernest Thompson Seton, whose fantasies, Burroughs believed, were corrupting the minds of the young. Protesting the absolute veracity of their eyewitness accounts, these 'new naturalists' claimed to have seen, among many other previously unsuspected phenomena, a fox luring hounds into the path of a train, an eagle swooping to catch in mid-air a chick that had fallen from its nest, a woodcock setting its own broken leg in a cast of mud, a lynx fighting off eight wolves, a wolf killing a caribou with a single bite that pierced its heart, a mother otter teaching her 'unsuspecting little ones' to swim by 'carrying them on her back into the water as if for a frolic, and there diving from under them before they realized what she was about'. Animals, in short, were as capable of creative thinking, and of developing their own cultures, as humans were. In 1903 Burroughs went on the offensive. In an article for the *Atlantic Monthly*, published under the headline 'Real and Sham Natural History', he denounced what he called 'the yellow journalism of the woods'. Ernest Thompson Seton's book *Wild Animals I Have Known*, he said, would better have been called *Wild Animals I ALONE Have Known*.

The President was entirely on Burroughs' side. He, too, was outraged that such books were being used to mislead children in American schools. In 1907 he decided to act. In an interview with *Everybody's Magazine*, he poured out his contempt. 'I don't believe for a minute', he said, 'that some of the men who are writing nature stories and putting the word "truth" prominently in their prefaces know the heart of wild things.' To the list of regular targets he added the name of Jack London, whose novel of 1906, *White Fang*, involved a bulldog which, in a 'very sublimity of absurdity', held its ground against a wolf three times its size. But Jack London was a sideswipe. Pure fiction was not the issue. The real enemy was fiction dressed as fact, and in Roosevelt's opinion the worst offender was the Connecticut pastor William J. Long, author of such titles as *Ways of Woodfolk*, *Secrets of the Woods* and *Wayeeses, the White Wolf*, which included the story of the caribou clinically despatched with a single bite to the heart. By measuring the gape of a wolf's jaws and the length of its teeth, Roosevelt cut Long's claim to shreds. Though hopelessly outgunned, Long himself fought like a cornered tiger, denouncing the president as less a lover of nature than its assassin. Others wondered whether it was appropriate for a President of the United States to use the authority of his office to assail a private individual. One sympathetic commentator likened Long to 'a dove shot at by an elephant gun'. But the fight was over. Roosevelt's dismissive epithet, 'nature fakers', entered the American language and Roosevelt himself, even as he packed his guns for Africa, emerged from the affair as one of the world's most improbable champions of non-human life. It is a glorious irony that this fierce proponent of 'the stern, manly qualities' of the hunter should now be remembered as the inspiration for that unsurpassable icon of anthropomorphic cuddliness, the Teddy Bear.

CHAPTER EIGHTEEN

The Wolf's Lair

FROM ANCIENT TIMES TO THE TWENTIETH CENTURY, NO WAR was ever won without horses. It was the Roman cavalry that defeated Hannibal's elephants, Octavian's cavalry that crushed Antony and Cleopatra, cavalry that remained the engine of warfare, and hence of human history, right up until the day Britain declared war on Germany in August 1914. During the four years of the First World War horses died by the million. Only humans perished in greater number. Dogs died too. So did mules, donkeys, pigeons, whales and slugs, though no one much cared about those. So did camels, which were used by British mounted infantry in the Middle East. There were diehards on both sides who, even as the tanks and machine guns lined up against them, clung to tradition. Whether in victory or defeat, they believed, there was nothing so glorious as a cavalry charge. The proper way to exploit a breakthrough by the infantry was for mounted troops to gallop through the breach. Horses, after all, were so much nimbler than tanks. The problem for horses and riders was that machine-gun bullets were less likely to bounce off them than they were from the flanks of the armoured divisions.

Who knows how many animals died? A widely accepted estimate puts the equine death toll, not counting mules and donkeys, at eight million. Only a minority of these died in cavalry charges. Their principal use was logistical. Horses hauled supply wagons, ambulances and artillery. They bore messages. They raised the men's morale. Like soldiers they died from shellfire, bombs and poison gas. Like sailors they drowned when their transports were sunk by submarines. Like horses in every kind of heavy occupation they died from injury, overwork, malnutrition and disease which, on top of their vast output of dung, had awful consequences for the stinking channels that passed for sanitation. Mules and donkeys suffered in similar ways, though nobody thought to count them. As the war progressed and animals died faster than they could be replaced, a dead horse was reckoned a more serious blow to the war effort than a dead human. This changed dramatically after the Armistice, when a lethal combination of expense and quarantine restrictions meant that many of the survivors could not be repatriated, leaving thousands to be shot, sold or sent to slaughterhouses.

Dogs, too, were heavily involved. They carried messages through trenches and across battlefields; they followed their noses to find wounded soldiers and warn of gas attacks, carried medical supplies to men awaiting rescue and brought comfort to the dying. They killed rats in the trenches, sniffed out hidden enemies and provided the companionship expected of best friends. Stories of canine heroism abounded: Dick, a black retriever who continued to bear messages even though fatally wounded with a bullet in his chest and a shell splinter in his back; Stubby, a Boston terrier who became the mascot of the 102nd Infantry, 26th Yankee Division, and whose sense of smell saved the lives of countless men. Stubby sniffed and barked through seventeen battles and was promoted to sergeant after capturing a German spy. After the war he was awarded a gold medal by the Humane Education Society, presented to him by the Commanding General of the US Army, John J. Pershing. When he died in 1926 he was accorded a lengthy obituary in the *New York Times*, then stuffed and presented to the Smithsonian Institute.

A creature did not need four legs to be a hero. Two legs and a pair of wings were enough. Both sides in the war used homing pigeons to keep officers in touch with their men. Tens of thousands of them were kept at divisional headquarters or in mobile lofts carried on the soldiers' backs. They were considered so valuable that the British Defence of the Realm Act made it a criminal offence to kill, molest or neglect one. Like the stables and the kennels, the pigeon lofts produced champions of their own. One of the bravest was Cher Ami, who flew twelve successful missions for the US

Army Signal Corps at Verdun. The last of these, on 4 October 1918, cost him a bullet through breast and leg, but onward he flew to save the lives of two hundred men trapped behind enemy lines in the 'Lost Battalion' of the 77th Infantry Division. The message he bore was misspelled but urgent. 'WE ARE ALONG THE ROAD PARALELL 276.4. OUR ARTILLERY IS DROPPING A BARRAGE DIRECTLY ON US. FOR HEAVENS SAKE STOP IT.' Thanks to Cher Ami they did stop it and the men were brought safely back behind American lines. Cher Ami sadly was not so fortunate. He died of his wounds on 13 June 1919, though not before the French government had awarded him the *Croix de Guerre*.

Such honours would have been unthinkable to the Ancients, or to the medieval barons in their forests: humans giving tribute to *animals*. Men expressing gratitude to actual wet-nosed dogs, not dog-headed gods, for the gift of enduring life. Other creatures gave vital service with no idea of what they were doing. Many soldiers were spared the effects of mustard gas by a chance observation made by a curator at the US National Museum's Division of Mollusks, Dr Paul Bartsch. When some slugs escaped into his boiler room, Bartsch noticed that they reacted to the boiler fumes by immediately compressing their bodies and shutting their breathing pores. It was an observation that seemed at first to be of little value, but Bartsch persisted. He did more tests and found the slugs could detect and react to mustard gas at concentrations far lower than those detectable by humans, thus giving soldiers advance warning of a gas attack and ample time to put on their masks. No medals were pinned on slugs after the war, but many men owed their lives to them.

If the slug was at one end of the scale, then the whale was at the other. While the tiny mollusc helped to prolong life, the huge mammal helped terminate it. Whale oil was widely used in the manufacture of soap, a process which coincidentally produced glycerine. When combined with nitric and sulphuric acids, this became nitroglycerine, an essential ingredient of the cordite used in bullets and artillery shells. It also made lubricants that remained liquid even in freezing temperatures and so were perfect for oiling weapons. It oiled the feet of British soldiers to protect them from trench foot, warmed them with whale-oil stoves, and greased the faces of pilots to insulate them from the cold. Soap factories during the war therefore concentrated on producing glycerine for the arms industry, and Britain enjoyed the great advantage of being in effective control of the world's whaling fleets. Thus it was able to starve Germany and Austria-Hungary of this crucial resource, obliging the German government *in extremis* to urge the country's fishermen to hunt seals and dolphins instead. The best estimate is that fifty-eight thousand whales were sacrificed to the British and Allied war effort, though this does not include the many bombed in mistake for submarines.

In Russia and Germany between the two world wars, attitudes to nature veered in opposite directions. In the Marxist-Leninist perspective, nature was an enemy that needed to be tamed for the benefit of the proletariat. In an essay of 1932, Maxim Gorky took aim at his fellow poets, deploring their worship of nature and submission to its 'foul tricks'. 'Praise of nature', he wrote, 'is praise of a despot, and in tone it is almost reminiscent of prayers.' Instead of worshipping the 'blind forces that destroy thousands of people and tear down the labours of their hands', they should 'summon humankind to the struggle against nature'. Under Joseph Stalin, no work of literature or art could be approved that strayed from the party line. Workers were to be depicted tearing down the forests, damming the rivers and generally obliterating every obstacle that wild nature placed in the path of economic progress.

Nazi Germany was wildly different. Here the voice whispering in people's ears was that of Friedrich Nietzsche. Or so it was made to seem. Civilisation, Nietzsche had said, was a sickness caused by man's denial of his animal instincts and his failure to see himself as a beast of action. But Nietzsche was a sinuous thinker who did not deal in simple truths. 'There are no facts,' he wrote, 'only interpretations.' One of his most prophetic statements came in his work of 1878, *Human, All Too Human: A Book for Free Spirits*:

The worst readers are those who behave like plundering troops: they take away a few things they can use, dirty and confound the remainder, and revile the whole.

This was to be the fate of his own work, largely at the hands of his sister, who after his death in 1900 became the chief custodian of his archive. His work did indeed contain some ideas that were useful to fascists and Nazis: the death of God, the subjugation of women, the rejection of democracy, the idea of the 'will to power' and the *Übermensch*, or superior human who lived by his own values. But these concepts were more often quoted than they were understood. By *Übermensch* he did not mean a blond-haired, blue-eyed 'Aryan'. By 'will to power' he did not mean the strong enslaving the weak. He meant rather an exuberance of spirit, a determination to fulfil one's own potential. Power over others, he suggested, might better be achieved by acts of kindness than by cruelty. He stood against nihilism, he stood against nationalism, he stood against any idea that the world might conform to a single way of thinking. He stood against the wastefulness of war. There are, he said, 'other means of honouring physiology than through army hospitals'. To raise a 'select crop of youth and energy and power and then to put it in front of cannons – that is madness'. Yet that is exactly what presumptive disciples proceeded to do in his name. The bad fairy in the story is his sister Elisabeth Förster-Nietzsche, who within a year of her brother's death cobbled together a compendium of his unpublished notes and jottings – unfinished material never intended for publication – which she then edited in such a way as to twist his philosophy into the shape of her own committed Nazism. The book she then published under his name, *The Will to Power*, had little to do with Friedrich's opinions but everything to do with her own. The staff and committee that administered the Nietzsche archive at Weimar were packed with National Socialists, including the notorious book-burner Alfred Bäumler and the philosopher Martin Heidegger, who encouraged people to believe that the truth of Nietzsche's thinking lay not in his own published works but in the manipulations of his sister. When Hitler visited the archive in 1933, Elisabeth presented him with her brother's favourite walking stick. The transformation was complete, the *Übermensch* transmuted into a strutting blond brute hell-bent on racial supremacy.

Shock was in store for those who believed love of animals would ensure respect for fellow humans. In 1933, less than two months after Hitler came to power, Germany opened its first concentration camp at Dachau and enacted new laws prohibiting cruelty to animals. There would be no more vivisection, no more abandoned pets, no more force-fed poultry, no more laboratory mice or rabbits. Instead, as the concentration camps spread and multiplied, there would be laboratory humans. Not being animals, Jews and Gypsies would have no protection from the law that banned operations without anaesthesia. Such were the values of the *Übermenschen*.

But the Nazis had their own ways of exploiting animals. There was propaganda value in Hitler's devotion to his German Shepherd, Blondi. It made him appear humane, caring and compassionate. There was propaganda value, too, in the contrast between animal-loving Aryans and cruel Jews whose method of ritual slaughter, *shechita*, meant cutting the throats of conscious animals. This, too, was banned by law in April 1933, reinforcing the perception of Judaism as inimical to civilised society. Thus animal protection laws bore the stamp of Nazi ideology. Six million Jews might die unmourned, but heaven help anyone who harmed a dog.

Hitler's Blondi, who would die with him in the Berlin bunker, was herself quintessentially German, a kind of canine Aryan. The breed was first described in 1899, the result of selective breeding by Max von Stephanitz, a breeder whose aim was to produce a superior kind of sheepdog. The desired characteristics were acuity, strength, obedience, loyalty and aggression, all virtues it would share with the German people. The German Shepherd was as close as the Nazis could get to their primeval animal champion, the wolf. Hitler's own image of himself as leader of the pack was brazenly lupine. There was no accident, or coincidence or irony in the fact that his secret headquarters in the woods near Rastenburg in East Prussia was called the Wolf's Lair, or that he was accompanied by a wolf-like dog. The wolf was the embodiment of the Aryan ideal: fierce, relentless, ruthless, a perfect example of the survival of the fittest.

Nietzsche was not the only victim of misrepresentation. Darwin suffered in the same way. What his theory of evolution actually said was that species were fitted for survival by adapting to their environments. What the Nazis meant by 'survival of the fittest' was the victory of the strong over the weak. Just as Max von Stephanitz had selected the strongest and rejected the weakest in breeding the German Shepherd, so the Third Reich would do the same for the German *Volk*. Just as Hermann Goering was encouraging his friend Lutz Heck, director of Berlin Zoo, to breed backwards from modern cattle to the primeval aurochs, so the German nation would expunge the alien blood that had poisoned it. The zoo was the ideal place to demonstrate the pyramid of life. From 1938, Jews were denied entry and no longer permitted to gaze upon the superior beings in their cages. As he revealed in *Mein Kampf*, Hitler believed that the first and most important species to be domesticated by humans in prehistory were not animals but other humans:

> For the establishment of superior types of civilization the members of inferior races formed one of the most essential pre-requisites. They alone could supply the lack of mechanical means without which no progress is possible. It is certain that the first stages of human civilization were not based so much on the use of tame animals as on the employment of human beings who were members of an inferior race. Only after subjugated races were employed as slaves was a similar fate allotted to animals, and not vice versa, as some people would have us believe. At first it was the conquered enemy who had to draw the plough and only afterwards did the ox and horse take his place. Nobody else but puling pacifists can consider this fact as a sign of human degradation. Such people fail to recognize that this evolution had to take place in order that man might reach that degree of civilization which these apostles now exploit in an attempt to make the world pay attention to their rigmarole.

It fell, therefore, to the Nazis to restore what had been lost. The Aryan race, Hitler declared, was superior to all others, and Darwin provided all the justification needed for their intended domination of the world. The *Übermenschen*, or Master Race, were the natural predators who would purify humankind. When men have lost their natural instincts, Hitler wrote,

> there is no hope that Nature will correct the loss that has been caused, until recognition of the lost instincts has been restored ... But there is serious danger that those who have become blind once in this respect will continue more and more to break down racial barriers and finally lose the last remnants of what is best in them. What then remains is

nothing but a uniform mishmash, which seems to be the dream of our fine Utopians ...

Those who do not wish that the earth should fall into such a condition must realize that it is the task of the German State in particular to see to it that the process of bastardization is brought to a stop. Our contemporary generation of weaklings will naturally decry such a policy and whine and complain about it as an encroachment on the most sacred of human rights. But there is only one right that is sacrosanct and this right is at the same time a most sacred duty. This right and obligation are: that the purity of the racial blood should be guarded, so that the best types of human beings may be preserved and that thus we should render possible a more noble development of humanity itself.

Pupils in German schools learned that humans no less than animals were subject to the laws of nature. This meant that Nazi eugenicists were as free to work on the human stock as Max von Stephanitz had been to work on sheepdogs. They called it *racial hygiene*. The Nazi eugenics programme began in July 1933 with the sterilisation of disabled people. The Nietzschean view of women, that their duty was to marry good Aryan husbands and produce the next generation of *Übermenschen*, was equally a priority. But eugenics was not exclusively a German preoccupation. The idea, and the word, first occurred to the English statistician Francis Galton in 1883, and there were well-established eugenics movements in Britain and the United States. The basic tenet of Galton's idea, which he had extrapolated from the work of his cousin Charles Darwin, was that human defects, like weaknesses in animals, were passed down from one generation to the next, and that the only way to halt progressive deterioration was to shut off the supply. But it was in America, and most particularly in California, that Galton's ideas were most stringently applied. Crime, sexual deviance, alcoholism and destitution were all read as signs of 'feeblemindedness', a lamentable condition which could be subdivided into a hierarchy of instability that descended through idiots and imbeciles to morons. For those held in public institutions the penalty was enforced sterilisation, which meant vasectomies for men and the excision of their Fallopian tubes for women. It was a report on the Californian project, *Sterilization for Human Betterment*, published in 1929 and reviewing 6,225 sterilisation cases in state hospitals, that provided the model for the Nazis' sterilisation law of 1933. But the Third Reich went further. It was not the mentally handicapped that Hitler regarded as the worst threat to the *Übermensch*: it was the presence in Germany of inferior, non-Aryan races such as Gypsies, Slavs and Jews. Thousands of enforced sterilisations were only the beginning. The de-sexing of racially unhygienic individuals grew into a euthanasia project in which the disabled and mentally unfit were gassed, at first by exhaust fumes inside specially adapted buses, and then in the gas chambers to which they were followed by thousands of Jews.

By perversion of science and logic, the theory of evolution had led to the Holocaust. The world's most famous dog-lover had crushed Pythagoras under his heel. Hitler kept Blondi with him until the end. In the Berlin bunker where she had shared his bed, her last service to her master was to confirm the lethal efficiency of cyanide.

The Second World War meanwhile had consumed as many animals as the First. Berlin Zoo in 1939 contained a population of 3,715. Thirty per cent of these died in the first fifteen minutes of the Allied bombing raids on 22 November 1943. More perished under Red Army artillery fire in March 1945, or were slaughtered and eaten by Russian soldiers. By the end of May only ninety-one animals survived. But these were losses of small significance when set against the wider costs of the war. Though 'cavalry' now was more likely to mean tanks than mounted soldiers, none of the armies could function without horses. Germany in particular cherished a proud tradition of horsemanship. Its riding schools were the best in the world, and its riders unequalled. At the Berlin Olympic Games in 1936 the equestrian events were dominated by German riders who won between them six gold medals and one silver. Many who served in the German army were countrymen with a deep understanding of heavy horses, and love of the horse was seen as a soldierly virtue. Thousands of the men who went to war in 1939 were still mounted cavalry who would fight in France, Holland and Belgium before being ravaged by the freezing Russian winter of 1941–2, which cost the lives of 179,000 horses. Supply trains and heavy artillery, too, still depended on horsepower. This was a formidable challenge. A supply wagon or heavy gun needed six horses to pull it, and as many men to harness them. Conditions in the field were attritional. Horses were weakened by heavy work and shortages of fodder, and as vulnerable as their handlers to bombs, shells and machine guns. Elegant animals that had seemed so refined and stylish in peacetime now struggled like ballerinas in a coalmine. Like the overworked cart-horses of Victorian England, they expired between the shafts and were either eaten by the protein-starved troops or were left to spread across the battlefield the characteristic stench of putrid flesh.

Other armies were not much different. The Russians, no less than the Germans, depended on horses for transport and supplies, and retained even more cavalry. These, too, suffered heavy losses in 1941. After the Battle of Stalingrad in 1942–3, the Red Army replaced some of them with camels. By 1939 the British army had demobilised most of its horses in favour of tanks and armoured cars, but it still needed many thousands of them around the Mediterranean. The Americans, too, went to war with huge numbers of animals. In Europe horses carried GIs on patrol. In the Philippines they carried them into battle. Mules bore food, weapons and sometimes even men. Twenty thousand dogs were employed in guard duties, bearing messages, guiding troops through hostile territory, aiding stricken airmen and raising morale as pets and mascots.

Pets were at the very heart of the British war effort. In May 1941 the War Office appealed to the public to 'take your great opportunity to actively win the war' by lending their dogs to the military. To general astonishment seven thousand pets were offered in the first two weeks, either out of a sense of patriotic duty or, in some cases, perhaps to save the cost of dog-food. These were hard times. On government advice, vast numbers of cats and dogs had already been put down in what would become known as the British Pet Massacre. This began in 1939 when a National Air Raid Precautions Animals Committee was set up under the jurisdiction of the Home Office. Its first act was to publish a pamphlet, *Advice to Animal Owners*, which urged city-dwellers to evacuate their pets to the countryside. If this was not possible, it said, then the kindest thing would be to have them humanely destroyed. There would be no food allowances for pets in the war, and no place for them in air-raid shelters. Accounts vary as to how many cats and dogs were euthanised in the ensuing panic. Some say two hundred thousand in two months; some say seven hundred and fifty thousand in a week. By all accounts it was a huge number, with many more to follow when the bombs started falling in 1940.

It was not just the RSPCA that reacted with horror. The Royal Army Veterinary Corps deplored such waste at a time when more dogs were needed for the war effort. The Germans and French had been quicker off the mark with dog recruitment programmes at the outbreak of war: Germany by now was reckoned to have a canine army of two hundred thousand trained dogs. Britain did have a few in service, mainly in North Africa and the Far East, but there was no co-ordinated recruitment plan. This all changed in the spring of 1941 when the War Office launched its appeal. The call was swiftly answered, though the pool of available animals had been greatly reduced by the massacre. Ten thousand dogs were offered, but only around a third of these were deemed acceptable for service, mainly as guard dogs but also for sniffing out mines. A few would be dropped into war zones by parachute. In May 1942, the army opened its first War Dogs Training School in greyhound racing kennels at Potters Bar, just north of London. Breeds considered most suitable for training were Airedales, Collies, Labradors, Boxers and, best of all, Alsatians, which was the name given in Britain to German Shepherds. No animal with any hint of Germany about it could hope to thrive in Britain, as owners of Dachshunds could painfully testify. Their pets were kicked or stamped to death in the street and their owners vilified as German sympathisers. Even a nation of dog-lovers had its limits.

It is not the least irony of the Second World War that the German war-dog should have become, and still remains, the first choice for policing, guard and guide duties throughout the world. In the English language, twenty-two years after the cessation of hostilities, the apologetic 'Alsatian' proudly reclaimed its ancestral name. No less than its homeland, the German Shepherd had stepped out from the long dark shadow of the wolf.

CHAPTER NINETEEN

The Third Hand

FIVE MONTHS BEFORE SHE DIED, JUST BEFORE CHRISTMAS 1877, the invalid Anna Sewell published her first and only novel, *Black Beauty*. She had been too weak even to transcribe her own words. Instead she had to rely on her mother to take dictation or copy out the notes she had scribbled on scraps of paper. That was how much it mattered to her. She had to get it done before she died.

Black Beauty was wholly realistic in the way it depicted the ill-treatment of horses in the nineteenth century. It was wholly *un*realistic in being narrated by a horse. Sewell's reason for writing it was to shame carters and cabmen into treating their animals less cruelly. What she achieved was one of the best-loved children's classics of all time. Though the treatment of working horses became progressively less of an issue through the twentieth century, *Black Beauty* remained as popular as it had been in the nineteenth. It was translated into French, German, Spanish and Italian, and sold by the million in America. The story is the fictional autobiography of a horse that begins life in the lush meadows of Squire Gordon's Birtwick Park but which in later life has to endure the agonies of the London cab trade before being rescued by two kind ladies and put out to grass. As well as the evils of heavy beatings, inadequate feeding and overwork, the book draws attention to the absurd vanities of people who docked their animals' tails or jerked up their heads with check reins. *Black Beauty* is undoubtedly anthropomorphic and unashamedly sentimental, but its accuracy and support for protectionism spared it the criticisms directed at other books written about animals for children.

Theodore Roosevelt's contempt for 'nature-fakery' was shared by the more lantern-jawed overseers of children's education, who deplored the over-sentimentalised view of animals that had so charmed the Victorians. Few, however, could see much harm in the Brer Rabbit of Joel Chandler Harris's *Uncle Remus* stories, first published in 1880, or in Rudyard Kipling's *Just So Stories* of 1902, with their wildly fantastical accounts of 'How the Camel Got His Hump', 'How the Leopard Got His Spots' and 'How the Whale Got His Throat'. These were charming diversions which not even the stupidest child could mistake for natural history. But the irony is that Roosevelt himself was responsible for one of the greatest triumphs of senti-mentalisation in the entire history of childhood. On a visit to Mississippi in 1902, the Great White Hunter took time off to hunt bears. Whether or not he bagged a trophy is not recorded, but much was made in the press of his refusal to shoot an orphaned cub. The cartoonist of the *Washington Star*, Clifford Berryman, marked the occasion with a cartoon entitled *Drawing the Line in Mississippi*, which showed the kindly president turning away from the cub and raising his hand to show he would not kill it. Morris Middleton, proprietor of a Brooklyn toy shop, saw Berryman's drawing and it gave him an idea. He and his wife got to work with needle and scissors to make a small, stuffed likeness of Berryman's cub. It had moveable limbs and button eyes, and it sold in an instant. Middleton sought and received permission from the president to name the fluffy toy in his honour, and so the Teddy Bear was born. The Middletons went into production but, being only a small business, struggled to keep up with demand. Bigger manufacturers swiftly moved in. One of these was the Tigue Manufacturing Company of Seymour, California, which claimed in 1906 that its weekly output of Teddy Bears consumed the fleeces of four thousand angora goats, thus inflating the price of a good breeding buck to a thousand dollars. Not everybody looked kindly upon this phenomenon. A priest in Michigan denounced the Teddy because he believed it would nullify girls' mothering instincts and lead inexorably to 'race suicide'. Others had more straightforwardly commercial reasons for worrying about the bear's impact on the market. According to one magazine editor:

The dear little girls who have always cried for dolls at Christmas are this year crying for Teddy Bears, and dolls are left on shelves to cry the paint off their pretty cheeks because of the neglect.

Coincidentally, and at almost the same time, a German toy maker called Richard Steiff had come up with a similar idea. His inspiration had nothing to do with Roosevelt: the president's failure to shoot a bear cub did not make headlines in Stuttgart. What *did* attract him was the local zoo, where he liked to sketch bears. By 1903 his drawings had fluffed out into a three-dimensional stuffed baby bear which he revealed to the world at the Leipzig Toy Fair. Here the story might have ended, had not a canny American buyer, mindful of what was happening back home, snapped up his entire stock of a hundred bears and placed an order for three thousand more. Next year twelve thousand were sold at the St Louis World's Fair, and from 1906, the year of America's great angora goat rush, Steiff adopted the name of 'Teddy'. Collected, coveted and copied like no other, the Steiff bear became, and remains, the aristocrat of the world's toy cupboards. Children throughout the western world have been cuddling stuffed animals of various kinds ever since, with no observable effect on the desire of grown-up young women to cuddle their husbands. The Michigan priesthood looked in vain for any effect on the birth rate.

Animals continued to dominate children's fiction. Beatrix Potter's *The Tale of Peter Rabbit* was first published privately in 1901, then commercially in 1902, introducing generations of children to the daring exploits of Flopsy, Mopsy, Cottontail and Peter in Mr McGregor's garden. Kenneth Grahame's *The Wind in the Willows* followed in 1908 with its four protagonists, Mole, Rat (actually a water vole), Mr Toad and Mr Badger defending their waterside idyll against the hostile incursions of weasel, stoat and ferret. Whereas Potter's Peter is rabbit through and through, Grahame's characters are anthropomorphic representations of Edwardian society which, as critics saw it, reflected the author's own anxieties about a changing world in which women and machines were threatening the social order. Then in 1920 came Hugh Lofting's *The Story of Doctor Dolittle*, which was uncompromisingly on the side of the animals. Dolittle kept mice in his piano, rabbits in his pantry, a squirrel in the airing cupboard. Not even the disgust of his patients and failure of his medical practice could damage his affection for the animals. He learned to speak with them; he rescued sick monkeys in Africa, and he brought back the fabulous pushmi-pullyu, a vaguely gazelle-like creature with a head at each end of its body. It is not a book that requires much decoding: Dolittle's message was simple. Animals are not to be persecuted or locked up in zoos. They are to be marvelled at, cherished and understood.

The Teddy Bear reclaimed the limelight in 1926, when A.A. Milne transformed his son Christopher Robin's stuffed toys into Winnie-the-Pooh and his friends Piglet, Kanga, Roo, Tigger and Eeyore. For the Rooseveltian anti-sentimentalists this was high noon. Their revulsion was pithily exemplified by Dorothy Parker in a review for the *New Yorker* in October 1928. Like an owl on a mouse, she swooped upon the moment when the Bear of Little Brain inserts a 'Pom' into his latest Hum in order to make it more hummy. 'And it is that word "hummy," my darlings, that marks the first place in "The House at Pooh Corner" at which Tonstant Weader Fwowed up.' Others rushed to defend the endearing little bear whose slowness of mind was transcended by his kindness and curiosity. In their view the cutesiness was a fluffy mantle for a well-packed stuffing of philosophical truths.

Even the Hums could be read as hymns to the imagination:

'But it isn't easy,' said Pooh. 'Because Poetry and Hums aren't things which you get, they're things which get you. And all you can do is to go where they can find you.'

The verdict of the world's children was unequivocal. In England Pooh still remains the best-loved children's character of all time, a fact that continues to enrage those like Dorothy Parker who can't see the woods for the treacle. If Pooh had been the cub in Roosevelt's sights, then most certainly he would have pulled the trigger.

Two years before Pooh, in 1924, a very different kind of forest creature appeared: one that might at first have pleased the late president and then by degrees goaded him to fury. This is how the German author Felix Salten introduced his hero:

He entered the world in the middle of a thicket, in one of those little, hidden parlours of the forest, which seemed to be exposed from all sides, but are really completely enclosed. There was only a little bit of room, just barely enough for him and his mother. He stood there, staggering uncertainly on his spindly legs and stared ahead dimly with unseeing, clouded eyes. He trembled and hung his head, still completely dazed. 'What a beautiful child!' the magpie exclaimed.

Thus begins *Bambi: A Forest Life*. Day by day Bambi's mother introduces him to their fellow creatures and educates him in the ways of the forest. One day he is terrified when 'a threadlike, little cry shrilled out piteously', followed by an even more ominous stillness. It is his first encounter with death. 'Yes, yes,' says his mother. 'Don't be frightened. The ferret has killed a mouse.' But Bambi is not comforted. 'A vast, unknown horror clutched at his heart.' After a long pause he asks:

'Will we kill a mouse one day too?' 'No,' his mother replied. 'Never?' Bambi asked. 'Never ever,' his mother answered. 'Why not?' asked Bambi, comforted. 'Because we don't kill anyone,' his mother said simply. Bambi became cheerful again.

We know by now that there is going to be more to this story than sentiment. The characters may speak with human voices but this is a real forest with real birds and animals in it. Bambi is frightened again by jays quarrelling over a plundered nest in an ash tree. He wants to know if he, too, will have to fight for food. No, says his mother, 'because there is enough for all of us'. Bambi is entranced by everything he sees. He befriends butterflies, which he at first mistakes for flying flowers; then grasshoppers, hares, squirrels, owls. But he knows also that there is a darker side to life. His mother warns him of mysterious dangers which he is not yet old enough to understand. But he does not have long to wait. One day, at the edge of a clearing by a tall hazel bush, a strange creature is standing. It is pale-faced and thin, holds itself remarkably erect and has a strange, acrid smell about it. *A kind of dread emanated from that face, a cold terror.* For a long time the creature does not move. Then it suddenly stretches out an extra leg from somewhere near its face ... Instinctively Bambi runs away, back into the safety of the forest.

> 'Did you ... see?' his mother asked gently. Bambi could not answer, he could not even breathe. He merely nodded. 'That ... was ... Him!' his mother said. And they both shivered.

Bambi soon sees all too clearly the dangers he has been too young to hear about. He watches the adored Prince, biggest stag in the forest, step out boldly from the trees into a meadow. He hears a crash like thunder. He sees Prince leap into the air and his own mother, aunt and cousins flee back into a forest that has fallen suddenly silent. Behind them scurries a frightened hare and a pheasant running with outstretched neck. Later a crow explains to Bambi that the upright stranger is dangerous only when He comes with a third hand hanging over his shoulder. This third hand is a terrible thing which the animals do not understand. Few of them have seen it for themselves, but all live in fear of it. They know very well what could happen:

> He would stand there, in the distance, and wouldn't move. You could neither explain what He did nor how it happened, only all at once there would be a thunderclap, fire sparked out and, far away from Him, you would fall down dead with your body ripped open.

'He's all fire inside,' says Bambi's mother. The forest in winter is an unforgiving place where something horrible happens every day. Hungry crows slowly and cruelly kill a young hare; a squirrel is bitten by a ferret and runs in agony up and down his tree. Every so often he sits and clutches his head while blood flows down his chest. Then suddenly he falls dead in the snow, where two magpies begin to eat him. On another day a popular and sociable pheasant perishes in the jaws of a fox. The whole forest has become a cruel hierarchy of tooth and claw: to eat or be eaten the single question with which each day begins and ends. Theodore Roosevelt would have struggled to find fault with such an unflinching account of nature in the raw. No honey drips upon the harsh imperatives of survival. But then nature itself is thrown into a fluster. It is not just one He that enters the forest. It is many. Not just one third hand that stretches out, but a multitude. Magpies and jays scream a warning. 'Run! Run!' But they are surrounded. Everyone is seized by a mad terror. He is here, in the very heart of the thicket! 'All around them was a roaring and shouting, and the thunder was crashing.' The pheasants are first to fall, then the hares as they run before the canopy of fire. 'Bing! Ping! Bang! roared the thunder.' Bambi's mother bounds away and Bambi rushes after her.

> The heightened desire to escape the din and get away from the stench that strangled him, the increasing desperation to flee, the longing to save himself, were at last unleashed. It seemed to him that he had seen his mother fall, but he could not be sure it was really her. He could not see properly. The unbridled terror of the thunder booming all around him had cast a veil over his eyes. He could not think, he could not make sense of anything around him. He ran. He crossed the clearing. A new thicket swallowed him up.

He passes a dying hare, a fallen deer, a bloodied fox rolling and gnawing the snow, but Bambi will never see his mother again.

All these books, and more, were adapted by Disney and others into cartoons, films and television series, sometimes many times over. Between 1947 and 2018 at least ten productions were based on *Winnie the Pooh*; four on *Peter Rabbit*, including a stage musical; three each on *The Wind in the Willows* and *Doctor Dolittle*. They aroused little controversy beyond the usual complaints of nature-fakery and saccharine sentiment. The one exception was Disney's *Bambi* of 1942. Typically of the cartoon genre, it spooned large helpings of syrup over Salten's novel and added a generous topping of whimsy. But the one thing that remained unchanged was the villain: the upright creature with the fatal third hand. To the heirs of Theodore Roosevelt, this was nature-fakery at its worst, the repudiation of man's own nature. Disney and his animators did make some concessions to accuracy: two young white-tailed deer were used as life-models in the studio. But while the movements of Bambi's body and limbs were more or less lifelike, the saucer-eyed baby-face with its range of human expressions was not. American hunting writers declared war. To begin with, the deer were all wrong. They appeared to resemble white-tailed deer but their antlers were more like those of mule deer. The young Bambi was wrongly depicted with spots. The deer were mating at the wrong time of year, in spring instead of autumn. The friendship between Thumper the rabbit and Friend Owl who might easily eat him was wholly unbelievable, and so on and on. But the worst things were the hunters. Unlike real, law-abiding sportsmen, the men in the film blazed away irresponsibly at anything that drew breath; they hunted with dogs, shot deer in the spring and torched the forest in the autumn. For all these reasons R.J. Brown, editor of *Outdoor Life*, declared *Bambi* to be 'the worst insult ever offered to American sportsmen and conservationists'. Disney's response was to point out that Bambi and all about him were German, and thus no American hunter need take offence. The fact that Bambi was an American white-tail and not a Black Forest roe was conveniently overlooked.

What everyone did agree was that the death of Bambi's mother was critical to the anti-hunting message. The cartoon format did nothing to soften its impact. 'It is one of the paradoxes of the movie business', wrote Pauline Kael, distinguished critic of the *New Yorker*, 'that the movies designed expressly for children are generally the ones that frighten them the most. I have never heard children screaming from fear at any of those movies we're always told they should be protected from as they screamed at Bambi.' A further paradox is that the hunters never actually appear on screen. The emotional impact depends entirely on sympathy for the animals. Writing with the hindsight of nearly fifty years, Ralph H. Lutts, author of *The Nature Fakers: Wildlife, Science, and Sentiment*, observed: '[The film] was targeted at children in their most impressionable, formative years. The memory of the incident remains with them even into adulthood.' But it was not just children. Even some adults, he said, were so affected by it that they were moved to hang up their guns. It was not the case, as some hunters had claimed, that opposition to hunting was unheard of before *Bambi*. Indeed, it had a long tradition. But it could certainly be said that *Bambi* reignited it and helped foment public outrage. The heirs of Roosevelt saw it as manipulation amounting almost to brainwashing. 'Naturally,' wrote George Reiger, conservation editor of the American pro-hunting magazine *Field & Stream*, 'once Bambi is raised in status from mere deer to Jesus Whitetail Superstar, man's hunting of deer becomes a crime comparable to the persecution of Christ.'

Those who sneer at the supposed sentimentality of the anti-hunting movement like to characterise their opponents as weak-minded sufferers of a *Bambi complex*, guided in their thinking not by science or history but rather by the nature-fakery of Felix Salten and Walt Disney. But this, too, is an over-simplification. The dividing line remains where it always was, with the Nietzschean *Übermensch* on one side and the Pythagoreans and Romantics on the other, both of them traditions far older than *Bambi*. There were also those who, knowing nothing of philosophy, simply recoiled from the idea of killing for fun. In the late 1940s yet another element was fed into the mix. Its author was an Australian anatomist called Raymond Dart. Years earlier, in 1924, when he was head of anatomy at the University of Witwatersrand in Johannesburg, a young woman called Josephine Salmons showed him a fossilised monkey-skull that had been found in a limestone quarry near the small town of Taung in the North West Province. Dart's curiosity was aroused by what seemed to him to be a new species of baboon, and by the fact that the skull had a neat round hole in it, almost as if it had been trepanned. Then another fossil arrived from the same quarry. This one was quite different, more like the skull of an infant ape and certainly not that of a monkey. It took little time for Dart to realise the significance of what he was looking at. His language when he spoke of it was scrupulously bland and academic, but a careful listener will hear the excitement leaking through.

'The specimen is of importance', he later wrote, 'because it exhibits an extinct race of apes intermediate between living anthropoids and man ... In the first place, the whole cranium displays humanoid rather than anthropoid lineaments.' He then proceeded in highly technical language to compare it to other anthropoids and chimpanzees. Measurements were taken of the brow, the nasal aperture, shape and thickness of the skull, and the teeth, which Dart found to be 'humanoid rather than anthropoid'. The specimen was juvenile, 'for the first permanent molar tooth only has erupted in both jaws on both sides of the face; i.e. it corresponds anatomically with a human child of six years of age'. Further: 'the canines in this jaw come, as in the human jaw, into alignment with the incisors'. Every comparison led him to the same conclusion: 'that the jaw and the teeth, as a whole, take up a parabolic arrangement comparable only with that presented by mankind'. Next he calculated the angle of the skull to the spinal column, which he found 'points to the assumption by this fossil group of an attitude appreciably more erect than that of modern anthropoids':

> The improved poise of the head, and the better posture of the whole body framework which accompanied this alteration in the angle at which its dominant member was supported, is of great significance. It means that a greater reliance was being placed by this group upon the feet as organs of progression, and that the hands were being freed from their more primitive function of accessory organs of locomotion. Bipedal animals, their hands were assuming a higher evolutionary role not only as delicate tactual, examining organs which were adding copiously to the animal's knowledge of its physical environment, but also as instruments of the growing intelligence in carrying out more elaborate, purposeful, and skilled movements, and as organs of offence and defence.

Better still, the skull measurements indicated a brain 'distinctive in type' that was 'an instrument of greater intelligence than that of living anthropoids'. Dart's paper, published in *Nature* on 7 February 1925, was headed 'Australopithecus Africanus: The Man-Ape of South Africa', but history would translate this mysterious, not-quite-human creature into something much more exciting and longed-for: *the Missing Link*. Dart himself referred to his new species only as a 'man-like ape'. The name he gave it, *Australopithecus africanus*, was intended to celebrate both 'the extreme southern and unexpected horizon of its discovery', and the vindication of Darwin's assertion in *The Descent of Man* that Africa would prove to be 'the cradle of mankind'. But it raised a question about the true links between apes and man. Apes flourish in luxuriant forests but the skull had been found in a region of grassy plains. 'We must therefore conclude', said Dart, 'that it was only the enhanced cerebral powers possessed by this group which made their existence possible in this untoward environment.'

> For the production of man a different apprenticeship was needed to sharpen the wits and quicken the higher manifestations of intellect – a more open veldt country where competition was keener between swiftness and stealth, and where adroitness of thinking and movement played a preponderating role in the preservation of the species ... In my opinion, Southern Africa, by providing a vast open country with occasional wooded belts and a relative scarcity of water, together with a fierce and bitter mammalian competition, furnished a laboratory such as was essential to this penultimate phase of human evolution.

A thought then struck him. His mind flew back to the earlier specimen from the limestone quarry, the skull shown to him by Josephine Salmons which had a neat round hole in the top. How could this be explained? In a book co-authored with Dennis Craig in 1959, *Adventures with the Missing Link*, Dart recalled the moment of realisation: 'Was it possible that the opening had been made by another creature to extract its brain for food? Did this ape with the big brain catch and eat baboons?' At first he thought it improbable: further discoveries at Taung suggested it had been a mere scavenger, living like a hyena on the scraps left by cats. But then other fossils convinced him that man-apes had armed themselves with more than just teeth and nails. They had learned to make lethal weapons from bone and horn with which they could slaughter animals as big as wildebeest and zebra. As an adult male australopithecine stood no taller than four foot six inches, these were considerable feats of skill and courage. From here it was but a short step to what would become known as the 'hunting hypothesis'. It was this, post-*Bambi*, that gave fresh encouragement to the hunters in their scuffle with the Romantics. For them, the hypothesis justified every bullet they had ever fired. It made clear that the practice of hunting by stealth was the one essential factor that had raised our earliest ancestors up on to their hind legs and transformed apes into humans.

'By the 1950s', writes the distinguished American anthropologist Matt Cartmill in his definitive history of hunting, *A View to a Death in the*

Morning, 'Dart was confidently asserting that Australopithecus was in the process of taking dominion over every beast of the field … and every creeping thing that creepeth upon the earth.' By this account, the authors of Genesis, writing three million years after the event, were simply bestowing God's blessing upon business as usual. Indeed, without that long-established dominion humankind simply could not exist. From those early kills flowed everything we take for granted. Hunting gave us not just bipedalism and tools: it fixed the entire direction of human evolution. From it emerged language, religion, the nuclear family and a process of sexual selection that rewarded raw masculinity with the most desirable mates. The ideal man would hunt, kill and provide for a grateful partner who, in return, would dedicate her life to child-rearing and domesticity. It took a while for Dart to win over the sceptics, but by the early 1950s it was widely accepted among evolutionary scientists that hunting was the lodestone of human existence and that mankind had been born with a taste for blood.

Enemies of *Bambi* rejoiced: they had been vindicated by science. To deny the right to hunt was to deny the right to be human. Yet Dart himself took a baleful view of what evolution had produced. 'The loathsome cruelty of mankind to man', he wrote in *Adventures with the Missing Link*, 'is the inescapable by-product of his blood lust; this differentiative human characteristic is explicable only in terms of man's carnivorous and cannibalistic origin.' Every atrocity ever recorded in the 'blood-bespattered, slaughter-gutted archives of human history', including most recently the Second World War, was testament to this. Thus in a strange way he found himself standing shoulder to shoulder with both Pythagoras and the crudest interpreters of Nietzsche. Over twenty years, support for the hunting hypothesis gradually ebbed away as Dart's finds were reinterpreted. The bone 'weapons' the man-apes had supposedly used to butcher their prey were nothing of the sort: they were the normal remains of kills made by big cats and gnawed by hyenas. The round hole in the skull of the Taung baboon, allegedly made by a two-legged predator, was a precise match for the fangs of a leopard. By the late 1970s the hunting hypothesis had pretty much gone the way of the unicorn. Reflecting on it all in 1993, Matt Cartmill put the professorial boot in: 'There is no good evidence that Australopithecus ever made tools or weapons, and it is hard to go on thinking of them as mighty hunters and skilful butchers.' There was no evidence that the meat in their diet amounted to anything more than scavenged scraps. They were not so much predators as prey. In the wider fraternity of apes, they were also not unique. What finally cut the ground from beneath Dart's feet was the discovery that chimpanzees, too, have a taste for flesh. 'If chimpanzees are predators,' wrote Cartmill in *A View to a Death in the Morning*, 'then predation was probably not a new departure for our own apelike ancestors. Therefore predation by itself cannot explain why our ancestors evolved into australopithecines and chimpanzees did not.'

This argument was of course conducted well out of sight of the audiences queuing for *Bambi*. And yet it precisely mirrored the division between those who believe hunting is a basic human instinct and those who condemn it as an abomination. Shooting is a costly business which, in the baronial tradition, is widely available only to the well-off. Nobody in the developed world now needs to hunt for the pot. The only benefit conferred by a gun that cannot be achieved by other means is the sheer pleasure of killing. The justification for this is atavistic: the acknowledgement of an evolved and natural urge so fundamental that we share it with weasel, stoat and polecat. This is why some working-class men, particularly Americans, also like to display their virility with firearms. But they are a minority. Even in America the percentage of men who hunt barely creeps into double figures. In most of the world, hunting is a symbol of power. Presidents, tycoons and crowned heads flex their trigger fingers on land from which ordinary people are excluded. Social polarisation means also political polarisation: shooters of game birds, stalkers of deer, trophy hunters and riders to hounds tend to the right of the political spectrum. You will not find many Marxists on a grouse moor.

The puzzle, then, is why the majority of men feel no urge to kill, and why public opinion weighs so heavily against the hunters. This might mean that no such urge exists, or perhaps it is peculiar to high achievers. It may be that those immune to it have been brainwashed into suppressing their natural blood-lust, or are unnaturally passive. *Wimps*, in the language of the macho men. It suggests, above all, that nature-fakery might not be exclusive to the Romantics. Primitive instincts do not translate well in city or suburb. A man's instinct to provide for his family might once have been satisfied by shooting a deer or a rabbit. Now it is better done with a debit card at the checkout. In most households the only relic of the primeval hunter is daddy's insistence on carving the meat, and the only wild beasts are a scatter of stuffed toys on the children's beds.

The battle over *Bambi* has been settled decisively in favour of Disney. Maybe now it has gone too far. We exist in the age of the theme park and themed merchandise in which proprietors of imaginary animals enjoy profits beyond the wildest dreams of those who deal in real ones. Children directly experience wildlife only in zoos and safari parks. Reality is being pecked to death by fantasy. Anyone who wants to influence, entertain or educate children will turn immediately to the anthropomorphised menagerie of birds and animals to which every child is exposed from the cradle. There is no moral that a fluffy animal cannot reinforce. A children's author in Australia used a transgender Teddy Bear to explain to young readers that children can be born into the wrong body. Although Teddy had been born a boy, it had always known it was a girl. One can only imagine, and smile, at what Teddy Roosevelt might have made of this scion of his sportsmanship.

In America, even adults now can have their attitudes compulsorily realigned by Disneyites. In Missouri in 2018, a man convicted of poaching deer was sentenced to a year's imprisonment during which, not less than once a month by order of the court, he was forced to sit through *Bambi*.

CHAPTER TWENTY

Louder Than Words

WHEN THE SOCIETY FOR THE PRESERVATION OF THE WILD FAUNA of the Empire launched itself as the world's first international environmental organisation in 1903, it looked like just another expression of colonial power. Though it styled itself somewhat disingenuously as 'a modest and unpretentious group of gentlemen', it could not shrug off its image as an aristocratic clique anxious only to preserve enough animals for itself to shoot. Its nickname, 'the penitent butchers', was well earned but also slightly unfair. To its credit, it did broaden its scope and argue for the protection 'from appalling destruction' of wild animals throughout the British Empire. As the Empire then covered a quarter of the globe, this was no empty gesture. The society since then has been through various name changes. After the First World War it dropped the 'Wild' to become just the Society for the Preservation of the Fauna of the Empire. In 1950, as the sun began to sink on the colonial era, it became simply the Fauna Preservation Society. This happened just two years after another American writer, Fairfield Osborn, president of the New York Zoological Society, picked up the threads of George Perkins Marsh's prophetic *Man and Nature* of 1864. Osborn's message in *Our Plundered Planet* was every bit as urgent as his predecessor's. In the latter years of the Second World War, it had occurred to him that humankind was engaged in not just one mortal conflict but two:

> This other world-wide war, still continuing, is bringing more widespread distress to the human race than any that has resulted from armed conflict.

It contains potentialities of ultimate disaster greater even than would follow
the misuse of atomic power. This other war is man's conflict with nature.

Osborn's book was an instant bestseller, glowingly endorsed by Eleanor
Roosevelt, Aldous Huxley and Albert Einstein. 'Reading it,' said Einstein,
'one feels very keenly how futile most of our political quarrels are compared
with the basic realities of life.' No author in the twentieth century has written more apocalyptically. 'Blind to the need of co-operating with nature,'
he said, 'man is destroying the sources of his life. Another century like the
last and civilisation will be facing its final crisis.' In the aftermath of a war
that cost so many lives, Osborn could not be accused of over-sensitivity.
His insistence on the need for population control must have seemed even
more shocking in 1948, when the world was still counting its dead, than
it does now. 'Even after wars, too many are left alive,' he said. Otherwise
he echoed George Perkins Marsh in deploring deforestation and the over-
exploitation of land, counting the cost in dried-up watercourses, silted
rivers, erosion and vanishing wildlife. It was a process of degradation 'as
deadly ultimately as any delayed-action bomb'. He was especially critical
of his native USA where, he complained, trees were being felled twice as
fast as they grew. 'The story of this nation in the last century as regards
the use of forests, grasslands, wildlife and water sources is the most violent
and the most destructive of any written in the long history of civilisation.'
And he saw all too clearly what must come. 'How about the valley of the
greatest river of them all, the Mississippi, its bed so lifted, its waters so
choked, so blocked with the wash of productive lands, that the river at flood
crests runs high above the streets of New Orleans? As in historical times,
the power of nature in revolt will one day overwhelm the bonds that even
the most ingenious modern engineer can prepare.' Few prophecies since
Noah's flood have ever been more tragically fulfilled.

It was in America, too, that Osborn identified the worst crime against
wildlife. When white men first set foot on the American continent they
found fifty million bison peacefully grazing north of the Rio Grande. By
1905 only five hundred remained – a loss of 99.999%. 'The uncomfortable
truth,' Osborn wrote, 'is that man during innumerable past ages has been
a predator – a hunter, a meat eater and a killer.' Comparisons with other

species worked only to man's disadvantage. 'His nearest relatives in the animal world most similar to him physiologically remained vegetarians. And at no time, even to the present day, have depended upon the lives of other living creatures for their own survival.' Subsequent revelations about the behaviour of chimpanzees might call for the insertion of 'mostly' before 'vegetarians', but his point still stands.

It was not just the New World that distressed him. The Old World, too, was faring badly. A visitor to Greece told him that 'during all his travels through the mountain section of the country he saw only two pair of partridges and one rabbit – all the natural wild life having been killed off'. In North Africa, wandering tribesmen moved 'from oasis to oasis, their herds stripping such grass as there is from the gullied slopes, leaving nothing but the raw unstable soil'. In southern Africa, despite all the remonstrations of the Society for the Preservation of the Fauna of the Empire, animal life was still being treated as a limitless resource:

> Alarming reports have come from southern Rhodesia to the effect that more than 300,000 native wild animals have been deliberately destroyed in recent years on the grounds that they were carriers of the tsetse fly pest. This move on the part of the Rhodesian authorities, unfortunately being imitated in neighbouring territories, may well prove to be a misguided and futile butchering of the superb wild life of those regions ... [This is] typical of man's lack of understanding of the place that wild living things occupy in the economy of nature.

Unlike the hunters, Osborn was as fearful for small, unseen creatures as he was for shootable megafauna. Burrowing animals such as moles, for example, were essential caretakers of healthy soil. But he had little confidence that his words would make any difference. The people who most needed to read such books were the ones least likely to do so. The preferred state of mankind was ignorance. 'It is amazing how far one has to travel to find a person, even among those most widely informed, who is aware of the processes of mounting destruction that we are inflicting upon our life sources.'

*

Meanwhile, distant from the forests and plains, a new science was taking shape. It grew from a seed planted years earlier at the University of Leipzig in Germany, where in 1879 Wilhelm Wundt had founded the Institute for Experimental Psychology. Wundt's big idea was to investigate the human mind by adapting the experimental methods used to study the body. At Leipzig he designed ways to measure people's speed of thought and their reactions to sights, sounds and sensations. This enabled him to break down observations and perceptions into their constituent parts in exactly the same way physiologists break down the interactions between vital organs. Where Wundt led, others followed. But his ideas did not appeal just to those interested in the *human* mind. Students of animal behaviour realised they too could make use of his methods. The first authoritative book on these earliest animal experiments was *Animal Intelligence*, published in 1898 by the American psychologist Edward Thorndike. His own best-known experiment involved cats and dogs, 'reduced by fasting to a state of utter hunger', being shut up in boxes with food left tantalisingly out of reach outside. The point was to record 'the process whereby they learned to work the various mechanisms which let them out'. Thorndike was followed in 1908 by the formidable Margaret Floy Washburn, alpha-feminist and the first American woman ever to earn a doctorate in psychology. She called her book *The Animal Mind*, but she was careful to explain that it might better have been called *The Animal Mind as Deduced from Experimental Evidence*. The old-fashioned 'Method of Anecdote' was scornfully dismissed:

> It consists essentially in taking the report of another person regarding the action of an animal, observed most commonly by accident, and attracting attention because of its unusual character. In certain cases the observer while engaged in some other pursuit happens to notice the singular behaviour of an animal, and at his leisure writes out an account of it. In others, the animal is a pet, in whose high intellectual powers its master takes pride.

This method, she said, suffered from at least one, and frequently from several, of five common drawbacks:

1 The observer was not scientifically trained and could not distinguish what he saw from what he inferred.

2 He did not have intimate knowledge of the habits of the species to which the animal belonged.

3 He was unaware of the animal's past behaviour.

4 He had a personal affection for the animal, and a desire to demonstrate its superior intelligence.

5 He wanted to tell a good story.

Ironically, but also rather charmingly, one of the examples she used to prove this last point was itself an anecdote, and one that featured no less a figure than Wilhelm Wundt. As a boy he had designed and built a fly-trap which he baited with sugar. Connected to it by a sliding door was a second box in which he placed a spider. Sometimes the door was left open; sometimes it was shut. When it was opened, no surprise, the spider immediately dashed out to attack the trapped flies. The experiment went on for some time, until Wundt noticed an outstanding example of arachnid intelligence:

> The spider was sometimes let into the cage, sometimes confined to her own box. But one day I made a notable discovery. During an absence the slide had been accidentally left open for some little while. When I came to shut it, I found that there was an unusual resistance. As I looked more closely, I found that the spider had drawn a large number of thick threads directly under the lifted door, and that these were preventing my closing it ...

What, he wondered, was going on in the spider's mind? There followed a lengthy dissertation on how the spider could have associated the open door with the availability of food and had then used her spinning skills to guarantee permanent access. As Washburn recorded, this fanciful idea was gleefully demolished in 1887 by George and Elizabeth Peckham, an American husband-and-wife taxonomic team who specialised in spiders and wasps. In a paper for the *Journal of Morphology* headed 'Some Observations on the Mental Power of Spiders', they exposed a classic category-five error:

Had Wundt been familiar with the habits of spiders, he would have known that whenever they are confined they walk around and around the cage, leaving behind them lines of web. Of course many lines passed under his little sliding door, and when he came to close it there was a slight resistance. These are the facts. His inference that there was even a remotest intention on the part of his prisoner to hinder the movement of the door is entirely gratuitous. Even the simpler mental states that are supposed to have passed through the mind of the spider were the products of Wundt's own imagination.

All such anecdotes rely on interpretations of animal behaviour which are as likely to be wrong as right. 'Dogs get lost hundreds of times', said Edward Thorndike, 'and no one ever notices it or sends an account of it to a scientific magazine. But let one find his way from Brooklyn to Yonkers and the fact immediately becomes a circulating anecdote.' In a revised edition of *The Animal Mind* in 1917, Margaret Washburn prescribed what she called the 'Ideal Method' of obtaining facts. In the case of a 'higher animal' this meant 'patient observation upon a specimen known from birth, watched in its ordinary behaviour and environment, and occasionally experimented upon with proper control of the conditions and without frightening it or otherwise rendering it abnormal'. This was trickier than it sounded. As with human subjects, the experimenter needed to acquaint himself with the peculiarities of each individual, bearing in mind that there could be striking differences in mental capacity between members of the same species. But this deeper acquaintance threw up yet more problems. While the observer must win the confidence of his subject, he must at the same time guard against the temptation to 'humanise' it, or to take pleasure in its achievements. As Washburn readily affirmed, this carried risks of its own. 'Absolute indifference to the animals studied, if not so dangerous as doting affection, is yet to be avoided,' she said. Only paragons of objectivity need apply.

Yet Washburn accepted that a degree of anthropomorphism – attributing human characteristics to animals – was impossible to avoid. Anthropomorphism had a long and distinguished pedigree. In *The Descent of Man*, Darwin himself asserted that dogs, cats, horses, and probably also birds and all the 'higher' animals, experienced vivid dreams. This was proved by the movements and sounds they made while sleeping, so 'we must admit that they possess some power of imagination'. Only 'a few persons', Darwin went on, 'now dispute that animals possess some power of reasoning. Animals may constantly be seen to pause, deliberate, and resolve.' This had been confirmed by George Romanes, whose observations of the capuchin monkey convinced him that emotional displays by animals were 'analogous to those in man', and that animals possessed intelligence and reason. This chimed perfectly with Darwin's purpose in *The Descent of Man* 'to show that there is no fundamental difference between man and the higher mammals in their mental faculties'.

But there was a hidden agenda here. Objections to the theory of evolution came from more than one direction. For George Bernard Shaw it was a matter of taste, aesthetics and hatred of science. This made for highly entertaining knockabout but was hardly fatal to Darwin's theory. The greater danger was the outrage of religious fundamentalists who refused to accept that there could be any similarity or connection between the mental and moral states of humans and the lower animals. It was therefore essential for Darwinians to show that, as Washburn put it, 'this gulf is not absolute but may conceivably have been bridged by intermediate stages of mental and moral development'. This meant that evolutionary writers were unreliable guides in the field of animal psychology, for they 'held a brief for animal intelligence'.

Washburn's own experimental subjects ranged from amoebae, snails and shellfish at the lower end of the scale to cats and dogs at the top. In none of these, she argued, could anyone prove the *absence* of consciousness. She focused particularly on insects, which she found had highly developed senses of taste and smell. When ants were offered honey laced with strychnine, they stopped feeding as soon as they sensed the contaminant. Wasps did the same, and held back even when offered pure honey afterwards. What fascinated Washburn above all was the insects' mating habits, which she characterised as 'one of the most remarkable phenomena connected with the sensory reactions of animals'. This was proved by an American entomologist, Charles Valentine Riley, who hatched out some Ailanthus silkworm moths. No other specimens of this insect were known to exist within several hundred miles of the breeding site in Chicago. To test the strength of their mating instincts, Riley took two individuals: a virgin female which he hung in a cage on a tree, and a male which he marked with a silk thread and then released a mile-and-a-half away. By next day the two were husband and wife. Fish, too, showed they had a sense of smell by swimming up to bags of food while ignoring identical bags filled with rubbish. To banish all doubt, researchers sealed some of the fishes' nostrils and cut the olfactory nerves of others. In both cases the sense of smell was lost.

No animal is more famously led by its nose than the dog. Washburn recalled a test which George Romanes had set for his own favourite gun-dog, a female setter. Romanes lined up twelve men, including himself and his gamekeeper, who were instructed to walk in single file, 'each man taking care to place his feet in the footprints of his predecessor'. Romanes himself was at the head of the file and the gamekeeper at the rear. After two hundred yards Romanes turned sharply to the right, followed by the first five men behind him. The other six all swung to the left, and the two parties walked away from each other for 'a considerable distance' before concealing themselves. The setter was then 'put upon the common track of the whole party before the point of divergence'. She followed the scent at such speed that she at first overshot the point at which the column had split, but quickly recovered herself and unhesitatingly took the path to the right. 'Yet', said Romanes, 'my footprints in the common track were overlaid by eleven others, and in the track to the right by five others. Moreover, as it was the gamekeeper who brought up the rear, and as in the absence of my trail she would always follow his, the fact of his scent being, so to speak, uppermost in the series, was shown in no way to disconcert the animal following another familiar scent lowermost in the series.' Where is the human who could do a thing like that?

One thing that humans *can* do is learn from experience. Could animals do the same? As every old-fashioned circus trainer knew, there was nothing better than pain to teach animals what to avoid, or, as Washburn put it, 'to manifest their ability to discriminate between stimuli'. She explained how an animal could be taught to make the correct choice between a lit passage and a darkened one. If it made the 'wrong' choice it suffered an electric shock, which it soon learned to avoid. But what did this prove? Did it mean that the animal now understood white to be 'good' and black 'bad'? No, said Washburn. Where punishment was the only method of training, 'the case would not be one of "white preferred to black", but one of "anything preferred to black".'

A better test was Edward Thorndike's 'puzzle-box'. This was ingeniously simple. A bird or animal would be shut in a box with food left outside, or outside the box with food shut inside. In both instances the challenge was to find out, and then remember, how to open the box. An article in the *American Journal of Psychology* in 1904 described how this had worked with English sparrows. The birds were shown boxes of food which could be opened either by pulling a string tied to a latch or by poking the string through some wire netting. Their movements at first were haphazard, and the box was opened first by a bird fortuitously pecking or clawing in the right place. But 'useless' movements soon ceased and, as Washburn explained, 'the birds learned not to attack other parts of the box, to use the bill instead of the claws, and to stand on the floor beside the box instead of hopping upon it'. Not all species were as clever as this. Similar tests on pigeons exposed them as strutting dunces. Similar methods were tried on rats, squirrels, cats, dogs, raccoons, porcupines and monkeys. Dogs were a disappointment. Thorndike found that only very gradually, and after many repetitions, could they learn to drop all pointless movements and perform only the one that worked. Monkeys by contrast learned almost as quickly as humans. Washburn concluded nevertheless that human intelligence had no conceivable rival:

> All of the experimental evidence which we have examined indicates that even the cleverest animal's intellectual ability falls far short of that demonstrated by rather dull human beings.

Yet only a few years earlier in Germany it had been seriously argued that horses and dogs really were comparable to humans. According to this well-supported hypothesis, their apparent shortcomings could be explained by our own failure to communicate with them or to educate them properly. In 1901 a Berlin mathematics teacher, Wilhelm von Osten, resolved to put this right by teaching arithmetic to a five-year-old horse named Hans. This required the animal to perform calculations with a degree of difficulty that would have challenged even human children of the same age. Hans answered the questions by tapping his front hooves on the ground: the right hoof counting in units, the left one in tens. A numerical system of vertical and horizontal columns was then added so that Clever Hans, as he became known, could also tap out letters. The letter A, for example, being in the third vertical column and the second horizontal one, was stamped out by three taps of the left foot and two of the right. How was Hans figuring all this out? A psychologist called Oskar Pfungst, who sat on the second of two commissions that examined the case, believed he had the answer. The person putting the questions, he said, was unintentionally indicating by slight movements of his head when the horse had tapped out the right number. The theory was then tested and confirmed by making identical movements on purpose. 'So', said Washburn, 'the matter rested, with the simple solution that the horse had, instead of really thinking, merely reacted to involuntary signals.'

But that did not end the matter. When Herr von Osten died, the horse passed into the ownership of a jeweller from Elberfeld, Karl Krall, who was unimpressed by Pfungst's explanation. To prove his point, Krall proceeded to educate several more horses including Hans himself and a pair of even smarter Arabians called Muhammed and Zarif. It took Muhammed just two weeks to learn addition and subtraction, and three days to progress from multiplication and division to fractions and cube and square roots. Finally, wrote Washburn, 'he as well as his fellow pupil began to offer original observations'. All this they could do even when they were unable to see a human. Similar abilities were demonstrated by Rolf, an Airedale terrier from Mannheim who tapped out answers with his paws and was said to be multilingual, and able to compose poetry and tell jokes. Many people, including serious zoologists and psychologists, were convinced that a new window had opened on to the untapped potential of the non-human mind. Washburn was not one of them. Certain indications, she wrote, 'point clearly away from the possibility that the horses are really mathematical geniuses'. She raised five objections:

1   The animals learned too quickly to be believable, faster even than a 'gifted human being'.

2   They solved difficult problems as quickly as simple ones.

3   They began tapping before even glancing at the problem written on the board in front of them.

4   The mistakes they made were not typical of real mathematicians. Common errors included reversing the numerals, for example 27 for 72, or miscalculating by a single unit, as in 21 instead of 22. These were mistakes most likely to happen if the horse muddled its forefeet or stopped tapping a fraction too soon or too late. They were not real arithmetical errors, such as failing to carry a figure over from one column to the next, which might be made by someone fluffing an actual calculation.

5   No really satisfactory results were achieved when no-one present knew the right answer.

'On the whole,' said Washburn, 'the phenomena do not present themselves with such authority as to compel a revision of our whole conception of the animal mind.' But lofty scepticism was no obstacle to the true believer. In 1912 Karl Krall wrote a book, *Thinking Animals*, which placed him at the head of Germany's burgeoning 'New Animal Psychology' movement which championed non-human intelligence. One of the more bizarre results of this came many years later, in the 1930s. Adolf Hitler apparently was persuaded by the 'New Psychologists' that dogs could be taught to speak and thus greatly increase their value to the military. An animal speech school, the *Tier-Sprechschule*, was set up at Leutenberg in the Thuringian Forest, where it ran throughout the war. The Nazis did recognise, however, that dogs might find it difficult to recreate the sounds of the human voice-box, and that sustained conversation was unlikely. Instead they used the late Rolf as their model and schooled their students in the language of paw-tapping. Even so, it was claimed that at least some of them could mimic the human voice and that one particularly outstanding performer, when asked 'Who is Adolf Hitler?', replied with an authentic SS bark: 'Mein Führer.'

Meanwhile, back in the scientific mainstream, a more profound and lasting change was taking place. The aim of comparative psychologists such as

Margaret Washburn, Edward Thorndike and their followers was to identify physiological or psychological characteristics common to all members of a species. The inherent weakness of this was that their experiments were done in unreal surroundings on a small number of species, most often rats or pigeons, which revealed nothing at all about an animal's place in its natural environment. This began to change in the 1930s when zoologists, including most importantly the Austrians Konrad Lorenz and Karl von Frisch, and the Dutch-born Englishman Niko Tinbergen, began to drag the subject back out of the laboratory and into the wild. Their discipline was biology, not psychology, and their particular branch of it was *ethology*, defined by Tinbergen as 'the biological study of behaviour'. The question they wanted to answer was a simple one: why do animals behave as they do? They were convinced that behaviour developed in exactly the same way as the body did, by evolution. Unlike the psychologists in America who focused on the *nurture* of animals, the ethologists were interested in the *nature* of animals living freely. Nature is full of astonishments. Tinbergen noticed, for example, the curious habit among black-headed gulls of removing broken shells from their nests as soon as the chicks had hatched. What was the reason for this? Did the sharp-edged fragments endanger the young birds' feet? Did their conspicuous inner whiteness alert predators to the presence of fresh chicks? Were they a breeding ground for bacteria? To find out, Tinbergen laid out a number of dummy nests with eggs in them. Some of these also contained shell fragments, and some did not. It took only a short while for the question to be answered. Many more eggs were thieved from the nests with shell fragments than from the ones without. The gulls somehow had understood that their chicks would be safer without visible signs of their hatching.

Even the most apparently pointless behaviours were found to have biological explanations. When young lions took over a pride, why did they kill all the cubs fathered by their predecessors? Whatever could justify, or even explain, such a cruel waste of life? The answer was self-interest. By destroying the genes of the previous generation they created opportunities for their own. The lionesses ceased lactating as soon as their cubs were killed and sought the attentions of the virile young newcomers. Even the most familiar behaviours revealed hidden secrets. Everyone knew, for example, that male frogs sang to attract mates. What was not understood was that the females of some species were most powerfully attracted to males with the lowest voices. The lower the note, the more desirable the singer. Bass beat baritone, and tenors could just hop it. Squirrels, too, could spring surprises. Everyone knew they buried nuts. What no one suspected was just how ingrained this behaviour actually was. Even when they were accustomed to regular feeding in captivity they would still dig down and build underground hoards. And squirrels never forgot. If they were reared on a solid floor and fed entirely on liquids, the burying instinct would kick in as soon as they met earth and nuts. Piece by piece, species by species, the ethologists rewrote the texts. Thanks to them we now know very much more than our grandfathers did about the way animals communicate, feel emotion, adapt to circumstances and choose their mates. Ultimate recognition of their achievement came in 1973 when Niko Tinbergen, Konrad Lorenz and Karl von Frisch were jointly awarded the Nobel Prize for Physiology or Medicine.

Not entirely coincidentally, another worldwide movement was gathering pace. The Society for the Preservation of the Wild Fauna of the Empire had already changed its name twice. Its transformation was completed in 1981 when it became the thoroughly modern Fauna and Flora International, one of the world's most effective champions of biodiversity. Here was a new word, and a new way of thinking that reflected a growing anxiety about the future of life on Earth. Ten years earlier, in 1971, a diverse group of Canadian mystics had founded a charitable organisation which took upon itself the almost biblical task of ensuring 'the ability of the Earth to nurture life in all its diversity'.

They called it Greenpeace.

CHAPTER TWENTY-ONE

Warriors of the Rainbow

GEORGE PERKINS MARSH IN THE NINETEENTH CENTURY AND Fairfield Osborn in the twentieth issued a clear warning to the world about what it was doing to itself. The question they left unanswered was: what were we going to do about it? It was not just a touch on the tiller that was needed but a whole new direction of travel and a visionary to point the way. The man who stepped forward, the long-awaited Messiah, was Aldo Leopold. Born in Burlington, Iowa, Leopold was a lifelong lover of mountain, field and forest. As a young man he trained as a forester, then progressed to become Professor of Game Management at the University of Wisconsin, where he developed a radically new philosophy of land management. He could hardly have thrown down a more provocative challenge to prevailing ideas – *misconceptions*, he would say – about wild places and the animals that lived in them. Contrary to every notion of economic land-use, he promoted the idea of wildness as something to be cherished. In 1924 he was largely responsible for the designation of the Gila National Forest in New Mexico as America's first official wilderness. Leopold died aged sixty-one in 1948, ironically the year of Fairfield Osborn's *Our Plundered Planet*. His own most influential work, *A Sand County Almanac*, was published posthumously. It sold by the million and confirmed him as the most profound environmental thinker of the century. The *Almanac* provided more than just enlightenment: it was a scientific, philosophical and ethical blueprint for conservationists that became indelibly imprinted on the minds of people who had never read or even heard of it.

Leopold himself was something of a 'penitent butcher', a hunter who, he confessed, 'had never heard of passing up a chance to kill a wolf'. His conversion from killer to conservationist came suddenly one day when he shot an old matriarch playing with her cubs and watched 'a fierce green fire dying in her eyes':

> I realized then, and have known ever since, that there was something new to me in those eyes, something known only to her and to the mountain. I was young then, and full of trigger-itch; I thought that because fewer wolves meant more deer, that no wolves would mean hunters' paradise. But after seeing the green fire die, I sensed that neither the wolf nor the mountain agreed with such a view.

The fruit of his soul-searching was 'the land ethic': the idea that man's relationship with nature had to be respectful and caring, not just exploitative. He saw the folly of his youthful assumption that shooting wolves was an act of mercy to the deer:

> Since then I have lived to see state after state extirpate its wolves. I have watched the face of many a newly wolfless mountain, and seen the south-facing slopes wrinkle with a maze of new deer trails. I have seen every edible bush and seedling browsed, first to anaemic desuetude, and then to death. I have seen every edible tree defoliated to the height of a saddlehorn. Such a mountain looks as if someone had given God a new pruning shears, and forbidden Him all other exercise. In the end the starved bones of the hoped for deer herd, dead of its own too-much, bleach with the bones of the dead sage, or molder under the high-lined junipers.

We abuse land, he said, because we think of it as a commodity that belongs to us. Not until we see it as a community to which we belong will we learn to treat it with the love it deserves. This is the founding principle of ecology, 'that the individual is a member of a community of interdependent parts':

> [Man's] instincts prompt him to compete for his place in that community, but his ethics prompt him also to co-operate (perhaps in order that there

may be a place to compete for). The land ethic simply enlarges the bound-
aries of the community to include soils, waters, plants, and animals, or
collectively: the land.

The question to be answered, he said, was whether improvements in our
'standard of living' were sufficient to justify the eradication of nature. 'For
us of the minority, the opportunity to see geese is more important than
television, and the chance to find a pasque-flower is a right as inalienable
as free speech.' It had been ninety years since Charles Darwin allowed the
first glimpse of where our species had come from, showing humans to be
nothing more than 'fellow-voyagers with other creatures in the odyssey
of evolution'. This should have implanted a feeling of kinship with other
species, and a sense of wonder at the scale and richness of the 'biotic
enterprise'. Man might be the captain of the adventuring ship, but he was
not the sole reason for its voyage.

This was precisely the point of the land ethic: to convert *Homo sapiens*
from conqueror of the natural world to a plain member of it. But it was
not a message the conquerors cared to hear. In their earliest existence
humans established their dominance with axe and fire. With each new
technological advance, from plough to bulldozer and from hoe to crop-
sprayer, the dominance intensified. Through two world wars the world's
most brilliant minds had been devoted to the science of destruction. Now
their attention was fixed on the landscape, and the extirpation from it of
everything without economic value. As Leopold had warned, a method of
conservation based entirely on economic self-interest was always bound to
fail. 'It tends to ignore, and thus eventually to eliminate, many elements in
the land community that lack commercial value, but that are ... essential
to its healthy functioning.' This was the theory, but the world still needed
a visible event to focus its attention. In 1962 it got one.

Rachel Carson was a fifty-five-year-old American marine biologist who
was dismayed by the effects of synthetic pesticides. Her dismay turned to
outrage when the US Agriculture Department decided to blanket-spray
millions of acres every year in an attempt to eradicate the gypsy moth. The
'all-out chemical war', as she called it, began in 1956 when nearly a million
acres of Pennsylvania, New Jersey, Michigan and New York were drenched

with a mixture of DDT and fuel oil. The war intensified in the following year with a three-million-acre plan of attack that included densely populated residential districts of Long Island. The gypsy moth, as Carson pointed out, is a forest insect with no interest in cities, parks or gardens. And yet down came the sprayer planes, raining poison from the air as indiscriminately as the wartime bombers had rained down fire:

> They sprayed truck gardens and dairy farms, fish ponds and salt marshes. They sprayed the quarter-acre plots of suburbia, drenching a housewife making a desperate effort to cover her garden before the roaring plane reached her, and showering insecticide over children at play and commuters at railway stations.

Few people outside the Agriculture Department thought this was a good idea, and public opinion at last was engaged on the side of the environment. Armed with a formidable arsenal of scientific data, research and literary talent, Carson seized the moment. In *Silent Spring* she imagined a not-too-distant future in which spring would sound no different from midwinter:

> There was a strange stillness. The birds, for example – where had they gone? Many people spoke of them, puzzled and disturbed ... The few birds seen anywhere were moribund; they trembled violently and could not fly.

There were no bees to pollinate the apple trees. On poultry farms no chicks would hatch. Newborn piglets survived only hours or days. Roadside verges were brown and dead, as void of life as the fishless streams. The cause of all this was plainly visible: a granular white powder that lay along gutters and eaves weeks after it had fallen from the sky. Carson raised questions that people have asked ever since. Who owns nature? Who has the right to decide what should live and what should die? *Silent Spring* had two lasting effects: it stirred public opinion in a way no environmental book has done before or since, and it led directly to the banning of DDT throughout the developed world. Carson herself did not live long enough to enjoy her achievement. She died only two years later, in 1964, leaving behind what has been described, with good reason, as 'the handbook for the future of all life on Earth'.

Others, too, had been agonising over wildlife. Even before *Silent Spring*, in April 1961, Lord Shackleton, son of the Antarctic explorer Ernest Shackleton, devoted his maiden speech in the House of Lords to the lethal effects of agricultural chemicals. The International Union for the Conservation of Nature, a Swiss-based international group with an all but invisible public profile, had wider concerns about the survival of endangered species, particularly in post-colonial East Africa. These concerns were brought to a wider public by Julian Huxley in a series of articles for the English Sunday newspaper the *Observer*. Huxley had only recently returned from an extended visit to ten African countries on behalf of UNESCO, of which he was director general. His shock at what he saw was reflected in the strapline of his first *Observer* article on 13 November 1960: 'Millions of wild animals have already disappeared from Africa this century. Does the wildlife of the continent now face extinction – threatened by increases in population and the growth of industry in the emergent nations? What, if anything, can be done to safeguard it?'

Not everyone agreed with Huxley's ideas, which included culling surplus wildlife for food – a strategy he thought less damaging than sacrificing precious wilderness to agriculture. But his words carried weight. Among the many people who wrote to him was Victor Stolan, a Czechoslovakian hotel-owner who proposed the establishment of a new international fund-raising body. This, he said, should be run by men of rank and authority who could persuade wealthy sympathisers to stump up the necessary millions. 'Nobody', he said, 'is in too high a place to lend a hand to defend creation.' Huxley's response was to put Stolan in touch with Max Nicholson, director general of the Conservancy Council, an agency of the British government responsible for ecological research. Though Nicholson regarded the Czech émigré with high British snootiness – 'rather too much the naive enthusiast and rather too little the practical man of affairs', he complained to Huxley – he nevertheless set off to do exactly as the 'naive enthusiast' had suggested. The result was an influential group of international figures

coalescing to form a well-subscribed new fundraising organisation dedicated to the preservation of the world's wildlife and working in partnership
with existing organisations such as the IUCN. On 11 September 1961,
the World Wildlife Fund was officially registered as a charity under Swiss
law and opened an office at Morges. Its president was Prince Bernhard of
the Netherlands, with the Duke of Edinburgh among a board of trustees
that fully lived up to the lofty ambitions of the forgotten Stolan. Executive
power devolved to the vice-president, the English naturalist Peter Scott,
son of Robert Falcon, 'Scott of the Antarctic'.

The younger Scott was an extraordinary son of an extraordinary father.
He was a distinguished wartime naval commander, an Olympic sailor,
British gliding champion and a popular artist whose prints – typically of
flighting wildfowl – were common adornments of urban households. He
was also an expert ornithologist and a household name through the wildlife
series, *Look*, which he presented on BBC television. Like Leopold, he was
something of a reformed killer. He had always loved watching birds, but
he also enjoyed shooting them. 'Part of the explanation of this paradox',
wrote his biographer Elspeth Huxley, 'lay in the fact that wildfowling was a
sport at which he excelled, and very few people willingly give up a skill they
are very good at'. During the time he was most trigger-happy, before the
Second World War, wildfowling provoked little opposition. Nevertheless,
Scott did begin to worry about the scale of his own success. In the winter of
1931–2, aged twenty-three, he reflected uneasily on a single day's shooting
with a friend that had cost the lives of twenty-three greylag geese. Better,
or worse, was to come. One December night in the following year, Scott
and a companion paddled out with a punt-gun – a huge shotgun mounted
like a cannon on a flat-bottomed boat – and brought down eighty pink-
footed geese. Once again Scott hesitated. 'A great bag of Pinkfeet', he wrote
in his book of 1941, *Morning Flight: A Book of Wildfowl*, 'should only be
dreamed about. The species can ill afford to lose so many individuals.' He
continued to shoot, but agreed with his friends that they would take no
more than a dozen geese at a time. Yet arithmetic was not the only problem. 'My personal doubts had increased,' wrote Scott in his autobiography,
The Eye of the Wind, 'and been finally crystallised by a particular incident.'
He was one of six or seven wildfowlers who all fired at a single goose. It

did not fall immediately, but staggered and gradually lost height until it crash-landed too far out on the mud for anyone to collect it. Scott inspected the bird through binoculars. It lay quivering on its belly with its head up, both legs obviously broken. When the shooters returned after their lunch, it was still there in the same position. It was still there after their tea, and still there on the following morning. Scott, like Leopold, was appalled by what he had done:

> 'What right,' I said to myself, 'have we men to do this to a bird for our fun – to impose that kind of suffering? I should not want this for a sworn enemy and that goose was not my enemy when I shot him – although I was his.'

Penitence turned to action. In 1946, at Slimbridge in Gloucestershire, Scott established the Wildfowl and Wetlands Trust, an international conservation charity that in later years would enjoy the patronage of the Queen and the presidency of the Prince of Wales. Increasingly on the mudflats he was armed with easel rather than shotgun, and in the winter of 1951–2 he stopped shooting altogether. Then in 1961 came the WWF. Thanks to Julian Huxley, the new body was driven principally by fears about terrestrial wildlife in Africa. But this was not the only arena in which large animals were suffering. In the deep oceans the risks were, if anything, even more pressing, which was why one of Scott's first priorities was to shut down the whaling industry. To this end he made numerous impassioned speeches to the International Whaling Commission, emphasising time and again that the whales could not withstand the depredations the fleets were imposing on them. His determination only intensified when, for the first time in 1979, he saw what the death of a whale actually looked like. For four-and-a-half minutes after the minke whale was hit, 'it surfaced occasionally, spouting blood, then it sounded, diving deep. Eight minutes after being struck it was hauled up to the surface tail first and seemed to be dead.' Despite Scott's rage, the WWF's approach was always diplomatic and restrained. But there were others now in the field who were far less inclined to good behaviour. Aldo Leopold had described conservation as 'a state of harmony between men and land', but despaired of its effectiveness. 'Despite nearly a century of propaganda,' he wrote, 'conservation still proceeds at a snail's pace;

progress still consists largely of letterhead pieties and convention oratory.'
All that was about to change.

In October 1969 a group of mostly young activists in Vancouver came
together to protest against nuclear weapons. They called themselves the
Don't Make a Wave Committee and identified their first target as a five-
megaton bomb blast, code-named Cannikin, which the US Department
of Defense planned to detonate in a mile-deep shaft beneath Amchitka, a
volcanic island in the Aleutian group in south-west Alaska. This would be
the biggest underground test ever conducted by the Americans, though
it was still smaller than some of Russia's. At a Sunday-morning meeting
over coffee on 8 February 1970, with a suddenness that surprised even
themselves, they agreed a strategy. They would charter a boat, sail it into
the test zone and confront the bomb directly. A search of the Vancouver
docks led them to a sixty-six-foot halibut seiner called the *Phyllis Cormack*,
whose skipper John Cormack had suffered a succession of poor fishing
seasons and was open to new employment. What the committee now
needed was a memorable name that could be shared by both the Amchitka
campaign itself and the rechristened *Phyllis Cormack*. Someone quietly
suggested Green Peace, which everybody liked. After discussion it evolved
to become, first, GreenPeace and then *Greenpeace*. It was the perfect name,
they thought, because it linked the two most important issues of the time:
protecting the environment and saving the world from a nuclear holocaust.
Their strategy was twofold: to stop the test and to plant a 'mindbomb' – an
explosive image of volunteers placing themselves in harm's way that would
fire people's imaginations and make headlines across the world.

At dusk on 15 September 1971, with the name *Greenpeace* painted on
a banner, they sailed for 'the Battle of Amchitka'. The campaign was in one
sense a failure: they never reached the test zone. The ship was intercepted by
a US coastguard cutter that detained it for supposed customs violations. A
back-up boat, a retired naval minesweeper originally named the *Edgewater
Fortune* but now *Greenpeace II*, took over the chase but met winter storms
so severe that 'full speed ahead' meant only slowing the rate at which it was
driven backwards. There was no hope of reaching Amchitka before the test.

Yet the Don't Make a Wave Committee could still claim victory. They had detonated their mindbomb and public opinion had swung behind them. Richard Nixon's US administration could find no international or scientific support for its assertion that the environmental risks from a five-megaton blast would be justified by any improvement in world peace.

On 15 October the Canadian Parliament voted unanimously in favour of halting the test. The government of Japan and the State of Alaska also demanded cancellation, and on 2 November unions representing more than 150,000 workers in British Columbia stopped work in support of the activists. In a statement three days later, thirty US senators warned Nixon that 'to proceed with the test is to endanger national security and world peace, not to further it'. Newspapers agreed. 'Does US need reminding that it doesn't own the world?' said the *Toronto Star*, while the *New York Times* spoke of 'the folly of a species that burns and poisons and blows up its own home'. In Washington, less than five hours before the test, the US Supreme Court finally ruled by the narrowest of margins, four votes to three, against an injunction sought by conservation groups to stop the test. In Canada students marched in Ottawa, Calgary, Thunder Bay, St Hubert, Quebec and across the Thousand Island Bridge between Ontario and New York State. Peace rallies were held in sixteen cities across the US. Four thousand people marched through downtown Boston; three thousand gathered in Washington. The biggest turnout was in New York, where demonstrators marched thirty abreast and twenty thousand sat on the grass at Sheep Meadow in Central Park to hear speakers denounce a catalogue of political and social ills: the Vietnam War, racism, the brutal quelling of the Attica prison riots and what was about to happen at Amchitka. The mindbomb had struck. Four months later, in February 1972, the US Atomic Energy Commission announced that no further testing would be done at Amchitka. Job done.

Three things were now evident. Direct action earned publicity, publicity brought results, and 'Greenpeace' lodged more readily in the public mind than 'Don't Make a Wave Committee'. The change of identity was agreed on 31 January 1972. On 4 May, at the Provincial Societies office in Victoria, British Columbia, the committee formally registered its name as the Greenpeace Foundation. With Amchitka now dealt with, its attention switched to a French atmospheric nuclear test planned for Moruroa Atoll in Polynesia. This time, under sail in a thirty-eight-foot ketch originally named *Vega* but reborn as *Greenpeace III*, they did manage to breach the security cordon, where they were rammed by a French minesweeper. Once again they failed to stop the explosion, but once again they won public support. Newspapers around the world published pictures of the tiny ketch under the looming guns of the French warship. Their galvanising effect, not just on public opinion but on public *action*, was more powerful by far than any amount of government sabre-rattling. Greenpeace in its campaigning henceforth would recognise no boundary that could not be overstepped in its fight against nuclear weapons, nor any risk that was not worth taking. But the war at sea was no longer all about bomb tests. To the dismay of the nuclear fundamentalists, another matter was beginning to weigh just as heavily on some of the activists' minds. It was an issue of 'green' rather than 'peace', and it was one that had long preoccupied Peter Scott.

No animals were heading for extinction faster than the great whales. By the 1920s humpbacks had already been reduced to a point at which hunting was no longer viable. Blue whales went the same way in the 1940s, soon followed by fin and sei, to leave the smaller minke as the only species surviving in harvestable quantities. Until 1946, when the International Whaling Commission was established to control the industry and set annual quotas, the whalers had faced no constraint. They operated in international waters that lay far beyond the reach of any world or national authority. Restrictions therefore would have to be voluntary, imposed by the industry itself. But any hope that the IWC would promote conservation over exploitation were as short-lived as a minke with a harpoon in its head. The quotas were set by a 'scientific committee', appointed by the commission itself, which did little more than rubber-stamp whatever the whalers wanted. Scientific data were stretched so thin that they lost all substance. In 1972 the committee calculated that the whale population in the southern oceans lay somewhere between 80,000 and 300,000 – a range so preposterous that it served no purpose other than to prove its authors' lack of competence. As Elspeth Huxley complained in her biography of Peter Scott, the IWC was founded without any hope, or even intention, of being an effective regulator:

Far from achieving its ostensible aim of curbing over-hunting, an annual
catch of all species of around 40,000 in the 1930s rose to 67,000 in 1962.
No resolution could be passed ... without a majority of three-quarters, and
any member could invalidate a resolution merely by lodging an objection
within ninety days. In other words not only did the Commission have no
teeth, it had no bark either, because it did not want one.

The one glimmer of hope was that membership of the IWC was open to
all nations, not just those with whaling fleets such as the Soviet Union,
Japan, Norway and Iceland, and that representatives of non-governmental
organisations such as the WWF could speak at meetings, though they could
not vote. Since 1965 the WWF's representative had been its vice-president
Peter Scott, who despised the commission's political posturing and its
hypocritical emphasis on 'the freedom of the seas' and 'rights of sovereign
states'. 'There is no doubt', he wrote, 'that what is going on is a world scandal of considerable magnitude.' It was a scandal of which the world was
becoming increasingly aware. In June 1972, a month after the Don't Make
a Wave Committee metamorphosed into Greenpeace, a United Nations
Conference on the Human Environment was held in Stockholm. Peter Scott
spoke on behalf of the WWF and played a significant part in achieving
what, for him, was the most fervently desired outcome: a unanimous vote
in favour of a world moratorium on commercial whaling. To the surprise
of no one, the IWC preferred the advice of its own scientific committee.
At a meeting two weeks after the conference, only four of the fourteen
eligible members voted for a ban. The scientific committee went on setting
its unscientific quotas and the whalers went on firing their harpoons. But
the anti-whaling campaign was about to take a dramatic new turn. Also
present in Stockholm during the UN conference was Patrick Moore, an
ecologist and future president of the Greenpeace Foundation, who joined
an anti-whaling protest with members of the WWF and Friends of the
Earth, all marching together behind an enormous dummy whale.

Divisions now widened between the Greenpeace anti-nuclear hard-
core and the ecology wing who wanted to save the whales. The more they
learned about whales – the size and complexity of their brains, the mutual
understanding between captive orcas and their trainers, their apparent

enjoyment of classical music, their language of song – the more they were determined to protect them. Nuclear disarmament might be the most pressing issue but it was not the only one. Conservation, too, was a matter of human survival. They noted the words of Peter Scott: 'If we cannot save the whale from extinction, we have little chance of saving mankind.' What would be the point of fighting to save a lifeless planet? Greenpeace and the WWF now shared a common purpose, though their backgrounds, personnel and methods could not have been more different. There were no crowned heads in Greenpeace; no men of wealth, no diplomats, no world-ranking scientists, no global industrialists. They looked and often behaved more like pot-smoking mystics or roadies for a rock band. There was not a business suit in sight; only beards, ponytails and sandals. Back in the days of the Don't Make a Wave Committee, they had funded the Amchitka mission with a concert at the Vancouver Coliseum by Joni Mitchell, James Taylor and Phil Ochs. This raised more than $17,000 and was hailed as the 'counterculture event of the year'. Now establishment and countercultural forces, in their contrasting ways, formed the two arms of a pincer movement closing in around the whalers. Where the WWF did nothing without consulting the science, Greenpeace did nothing without consulting the ancient Chinese book of divination, the *I Ching*. It is hard to imagine Peter Scott, Prince Bernhard or the Duke of Edinburgh doing as Greenpeace's mystics did when they waded knee-deep into a bay and tried to summon whales by thought transference.

But, as the anti-nuclear confrontations had shown, mysticism was no obstacle to bravery. The fashionably lower-case title of Rex Weyler's history of Greenpeace in the 1970s, *greenpeace – how a group of ecologists, journalists, and visionaries changed the world*, is but a small exaggeration of what they actually achieved. There was hardly a newspaper or a news channel anywhere in the world that did not print or broadcast pictures of activists in their inflatable Zodiacs harassing the Russian and Japanese factory ships, interposing themselves between the hunters and the hunted, daring the harpooners to fire over their heads. Just as before, the mindbombs found their mark. Outside the whaling nations, political and public opinion hardened against the whalers. Not only was whaling cruel, it was also unnecessary. In earlier times whale oil had satisfied a number of essential human needs as a lubricant and fuel for oil-lamps. Whalebone had been the mainstay of the corsetry trade. But nobody needed those things now, and the use of whale oil in cosmetics, shoe polish and pet food could not be justified when so many less damaging alternatives were available. Nor was there any substance in the Japanese claim that whale meat was an essential part of their national diet. As Huxley pointed out, it 'accounted for less than one tenth of one per cent of their protein intake, and anyway would have priced itself out of the market without a government subsidy'.

Greenpeace and the WWF continued to plough their separate furrows, but their tracks were converging. Helping hands were extended. In 1977, the WWF's Netherlands office ran a fundraising campaign for Greenpeace and, live on Dutch television, handed over a cheque for £45,000. This was another turning point. Greenpeace spent the money on the *Sir William Hardy*, a 134-foot rusting Aberdeen trawler that had last seen service as a research ship for the UK Ministry of Agriculture, Fisheries and Food and was now tied up in the Thames. Greenpeace bought her for £32,500, fitted her out as a campaign vessel and renamed her *Rainbow Warrior*. For the mystics this was a name of utmost significance, symbolic of their brotherhood with the Native Americans whose spiritual symbols had adorned their earlier boats. It was borrowed from the title of a book, *Warriors of the Rainbow*, a collection of Native American myths and prophecies. In one of these an old woman promises her grandson:

> When the earth is ravaged and the animals are dying, a new tribe of people shall come unto the earth from many colors, classes, creeds and who by their actions and deeds shall make the earth green again. They will be known as the Warriors of the Rainbow.

The passion for Native American mythology reached across the Atlantic. When Greenpeace launched its German branch at Hamburg in 1981, two activists climbed up an industrial chimney and unfolded a banner which, translated into English, read: 'When the last tree is cut down, the last fish eaten, the last stream poisoned, you will realize that you cannot eat money.' This dystopian prophecy was attributed to the Cree tribe of the northern United States and Canada. It hardly mattered whether or not this was true.

The important thing was to reaffirm Greenpeace's solidarity with people whose respect for nature contrasted so starkly with the commercially driven vandalism of the industrialised world.

For a while *Rainbow Warrior* was the most famous ship afloat. It accelerated Greenpeace's harrying of whaling fleets, disrupted seal hunts in the Orkneys and Newfoundland, led campaigns against nuclear tests and the dumping of nuclear waste which brought it repeatedly into confrontation with the French navy. In July 1985 came the biggest mindbomb of them all, when French agents mined and sank *Rainbow Warrior* in the port of Auckland, New Zealand, killing a Portuguese photographer in the process. The most famous ship afloat now became the world's most famous wreck. Furious French denials of responsibility continued all through July and August until late September that year when the Defence Minister, Charles Hernu, confessed that intelligence officials had lied to him. The chief of the French foreign intelligence service, Admiral Pierre Lacoste, was dismissed by President Mitterand and Hernu resigned. In 1987 an arbitration tribunal in Geneva ordered the French government to pay Greenpeace $8.1 million in reparation. The scandal may have cost Greenpeace its ship, but the dividend in public support was beyond price. France's violent response to non-violent protest had definitively cast Greenpeace as the champions of peace and the nuclear power as a ruthless villain careless of human life.

In Britain in 1973 Peter Scott became the first person ever to be knighted for services to conservation. A year later he was installed as Chancellor of the University of Birmingham, where one of his first acts was to confer an honorary degree on Konrad Lorenz. But none of this diverted him from the whales. He recognised that the IWC's Achilles heel was the right of non-whaling nations to join and vote. At its foundation in 1949 the commission had only fifteen members: Argentina, Australia, Brazil, Canada, Denmark, France, Iceland, Mexico, the Netherlands, Norway, Panama, South Africa, the Soviet Union, the United Kingdom and the United States. In 1951 they were joined by Japan. Scott's approach to the membership was diplomatic but wily. In what Elspeth Huxley described as *a policy of encirclement*, he concentrated his attention on nations known to oppose whaling. If enough of these could be persuaded to join, then they could outvote the whalers. Membership began gradually to expand. Brazil signed up in 1974, New Zealand in 1976, the Netherlands in 1977, Korea in 1978, Chile, Peru, Spain and Sweden in 1979, swelling the number to twenty-three. In the summer of that same year, ahead of the IWC's annual meeting in London, between twelve and fifteen thousand protestors led by Greenpeace UK marched to Trafalgar Square, where they were addressed by an emotional Scott. The persecution of the great whales, he said, was 'an affront to human dignity'. Would people be happy to see cows harpooned in fields and dragged away to die in agony? If cruelty to a cow was unacceptable, then why was it permissible for an intelligent and sensitive creature such as the whale? Despite its increased membership, the IWC once again put its fingers in its ears and voted against a moratorium. But the membership went on growing. By 1985, the year *Rainbow Warrior* was sunk, it stood at forty-one, with the newcomers now including China, India, Switzerland and Germany.

It was enough. At its thirty-fourth annual meeting in 1982, the commission at last agreed a moratorium, to take effect from 1986. Among the conservationists there was great exultation. 'We have won,' said Scott. 'It seems to be a great victory in one of my lifetime's battles, and I feel a great lift.'

It was indeed a victory of sorts. The importance of the 'Save the Whale' campaign cannot be over-estimated. It was the very foundation of the worldwide conservation movement. For the first time it aroused widespread public indignation not just about the suffering of individual animals but about the future of entire species. It also inspired newspapers to devote regular space to environmental issues. But the celebrations were premature. The whalers had been wounded, certainly, but it was not a clean kill. Legal fleets were replaced by pirates who had even less regard for the animals' suffering or for the survival of the species. Even more insidiously, the exemption of 'scientific whaling' from the moratorium created a legal loophole through which the Japanese whale-meat trade could sail without hindrance. Conservationists may have shown themselves to be a force to be reckoned with, but cynicism and greed were still in the game.

CHAPTER TWENTY-TWO

Meat

ASH AND BONE FRAGMENTS TELL US THAT PEOPLE HAVE BEEN dining on roasted meat for around two million years. Some would argue that this is quite long enough for flesh-eating to be accepted as part of our genetic inheritance, as natural to humans as bone-crunching is to a hyena. But we are not hyenas. We have choices, and with choices come responsibilities. Meat-eating has gnawed at our consciences for as long as philosophers have known how to write. Pythagoras in the sixth century BC preached vegetarianism because he believed animals possessed souls and that cruelty to animals was only a short step from cruelty to humans. He remains a champion for proselytisers two-and-a-half thousand years later. Others argue that killing and eating animals is not the point. God, history and common sense give us that inalienable right. The choice therefore lies not between indulgence and abstinence, but rather between kindness and cruelty. All that should concern us as moral beings is the way animals are treated while they are alive. But this only invites more questions. If we are going to concern ourselves with the quality of life in an Aberdeen Angus, then why should we feel any less concern for, say, the bone-crunching hyena? Conversely, if we care so little for the hyena, then why should we care any more for the bullock? Back comes the answer: as humans we are *responsible* for the bullock. Only the good Lord is responsible for the hyena. But back again comes the objection: *it is not that simple*. It never is.

*

It is not just membership of a particular species that fixes an animal in our scale of values. The role of an animal *within* a species can matter just as much. One of the best illustrations of this, more than thirty years ago, was the case of Herzog's mice. The University of Tennessee in the 1980s was home to some of the most privileged mice on the planet. The temperature and humidity in their living space were carefully controlled. Their bedding was fresh, their diet tailored to ensure their fitness and health. Altogether they were treated like honoured guests. But there was a downside. Although they would be cherished for as long as they lived, their ultimate destiny as laboratory animals was to die as martyrs to science. Yet even at this last extreme their comfort was paramount. To ease their passing, their very own dedicated vet would waft them away on clouds of anaesthesia. Few humans live and die as peacefully.

But these were not the only mice in the university. Beneath floors and furniture, behind skirting boards, wherever they could find a place to hide, lived another quite separate population – genetically identical to the five-star specimens in the laboratory, even directly related to them, but socially a world apart. These animals were pests whose well-being was of no interest to the US Department of Agriculture or to the university's animal care committee. They were the responsibility of the caretakers, who trapped them on sheets of cardboard smeared with glue. The irony of their sticky end was not just that it would have been a crime if perpetrated against their upstairs cousins. It was that the gluepot victims had once been five-star mice themselves. Their fatal error had been to escape, and not to understand the small print of human ethics.

But the twists in the moral maze didn't stop even there. It was a core principle of the animal care committee that animals kept for study must be fed their natural diets – which, for the zoology department's snakes, meant live mice. The ethical proviso was that this must be done solely for dietary reasons and must not be part of any experiment. If the zoologists wanted to augment their snake project by studying, say, the fear responses of the mice, then they would have some hard questions to answer. The mice themselves would have become subjects of an experiment, and being fed to snakes clearly would cause them to suffer. The animal care committee therefore would need to hear some very compelling arguments before allowing the work to proceed.

The story of the Tennessee mice was told by an American psychologist, Harold A. Herzog, in the *American Psychologist* magazine. He drew the obvious conclusion. The moral judgements that humans make about other species 'are neither logical nor consistent … The *roles* that animals play in our lives, and the *labels* we attach to them, deeply influence our sense of what is ethical.' In plainer language, we are prejudiced. If you take the labels we attach to animals of different kinds – Food, Pet, Vermin, for example – and randomly shuffle the pack, then the results are almost viscerally disturbing. Pony-veal? Cat-poison? Dog-shoots? There are two distinct ways of responding to such difficulties, though both require us to accept that, for as long as humans take animals for their own use, paradoxes are inevitable. No amount of philosophical tap-dancing will persuade us to cuddle the skunk or curry the canary.

Animal protection societies throughout the world are dedicated to *welfare*. They do not challenge the presumed right of humans to exploit other species. What they do say is that people should recognise a duty of care to animals under their control, and must accept that this means treating them kindly. No animals arouse more controversy than those reared for the table. Since the British Parliament enacted the Ill Treatment of Cattle Bill in 1822, no class of animal has been subject to more legislation, and no legislation has come under more sustained attack. It was less than a year after the Ill Treatment Bill that Elizabeth Heyrick published her incendiary pamphlet on the failure of the law to protect animals at markets. As it began, so it has continued. The only thing that changes is the nature of the cruelty. The issues that inflamed Elizabeth Heyrick in the first half of the nineteenth century were very different from those that enraged her successors in the latter half of the twentieth. Heyrick herself would not have recognised her own country, nor any other country in Europe or America, in the 1960s. The industrial revolution had completed the transformation of towns and cities and was now moving out into the fields. In this new landscape the modern meat production unit was as different from the pre-war farm as a

car plant from a blacksmith's forge. In place of the pastures were factories –
automated plants in which the products rolling off the lines were living
animals. For eggs, meat and milk, no less than cars, coats and saucepans,
we had reached the age of mass production.

Many would say that we had also reached the age of mass suffering.
Livestock farming from prehistory to the Second World War had been a
gradual process of evolution in which each generation of farmers shared
a kinship with the generations that came before and after. It made little
difference that centuries of selective breeding had produced cows that
yielded more milk or beef, pigs that gave more bacon, hens that laid more
eggs. Farming still looked much the same as it always had done. It was
a thing done in fields and barns by men and women who lived close to
their livestock. Grazing animals were as much part of the landscape as
the grass, the hedgerows and the trees. Cockerels crowed, hens pecked
and scratched in the open air. All this changed after the war. Instead of
hens foraging in the open, huge flocks of 'broilers' were crammed into
sheds where they were fed and watered by machines. Not an inch was
wasted. The birds were packed in so tightly that each one had no more
space than it could stand up in, often as little as half a square foot, about
the size of a single sheet of typing paper. They would have more room in
the oven. Many were de-beaked to stop them pecking each other, though
in such tightly packed communities little could be done to halt the spread
of disease. Farm budgets allowed for a mortality rate of between two and
six per cent, but this was often exceeded during outbreaks of fowl pest.
Respiratory disease and cancer added to the wastage before the survivors,
having reached slaughter-weight in just forty-two days, were taken away,
twelve to a crate, to be hung upside down from a moving belt that carried
them onward to a slaughterman who slit their throats at the rate of one
every two seconds. Birds damaged by rough handling, along with those
whose legs had collapsed under their bodyweight, were chopped up into
breast, thigh and leg joints while undamaged ones embarked on the final
stretch of their journey to Sunday lunch. The economies of mass production
assigned no value to compassion. With food rationing a recent memory for
many after the war, the first and only priority was to satisfy public demand
for affordable meat.

Laying hens fared even worse. Instead of being packed into sheds they were shut inside tiny individual cages. Here, unless they were culled for failing to meet their quotas, they would labour in the gloom for a single calendar year before they were worn out and sent off to make pie-filling. Like the broilers, battery hens ran the risk of disease and sudden death from 'bone atrophy', cancer or exhaustion. As with the broilers, too, quality declined with cheapness. Yolks were smaller and paler than before, whites watery, shells thin. A writer in the UK's *Poultry World* magazine in 1962 lamented: 'Some years ago it was hardly possible to cut off the top of an egg without touching the yolk. Now you are more than a quarter of the way down the egg before the yolk is reached.'

Unluckiest of all were male calves born to milk cows. Being no good for beef, they were more of a liability than an asset. Most lived for only a few days – motherless, terrified and unfed – before they were rendered into pastes, pies, gloves and shoes. But these were the more fortunate ones. Some of those from more versatile breeds had to suffer the extended torments of the veal trade. This meant spending the whole of their three months of life squeezed into crates less than two feet wide, too small for them to turn or even lie down in comfortably. Some had their heads pinned between bars which allowed them to slide up or down but otherwise clamped them like prisoners in the stocks. Quality of life was not an issue. All that mattered was to give consumers what they wanted: the whitest possible veal. Even in the industrial age, methods used to achieve this owed more to superstition than to science. British producers thought that fortnightly blood-lettings from the animals' necks would do the trick; the Dutch preferred to withhold light and food. Calves were kept in the dark and fed skimmed milk or milk substitutes instead of the mother's milk their bodies needed. For the Dutch in particular, it serviced an international trade with lucrative markets in Germany, France, Italy and Britain. Like the chickens, veal calves were vegetablised and concealed from public view. The same went for overcrowded piggeries where animals were fattened in overheated 'sweat-boxes' and forbidden all but the dimmest of light, and where pregnant pigs were trapped behind bars in 'sow stalls' barely wide enough for their bodies.

What made factory farming acceptable to its customers was their sheer ignorance of how it worked. The food packaging and advertising industries continued to project a picture of farming as if nothing had changed since the invention of the three-legged milking stool. Images showed happy animals grazing in idyllic landscapes, while marketing slogans were spun around words like 'natural' or 'farm-fresh'. It was not so much a distortion of the truth as an inversion of it. What was being sold was a myth.

The person who exploded the myth was an English Quaker and conscientious objector called Ruth Harrison, whose disturbingly detailed observations of intensive farming units were recorded in her book *Animal Machines*. This was an essential but distressing read for anyone interested in animal welfare. 'How far', she asked, 'have we the right to take our domination of the animal world? Have we the right to rob them of all pleasure in life simply to make more money more quickly out of their carcasses?... At what point do we acknowledge cruelty?' The answer to this last was the bleakest of all: *not until they cease to be profitable*. To show what this meant in practice she published photographs of broiler houses, battery cages, slaughter rooms, veal crates and sweat-boxes. Even so, nothing was more damaging to the meat industry than its own unguarded words. In February 1962 the influential *Farmers Weekly* quoted the director of a leading farm livestock research centre, Dr K.C. Sellers, who argued that 'pigs were kept to make money, and one should not get over-sentimental about them ... I think the test of a "sweat-box" is whether or not it pays.' In *Animal Machines*, Harrison explained that sweat-boxes worked by using the heat generated by the pigs themselves to keep the temperature to a minimum of eighty degrees Fahrenheit. Moisture from urine and sweat then 'rises up in the intense heat taking with it all bacteria, which find their way out of the houses with the steam, or remain caught in the stalactites hanging from the ceiling'. It was a health regime of sorts, but not one that any caring human would impose on sentient creatures whose well-being was deemed important.

At the end of her book Ruth Harrison proposed a new welfare charter that would abolish battery cages and intensive veal units, and ban the importation of eggs and veal from factory farms. 'Deficiency diets' such as those designed to cause anaemia in veal calves should be illegal, as should permanent tethering of animals and keeping them in the dark. *Animal Machines* produced surprisingly rapid results. In response to its publication in 1964 the UK government appointed a committee of inquiry under the chairmanship of Francis Rogers Brambell, Professor of Zoology at the University of Bangor. By the normal standards of official investigations, Brambell's work was done at lightning speed. *The Report of the Technical Committee to Enquire into the Welfare of Animals Kept under Intensive Livestock Husbandry Systems*, more commonly known as the Brambell Report, was published by Her Majesty's Stationery Office in 1965. Its first achievement was to define the conditions necessary to ensure an acceptable quality of life for farmed animals. These have been known ever since as the Five Freedoms. Its second was to persuade the government to set up a new statutory committee to advise on animal welfare. The result, in 1967, was the Farm Animal Welfare Advisory Committee (FAWAC); then a year later came the Agriculture (Miscellaneous Provisions) Act, which made it a criminal offence to cause 'unnecessary suffering of pain or distress' to livestock on agricultural land. By 'livestock' was meant not just poultry, pigs, sheep and cattle but also horses, goats, deer, rabbits and others such as mink and foxes which were kept for fur. Protection did *not* stretch to pet rabbits, even when they were kept on a farm, nor to ornamental ducks or pheasants reared for the gun. Cruelty in that case was impossible to define in any terms that would allow shooting to continue. Subsequent variations of the Act then introduced specific welfare codes for each commonly farmed species. In 1979 FAWAC was replaced by the Farm Animal Welfare Council (FAWC) which had additional responsibility for the welfare of animals not just on the farm but also in transit, at market and in slaughterhouses. One of its very first acts was to formalise Brambell's Five Freedoms:

1 **Freedom from Hunger and Thirst** by ready access to fresh water and a diet to maintain full health and vigour.
2 **Freedom from Discomfort** by providing an appropriate environment including shelter and a comfortable resting area.
3 **Freedom from Pain, Injury or Disease** by prevention or rapid diagnosis and treatment.
4 **Freedom to Express Normal Behaviour** by providing sufficient space, proper facilities and company of the animal's own kind.
5 **Freedom from Fear and Distress** by ensuring conditions and treatment which avoid mental suffering.

These are not as straightforward as they sound. When considering the Fourth Freedom, for example, one of the commonest ways to assess the 'normal behaviour' and 'natural requirements' of a domesticated animal is to observe its closest wild ancestor. For the chicken, this is the wild red junglefowl of south-east Asia – a species that lives in small flocks, flies and roosts in trees, and whose hens build proper nests in which they hatch and rear their chicks in seclusion. But none of these fundamental behaviours is available to birds in intensive production units, which might lead us to conclude that, for all the law's fine words and good intentions, they must live in permanent agonies of frustration and rage. The problem is that the selective breeding of chickens has been going on for at least four thousand years, so that the modern farmed hen no more resembles a red junglefowl than Donald Trump does a Palaeolithic hunter-gatherer. What can be gained from comparing a lightweight, fleet-footed, fully flighted bird with a flightless and near-sedentary laying hen or broiler? How do the needs of a dairy cow compare to those of the ancestral aurochs? How far has seven thousand years of breeding distanced the modern bacon pig from the wild boar?

What has to be weighed is the discomfiting fact that some animals have been so fundamentally altered by human interference that their 'natural' environment is no longer natural at all. A broiler chicken released into the jungle would fare no better than Donald Trump. Neat and tidy comparisons with wild species are no longer possible: there is no longer any such thing as *the* pig, *the* cow or *the* chicken. It could be argued that the natural environment of an animal bred for the intensive production unit *is* the intensive production unit. This is not a view popular with welfare campaigners but it has to be accounted for.

Ruth Harrison's influence, like Rachel Carson's, was not confined to her homeland. Just as *Animal Machines* inspired the UK government, so the Council of Europe was persuaded in 1976 to adopt the European Convention for the Protection of Animals Kept for Farming Purposes. This committed its member states to observe and maintain standards very similar to those proposed by Brambell. The Five Freedoms thereafter spread to the United States and beyond to become the global gold standard. But what did any of this mean in practice? How much better off were farmed animals than they were before Ruth Harrison revealed their suffering? Many would say: not much. Even within FAWC, there were people who clung to beliefs about chickens that owed more to Descartes than to Ruth Harrison. Across the world, commercial and political pressures were heavily weighted in favour of more and more intensive production, and meat production remained as remote from the public eye as the conversion of oil into plastics. The only time animals would see sunlight, and the only time anyone outside the factory would see *them*, was between the slats of a lorry heading for the slaughterhouse. How could people who professed to love animals eat the products of such regimes? Were they even now, post Harrison, being misled by weasel words such as 'farm-fresh' or 'corn fed'? Did the promise of cheap meat outweigh every other concern? Or were the animals simply too distant, too invisible, too unimaginable, for anyone to think about them? Or perhaps we just find ways to distance ourselves from the circle of blame.

James Serpell, Professor of Ethics and Animal Welfare at the University of Pennsylvania, explains in his book *In the Company of Animals* that self-forgiving 'distancing devices' fall into four main categories: *detachment*, *concealment*, *misrepresentation* and *shifting the blame*. *Detachment* comes in multiple forms, but most obviously from the unbridgeable distance between urban consumers and the animals that stock their freezers. If you never knew the pig that filled your bacon sandwich, then you'll be unlikely to feel much in the way of remorse. Much the same applies to the farms themselves. They are so vast and impersonal – thirty thousand identical chickens here, a thousand pigs there – that there is no chance of any individual being recognised as anything more than an industrial production unit, to be counted rather than named. In such a highly mechanised and computer-controlled industry, contact with humans is minimal. Only at the slaughterhouse is there direct human involvement. Here, workers desensitised by killing necessarily achieve their own form of detachment, though many do suffer later from post-traumatic stress disorder (PTSD). But the question remains. Factory farmers are not all monsters. Why is it, then, that they accord such low priority to animal welfare? The answer, says Serpell, is not all about economics:

> Livestock producers are generally unwilling to consider the welfare of their animals because this would entail thinking about them as subjects rather than objects; as persons rather than things, and this would raise imponderable questions about the morality of their treatment. Far easier and less painful to regard them as Cartesian automata ...

The second device, *concealment*, is handmaid to the first. What the eye doesn't see, the heart doesn't grieve over. And what the eye will *never* see in a factory-farmed landscape is an animal. On supermarket shelves, too, packaging conveys little idea of the creature that provided its contents. In some supermarkets, pieces of chicken are sold in pouches that allow cooks to transfer them to the pan without ever touching raw meat at all. Nor is any butchered cow, pig or calf ever called by its rightful name. We eat only euphemisms: *beef, pork, veal*.

Serpell's third device, *misrepresentation*, might just as well be called 'vilification'. If the character of an animal is blackened sufficiently to make people hate or fear it, then there is less likelihood of anyone caring about how it is treated. Wolves, rats and hyenas are classic examples. Their very names are adopted by humans to insult each other, generally for behaving in ways that bear no resemblance to the animals at all. Fictional stereotypes are another means by which negative images are falsely attached to species of undeservedly low esteem. There is nothing intrinsically loveable about a rabbit or intrinsically hateful about a fox or a weasel, though one would struggle to see much parity in their treatment. The farmyard gets off relatively lightly, though few people called 'pig', 'swine', 'chicken' or 'cow' will regard it as a compliment. This is particularly harsh on the pig, whose 'filthy' image owes nothing to its nature but everything to the way it is kept. If pigs could speak, then their epithet for a mucky individual would surely be 'man'.

One inconvenience of human nature is the nagging inner voice. There are only two ways to avoid stirring the conscience: lead a blameless life, or *shift the blame*. In the impersonal, mechanised, production-line processes of the factory farm, that is easily done. No single person bears responsibility for the whole. Breeding, fattening, slaughtering, butchering and marketing are all done by different people, and the buck stops with the consumer whose lust for cheap meat justifies the entire enterprise. *We are all to blame* then translates very conveniently into *no one is to blame.* As Serpell puts it: 'We have created an artificial distinction between us and them, and have constructed a defensive screen of lies, myths, distortions and evasions, the sole purpose of which has been to reconcile or nullify the conflict between economic self-interest and sympathy and affection.'

CHAPTER TWENTY-THREE

Cruelty and Compassion

FOR THOSE WHO DID CARE ABOUT FARM ANIMAL WELFARE, *Animal Machines* was a baton that needed to be passed on. The man who grasped it was a Hampshire dairy farmer called Peter Roberts. As a farmer himself, he was dismayed by the new methods. His relationship with his animals was unashamedly old-fashioned. When cows went to the slaughterhouse he stood with them until they died. None of his surplus male calves were sent to market, for fear they would end up in veal crates. For all these reasons and more, he fully shared Ruth Harrison's abhorrence for the cages and crates, and for everything else that went on in factory farms. His angry letters to newspapers received strong support from the public but little or none from the animal welfare charities. It seemed to him that there was only one way forward. He and his wife Anna would have to establish a charity of their own – one uncompromisingly dedicated to the abolition of the 'needless misery of factory farmed animals' and restoring kindness and compassion to the vocabulary of the countryside. Compassion in World Farming began in 1967 as a 'cottage charity' run from his kitchen table. As he would say nearly thirty years later: 'There is nothing more powerful than an idea whose time has come.'

Having launched his charity, Roberts ceased farming, became a vegetarian and set up a company selling 'textured vegetable protein', an early meat substitute made from soy. Vegetarians in those days were few in number and widely regarded as cranks. So too were meat-eating animal-lovers who risked charges of hypocrisy when they lobbied for higher welfare standards. Like every other issue in the long and tortured history of man and beast, the arguments around meat were complex, confused and anthropomorphic. People would project their own feelings on to suffering animals and the inevitable question, *How would we like it?*, invited the obvious answer, *Not at all*. But, as every serious thinker since Aristotle has been anxious to point out, human beings are not like other animals. They are unique.

We are the only species known to fear death. The only species that worries about what it eats and drinks. The only species that feels guilty about its treatment of others. Modern man is afraid of dark and dirt. He is afraid of sunshine. He fears everything from the aggression of his own species to the chemicals in his lunch. What he suffers, you wouldn't do to a pig. Earning his keep means long hours of dull, repetitive activity spiked with stress loads that ulcerate his stomach and make his head hurt. He needs counsellors to reassure him that his fears are permissible, and pays huge anxiety taxes in the form of insurance premiums against every vile thing the world might do to him. Often he is bored. He feels terrible, agonising grief when bereaved or separated from members of his own species. Sometimes he is so unhappy he kills himself. If you did this to an animal – made it commute to work every day and put it in fear of walking among its own kind – you would have to answer to the law. But this is precisely our defence against hypocrisy. It is from our own suffering that our feeling for animals comes. We know what it is like to endure pain, hunger, grief, boredom, frustration and rage, and our humanity tells us not to inflict it on others. Anthropomorphism – the transference of human values to animal lives – is harder to eradicate from the human psyche than fear of snakes. Hence the need to keep our distance, to avoid the hard questions. What we don't know, we needn't care about.

How much suffering would be spared if we stopped rearing animals for the table? In theory, if the average British person lived for seventy years without consuming animal products, then it would save the lives of eight cows, thirty-six sheep, thirty-six pigs and five hundred and fifty chickens, and relieve the huge metabolic effort required for hens and cows to provide ten thousands eggs and eighteen tonnes of milk. One must say *in theory*, for without consumers the lives would never have existed in the first place. An entirely vegetarian society would mean not meadows filled with happy lambs, but no lambs at all. The cost in animal lifetimes would be total. As the paradoxes and ironies of the meat versus vegetable debate go, this is one of the most obvious. A subtler question might address the true cost of a plate of vegetables. How has tilling the soil served the 'rights' of species whose habitats it has destroyed? Forests have to be felled, and wildlife lost, whether or not the soya is for human consumption or for livestock. All of James Serpell's distancing devices come into play here: *detachment* from the animal victims, *concealment* of their suffering, *misrepresentation* of the true picture and *shifting the blame* to the manufacturers of agrochemicals and the governments that fail to control them. It is like the difference between hand-to-hand combat and a remotely detonated bomb. Vegetables kill at a distance; meat kills at close quarters. Every mouthful has its consequences.

But the lack of any perfect solution is no argument against seeking the best one available, however imperfect it may be. This brings campaigners to an irreconcilable parting of the ways. In one direction lies *animal welfare*; in the other, *animal rights*. All animal welfare organisations by definition have chosen the first path, broadly delineated by the Five Freedoms. Although Peter Roberts himself was a vegetarian, Compassion in World Farming did not set out to persuade people to follow his example. It encouraged consumers rather to make informed, welfare-friendly choices – pasture-fed, not feedlot; free range, not battery or broiler – and to understand that we must all accept our share of responsibility for the animals kept to feed us. This does not mean according 'rights' to species that are incapable of discharging the responsibilities that go with them, but it does mean treating them humanely and taking care not to inflict *unnecessary suffering*. But what, then, constitutes 'necessary' suffering, and how can we balance the profit-and-loss account of animal lives against human gain? This takes us back to Harold A. Herzog and the Tennessee Mouse Syndrome. The issue is the same. By tacitly accepting different ethical standards for different groups of animals, we only reinforce the paradox. This is precisely why the animal rights movement dismisses the welfare argument as 'speciesism'.

It could be argued that the case for animal rights began in 1789 with Jeremy Bentham's well-worn rubric on reason versus suffering. In terms of public consciousness, however, it did not take hold until 1975, when the Australian philosopher Peter Singer published *Animal Liberation*. The American philosopher Tom Regan's *The Case for Animal Rights* followed in 1983, and these two books have underpinned the vegan and animal liberationist causes ever since. Like most ideas about inter-species relationships, the rights argument rests on Darwin. All forms of animal life have evolved from a common root, so that each species represents a twig on the same evolutionary tree. Thus it follows that they have many important characteristics in common, such as the ability to feel pain, hunger and fear. Both morally and physically, therefore, the differences between species are just like the differences between races or sexes, only bigger. If you reject racism and sexism, then it follows that you must also reject moral distinctions made on the grounds of species. In the words of Tom Regan, every animal, human and otherwise, is 'the subject of a life' and all possess the same moral rights. High among these must be the right not to be eaten. Killing other animals in order to eat them, wrote Peter Singer, 'is a clear instance of the sacrifice of the most important interests of other beings in order to satisfy trivial interests of our own'.

Nearly fifty years after *Animal Liberation*, the argument still rages, welfare versus rights. It has not always been subtle. 'Before they're roasted in garlic and rosemary,' ran the headline on an RSPCA advertisement in 1996, 'they're soaked in urine and excrement.' Hold your nose and pass the mint sauce. The most strident voices came from America, where the radical campaign group People for the Ethical Treatment of Animals, better known as Peta, emblazoned its 'Meat is Murder' slogan on advertisements, billboards, T-shirts and a 1985 album by The Smiths. Peta refused to be inhibited by anything like conventional good taste. When the police in Chicago published the city's homicide figures in 2017 – six hundred and fifty dead – its response was *So what?* Why obsess about such a tiny cull of humans when animals across the world were being murdered in their billions? To underscore the message, it published an alluring photograph of a woman's leg, garnished on a plate ready for the carver. 'Meat is murder'. Prime cuts from female bodies were a hallmark of Peta's determination to shock. Posters showed a scantily clad Pamela Anderson with her body labelled as joints of meat: *leg, round, rump, ribs, shoulder, breast*. Another campaign flaunted a bevy of supermodels amply fulfilling their promise that 'We'd rather go naked than wear fur.' Stunts included swimsuited women at the Wimbledon tennis championships handing out strawberries with vegan cream, and a semi-naked young woman in Kerala, India, painted to look like barbecued meat. As everyone in the advertising industry knows, nothing sells like sex. But not everyone welcomed this approach. The fact that Peta's founder, Ingrid Newkirk, was a woman did not appease the feminists. 'Put your breasts away, Peta. Your cheap stunts do nothing for animal welfare', said a headline in the *Guardian*, ignoring the fact that Peta's interest lay in animal *rights*, not welfare. Other critics denounced the charity as misogynistic, 'vile' and 'hate-filled'. They argued that the intended message of the breast-and-leg imagery, that attractive women are literally made of the same stuff as steak and cutlets, could not justify the conflation of sexualisation with the exploitation of animals. But who cared? In a world already saturated with sexual imagery, moral outrage was not likely to be aroused by yet another breast or bottom. Love it or loathe it, Peta now claims to be the biggest animal rights organisation in the world, with a membership of six-and-a-half million.

Size, however, is not everything. Slogans and supermodels may catch the eye, but they do not carry much weight with policy-makers. Fixed positions are not easily shifted. As Peter Scott found with his anti-whaling campaign, change does not come without the steady accumulation of evidence, the clear articulation of achievable goals and the building of an unanswerable case. A measured speech at the UN or World Trade Organization can be worth far more than a sensational headline. It is impossible to imagine Peter Roberts campaigning with naked women, and hard to believe that many of the improvements in farm animal welfare could have been achieved without the dogged persistence of the organisation he founded.

One of his first priorities was the veal crate, and in 1984 came the chance to act. His target at first looked improbable: a community of 'white canons' at Storrington Priory in West Sussex, where Roberts had found six hundred and fifty calves chained by the neck in crates. Like all intensively-reared veal calves they had insufficient space to turn round, stretch or lie down comfortably. They were fed nothing but milk, and by the time they were ready for slaughter at the age of six months were often too weak to walk. These of course were standard methods common to veal producers across the world, but what made Storrington different – and, crucially, newsworthy – was the fact that the cruelties were being inflicted by religious ascetics. Roberts might also have had in mind the fact that the Catholic Church was, at best, ambivalent in its attitudes to animals and that the countries of southern Europe, where its influence was strongest, had some of the lowest welfare standards in the western world. CIWF launched a private prosecution, charging the monks with nine counts of cruelty under the 1911 Protection of Animals Act and the 1968 Agricultural Act. It caused such a sensation that even some local Catholics felt the need to worship elsewhere, and their anger was conveyed to the Pope. The business of the court, however, was to decide whether the treatment of the calves was illegal, not whether it was inhumane. The case was lost, at a cost to CIWF of £12,000, a heavy burden for what was then still a small charity. Strategically, however, it was a victory beyond price: the only defence that could be made of the monks was that their actions were not proscribed by law. But people knew cruelty when they saw it, and the government and meat industry alike knew the likely cost of public outrage.

In 1987 the British government took the first steps towards making veal crates illegal. Ten years later, following a Europe-wide petition organised by Peter Roberts, the European Union awarded legal status to animals as sentient beings. In 2007 the EU followed Britain's lead and prohibited veal crates in all twenty-seven member states. In 2012 it banned 'barren' battery cages for laying hens and a year later it did the same with sow stalls, which, following a mass letter-writing campaign by CIWF to Members of Parliament, had been illegal in Britain since 1999. Year by year, country by country, the table-top charity grew into a powerful international NGO with offices across Europe, the USA, South Africa and China. Its voice was unignorable, though this did not mean that governments, let alone commercial producers, rushed to do its bidding. Change costs money, and not everyone thinks virtue is its own reward. On the other hand, few commercial organisations like to be identified with cruelty, or fail to recognise the advantages to be gained from a bit of affordable self-righteousness. Laying hens have been the principal beneficiaries of this, though countless generations will have to hatch and die before the last battery hen says goodbye to the last battery cage. In the USA in 2015 the fast-food giant McDonald's announced that it would switch to cage-free eggs, though it would take ten years to effect the change. Hundreds of other food companies across the world, including all major British supermarkets, have followed its example. The German state banned cage production in 2015, effective from 2025, and in early 2020 the poultry industry in the Slovak Republic said it would end caged systems by 2030. One result of all this is that, in most parts of the world, people who engage emotionally with issues of animal suffering are no longer derided as cranks or misguided idealists. Such is the slow drip of progress.

In many places it is even slower than it looks. Changes in the law do not immediately transform animal lives. The outlawing of barren battery cages, for example, did not mean the doors were thrown open and hens released into the sunshine. Some EU countries simply failed to enact the ban. Others complied with it by replacing the barren cage with a new kind of 'enriched' cage, which nods towards the Fourth Freedom by allowing a fraction more space and providing such minimum comforts as scratch areas, perches, nest boxes and the company of others. With ten birds packed into an area big enough to provide each bird with only a postcard's-worth of extra space, that company is necessarily intimate. 'Normal' behaviours such as preening and dustbathing remain impossible, wing-stretching is an occasional luxury, and natural daylight is never seen. Larger units, known as 'colony cages', are scaled up to contain as many as eighty birds. Campaigners have vigorously rejected the industry's assurance that these changes add up to 'significant benefits' for the birds. A joint statement by welfare organisations including CIWF, the RSPCA, the Humane Society of the United States, Eurogroup for Animals and the World Society for the Protection of Animals declares that the improvements bear only a 'distant resemblance to the things that matter to hens'. Ultimately, it says, 'they confine the hens and make normal behaviour impossible. A cage is still a cage.' For the birds, the consequences are 'frustration, bone weakness and osteoporosis'.

And so it goes on. Two-thirds of the seventy billion farm animals raised in the world every year are kept indoors. Even in places where there is ample outdoor space, dairy cows live like scaled-up battery hens. The word 'machines' is often used to describe their relentless productivity, but few real machines are driven so hard that they have to be scrapped after just two or three years' work. A 'normal' cow, of the kind still projected by the advertising and packaging industries, would have a life expectancy of twenty years. The metabolic load on a factory cow is colossal. To yield milk, it first has to produce a calf. In their natural state, like human mothers, cows produce enough milk to suckle and wean a single infant. The beach-ball udder of a modern dairy cow requires it to waddle with as much as six-and-a-half gallons of liquid between its hind legs, eleven-and-a-half times more than it would need for its own calf. The average daily output of a European dairy cow, spread over two milkings, is twenty-two litres, or just under five gallons, and as much as sixty litres when the flow is strongest. In America the average is even higher, at thirty litres a day. These are more than double the yields that would have been expected from any cow in the 1970s. The distension of the udder means that the animal cannot plant its hind hooves squarely to the ground, with consequences, such as swollen joints, sores and lameness, which are hard to reconcile with the absence of pain, suffering and disease required by the Third Freedom. The calf itself is taken away shortly after birth, so receives none of its own mother's milk, a denial which complies with the First Freedom only if 'full health and vigour' is taken to mean fitness to develop into another milk machine. This of course applies only to females. A few males in dual purpose breeds may be raised for beef; some will be sold into the veal trade; thousands more will be shot.

A typical modern Holstein-Friesian heifer will be artificially insemi-nated at between fifteen and twenty-one months and produce its first calf nine months later. In its short lifetime it will bear just two or three more, inducing it to give milk for ten months of each year until it is worn out and culled. A lucky few are let out in the grass-growing season, but most of those in Europe and America spend their entire lives in sheds. This is wholly a question of economics. Old-fashioned grazing does not provide enough nutrients to maintain a factory cow at peak output: only concen-trated grain feeds can do that. 'Sheds' in one way is a misnomer. Particularly in America, they can be enormous, with 'herds' numbering in the thou-sands. In other ways the term could not be more apposite. Investigations by CIWF and others in Europe revealed housing so primitive that cows had only bare concrete with no straw or other bedding for them to lie on. In Europe's most prolific dairying country, Germany, many were tethered by chains in cubicles so small that their movements were limited to just a few steps in any direction. Some had their hind legs shackled to prevent them skidding apart on concrete slippery with excrement. Others had their tails permanently tied up to stop them flicking the humans at the milking machines, which had the secondary effect of rendering them useless for whisking flies. In Spain some had their tails illegally docked. Everywhere there was a permanent threat of mastitis, a painful inflammation of the udder which spreads rapidly wherever housing and hygiene are poor. In some British herds the infection rate has reached seventy per cent.

Beef cattle have a better chance of spending some of their time on grass, though many will be brought inside during the winter, and some will spend their entire lifetimes in sheds. In the western world, most of the anger is aimed at American feedlots, which may house as many as one hundred thousand animals at a time. Viewed from the air, the farms look like gigantic chequerboards of open pens, more formally known in the USA as Concentrated Animal Feeding Operations, or CAFOs. This is where bullocks are brought, typically at the age of ten months, to be fattened for slaughter. More than seventy-five per cent of American beef passes through these pens, each of which contains between sixty and a hundred and fifty bullocks. In January 2018, the US Department of Agriculture's National Agricultural Statistics Service estimated the national total of cattle then in feedlots at fourteen million. Welfare organisations oppose this on multiple grounds. Any kind of close confinement is anathema to those who believe cattle belong in fields, and it is hard to argue that the 'golden standard' of the Five Freedoms is being rigorously observed in such places. In particular, an elastic interpretation of the Fourth Freedom is needed if milling about in a densely packed, earth-floored pen is to be called 'normal behaviour'. Freedoms Two and Three are also compromised. Discomforts include soiling with mud and excrement during wet weather, and the inhalation of dust during dry periods. More than half the cattle arriving at American slaughterhouses are encrusted with dirt. Health and well-being may also be damaged by extremes of hot or cold weather. On average every year in the US, five thousand head of cattle die from heat stress. During a heatwave in 2011, fifteen thousand died in just five states. The effects of heat are exacerbated by the inflated bodyweights now demanded of beef carcasses, which means it takes longer for the animals to cool down. The problem is worsened by the higher heat absorption of animals with black hides, and the metabolic effects of concentrated diets. It has been reported that some small reductions in the mortality rate are now being achieved by the introduction of sunshades.

Neighbouring humans may also suffer. Albeit in the pre-Trump era, the United States Environmental Protection Agency confirmed that feedlot farming 'can pose a number of risks to water quality and public health, mainly because of the amount of animal manure and wastewater they generate'. More broadly, Europeans view with horror the Americans' use of growth hormones to accelerate weight gain and increase muscle mass. These growth-promoters are given to ninety-six per cent of all cattle in American feedlots, but are illegal in the UK and throughout the European Union. Farmers and American trade officials cite the US Food and Drug Administration in support of their contention that these 'growth-promoting steroids and steroid-like compounds', or GPSCs, pose no risk to human health or to the environment. This, they say, is scientifically proven. Others hesitate over the word *proven*. 'After administration,' said a scholarly article in the peer-reviewed US *Journal of Soil and Water Conservation* in 2013, 'a portion of these natural or synthetic steroids and their metabolites are excreted into the environment either in animal faeces or urine.' Studies of the effects on fish showed, for example, that male minnows downstream of a large feedlot had 'significantly smaller testes, diminished secondary sexual characteristics, and a reduction in testosterone synthesis' compared with those in other waters. So what does this mean for humans? A World Health Organization report in 2002 concluded that there was clear evidence of adverse impacts on some wildlife, but inconsistent and inconclusive evidence of effects in people. There is a widely accepted association between endocrine disruptors and testicular, breast and prostate cancers, and with changes in male/female birth ratios. But these known risks are all associated with high doses, not the chronic low levels blamed on feedlots. In this case, says the WHO, our understanding is 'much more obscure': human health is subject to so many other factors – diet, lifestyle, sexual behaviour, genetic susceptibility – that the influence of low-level steroids is all but impossible to isolate. The reactions to this scientific black hole neatly encapsulate the contrasting European and American attitudes to risk. In Europe, the precautionary principle is paramount: growth hormones will be deemed dangerous until they are proven safe. In America, nothing trumps the dollar: the hormones will be deemed safe unless proven dangerous. Both these attitudes, however, have one thing in common. The arguments all focus on risks and benefits to *humans*, not on animal welfare.

Though some feedlots have sprung up in the UK they are only a fraction of the size of those in America. In northern Europe generally, rainfall is too heavy to make open pens a realistic option. The animals would wallow like buffaloes in permanent swamps. Indoor housing is the usual preference, though this is no guarantee of higher welfare. CIWF and others complain about permanent tethering, inadequate space and poor lighting, uncomfortable slatted floors, insanitary housing, and absence of pain relief during surgical procedures such as dehorning.

In popular culture, the word 'pig' is code for filth. For comparative psychologists, however, it indicates a superior animal whose intelligence bears comparison with dogs' and chimpanzees'. In the English-speaking world, for reasons of delicacy, it is a word that stops short of the dinner plate, where it transmutes into pork or bacon. The French, too, prefer to serve *porc* rather than face the distasteful realities of *cochon*, though the Spanish, Italians and Germans are happy to tackle *cerdo*, *maiale* and *Schweinfleisch*. The number of pigs slaughtered around the world each year is around 1.4 billion, half of which are bred in China. Some of these are extensively reared in conditions not too different from their natural way of living in small groups of sows with their young, but at least half the world's *porc*, *maiale* and *Schweinfleisch* is produced in factory farms where the word 'natural' means little more than 'alive'. Film of these on the CIWF website comes with parental warnings: 'Watching this clip may be distressing', 'Potentially upsetting scenes of animal suffering'. For those who share the European Union's view that animals are sentient beings, the warnings are not misplaced. One American website even asks for age verification before the full horror can be revealed.

Writers and theologians forever strive to discern some sense of purpose in the chaos of our existence, to achieve some better understanding of 'what it means to be human'. Whatever we think we understand about humanity, it will be unlikely to survive exposure to the covert video recordings made in farms and slaughterhouses by the Humane Society of the United States. The behaviour it recorded has nothing to do with being human, if 'being human' means possessing a moral dimension that distinguishes *Homo sapiens* from all other species. It has nothing to do even with the necessary hardships of mechanised routines. What we see is not mere carelessness. The men in the videos know what they are doing, which is deliberately to inflict pain and injury: cruelty for cruelty's sake. We see piglets tossed and punted like footballs; screaming sows dragged by their snouts; fallen cows – 'downers' in the jargon of the slaughterhouse – dragged by chains or shovelled like living garbage by forklifts; calves too weak to stand being abused, kicked and hauled by their tails; others being sprayed with water to maximise the agony of the electric prods; animals with broken legs being forced to walk. At the end, we see calves not properly stunned before slaughter, some remaining conscious even after their throats have been cut; a calf being skinned alive. On and on it goes, one perversion after another. How is it to be accounted for? The perpetrators were not small-scale rogue operators working beyond sight of the law. America does not do 'small scale'. They were vast industrial enterprises. Nor were they isolated incidents or temporary lapses of self-control. They were the industry standard.

Americans were shocked by what they saw, not least by the fact that the sick cows being dragged into the slaughterhouse were destined for the National School Lunch Program. The result was criminal prosecution and the recall of one hundred and forty-three million pounds of beef, the rough equivalent of two hamburgers for every man, woman and child in the United States. The calf slaughter plant responsible for the worst excesses was shut down. And yet it was not the perpetrators of cruelty that lawyers, state legislators and the industry sought to criminalise, but the whistleblowers who brought the abuses to light. So-called 'ag-gag' laws in some states have banned photography and videos taken in farms and slaughterhouses without the owners' permission, and made it a criminal offence for undercover investigators to take jobs on factory farms. Following pressure from newspapers, the HSUS and more than seventy other campaigning groups, many of these laws have been struck down as infringements of the First Amendment, which protects freedom of speech and of the press. The very fact of the industry's desire for secrecy testifies to the fact that the abuses are not the work of a malign minority. 'It's important to understand', said the agricultural trade magazine *Feedstuffs*, 'that companies and producers can't just say "bad apple" and move on because – to consumers who have seen these videos again and again – there are no bad apples anymore. The bad apple, to consumers now, is the industry.'

Criminality, however, is not the issue. It happens only because the factory farm creates a context for it. The case against intensive farming is not that it is staffed by psychopaths but rather that it is abusive by design. If anything has changed in these places since Ruth Harrison first drew attention to them, then in welfare terms it does not look very much like a change for the better. For many piglets, their first experiences at the hands of humans are tooth-clipping and castration, both commonly performed without anaesthetic. The sounds they emit while undergoing these procedures are not for sensitive ears. The renaming of sow crates as 'gestation crates' has made no difference to the reality. Pregnant sows are still confined for the whole of their sixteen-week pregnancies in metal cages too narrow for them to turn round in, and in which even lying down and standing up are possible only with difficulty. The Fourth Freedom is breached in every way imaginable. It would require unachievable levels of cynicism to suggest that being trapped in a cage, deprived of any opportunity to exercise, explore or forage outdoors – all of which an unconfined sow would do by instinct – could pass as 'natural behaviour'. CIWF's video-clips show the animals biting the bars of their cages, behaviour which CIWF suggests is evidence of what in human terms would be called clinical depression. Despite its illegality in Europe, this still goes on in some EU member states and is normal practice in much of the rest of the world, including America.

After the gestation crate comes the farrowing crate, another cage in which the sow will give birth, and in which she cannot follow her natural instinct to build a nest for her litter. The piglets instead are put into a small cage adjacent to her own, where she has to suckle them through the bars. There they remain for just three or four weeks before they are taken away from her, at least ten weeks earlier than they would be weaned naturally. Two weeks later the sow will be artificially inseminated and the whole cycle begins again. The average production rate of a factory sow is a fraction over two litters per year, and ten or twelve piglets per litter. Such an exhausting work rate cannot be sustained for more than three years, after which she is dispatched to the slaughterhouse, job done.

Her estranged progeny will be fattened in crowded sheds with straw-less, slatted concrete floors, cut off from fresh air and daylight. Boredom and frustration are the inescapable consequences of close confinement in a barren environment where the only outlets for their pent-up energies are to fight and bite each other's tails. Welfare campaigners cite all these things as blatant infringements of the Five Freedoms. Intensive farming presents us with stark choices. Who pays the price? Should it be the animals through their suffering, or consumers paying the extra cost of higher welfare? There are two simple answers to this, and one very complex one. The simple ones are black-and-white absolutes: follow the market and wring every possible egg, drop of milk or ounce of flesh from animals driven to the highest metabolic work-rates they can survive. Or ban the consumption of animal products altogether. The complex answer is the one that CIWF and other welfare organisations around the world are striving to achieve. To make the best of it. To inform and engage public opinion. To put an end to factory farms and all the crates, cages and mutilations that go with them. To respect the sentience of sentient creatures. The task is formidable; the combined forces of commercial interest and political inertia stand as Goliaths in the path of reformers armed with nothing but compassion. In many parts of the world where humans themselves endure poverty, repression and suffering, the comfort of pigs is not a priority. But welfare campaigners are not alone in their opposition to factory farming. Land use is central to the debate around climate change. One of the most persistent misconceptions about intensive farming is that taking animals out of the fields and cramming them into sheds is a way of 'saving land'. It is not. The concentrated, grain-based diets of intensively-farmed animals are voracious swallowers of land, growing crops for animal consumption when, in the view of many, it would be better used for growing food for humans. Producing feed for factory-farmed animals, says the current head of CIWF, Philip Lymbery, in his deeply disturbing book *Farmageddon*, occupies a third of the world's croplands, and livestock altogether consumes a third of the global cereal crop:

> So much land is used for industrially farmed animal feed that if it were all in one field, that field would cover the entire surface of the EU, or half the surface of the US.

To make room for all this, vast tracts of Amazonian rainforest have been replaced with soy. Native people have been expelled from their ancestral lands, sometimes even killed in battles with loggers or police. In developing countries, says Lymbery, growing crops for animals rather than people is 'a new form of colonialism, carved up by richer nations in the cause of cheap meat'. As it was in the days of mineral exploitation in Africa, so it is now. All the benefit is to the colonisers and the markets they serve. For the villagers there is neither crop nor meat. But environmentalists see the problem on a world scale. It is a commonplace of climate activism that avoiding meat and dairy products is the most meaningful gift any individual can make to the global environment, or to their descendants who will have to live in it. Research led by the University of Oxford suggests that if everyone did this, then Philip Lymbery's global field would be reduced by seventy-five per cent. The agriculture industry's greenhouse emissions would be cut by sixty per cent, displaced wildlife could reclaim at least a portion of its lost habitats, and biodiversity would become more than just a pious hope. As it is, eighty-six per cent of land-dwelling mammals in the world are either humans or livestock kept to feed them. Others are critical of the meat industry for its over-reliance on the prophylactic use of antibiotics, which remains standard practice in the US though banned in the EU. This is another calculation in the profit and loss account. Over-use of antibiotics risks the spread of resistant bacteria that could affect as many humans as animals. Resistant bacteria worldwide already cause seven hundred thousand human deaths annually, which the charity Antibiotic Research UK warns could rise to ten million by 2050 if nothing is done to prevent it. No one alive in Pittsburgh or Cincinnati, however, will be unable to afford the price of a steak. The other big issue, the elephant in the cowshed, is climate change. Cattle and other ruminants belch out thirty-seven per cent of the methane attributable to human activity, between seventy and a hundred and twenty kilos per cow per year.

As the US is as much a world leader in climate scepticism as it is in the consumption of beef, the best hope of methane reduction might lie in genetically re-programming cattle to belch less gas. An international research project involving scientists in Australia, Israel and across Europe and the US has demonstrated that this is at least a possibility. 'What we showed', said Professor John Williams of the School of Animal and Veterinary Sciences at the University of Adelaide, 'is that the level and type of methane-producing microbes in the cow is to a large extent controlled by the cow's genetic make-up. That means we could select for cattle which are less likely to have high levels of methane-producing bacteria in their rumen.' Better still from the industry's point of view, Professor Williams held out the possibility that energy saved by the animal in reducing its methane output could generate more efficient meat production – a 'win, win situation' as he puts it. Scotland's Rural College is leading a parallel 'Grass to Gas' project with sheep.

Cleaner belches are one vision of a scientifically engineered future. But it is not one that impresses those who believe it is human behaviour, not the DNA of the cow, that needs to be altered. Vegans and other opponents of the factory farm prefer to pin their faith on meat that needs no animal at all. It is impossible now to walk into any fast-food outlet and not be offered meat- and dairy-free iterations of products traditionally made from animals: hamburgers, cheeseburgers, hotdogs, sausage rolls, doner kebabs, bacon, pasties, sausages, chicken nuggets. Supermarkets have developed meat-free ranges including chicken buckets, 'bacon style' rashers, Mac and Cheese Melts, chorizo sausage, hoisin duck, Greek kebabs, fish fingers and dozens more. Famously, the US brand Beyond Meat created a burger which, by jiggery-pokery involving beetroot juice, 'bleeds' when cut. The pot of gold at the end of the vegetarian rainbow is a substance that is indistinguishable from meat but is made entirely from vegetables. Yet there are limitations. Committed meat-eaters refuse to concede that it has the flavour, or 'mouth-feel', of the real thing. And there is resistance to the *ersatz*: if you want to eat vegetables, then why not just do it? Why pretend they are anything but themselves? Aren't they delicious in their own right? And what about all the additives, preservatives and chemicals essential to fleshless meat that no health-conscious home cook would keep in their own kitchen? How does this match the vegan ideal of eating naturally?

The alternative to all this was foreseen as long ago as 1931 by the former UK Chancellor of the Exchequer and yet-to-be Prime Minister Winston Churchill. In an article headed 'Fifty Years Hence', first published in the Canadian *Maclean's* magazine and later in the British *Strand* and American *Popular Mechanics* magazines, he cast his mind half a century into the future. By that time, he wrote:

> With a greater knowledge of what are called hormones, i.e. chemical messengers in our blood, it will be possible to control growth. We shall escape the absurdity of growing a whole chicken in order to eat the breast or wing, by growing these parts separately under a suitable medium. Synthetic food will, of course, also be used in the future. Nor need the pleasures of the table be banished. That gloomy Utopia of tabloid meals need never be invaded. The new foods will be practically indistinguishable from the natural products from the outset, and any changes will be so gradual as to escape observation.

Churchill's grasp of biological science might have been rudimentary and his time-frame optimistic, but his augury would have aroused the envy of a Sybil. The fortunes already made from fake meat may come to look like chicken feed against the potential of *artificial* meat grown from animal cells, and thus structurally and chemically identical to the real thing. Lab-grown steak is already a reality. On its way to the market it will face many obstacles, including opposition from the farming and meat industries and, in Europe, EU rules that discourage genetic manipulation of the things we eat. But, even against the opposition of America's cattle-men, it is hard to imagine the industry turning its back on a commercial opportunity. The first hamburger grown from cell culture, at the University of Maastricht in 2013, was created from tens of billions of laboratory-grown cells and cost £225,000 to produce. Reactions were polarised. 'Weird and unacceptable' was the reported verdict of Dr Tara Garnett, head of the Food Climate Research Network at the University of Oxford. 'The consistency is perfect ... This is meat to me,' said the American food writer Josh Schonwald when the burger was served at a news conference in London. The man who grew the meat, Professor Mark Post, told journalists that a single sample from one cow would be enough to make eighty-thousand quarter-pound burgers.

The next great challenge, lab-grown steak, was achieved in Israel in 2018. Now comes the race to bring artificial meat to the market, with loosely structured products such as burgers and nuggets leading the rush to the shelves. In December 2020 the Singapore Food Agency issued the world's first official approval for an artificial meat product when 'chicken bites' made by the US company Eat Just passed its food safety review. Advocates of the new technology claim it heralds the end of intensive livestock farming and fulfils all the campaigning ambitions of CIWF and the HSUS. Meat production in the future, they say, will be ethical, efficient and sustainable with no cruelty to animals, no antibiotics and no more effluents creating dead zones in the oceans. Even Peta signed up to the idea of cellular farming. Lab-grown meat, it said, 'will spell the end of lorries full of cows and chickens, abattoirs and factory farming. It will reduce carbon emissions, conserve water and make the food supply safer.' Others are less ready to sign up to this pain-free utopia. Science is no substitute for the animals that God created. Lab-meat will never taste as good as the real thing and the public would rather eat Brussels sprouts than accept anything so unnatural. Even the environmental benefits are illusory. Methane-emitting cows, they say, will simply be replaced by carbon dioxide-emitting laboratories at even worse cost to the climate. One absurdity replaced by another. But who knows? The future, like the past, is a foreign country speaking a different language. In the future as in the past, animals will stand or fall by virtue of their usefulness.

The market is god, and god will decide.

CHAPTER TWENTY-FOUR

Crossing the Divide

NOT MANY DAYS PASS IN BRITAIN WITHOUT SOME RELIGIOUS OR social commentator announcing a pressing desire *to understand what it means to be human*. The answer when it comes will be either a homily built around a recent news event or, more often, something said or done by Jesus. Science is rarely mentioned. Darkness seldom lightened.

A better question might be *what it means not to be an animal*. It is here, on the biological fault-line, that the fixed canons of theology and behavioural science begin to coalesce, though what they hold in common is more faith than reason. Historically, both have been committed to the idea of human exceptionalism, the belief that some kind of impermeable barrier stands between humankind and all other forms of life. We are jealous of our special status. Our upright stance, our large and subtle minds, our language, technology, self-awareness, morality, memory, sense of justice, forward planning and rich emotional lives are uniquely human and thus fully justify the right of dominion we claim over others. To suggest that such faculties might be shared by non-humans is blasphemous in the minds of religious fundamentalists, and heresy in the minds of behaviourists who cling to the Cartesian faith in animals as unreasoning, non-sentient beings. Where humans *think*, others *respond to stimuli*.

The big problem with sealing off the human/animal divide is of course Darwin. All but the most obstinate of (mostly American) creationists now accept that *Homo sapiens* shared much of its ancestry with apes. But their acceptance is limited to the evolution of limbs and organs. It firmly excludes the 'soul' and the uniquely capacious brain that no human-exceptionalist could believe emerged from the skull of an ape. From this perspective we are as different from other species as the sun is from a hole in the ground. What other animal can feel empathy or enjoy friendship? Who else can resolve conflicts by negotiation or political intrigue? Who else plans for the future, prostitutes its females or commits premeditated murder? Who else cheats and tells lies?

None, say the heirs of Descartes and Soapy Sam Wilberforce. What it means to be human is to dwell in the image of God. Yet resistance is crumbling. You cannot go on insisting the world is flat if everyone can see it is round. You cannot go on insisting that there is no continuity across the human/animal divide when everyone can see that there is. While the behaviourists peer out from psychology departments like beleaguered bishops, ethologists in the zoology departments are marking so many similarities between humans and their closest relatives that some are now suggesting it is only a matter of pride that awards *sapiens* a whole genus of its own rather than placing it with chimpanzees and bonobos in the genus *Pan*. Also under assault is the idea that all life-forms exist in a strict vertical hierarchy from highest to lowest with microscopic invertebrates at the bottom and – who else? – humans at the top. Behaviourists consider animals to be inferior to humans because they perform less well at human skills. But the inequity here is easy to spot. Humans do not judge themselves inferior to animals because they perform less well at flying, swimming, sensing a thunderstorm, following a scent or swinging through trees. All species are adapted to thrive in their own environments. A fish is not inferior to a bird because it cannot fly. A cat is not inferior to a fish because it cannot breathe under water. Humans are not inferior to elephants because we cannot lift tree-trunks with our noses. What it means to be human, what it means to be a chimpanzee, what it means to be *anything*, is less a matter of faith than of straightforward belief in what we see, hear and feel.

Behaviourists have constantly redefined 'human' traits such as sentience, cognition, memory, altruism and technical skill in ways designed to place them beyond the reach of other species. Exhibit A is the size of the human forehead. Inconveniently, however, the brains of dolphins, elephants and whales are even larger than ours, and those of monkeys and small rodents bigger in proportion to body-size. This has inspired some exceptional mental gymnastics. As Matt Cartmill explains in *A View to a Death in the Morning*, scientists have 'laboured to redefine brain size, dividing brain weight by basal metabolic rate or some other exponential function of body weight to furnish a standard by which animals' brains can be deemed smaller than ours. The unique bigness of the human brain thus turns out to be a matter of definition.' One such definition is the overall number of *neurons*, the nerve cells that transmit electrochemical signals in the brain and which are often likened to the wiring of a computer. The human brain contains an impressive one hundred billion of these, but an elephant has three times more. Ah, say the behaviourists, but the great majority of these, more than ninety-seven per cent, are in the cerebellum, which regulates *movement*, whereas humans have far more in the cerebral cortex, which regulates consciousness, thought, awareness, memory and language – all the things that make us unique. It is a fundamental principle of Darwinism, however, that the differences between species, including most importantly those between humans and animals, are matters of degree rather than of kind. The DNA of apes and humans differs by just 1.2%. It is unarguably true that humans have bigger brains than apes, and not even the most ardent primatologist would argue for parity in cognition. But that is not the point. You have only to look at a chimpanzee or a bonobo to understand that *what it means to be human* is materially similar to *what it means to be an ape*. Look at the upright stance, the opposable thumbs, the expressive contortions of the face.

The whole point about evolution is that it is *evolutionary*, a process that builds continually upon all that has gone before. The German writer Peter Wohlleben, in *The Inner Life of Animals*, likens it to a computer system. 'Just as code from earlier operating systems is integrated into the latest Windows program, the genetic programming of our ancient ancestors still works within us.' So why should we doubt, or be surprised, that the innate structures of humanity – intelligence, emotions, memory, altruism, empathy – are common to all who share our primate ancestry? And why, then, should we suppose that they are not shared also by dogs, pigs, dolphins or whales? 'We cannot assume', says the Canadian primatologist Anne Russon, Professor of Psychology at York University, Toronto, and a world authority on orang-utans, 'that how we think is necessarily how orangutans think … But, if you work on the premise that to predict how a species will behave, the smart thing to do is to assume that it will behave like other species that it most resembles. Based on how closely the non-human great apes are related to other living species genealogically, in terms of how recently they shared a common ancestor with other species, they are more closely related to humans than they are to any non-human species. On that basis, for the great apes, the proper assumption is anthropomorphism.' Those are the five syllables which, perhaps more than any others, raise the hackles of 'anthropodeniers' who regard any suggestion of human likeness in animals as proof of arrested development.

A younger generation of ethologists now deems it obvious that we share with other species not just the disposition of our vital organs but the roots of our psyche, our culture, our souls. Tribes of apes, elephants, whales and dolphins, like tribes of humans, are not just *populations*. They are *societies*, with all the hierarchical and political complexities of their human equivalents. And, like human societies, they are composed of *individuals*.

Time magazine in 2007 named the Dutch ethologist Frans de Waal as one of the world's hundred Most Influential People. Few people in the twenty-first century have done as much to improve our understanding of the way animals think and behave. His many books on chimpanzees and bonobos discuss them in terms that would fit just as snugly in studies of humans. As in human societies, dominant males rule by consent. Bullies are not tolerated, though Machiavellian schemers are as meddlesome in chimp societies as they are in human. Older females accept responsibility for keeping the peace, resolving disputes and consoling those grieving or in distress. Strong family bonds ensure caring relationships, and reciprocal deal-making ensures social stability. Debts are remembered and honoured as keenly as grudges. But apes are not angels. Vices, too, are shared with humans. Violence grows out of jealousy. Rivalries and resentments may result in murder.

All this is underpinned by a powerful sense of fairness. To prove it, de Waal enlisted a couple of capuchin monkeys, a cucumber and a bunch of grapes. Like most primates, brown capuchins will happily accept a gift of cucumber. Like all primates, however, they would much prefer a grape. In de Waal's experiment two monkeys were each set a task and rewarded with cucumber when they completed it. Result: mutual contentment. But when the test was repeated, only one of the monkeys was rewarded with cucumber; the other was given a grape. Result: the short-changed individual erupted into a violent tantrum and hurled the suddenly despised cucumber back at the researchers.

But of course the anger could be attributed to mere envy or self-interest. A true sense of fairness has to cut both ways. In a moral society, an individual should be as sensitive to the rights of others as to its own. The only alternative is eternal conflict, and no one in that state sleeps easily.

A sense of fairness, no matter how imperfect, is fundamental to any workable human society. So how might it have evolved? The question was explored by one of de Waal's colleagues, Sarah Brosnan, who applied a similar test to chimpanzees. But there was an important difference. This time she observed the reactions of the favoured grape-receiver as well as the one fobbed off with a carrot. Unsurprisingly, the carrot produced exactly the same reaction in the disappointed chimpanzee as the cucumber had done in the capuchin. Much more surprisingly, the one given the grape was also unsettled. It gladly accepted a grape if its partner got one too, but did so less willingly if the rewards were unequal. Sometimes it was so unsettled that the grape was refused. The apparently humanlike sense of fair play was confirmed by another of de Waal's colleagues, Darby Proctor, using a test which previously had been applied only to humans. The so-called Ultimatum Game was devised in 1982 by the German economist Werner Güth and his colleagues as a way of assessing attitudes to fairness, negotiation and trade. The rules are simple. One of two players, the 'proposer', is given a sum of money to split with the other. He can do this in any ratio he likes, from 50:50 to 99:1. The other player, the 'responder', then has to decide whether or not to accept the offer. If he does, the money is divided exactly as the proposer specified. If he doesn't, neither player receives anything at all. The tendency for fair offers to be made, and for low offers to be rejected, is interpreted as proof that humans do not willingly tolerate injustice, and that they will not allow themselves to be demeaned. Taken together, this demonstrates a *sense of honour*. In the chimpanzee test, the proposer was offered a choice of two coloured tokens. If she picked the first colour, say red, then she and her partner would each receive three slices of banana. If she chose yellow, then she would get five slices and her partner only one. Both animals quickly understood the rules of the game. As in the human version, the proposer's offer had to be accepted or rejected by the responder. The proposer was not allowed to pass the selected token directly to the researcher: she had to hand it through the bars to her partner, who then had to decide whether or not to pass it on. Like humans, chimpanzees resented raw deals: a responder offered only one of six available banana slices would bang on the bars and spit mouthfuls of water at the selfish individual on the other side. 'In the majority of trials,' de Waal reported, 'choosers preferred the token that produced equal rewards. At first sight this decision seems costly, but not if we factor in the value of social relationships. Being too selfish might cost a friendship.'

Peter Wohlleben noted similar reactions in his horses. The elder of the pair, twenty-three-year-old Zipy, could no longer digest grass and needed a supplement of grain. Witnessing this, her younger companion, Bridgi, pranced around with flattened ears, showing every sign of petulance. All it took to calm her down was a handful of the precious grain. Though she received far less than Zipy, and though she had to pick her tiny portion out of the grass, Bridgi nevertheless accepted that justice had been done. It was a matter of principle.

Early in 2009, scientists at the University of Vienna took a similar look at pets. Their findings were published in the *Proceedings of the National Academy of Sciences* under the precise if unmelodious title 'The Absence of Reward Induces Inequity Aversion in Dogs', and showed a marked similarity to Sarah Brosnan's monkey test. First the dogs were taught to raise or shake a paw. Then they were tested in a range of different settings, with or without rewards, and with or without the presence of another dog. The results were striking. A dog performing alone would obediently 'give the paw' regardless of whether or not a reward was offered. The same was true of dogs performing in pairs when both were treated equally. But everything changed when one partner alone was rewarded. Then the offended animal would at first hesitate before obeying, then withdraw co-operation altogether. The response was less dramatic than the uncontrolled fury of the chimpanzees, but just as clear in what it showed. The researchers concluded that 'sensitivity to others' efforts and payoffs compared with one's own costs and gains' was likely to have been the driving force in the evolution of co-operation – an essential prerequisite for any functioning society, whether among dogs, apes, lions, orcas, humans or any other species that lives in groups.

Everything from the hunting behaviour of wolves and hyenas to the choreographed movements of a pair of Indian elephants carrying a tree trunk depends on co-operation. In 2015 another group at Vienna tested a pair of ravens. Researchers threaded a piece of string through the bars of their cage, attached it to a piece of cheese and gave each bird one end to hold. It took them very little time to work out that the only way they could get at the cheese was for them to work together. Each had to pull its own end of the string, each with the same degree of force and rhythmically in unison. But co-operation depended on fairness. They would work together only if there was an equitable distribution of the cheese. Any bird that snatched more than its share would forfeit its partner's trust. Apes not surprisingly perform even better. One of the world centres of primate studies is Emory University in Atlanta, Georgia, where Frans de Waal is Professor of Primate Behaviour in the Department of Psychology and director of the Yerkes National Primate Research Centre. Here a whole colony of chimps was left to decide for itself how to manipulate a complicated system of moveable bars in order to access food. This required two or three chimps at a time to work co-operatively at different bars. Despite occasional quarrels and minor scuffles, co-operation scored a clear victory over competition. Work continued almost non-stop for a total of 3,565 co-ordinated pulls. Given such a weight of evidence, de Waal argues, it is truly bizarre that social scientists were able so easily to convince themselves that co-operation between humans was a 'huge anomaly' in the realm of nature. Who now can really believe that animals do not work co-operatively towards shared goals? What we are seeing here is the evolution of a negative impulse, envy, into a positive one, the desire to share. This, says de Waal, is emotional intelligence.

But here are two more trigger-words in the lexicon of exceptionalist dissent: 'intelligence' and 'emotion'. In the old way of thinking these are defining features of one species alone, and anyone who says otherwise is as misguided as the dog-lover who thinks his pet is brighter than his human neighbours. This is a pool into which even Darwin dipped his toe with caution. While it was assumed by most evolutionists that mammals enjoyed some kind of consciousness, notions of intelligence, reason and emotion were matters of dispute even among Darwinians. The man himself had little doubt, though the distinction between 'higher' and 'lower' life-forms remained crucial. In *The Descent of Man*, he says:

> No-one supposes that one of the lower animals reflects whence he comes or whither he goes – what is death, or what is life, and so forth. But can we feel sure that an old dog with an excellent memory and some power of imagination, as shewn by his dreams, never reflects on his past pleasure of the chase? And this would be a form of self-consciousness.

Of course he understood that those blinded by Genesis would reject any suggestion that 'human' faculties, however primitive, could exist in the minds of others, or that there could be any concept of 'mind' in an animal at all. Anyone not convinced by 'what he may observe with his own dogs, that animals can reason,' wrote Darwin, 'would not be convinced by anything I could add'. But it would be very hard, perverse even, not to be convinced by all that has happened since he wrote those words in 1871. Crucially, if we accept an evolutionary explanation for the origin of life and the diversification of species, then similarities between humans and non-humans should be no surprise. Indeed, it would be unintelligent to doubt the intelligence of others. One of the most significant leaps in our understanding happened in Tanzania seventy years ago when the primatologist Jane Goodall dispelled two persistent and deep-rooted misconceptions: first, that only humans could make and use tools; second, that chimpanzees were non-violent vegetarians. Having first seen chimps at termite mounds using grass stalks to fish termites out of their holes, she watched in astonishment as they peeled leaves from twigs and carefully fashioned them into more efficient rods. They were not just making intelligent use of found objects, they were *toolmaking*. The impacts of this discovery were seismic. As Goodall herself wrote in *My Friends the Wild Chimpanzees*, one vital element in the birth of humanity widely accepted by anthropologists was that 'man starts at that stage to make tools to a regular and set pattern'. She allowed that the grasses and twigs used by chimps for termite fishing might not entirely satisfy that definition, yet it was enough to set her mentor, Louis Leakey, the palaeoanthropologist who did more than any other to prove that humans evolved in Africa, into a fluster. 'I feel that scientists holding to this definition', he wrote to Goodall, 'are faced with three choices. They must accept chimpanzees as man, they must redefine man, or they must redefine tools.'

Later observers recorded innumerable examples of chimpanzees making tools for a variety of purposes. Twigs and sticks are used for collecting honey, shelling nuts and picking brains from the skulls of monkeys. Leaves are applied in much the same way that humans use paper in their bathrooms, to clean their bodies and catch their faeces (from which, in a distinctly unhumanlike way, they may pick out bits of undigested food). Chewed and compressed, they become sponges to soak up water from tree-holes. Frans de Waal has since calculated that chimps spend twenty per cent of their waking life working with tools. Typically, he writes, a chimp community will employ up to twenty-five different kinds. But apes are not the only non-human tool-users. Macaques use stones to crack oysters; sea otters float on their backs while cracking shellfish against stone anvils on their chests. Less well known, but considerably more surprising, is the ingenuity of the New Caledonian crow, *Corvus moneduloides*, which is the only non-human species known to make hooks. These it fashions from leaves or twigs and uses to fish for grubs. Such crafted tools do not appear in the human record until the Lower Palaeolithic, or Old Stone Age, which is the stage at which de Waal suggests tool-using animals have now arrived. One must wonder, however, whether a cave-man transported from the Stone Age would display the ingenuity of urban crows in Japan, which lurk by traffic lights and use passing cars as nutcrackers.

The creation, transportation and use of tools illustrates two more qualities which humans in the past have claimed exclusively for themselves: memory and forward planning. There is no point setting out to hunt with tools unless you remember to take them with you; and no point setting out at all unless you know where you are going.

On 10 September 2007, the *New York Times* published an obituary of a parrot. It was, of course, no ordinary parrot. An obituary in the *Times* is not awarded lightly. Among the scientific community at least, Alex, a thirty-one-year-old African grey, was the most famous bird in the world. His last words, addressed to his owner Dr Irene Pepperberg, a comparative psychologist at Brandeis University in Massachusetts, were 'You be good. I love you. See you tomorrow.' Alex had a genuine vocabulary – meaning he could understand what he was saying, not merely 'parrot' the language of others – of more than one hundred English words. He could also count up to six, identify colours and shapes, and differentiate objects by size. When he was shown a familiar object such as a key he could name it correctly, regardless of variations in size or colour. He was also the only non-human animal ever known to have asked a question. 'What colour?' he said when he saw himself in a mirror, and quickly understood that he was grey. Like the human child whose accomplishments he replicated, Alex could also become petulant when bored. Then he would deliberately give wrong answers and demand to be returned to his cage. *Wanna go back!* Inevitably there were sceptics who invoked the memory of Clever Hans, but it encouraged many more to think more open-mindedly about the intellectual abilities of birds in particular and animals in general. One of the most astonishing aspects of Alex's career was his ability to communicate with humans far more effectively than apes trained in sign language could do (and, for that matter, far better than any human can speak in the language of another species). This requires intelligence, and a capacious memory.

Apes, too, will confound anyone still clinging to the wreckage of spe-ciesism. De Waal describes a test which required subjects to remember numbers flashed randomly on a touch screen. The champion at this was a chimpanzee called Ayumu, who could outperform any human. 'Trying the task myself,' de Waal wrote, 'I was unable to keep track of more than five numbers after staring at the screen for many seconds, while Ayumu can do the same after ... just 210 milliseconds.' No animal could survive without memory. Members of a community must be able to remember and recognise each other. Chimpanzees may all look the same to us, but not to each other. Their ability to remember and recognise each other's faces is no less acute than our own. Nor is this ability limited to primates. Wasps, cows and sheep can do it too. More importantly in terms of self-awareness, some animals can recognise *themselves*. After the revelation of tool-use, the second great breakthrough of the twentieth century was the 'mirror test'. This was devised in 1970 by an American psychologist called Gordon Gallup, who anaesthetised a chimpanzee, painted a red dot on its forehead while it slept and then showed it a mirror when it woke up. The chimp's hand immediately flew to the mark, thus proving that it had recognised the reflection as an image of itself and not of another animal. Not every species can do this. Bonobos, orang-utans, dolphins, Asiatic elephants and pigeons all pass the test. Gibbons, many species of monkey, grey parrots, pandas and, most surprisingly, gorillas all fail. So do most human children under the age of two and all dogs. This does not prove that dogs, toddlers and gorillas lack self-awareness; it shows only that the mirror test is not the only way of gauging it. If one species is proven to be self-aware, then no one reasonably can doubt that others are too. That is the true lesson of Gallup's test.

Psychologists have a word for everything. All the stuff people involuntarily fill their minds with – where they've been and why, who they met, what they ate for lunch, what the weather was like, how happy or sad they felt, what they were wearing: in the jargon this is 'episodic memory'. We don't intend or necessarily need to retain it all but, for a while at least, we do.

It is another of those traits once thought exclusively human. Episodic memory is at work, for example, when we suddenly fancy a doughnut, remember which shop sells the jammiest ones and go to buy more. This long-term retention of detailed information is entirely different from what behaviourists call 'associative learning', which is what happens when a dog is 'conditioned' to expect a reward for obeying a command. But an animal capable only of associative learning would not last long in the wild. Chimpanzees in the forest are like shoppers. They remember from one year to the next which trees yield the best fruit, and where they are in the forest. The further away the trees are, the earlier they set out to visit them. Dogs, too, have episodic memory. This was proved by scientists in Budapest who trained a group of dogs to watch their owners perform some simple task – climbing on to a chair, for example – and then to mimic the action when commanded 'Do it!' This of course is the kind of associative learning for which dogs are famous. To confirm episodic memory, the test needed another element. Instead of copying their owners' actions, the dogs were re-trained immediately to lie down. Once they had got used to this and done it for a while, the 'Do it!' command was suddenly sprung on them again. Every animal was tested in this way twice, each time following a different action. After a minute's delay, 58.8 per cent of the dogs performed the correct task. After an hour, 35.3 per cent still did so. This, said the researchers, was proof of episodic memory because the command was unexpected, the witnessed actions had not been given any special significance and the memory faded over time.

With exemplary academic caution, the lead researcher, Claudia Fugazza, would speak only of 'episodic-like' memory, but her findings were widely accepted as proof that such abilities were not unique to primates, let alone to humans, and were likely to be widespread throughout the animal kingdom. Observation bears this out. When drought strikes, for example, a troop of elephants will faithfully follow a matriarch to a distant waterhole, staking their very lives on her memory. Bad experiences also lodge in animals' memories. Researchers at Queen's University Belfast proved that even shore crabs will learn to avoid places where they have suffered electric shocks, just as farm animals avoid electric fences. The crabs' aversive behaviour is convincing evidence that you don't need a backbone to feel pain. In that case, argues Frans de Waal, we should consider them to be sentient, at least 'in the sense of having subjective feeling states' – something perhaps to be borne in mind before we next boil a live lobster or swat a wasp. It may be that the Jains of India, who refuse to harm even the tiniest micro-organism, have science on their side as well as faith.

*

The chimpanzees' shopping expeditions are instructive in another way too. They demonstrate not just episodic memory but also forward planning, yet another intellectual accomplishment formerly ring-fenced by human exceptionalists. However, though they have rowed back somewhat from their Cartesian intransigence, the sceptics still work as hard as they can to skew the debate in favour of their own species. Instead of devising tests to measure the specialised skills that fit animals to their own environments and communities, they prefer to test them against skills, such as spoken language, which are specialisms of *Homo sapiens*. The game is fixed. It is as if they believe every species should aspire to evolve into humans, and that those stuck in the trees, sea or sky have somehow fallen short. But what sense does it make to test apes against children? As de Waal puts it, this is 'an illusion of the same order as throwing both fish and cats into a swimming pool and believing you are treating them in the same way'. Even so, apes raised by humans are just as good at imitating their guardians as young children are, and better than children at grasping the meaning of adults' behaviour. They do not just 'ape' them uncomprehendingly. Learning by example, complying with societal norms, is yet one more way in which apes and humans reflect each other.

The last bastion of human exceptionalism is language. Without vocabulary and syntax, the hardliners say, no organism can be truly cognisant or capable of reason. But every parent knows that children can think, and develop some understanding of cause and effect, before they learn to speak. Dogs dream without human language. Chimpanzees and parrots learn to count without human language. Apes can plan ahead, and many species behave co-operatively without speaking English, German or Chinese. What they *can* do is *communicate*. No prey species, for example, is deaf to its companions' alarm calls. Some, like vervet monkeys, have different alarms for each common predator – leopard, eagle and python – and different responses to each. The leopard alarm dispatches the vervets immediately into the trees; the eagle call sends them diving under the bushes; the python call raises them on to their hind legs, fearfully scanning the ground. All species can distinguish the calls of their own kind. In *The Expression of the Emotions in Man and Animals*, published in 1872, Charles Darwin observed, for example, that humans and apes share a range of mutually recognisable facial expressions. His own summary of Chapter V, 'Special Expressions of Animals', could just as well apply to humans:

> The Dog, various expressive movements of – Cats – Horses – Ruminants – Monkeys, their expressions of joy and affection – of Pain – Anger – Astonishment and Terror

Darwin's point here is that the emotional apparatus of sentient life flows as easily across the human/non-human divide as breathing and the circulation of the blood. They are just as much part of our shared inheritance. The muscles that control and create expressions in the human face are called *mimetic* muscles. In 2008 a multinational research team reported in the *Journal of Anatomy* that the differences between the mimetic musculature of chimpanzees and humans were 'minimal'. Thus we see exactly what we should expect – a wide range of shared expressions from puzzled frown to laughter and fury. Body language, too, has travelled along the same evolutionary channel. The only emotional display unique to humans is the one described by the Anglican bishop Dr Thomas Burgess in his learned work of 1839, *The Physiology or Mechanism of Blushing*.

'Endowing Man with this particular power of exhibiting his internal emotions', he wrote, 'was all part of the Creator's grand design, intended to have a salutary effect in curbing immoral behaviour. 'The civilized', he noted, 'being more prone to blush than the savage.' It would have been a great comfort to him to know that non-human species do not blush at all. But it might not have pleased him quite so much if he had looked instead at facial expressions and gestures. Then he would have found himself sharing common ground not just with dark-skinned humans but also with horses, dogs and apes. A horse, cat or donkey will curl its lip when it encounters an unfamiliar smell; the reverend gentleman would have done the same. His skin would have tingled with goosebumps when he felt cold, afraid or ashamed. An excited chimpanzee with his hair standing on end is feeling the same. Among apes and humans, emotional displays are both shared and understood. See a chimp or bonobo frown when puzzled or annoyed. See a dog avoid eye contact when caught stealing. See a winning athlete raise his arms and pump out his chest, chin up and teeth bared. Watch the rolling swagger of a world leader strutting in the public gaze. Map all these movements on to an alpha chimpanzee and you will struggle to notice the difference.

Ears tell a similar story. Humans express emotions by changing the frequency of their vocal sounds; so do horses. Our anthropocentricity drives us to invest much more effort in trying to teach birds, dogs, chimps and even elephants to articulate human words than in trying to understand the animals' own languages. Sometimes we literally cannot hear them: elephants communicate at a pitch too low, and bats and mice too high for the human ear. But scientists increasingly are beginning to listen, and the results are thrilling or discomfiting according to your point of view. For many years after their alarm calls were recorded in Kenya during the 1970s, vervet monkeys were the superstars of non-human communication, masters of what scientists cautiously labelled a 'language-like' form of communication. These were not just involuntary expressions of fear, but properly formed sounds with precise meanings. But *language proper*, with different forms and figures of speech, syntax or grammar? That was another matter entirely. Nineteenth-century bishops and twentieth-century behaviourists could all agree on that. When all else was stripped away, it was language that made us human. Forty years later, the world is beginning to sound very different.

For more than thirty of those years, Professor Con Slobodchikoff of Northern Arizona University has been watching and listening to prairie dogs. What he heard is something far too sophisticated to be called merely 'language-like'. The animals' alarm calls did not just indicate whether the threat came from hawk, dog or coyote: they also specified an intruder's size, colour and speed. When the threat was human, they produced different sounds for people wearing different coloured shirts, and different calls for a man with or without a gun. In Slobodchikoff's opinion this is a vocal system so flexible and so complex that the only possible word for it is *language*. Songbirds, elephants, whales and dolphins all have vocabularies that might not be far different in their expressive range than the proto-languages of the earliest humans. The human brain is three times larger than a chimpanzee's but the area that controls speech is lodged in the left side of both, and vocalisation is an essential part of the chimp's behaviour. Thus another supposed line of demarcation is rubbed away. Communication does not separate humans and non-humans. The difference between us and them is, as Darwin proposed, only a matter of degree, a slope and not a cliff.

Much of what humans communicate, and much of what passes between animals, is emotion. Few non-scientists who spend time with animals have ever doubted that they feel and display the same emotions as humans do: fear, joy, despair, shame, embarrassment, grief, gratitude, resentment, disgust, envy, hatred, love. A younger generation of scientists now thinks the same. Yet the scepticism of older behaviourists has not yet gone away. They deplore all talk of non-human mental states as unscientific, romantic and naive. You cannot look directly into the mind of another, they say. Therefore we have no 'observable data', and without observable data there is no science. But this argument is easily stood on its head. Absence of evidence is not evidence of absence. A lack of data does not prove that emotions in animals do not exist (fundamentalists do not require data to proclaim their faith in God), and the deniers still have Darwin to contend with. What reason is there to doubt that animal and human emotions, like human and animal bodies, have developed through natural selection along the same evolutionary pathways? Ethologists argue from this that emotions are *biological*, as necessary to the continuance of life as the organs of the body. The process of natural selection would not have burdened animals with them unless they conferred some evo-lutionary advantage. How could any species survive if it felt no fear? How could a mother raise a baby without love? How could any society flourish without empathy?

Emotions are the engines that drive actions. They are both visible and, in many cases, contagious. Fear spreads faster than a virus. But emotions amount to much more than just raw fear or the fight-or-flight mechanism which the behaviourists interpret as instinctive reflexes. In *Through a Window: My Thirty Years with the Chimpanzees of Gombe*, Jane Goodall describes the grief of a young chimpanzee after the death of his mother. Like a distraught human with nothing left to live for, he withdrew from the community, stopped eating and sank into a deep depression.

The last time I saw him alive, he was hollow-eyed, gaunt and utterly depressed, huddled into the vegetation close to where Flo had died ... the last short journey he made, pausing to rest every few feet, was to the very place where Flo's body had lain. There he stayed for several hours, sometimes staring and staring into the water. He struggled on a little further, then curled up – and never moved again.

Across many species, including birds, displays of grief by bereaved mothers are as painful and desperate as those of any human. A chimpanzee may cradle her dead baby for several weeks, ignoring the stench until the corpse disintegrates in her arms. An elephant will hang her head over a dead calf, and a dolphin will float with her dead baby for days on end. In 2018 an orca was seen to carry her stillborn calf aloft for seventeen days. Breeding partners, too, are bitterly mourned. Konrad Lorenz likened the grief of a bereaved greylag goose to that of an orphaned child. 'The eyes sink deep into their sockets, and the individual has an overall drooping experience, literally letting the head hang.' But grief does not come from nowhere. First there has to be something to grieve. 'Grief is the price we pay for love,' said Queen Elizabeth II at a memorial service for victims of 9/11. But do birds and animals really love each other in the romantic sense understood by humans? The answer varies from species to species. Some, like rabbits, warthogs and bonobos, guarantee the spread of their genes by promiscuously mating with as many partners as they can manage. Others prefer lifelong pair-bonding with its promise of mutual support and nurtured offspring. Then the processes of courtship and monogamous union, till death do us part, bear comparison with human marriage.

Watch how a human relationship begins and develops: the repeated touching, the lingering embrace, the joined hands, the longed-for intimacy and growing stability of a settled marriage. Now watch the courtship of a pair of right whales, first tentatively and then continually touching each other with their flippers, the touches stretching into a long slow caress that ends with a hug. Watch a young raven showing off to his intended mate with daring displays of aerobatic flight. Watch the impressed female join him in an aerial dance, somersaulting and locking their toes as if holding hands. On the ground they coo soft nothings and stroke each other with their beaks before bonding for life. Where are the data that say this is not love? Watch an elephant reach out with its trunk to comfort a bereaved mother or guide a blind companion. Think about the brown bear at Budapest Zoo that rescued a drowning crow from the moat. What word better describes deeds like this than *compassion*? And what is compassion if not concern for others, born out of empathy and altruism, the base materials of all functioning societies? Chimpanzees, like humans, rush to the aid of those in distress. If a vampire bat fails to find a blood-victim one night, then another will regurgitate part of its own meal to tide it over. Just as human societies deliver food to the frail and elderly, so do chimpanzees bring food and water to those too old to fend for themselves. Bonobos seem to take pleasure in the simple act of giving. This goes beyond even compassion or sympathy for the plight of another. This is *empathy*, the ability of one individual to imagine himself in the place of others and to understand their feelings by identifying with them. From here it is but a short step to what psychologists call a *theory of mind*, the awareness that others possess knowledge, feelings and intentions different from one's own. Apes, monkeys, ravens and humans are among the species endowed with this special understanding of others. But it is not all back-slapping and shared bananas. Empathy inspires cruelty as well as kindness. No torturer applies his craft without understanding the pain he will cause. Apes, too, know all about pain and how to inflict it on enemies and rivals, even to the extreme of premeditated murder.

To understand the cruelties of tyrannical rulers and regimes, therefore, we need look no further than our evolutionary fellow-travellers. Hitler, Pol Pot and Saddam Hussein rode on the backs of power-crazed, resentful chimpanzees. To trace the roots of modern politics we have to look back far beyond Machiavelli to the machinations of conspiring apes, to the skill with which alpha-female chimpanzees resolve conflicts and soothe hurt feelings, to the deceit and sometimes brutal effectiveness of alliances. All these things are a construction kit for the modern human. Almost everything we do relies upon reciprocity, the grandmotherly virtue of do-as-you-would-be-done-by, or give-in-order-to-get. The altruism of the vampire bat is grounded in self-interest, the expectation that one good turn deserves another. What are industry and commerce if not complex networks of reciprocity? What is a redistributive tax system if not a vampire-style blood-sharing deal? What is morality if not the grown-up scion of ancient envy, the primal sense of unfairness in creatures unfairly rewarded?

It is difficult – for this writer, impossible – to conceive of any aspect of human behaviour that, for better or worse, does not find some echo in the minds and bodies of others. Virtue and vice are there in the evolutionary blueprint. Every human trait has a non-human champion. The importance we attach to cleanliness; our disgust at putrefaction and reluctance to foul our own nests are shared by a plethora of others, not least by the naturally fastidious pig. The most abundant sources of emotional hand-me-downs are surely our own closest relatives. Like us, chimpanzees signal affection by touching, kissing and cuddling. Like us they are strongly motivated by sex, a commodity which females are willing to trade for fruit and meat, but like us they avoid inbreeding by choosing partners from different family groups. Like us they work with tools, harbour grudges, reward favours, make lasting friendships and live in patriarchal communities. Like us they resist invasion and defend their territories with as much violence as it takes to destroy or be destroyed by the invaders. Whence came humans' thirst for war? Having descended from apes, wrote Richard Wrangham, the British-born Professor of Biological Anthropology at Harvard, modern humans are 'the dazed survivors of a continuous, five-million-year habit of lethal aggression'.

It could have been different: the chimpanzees' smaller cousins, the bonobos, are one of the most peace-loving species on the planet. But for us the die was cast when some smart bipedal opportunist picked up a stick or a stone and realised its lethal potential. We see it still in country after country, conflict after conflict, the endless search for ever more deadly sticks and stones, in every quarter of the world. But this does not mean we are incapable of using our brains to exercise self-restraint. So here is another opportunity for the exceptionalists to claim human exclusivity. What other genus than *Homo* exercises self-control? The answer is the very same one that put the stick in our hands. The Ultimatum Game, though designed to reveal a sense of fairness, is just as much a test of self-control: the animal forgoes an immediate reward in return for friendship. Our inherited capacity for self-restraint is one of the things we most admire in ourselves. Few parents in the developed world fail to teach their children to forgo a chocolate bar before lunch.

Pleasure, too, is an important part of our inheritance. We share a sense of fun. When we are supremely happy we jump for joy. So do chimpanzees. So do rats, dogs, cats and horses. All these, like ourselves, indulge in activities which have no other observable purpose than to create amusement, and for which the only word in human language is *play*. Buffaloes, like children, will run and slide across ice apparently for the sheer exhilaration of it. Crows have been observed sliding down roofs on salvaged plastic lids. As soon as they reach the bottom they pick up their toboggans, climb back to the top and do it again. For the behaviourist with his clipboard and laptop this does not count as 'observable data'. It is mere anecdote and proves nothing. More naive and romantic observers, however, might be inclined to think that what looks like fun *is* fun. It is ingrained in our own selves. A human's excitement in chasing a ball around a field is no less than a dog's. The only difference is in the rules. Young orang-utans and chimpanzees laugh contagiously when they play with each other, just as children do. Like children too, they laugh when they are tickled. If laughter is one of the great joys of being human, it is also one of the great joys of being an ape or a rat.

Darwin's view that emotions flowed across the human/animal divide is beyond rational dispute. Neuroscience is showing us that the similarities between the rat and the human brain are so slight that the former can be used to inform studies of the latter. 'Dogs trained to lie still in a brain scan', writes Frans de Waal in *Mama's Last Hug*, 'show activity in the caudate nucleus when they expect a hot dog in the same way this region lights up in businessmen who are promised a monetary bonus'. Thus science, finally, is steering us in the same direction as our eyes and our ears. It is not that emotions *cross* the inter-species boundary. There is no boundary at all. No them and us. Just us. All of us, in this world together.

CHAPTER TWENTY-FIVE

Rather Them Than Us

AT VERSAILLES ON 19 SEPTEMBER 1783, THE LAST BOURBON king of France, Louis XVI, and his unpopular queen Marie-Antoinette were joined by a crowd of thousands to watch the Montgolfier brothers show off their miraculous new hot air balloon. The point of the demonstration was twofold: to show how well the balloon could float through the air, and to prove that flying was safe. To test the latter hypothesis, Louis had proposed sacrificing a couple of convicts. Risking royal displeasure, the brothers sent up instead a sheep, a rooster and a duck. Happily for all concerned, after an erratic, wind-blown flight that ended two miles away in a wood, all three pioneers stepped unscathed from their cage, though the rooster had taken a kicking from the sheep. From lift-off to touchdown the flight had lasted just eight minutes.

Montauciel the sheep and his two fellow travellers were the first animals to deputise for humans on a flying machine, but they were far from the last. Up into the sky, then on through the stratosphere, hurtled an assorted menagerie that extended from insects to dogs, chimpanzees and finally to men and women. The very first creatures sent into outer space, on 20 February 1947, were fruit flies launched from the United States to an altitude of sixty-eight miles in a captured German V2 rocket. Unlike many of those who followed them, they survived both the three-minute ascent and the parachute back to Earth. The first mammal in space, on 11 June 1948, was an anaesthetised rhesus monkey named Albert, who died of suffocation even before his capsule had reached its maximum height

331

of thirty-nine miles. He was succeeded in the following year by Albert II, who survived an ascent to eighty-three miles only to die on the way home when his parachute failed. The line of succession continued through Alberts III, IV and V, none of whom survived. It was not for another ten years, until 28 May 1959, that a rhesus monkey named Able and a squirrel monkey named Baker returned alive together from a journey into space, having rocketed to a height of 360 miles, survived a gravitational pull thirty times greater than that on Earth and been weightless for nine minutes. Able's luck was short-lived – she died during an operation to remove an electrode from her body – but Baker survived to die of natural causes in 1984. While the US launched a variety of monkeys, the Soviet Union took the less expensive option of stray dogs picked up from Moscow streets. One of these, a young husky named Laika, aboard Sputnik 2 on 3 November 1957, became the first animal to orbit the Earth. It is not known how many orbits she actually completed before her life-support system failed and she died from heat-stress. Other space adventurers included worms, beetles, spiders, newts, rats, mice, rabbits, cats and a pair of tortoises which, riding aboard the Soviet Zond 5, won the race to circle the moon in 1968.

The animals between them proved that gravitation, weightlessness and radiation in space were all manageable and survivable, and added to the already long list of human surrogates that were the advance guard of physiological, psychological and medical research. Science long ago took the view that dog, monkey, rat and tortoise were, in their various ways, sufficiently similar to humans to be employed as their special representatives, in space as on Earth. This not merely implies, but *insists*, that animals share human characteristics. Otherwise, what would be the point? And the word for that way of thinking is the one least likely to spring from the lips of a scientist: *anthropomorphism*. Despite the best efforts of Charles Darwin, George Romanes, Margaret Washburn and many others, it remains a curse-word, used to vilify uncritical sentimentalists who prefer anecdote to data. While *zoomorphism* – assigning bestial qualities to humans, and thus understanding a 'higher' form of life by comparison with a 'lower' – is held to be scientifically valid, the opposite is condemned in the same breath as alchemy and divination. But this is to proceed with one eye closed. If non-human organisms really do in some respects resemble *Homo sapiens* then 'anthropodenial', as Frans de Waal has called it, serves only to blind us to observable facts. What cannot be denied is that anthropomorphism is as old as humanity, and has been a profound and far-reaching influence in shaping the way we live. How else than by attributing thoughts, feelings and motivations to other species did our earliest ancestors establish a relationship with them? How, without anthropomorphism, could we have thought of livestock farming or the keeping of pets? More latterly, how could the welfare and animal rights movements have flourished without anthropomorphic ways of thinking? How else would wildlife documentary-makers, routinely abused for distorting the science, engage public sympathy? How else would children's authors or animators win their adoring audiences?

It remains true, however, that anthropomorphism *can* very easily drown itself in sentimentality. The results are visible every day in parlours, parks and gardens. Pet-ownership has a history of ridicule that stretches back to ancient Rome. It has been mocked as an aberration comparable to prostitution: the desperate recourse of inadequate people unable to form relationships with others of their own kind. Unlike stock-keeping, it confers no evolutionary advantage and therefore is both perverse and pointless. If it has any rational basis at all, then it must lie in what psychologists have called the 'cute response' triggered by kittens and puppies with their huge eyes and soft plump bodies demanding love and protection. This is why pug-faced dogs are bred to resemble human babies. But research increasingly suggests this is far from the whole story. It does not explain why, if pet-ownership is such a reliable signifier of human weakness, pet-owners – at least in the western world since the late twentieth century – have become the majority. The sixty-six million people who live in Britain own between them an estimated fifty-one million pets. Twenty per cent of German households have a dog, and twenty-three per cent have a cat. Are we all becoming less adequate human beings? Can it be believed that our dog-walking friends are all socially inadequate? As James Serpell noted in *In the Company of Animals*, 'No-one seems to have noticed that in the US there are nearly as many cats and dogs as there are television sets.' Writing in 1986, he found it extraordinary that so much research had been devoted to the effects of television and so little to the effects of pet-ownership. The only way to interpret this, he said, was as 'a symptom of prejudice'.

Thirty-five years later we know a little more.

Science now suggests that pet-owners' eagerness to attach human emotions and motivations to their animals is very far from the category error of ancient prejudice, and that it is a source of *strength*, not weakness. It could be that science finally is waking up to what everyone else has always known and understood. Pets are good for you.

James Serpell argues that people keep animals for the same reason they wear warm clothing: 'because by doing so they enhance their own health and quality of life'. Pet-ownership is socially beneficial because it enrols people in a network of like-minded others – there is always someone to chat to in the park – and the animal itself is a source of comfort at times of stress. It promotes a sense of usefulness that comes from being responsible for the well-being of another, and of personal value expressed through the animal's loyalty. All this translates into better physical health. In general, people who feel socially supported and shielded from loneliness have less chance of heart disease, strokes, cancer or depression. Studies of heart-attack survivors at the universities of Maryland and Pennsylvania showed that their blood pressure fell to below even normal resting levels when they were reunited with their dogs. Researchers at the University of Ohio reported 'marked and sustained improvement' in psychiatric patients partnered with dogs, and a study of nearly six thousand subjects in Melbourne confirmed the inverse relationship of pet-ownership with heart disease. As with more conventional therapies, what seems to matter is the size and regularity of the dose. The closer the attachment, the greater the gain, which is perhaps why dogs are better for their owners than cats.

This comfortable generalisation, however, runs out of road when closeness turns to intimacy. Bestiality is illegal in most US states, where prosecutions are more numerous than a suburban dog-walker might suppose. Reliable figures nevertheless are hard to come by, though the

American sexologist Alfred Kinsey reported in the 1940s that roughly eight per cent of American men, and half of all 'farm-bred males', admitted having sexual contact with other species. The bias towards farm boys meant that the most frequent, if not most fragrant, recipients of their favours were unspecified 'ungulates' rather than pets, though the 3.6% of adolescent females who confessed to bestiality were more inclined to dogs. Insofar as the boys were concerned, Kinsey attributed their zoophilic yearnings to the absence of women on remote farms and ranches. 'To a considerable extent,' he wrote, 'contacts with animals are substitutes for heterosexual relations with human females.' Several later studies, however, have shown that some men, given a choice, do prefer animals. In 2009 the science journal *Archives of Sexual Behavior* reported on the case of a forty-seven-year-old medical doctor and father of two who found his wife to be an inadequate substitute for a horse. He and many other well-educated professionals dispelled the myth, promulgated by Kinsey, that zoophiles were all either mentally deficient or too unsavoury to be attractive to women. So why is it that most people feel such revulsion at the very idea of inter-species sex?

'Unnatural' sex always draws a visceral response, an emotional reflex that presumably evolved over millions of years. Darwinian theory dictates that this necessarily must convey some evolutionary benefit. There is horror from the animals' perspective too. Animal rights and welfare organisations are appalled by what they regard as sexual abuse, cruelly inflicted upon innocent creatures by human predators. When another US state voted for prohibition, the Humane Society of America hailed it as 'a great victory for the animals of Ohio'. Forty states now have laws against bestiality, half of which class it as a felony. Yet the zoophiles themselves complain that they are victims of injustice, as unfairly treated as homosexuals were at the turn of the twentieth century. What they practise, they insist, is *love*, not abuse, the very antithesis of cruelty. To say the very least, it would require a revolution in public opinion for their plea for tolerance to arouse anything much kinder than contempt. British newspapers bristled with indignation in the autumn of 2017 when they learned of 'sick tourists' travelling to Serbia to enjoy the favours of cows, goats, sheep, donkeys, dogs, cats and geese at 'animal brothels'. Rates for sex, it was reported, ranged between seventy and one hundred and fifty euros, plus a surcharge of fifty euros for filming. Alfred Kinsey would hardly know where to begin.

Conventional animal-lovers also delight in excess. They show extremes of love and mourning, extremes of anthropomorphic projection, extremes of ostentation and expense. For unconditional love, it would be hard to beat the example of a bereaved hairdresser in Texas. Though the woman was not exactly overjoyed when her pet Rottweiler ate her four-week-old baby daughter, she was distraught when told the animal itself would have to be destroyed. 'I can always have another baby but I can't replace my dog Byron.' Other bereaved pet-owners have committed suicide, and men have divorced wives who loved their dogs more than they loved their husbands. The temptation to regard animals as small pet humans is difficult for many owners to resist, despite all that the word 'owner' implies. This imposes peculiar pressures on pets, most especially on dogs, in ways unknown to their wild forebears. In the manner of gods, we like to create beings in our own image, or to our own design. Wolves and wildcats are now vastly outnumbered by their tame descendants, many of which are unrecognisable as members of the same species. Cosmetic breeding, the creation of four hundred distinct dog 'breeds' (in nature they would be called sub-species), represents an extraordinarily consistent human effort spread across thousands of years. The late archaeozoologist Juliet Clutton-Brock in *Domesticated Animals from Early Times* suggested that the Pekingese should be seen as 'one of man's greatest achievements', though 'most improbable' might be nearer the truth.

Animal welfare groups now campaign against what they see as the purposeful creation of animals with genetic defects. By 'defects' they mean respiratory problems, skeletal deformities, malformed eyes and teeth, excessive skin-folding, over-long ears, deafness, hairlessness, vulnerability to injury and aggression. The problem they face is that these are the very characteristics that distinguish one breed from another – the squashed face of the bulldog, the miniature legs of the dachshund, the bulging eyes of the Boston terrier, the short skull and truncated nose of the Persian cat. Breed standards – the blueprints against which show judges award points – are catalogues of deformity. Ban deformity and you ban the breeds. The most notorious example, ironical in a country such as Britain whose emblem it has become, is the bulldog – an animal so incompetent that nothing like it could have survived to evolve naturally. It has been designed to have such an enormous head and such narrow hips that it is rarely able to give birth other than by caesarean section and is more vulnerable than any other breed to hip dysplasia.

Like many other show breeds the bulldog is incapable of independent survival, a corruption of nature that throws evolution into reverse. In Darwinian terms this is *un*natural selection, the survival of the weakest. In one breed after another, nature's revenge is cruel. The unnaturalness of this process is most obvious in the animals' brains. When wild species evolve to become larger or smaller, so their brains swell or shrink proportionally. Not so in designer dogs, whose bodies get bigger or smaller around brains that remain roughly the same. The most obvious result of this is that the smaller breeds have much larger heads in proportion to their pelvises and, like the bulldog, have difficulty giving birth. It is a perfect example of the way selecting for a desired trait will often drag less desirable ones in its wake. Hips are misaligned. Eyes scoured by inwardly-turned lids. There are respiratory diseases, horrible skin infections, thyroid deficiencies, sexual dysfunction (the bulldog, belying its virile image, is frequently unable to mate), blindness, deafness, heart murmurs, cancers. Dog-lovers are often prominent in protests against other forms of animal exploitation in laboratories, factory farms and zoos. The irony is that if the English bulldog were the genetically engineered product of a biotechnology company, then our view of it would be very different. As a society we are revolted by the idea of scientists deliberately programming mice to develop illnesses or deformities, but are ready to reward dog-breeders who do the same. Illogicalities abound. We imprison budgerigars (birds of flocking habit) alone in tiny cages but recoil in horror at doing the same to robins (birds of solitary habit), when the opposite would make better sense. We swerve to avoid wild rabbits on country roads but allow tame ones to be eaten alive by maggots.

In Britain, the rabbit is the fourth most popular pet after dogs, cats and fish. It is also one of the most misunderstood. Unlike the carnivorous cat and dog, the rabbit is a prey species, on the menu of every hunter from weasel upwards. Its natural condition therefore is trepidation, and without sensitive handling it will spend its entire life in fear. Without companionship it suffers from boredom and frustration, leading to the kind of aggressive behaviour that will accelerate the downward spiral of neglect common among young owners. Its health suffers through lack of exercise, faulty diets and inadequate housing. As a bare minimum it needs enough space to stretch upright on its hind legs and to take three or four hops in either direction – a distance of perhaps eight feet. Osteoporosis is a common result of enforced inertia, and obesity the result of feeding chocolate to an animal that thrives on hay. All pet species, most especially dogs, run the risk of gastronomic abuse. A survey in 2018 revealed that sixty per cent of cats and fifty-six per cent of dogs in the US were overweight or obese. In Britain, vets estimate that nearly fifty per cent of dogs are overweight, shortening their lives by an average of two years. Many are so fat through overfeeding and insufficient exercise that their bones and muscles can no longer support their weight. To compound the illogic, any member of the public who sees an underweight animal will call the RSPCA. But no one calls to report an *over*weight animal, even though its treatment may be just as cruel. Cats suffer too. When they rub themselves around their owners' legs it is social contact they are looking for, not food. But food is what they get.

It is not just bodies that are warped by cosmetic breeding. Animals' mental states, emotions and behaviour are bent out of shape too. The fidelity bred into a pet dog, for example, may result in over-dependence on the human, and panic when it is left alone. From the owner's point of view, the very worst thing a pet can do is to behave 'naturally' rather than in the neo-humanoid way expected of it, in which case it will risk incarceration, thrashing or abandonment. What is behaviour in a wild animal is *mis*behaviour in a pet. No reliable data exist on the numbers of pets discarded each year, but some rough idea may be taken from the numbers brought into rescue centres. In the US this has declined from a peak of thirteen million cats and dogs in 1973, but the total still ranges between six and eight million. Despite being mainly in good health and suitable for rehoming, three million of these are destroyed. The risk of divorce is even greater with exotics such as snakes, monkeys and cheetahs, which are kept more for status than companionship and are not easily persuaded to give up their wild habits.

Rights advocates dislike the very word 'pet'. They prefer to emphasise the mutuality of the relationship by speaking rather of 'companion animal'. Some go further, arguing that the rights of animals must include the right not to have their freedoms constrained by human ownership in any circumstance whatsoever. When interviewed by the author of this book for the *Sunday Times Magazine* in 2003, the leading British theologian of animal rights, Andrew Linzey, condemned the buying and selling of pets as completely as he rejected the consumption of meat. 'It is a question of justice,' he said, 'not of taste, or philanthropy or feelings ... Human beings have been given power over creation not to despoil what God has made but to serve it and protect it. We have nothing less than a sacred commission to serve the earth, to honour life and love our fellow creatures.' For those without religious faith, the ideas of 'honour' and 'love' work just as well if 'nature' is substituted for 'God': the responsibility is the same. But is not pet-keeping a valid expression of that love? 'It can be,' Linzey said, 'but we need to distinguish between selfish loving and altruistic loving. Most pet owners get more out of their pets than pets get out of their owners.' Rights activists also object to pet-ownership on the grounds that other species have to die in order to feed them, though this overlooks the fact that the nature of all carnivores, whether wild or domestic, is to consume the flesh of others, and that those destined for the stomachs of pets will have easier deaths than those pursued by hyenas. But there is an environmental issue too: it has been estimated that pet food accounts for twenty-five per cent of the global impacts of meat production in terms of land-use, the con-sumption of water, fossil-fuels, and pollution.

For welfare organisations, the principal concerns after cosmetic breed-ing and overt cruelty are the environments in which the animals are kept. 'Most environmental conditions provided by pet-owners', Andrew Linzey said, 'are totally unsuitable for the animal – in some cases even worse than in the laboratory or farm.' One useful and oft-quoted definition of cruelty is to deny an animal the right to perform its natural behaviours. These may include freedom of association with others of its own species, freedom to possess and wag an undocked tail, appropriate access to food and water, and freedom to exercise. It can be argued that one or more of these is breached whenever a solitary animal is kept inside a human home. But the conundrum here is the same as it is in factory farms. The animals are not bred to be wild. They are bred to be domestic. So what exactly *are* the behavioural needs of a selectively bred animal designed for the home? What is its true nature? It would be hard to argue that it is any kindness to a budgerigar to deny it the freedom of flight, a rabbit the freedom to run, or a small rodent any acquaintance with its own species. But it would be equally hard to deny the obvious contentment of so many dogs and the apparent ease of their relationships with their owners.

So why do we do it? What part of our human nature is it that prompts us to keep animals as ornaments, companions or playthings? When or how was this inserted into our genetic identity? The common assumption is that pet-keeping is a uniquely human phenomenon. But this was disproved in 2001 when an article in the *American Journal of Primatology* reported that wild chimpanzees at Bossou in Guinea had been seen catching tree hyraxes – nocturnal mammals which resemble large guinea-pigs – and keeping them alive rather than eating them. One adolescent female carried a hyrax for fifteen hours, groomed it and slept with it, much as an adolescent human might do with her puppy. However one chooses to interpret this, on a linear scale it looks a lot closer to pet-keeping than it does to predation, and yet another breach in the crumbling wall of human exceptionalism.

Moral objections to pet-ownership are confined to a relatively small number of people whose position on animal rights is absolute. The same cannot be said about medical and physiological research. Nothing unites rights and welfare activists, or inflames public opinion, more than a photograph of a monkey gripping the bars of a laboratory cage or strapped to an apparatus with wires poking out of its head. Commercial and university research establishments are characterised as hell-holes staffed by monsters, and have attracted the attention of people armed with firebombs and baseball bats.

Any visitor to such a place has to pass through a security system designed to exclude everything from an eco-terrorist to a microbe. When the author of this book, after prolonged negotiation, was given admittance to a university laboratory in England, he had to exchange his own clothes for paper underpants, pyjamas, zip-up boiler suit, overshoes, hairnet and mask. If animal laboratories were truly hell-holes, then this was a peculiarly sterile vision of hell. Heaven forbid that a bacterium should find its way to the transgenic mice. Even my spectacles had to be left at the door. At other institutions I was able to observe experiments on monkeys, dogs, pigs, rodents and fish. Here is an edited version of what I wrote at the time:

Many times over I have heard hopeful news for cancer, Parkinson's and dementia sufferers. I have heard bad news for manufacturers of salty snacks and fizzy drinks, and endless confirmation that the scientific and ethical dilemmas of medical research are seldom simple. World experts on neuro-science and pharmacology have patiently explained the breakthroughs they are working towards, but always on condition of anonymity. In one lab I had to surrender my watch in case it concealed a camera. At one institution, a breeding centre for macaques, I was photographed, had my passport copied and not allowed to move without an escort. At another my car was searched.

The monkeys preferred for laboratory use are macaques. At the breeding unit, as far as I can see, these are happy monkeys, secure in their identities and comfortable with handlers who know them by name. The building is modern, airy and filled with light. Our arrival in the glass-roofed service corridor is greeted with a cacophony of squeaks that sounds like a race between rusty wheelbarrows. In fact the source is a range of mirrors, one outside each glass-fronted room, which the monkeys can swivel by turning a handle. They simply want to see who is coming. Inside each climate-controlled 'free-roaming room' is a colony of a dozen or so macaques, ranging from alpha males right down to suckling infants. Instead of trees they have an aerial jungle of climbing frames, swings and play equipment, much of it made from fire-hose.

It all looks believably natural. Mothers groom their babies. Youngsters race through the branches of the surrogate trees. Alpha males never let anyone forget who is boss. They have an enviable diet. The fruit in the cold store looks as if it might have come straight from Waitrose. There are fresh eggs (they like them hard boiled) and a muesli of mixed grains and seeds. All this is scattered for them to forage among the straw and wood shavings on the floor. Sitting among them and feeding them party-treats – McVitie's digestive biscuits, popcorn and Ribena – was a joyful, life-affirming experience I'll not forget. And yet ...

There are hints that this five-star mini-resort has a darker side, and that all this luxury will have to be paid for. Each animal has its name tattooed across its chest, the initial letter indicating the year of its birth. This year it is T, so here are Tim, Tallulah, Titan, Toots and Tigger. There are 237 monkeys in all, ranging from newborns to a greybeard of 21. Some will be kept for breeding. The rest will be taken to institutions where their living brains and bodies will be used in research. Some will improve our knowledge of infection; some will help prevent blindness; many more will be used in neuroscience. Knowing this, it is hard to enjoy the party without a pang of guilt.

Typically they will be immobilised by a surgically implanted 'head-post'. Electrodes then will be planted inside their skulls to monitor their brain activity while they perform a range of tasks involving memory, learning or physical dexterity. Drugs may be used to stimulate or inhibit particular kinds of behaviour, and parts of the brain may be removed. Some of them will suffer strokes. None of this is easy to think about, never mind look at. For medical science, the aim is a better understanding of the brain, and especially of neurological diseases such as Parkinson's and dementia. That is the human benefit. It is hard to know how much the monkeys suffer. Controversy haunts the official grading system – mild, moderate, substantial – which the Home Office uses to categorise pain. Under this mechanism, removing part of a monkey's skull and delving into its brain is merely 'moderate'. Many experienced observers, not just animal rights campaigners, think that 'substantial' – a category requiring intense ethical scrutiny, and defined as likely to cause a 'major departure from the animal's usual state of health and wellbeing' – would be nearer the mark.

Even so, scientists argue that laboratories in Britain are the most tightly regulated in the world. Each laboratory has to be licensed. So does every researcher, and every procedure the researcher performs. No experiment is (or should be) allowed if there is a non-animal alternative. Some people still think this is not enough. For them, experiments like this are too distressing ever to be justified. Others see a moral imperative in attacking human disease.

After visiting the macaques I talked to a man who had suffered severely from Parkinson's disease for fifteen years but who could now function near normally thanks to a technique known as deep brain stimulation (DBS), which was pioneered in monkeys. This is one example among billions – billions which include every one of us, not just those who have been cured of life-threatening diseases. From cancer drugs to over-the-counter analgesics, nothing gets into humans that hasn't first been tried on animals. It is not just medicines. Cosmetics testing is now illegal in the UK (though not in the US), but every compound in the past will have had its safety confirmed by animals. The same goes for many industrial or household products – cleaners, disinfectants, dyes, agri-chemicals and food additives. In most cases it is a legal necessity. So let us be in no doubt. It was us, the public, through our elected representatives, who demanded the 3.7m 'procedures' on living animals that were conducted in the UK last year. The monsters in the hell-holes are our servants, and we are working them harder than ever. It is not their consciences we should be examining; it is our own.

Hypocrisy, exaggeration and soaring rhetoric distort both sides of the argument. Monkeys, dogs and cats excite the most revulsion and the most vehement opposition, but in fact these three added together account for less than 0.5% of Britain's annual total, and monkeys just 0.12%. The overwhelming majority, 66%, are mice, a throwaway species whose common fate in the outside world – to be poisoned, caught in traps or in the claws of cats – does not provoke much in the way of organised protest. Only labs do that.

I am given access also to Huntingdon Life Sciences, the most infamous commercial testing establishment anywhere in Britain, and very likely in the whole of western Europe. In 1997 it was made notorious by undercover filming that showed technicians abusing beagles. Two people then were convicted of criminal offences, the company lost many of its most important clients and has had a long, uphill struggle to restore its reputation in the pharmaceutical industry, if not yet with the public.

The main UK unit employs 900 people on a sprawling site in open countryside north of Huntingdon. The character of the place is hard to grasp – a weird amalgam of defence establishment, hospital, university and zoo. Every year it carries out some 2500 experiments for a client-list of

450. It is desperate to be understood. Before being allowed into the animal blocks I have to pass through a kind of philosophical foot-bath in which to be cleansed of my preconceptions. In fact what they say is what I have heard from every other scientist I have spoken to. No-one likes using animals. It's an option of last resort. Sir Mark Walport, director of the Wellcome Trust, has told me: 'Science is about finding the least invasive, most ethically acceptable alternative. It is an environment that always questions whether animal procedures are necessary or not. Scientists also think in terms of a hierarchy of species. They won't use a mouse if a worm will do. Won't use a rabbit if a rat will do. Won't use a primate if anything else will do.'

Because scientists like to customise their language, there is a new bit of jargon to wrestle with – testing in silico, which turns out to mean 'using a computer'. Programmes derived from previous experiments can help researchers check the safety of any new compound they are interested in. Does it contain anything that could interfere with DNA? Or damage the liver, kidney or cardio-vascular system? From 500,000 new compounds, only 50,000 will get past this electronic gatekeeper. After further tests using bacteria and mammalian cells, the number will shrivel to 500 and then to 25. In the bad old days all this would have been done with live animals, many of which would have been poisoned to death. Now it's only at this relatively late stage that rats or mice become involved.

Unfortunately it doesn't end there. Although the vast majority of safety testing is on rodents, the law requires testing on larger mammals before a drug can be given to human volunteers and, finally, to patients. At this institution 'larger mammals' means monkeys, dogs or pigs. The monkeys are macaques, imported from farms in south-east Asia. Animals behind bars are never a cheering sight, and anthropomorphic projection of one's own feelings – How would I like it? – are hard to suppress. That apart, it is difficult to find fault. I regret that animals have had to travel halfway round the globe, but the sources are inspected by the Home Office and the animals are captive-bred and supplied with family histories.

The housing for the macaques is adequate rather than luxurious but the animals are in groups of at least three, some as many as ten. They have some 'environmental enrichment' – play equipment and cage-front balconies from which they can watch the world go by – and they seem healthy and well fed. Happy? Holding anthropomorphism at bay, I can say at least that they do not look unhappy. They are unafraid, active and curious. As I move between the cages, hands and feet shoot out, snatching at my tape machine, grabbing my collar. They are like mischievous children. Like children, too, they are wholly trusting, and it is hard not to be touched by this. In a few weeks or months, the end will come. They will be wafted away, painlessly on clouds of anaesthetic, but they will no longer be possessors of lives. If the scientists' calculations are right, they will have suffered no major discomforts and their autopsied organs will confirm the safety of compounds that could extend the lives of men, women and children. That is the deal.

It's a similar story with the pigs, which are not full-scale porkers but dog-sized miniatures from Denmark purpose-bred for the lab. They are plump and squealy, cleaner and better housed than any pigs I have seen on farms. And then there are the dogs … In the long term they might be replaced by pigs, but for now the demand for them remains high. They are beagles, locally bred, waggy-tailed and hyperactive. Currently there are 560 of them on site, living 32 to a room. The din they kick up is indescribable. I am offered earplugs but still I feel it as physical pain. They are, I am told, excited by strangers. They are also irresistibly seductive, leaping up and wanting to be petted.

In between the noticeboards in the technicians' room hang tokens of typically English sentimentality. Pinned up like family portraits are photographs of dogs that have been spared the lethal injection and re-homed. One of the technicians is about to adopt a retiree – a mate for the one she already has. But survivors are a small minority. The overwhelming majority will be killed and, despite the ubiquity of death, tears will be shed when favourites die. To some, this may look like hypocrisy. Others speak of 'respect', in the way old-fashioned farmers do when they prepare animals for slaughter. You might not desire it, you might even feel moved to campaign against it, but it is too simplistic to describe such a place as a hell-hole, or to characterise its people as monsters.

Neither do the procedures much resemble the torments of popular imagination. Pigs' heads are not sewn on to beagles' bodies. No animal is being systematically poisoned to death. Many will suffer nothing more painful than an injection. Others will suffer no ill effects whatsoever. The only suffering is their confinement in an animal house. I speak to one leading scientist who surprises me with his tolerance of anthropomorphism. 'Animal suffering is not something we are able to judge accurately,' he says. 'We cannot know their internal emotional state. We try to avoid anthropomorphism, but sometimes we can only imagine what it might be like to experience the procedure as a human. That's the only criterion.' It is a view I encounter time and again. 'If a mouse injures its paw,' says the head of a research establishment at the cutting edge of GM technology, 'I tell the technicians to imagine it's their own hand.'

The reasons are pragmatic as well as humanitarian. Animal procedures are costly, lab-quality beagles and pigs are hugely expensive, and sick or stressed animals give poor results. At Huntingdon the animals in each trial are arranged in four sub-groups. Three receive low, medium or high doses of the test-drug; the fourth gets a placebo. Some of the macaques are being given weekly injections of an anti-cancer compound; others are in a single-dose vaccine trial. The pigs are being orally dosed with a drug for diseases of the central nervous system. The dogs are testing a treatment for Alzheimer's.

During their lives they will be watched for side-effects – loss of appetite, lassitude, excessive salivation, unsteadiness. Afterwards their organs will be dissected in autopsy. To this extent, the campaigners against suffering have been remarkably successful. Analgesics are mandatory in most cases where pain is suffered, and animals involved in the most invasive procedures – i.e. 'vivisection' in its true sense – never know what is happening to them (though the studies of brain function, described above, are glaring exceptions). Each lab has a vet to advise if suffering becomes excessive. Government inspectors have unrestricted rights of access and staff are expected to be vigilant. For the benefit of whistle-blowers, notice boards list the telephone numbers of both local and government officials.

But this is where the anthropomorphic control mechanism splutters and dies. Pain is taboo, but death is not. In a case brought by anti-vivisection campaigners last year, the High Court ruled that, unlike pain, death could not be counted as a 'cost' to the animal. To the animal rights lobby, this is illogical. To any anthropomorphic self-projectionist, it is unthinkable. A life is a life, and the cost is supreme. For others, it is a matter of proportion. In the UK, 3m animals die in the cause of science each year. Between 600m and 700m are killed to be cooked and eaten.

'Double standards – I should say multiple standards – make ethical debate difficult,' says a university professor. 'Think about overweight pets. Pets with chronic disease conditions. Dogs in pain with untreated arthritis. This would not be acceptable in a lab. Think about lameness in cattle and sheep, and mastitis in dairy cows. It is accepted as part of the cost of meat and milk. We wouldn't accept this in laboratory animals.'

At the large university in the Midlands where my journey ends, there is wry amusement over a television documentary that showed farmers branding ponies with red-hot irons. 'There they were filming it,' says the chief vet. 'Oh yes, that's fine. Part of rural tradition. Very interesting!' Could they do anything like that to a laboratory mouse? Laughter all round.

The science here is not easy to understand. A professor carefully describes his work with genetically modified mice, which he is using to study the causes of dementia. It cannot be done without functioning brains in live animals, he says. 'You can't do research on human tissue. You can only test findings you've made from the animals.' And why is it important to humans? 'Because we can understand the bio-mechanisms by which the neurones die, and then interfere with those processes in order to … I hesitate to say stop, but at least slow down the process of neuro-degeneration.'

Elsewhere in the building rats are being monitored to see how their heart rates and blood pressures respond to fructose – an important ingredient in sticky drinks. This will help researchers to understand the link between childhood cardio-vascular disease and mothers' diets. Early observations suggest there may be bad news for Coca-Cola. After that, attention will switch to salty snacks.

Nearby are the fish – tiny zebra fish whose wild progenitors swam in the Ganges. These are contributing to stem-cell research, which might lead to the cure of almost anything. The burgeoning popularity of fish is one of the reasons why the expenditure of animals is going up. This lab alone uses 13,000 a year, and every one of them is a Home Office statistic. So is every birth of a transgenic mouse, regardless of whether or not it is used in an experiment. Simply nicking an animal's ear to take a tissue sample – equivalent to ear-tagging in farm animals, or ear-piercing in humans – similarly counts as a notifiable 'procedure'.

This is the context in which the anti-vivisectionists' headline claim – 'shocking 14% rise in animal experiments' – must be evaluated. Its unrestrained use of the word 'vivisection', evoking images of scientists cutting up live animals, also stretches the margins of objectivity. This is why the argument needs to be more of a debate and less an exchange of mortar fire. Animal procedures are not going to stop because objectors exaggerate the case against them. They will cease only when there are better alternatives, which is the best – realistically the only – hope for those who want to release mice, dogs and monkeys from the labs. In Britain the government set up an independent body, the National Centre for the Replacement, Refinement and Reduction of Animals in Research (NC3Rs), to encourage efforts to find alternatives to animals and reduce both the number and the suffering of those still deemed necessary. The Fund for the Replacement of Animals in Medical Experiments (FRAME) shares its ambition and has been striving for more than fifty years to develop 'physiologically relevant' models of human disease without killing anything.

No-one expects perfection. No procedure has yet been devised that can guarantee the elimination of rogues. As the recent exposure of cruelty to mice and rabbits in an incompetently run cosmetic surgery trial shows, the gold standard is still elusive. How elusive, it is impossible to say. I saw only those institutions that were prepared to open their doors. Many others, including leading universities and drug companies, declined to receive me. Perhaps this was because they didn't trust me to write objectively. Perhaps it was because they feared public reaction, or the attentions of activists. They wouldn't say.

I regret also that, with the exception of Huntingdon Life Sciences, I am unable to identify the sites I did visit. This is not the climate of openness that will allow the kind of mature debate the issue demands. Secrecy is the enemy of trust, and mistrust is the enemy of progress. Any monkey could tell you that.

*

That was written in 2009, when the total number of animal procedures in the UK was 3,619,540, spread across more than thirty species. The most heavily used creatures were mouse (2,628,556), octopus (398,101) and rat (333,865). Further up the scale of human concern were the beagle (5,864), macaque (3,644) and marmoset (619). Birds included domestic fowl (114,301), quail (2,896), turkey (2,896) and 9,064 unidentified others. By 2018, the latest year for which statistics are available at the time of writing, the overall number had nudged down to 3.52 million, a figure which the Home Office said was the lowest since 2007. The mouse was still by far the largest contributor, at 2,568,197, representing 72.96% of the total. Fish came a distant second at 514, 340 and rats third at 177,904. Further down the register were 10,424 horses, 4,481 dogs, 3,207 primates and 159 cats. Overall, 125,420 (3.6%) of the procedures were classified as 'severe'. The justifications for all this are human benefit and tight regulatory control. Much of the anger in past decades focused on the testing of tobacco products – the infamous 'smoking beagles' – cosmetics and household products, all now banned in the UK. Throughout the European Union it is illegal to sell or import any cosmetic product whose ingredients have been tested on animals. In Germany as in the UK, all experiments involving invertebrates must be officially approved. In Britain this covers everything from a simple blood test to major invasive surgery, and researchers must demonstrate that no non-animal alternative is available. Justifications for procedures on dogs include the development of treatments for muscular dystrophy, and monkeys with their humanlike prefrontal cortexes are the current best hope for finding answers to Alzheimer's and Parkinson's diseases.

All this contributes to a world total which is literally incalculable. Best guesses hover around 115 million annually, but could be wildly inaccurate as standards of record-keeping, where they exist at all, vary widely from country to country. The US, for example, recorded in 2017 a surprisingly small total of 932,954, which becomes rather less surprising when it is realised that the only animals counted are those protected by the Animal Welfare Act. These specifically exclude the most heavily used laboratory species – mice, rats, fish and birds – which the US, unlike Canada, the UK and the European Union, deems unworthy of notice. American consumption of primates (110,194 in 2017), dogs (74,853) and cats (19,368) is far higher than in any European country, and there is no reason to suppose the same is not true of mice, rats and all the other denizens of the zoological underclass. In Europe the highest rate of animal testing is in the UK, with Germany second. In 2018 Germany recorded a total of 2,826,066, of which mice, rats and fish accounted for 93%. But statistics like these can have a negative effect. The endless repetition of seven- and six-figure numbers dulls the imagination. It is too much to take in. The mind is anaesthetised by excess. Boredom ensues. The eye moves on.

In the end we face a choice between numb acceptance, qualified approval or implacable rejection. For well-understood reasons, animal rights organisations fiercely condemn all exploitation of animals and do not accept 'human benefit' as a moral justification for curtailing the lives of others. There are times when the scientific industry is its own worst enemy. Laboratory technicians may be better trained than handlers in factory farms but the dangers are the same. Where the end product of any system is dead animals, a coarsening of attitudes is always a risk. As in factory farms, and despite all the regulations, inspections and safeguards, undercover filming in research establishments still feeds the Frankenstein narrative. In 2019, the worldwide campaign group Cruelty Free International released shocking undercover footage from the Laboratory of Pharmacology and Toxicology near Hamburg in Germany. Macaques were shown being violently grabbed with metal tongs before being pinned upright and made to stand for long periods like medieval torture victims with shackles around their necks. Their distress was obvious not just during the procedures but also in the tiny, battery-style cages measuring less than a cubic metre in which they were held in solitary confinement. Dogs, too, were filmed in appalling conditions, kept in cages where they had to lie in their own blood and faeces. For the protestors it was an easy, if upsetting, win. The level of public and political protest resulted in the laboratory losing its licence. The disquieting thought is that without the penetration of the unit by an investigator working undercover, the cruelties would have continued without interruption, and there are many more institutions in Germany, Britain, the US and throughout the world that will continue to evade the prying lens. Suspicion will only be lifted when secrecy is replaced by transparency – or perhaps, a cynic might say, when the public benefit is more obvious and immediate.

There was no audible protest – rather, there were murmurs of optimism – when it was reported during the global pandemic in May 2020 that potential Covid-19 vaccines were being trialled on monkeys.

CHAPTER TWENTY-SIX

Articles of Faith

IN 2010, TWO SCIENTISTS FROM THE COMPLUTENSE UNIVERSITY in Madrid set out to investigate the feeding habits of the city's blackbirds. One of the things that especially interested them was the birds' 'flushing response'. In an urban environment, what were the things most likely to startle this rural species into flight? The answer was hardly a surprise. Humans were overwhelmingly seen as the most serious threat, followed by magpies, dogs, other blackbirds and cars. Ten years later, on a sunny afternoon during the Covid-19 lockdown in England, I receive an unexpected visitor in my garden. A male blackbird suddenly flutters down from the wall and perches on the chair next to my own, a distance of two feet at the most. On the previous evening the same bird had hopped along beside me as I watered the flowers, keeping up a ceaseless serenade of song and coming so close that I might have dropped a worm or caterpillar straight into his open beak. But how does this square with the Madrid study, and with the essential wariness of wild birds and animals? How did the blackbird and his mate know I was not a threat?

The answer, or part of it, is evolution. All blackbirds are not the same. Neither are all spiders, all mice, rats, jackdaws, sparrows, foxes or moths. Humans, too, are a varied tribe, though perhaps not as varied as they used to be. For the first time in history, the twenty-first century now finds more people living in towns and cities than in the countryside. This change will be permanent. The best estimate is that by mid-century two-thirds of the global human population will wake up every morning in a city. And they will not be alone. All around them myriad others will be waking up too, and waking up *earlier*. Evolution dictates that species adapt to their environments. If environments change, then so too must the species. Animals are opportunists. They found and took possession of the most fertile stretches of land long before humans came along and built on top of them. The earliest architects were not men but ants and beavers. Much has changed, but not the animals' knack of seizing opportunities. As a denuded, intensively farmed landscape became more and more difficult for them to survive in, and as more of the land became urbanised, so they began to follow their tormentors from the forest into what they perceived literally as an urban jungle, where buildings and cycle racks substituted for trees. Here they did not cease to evolve. On the contrary: the pace of evolution quickened. Naturalists began to speak and write of 'urban wildlife' as something distinct and very different from the life of forest, field and savannah.

To understand this, we need to travel in our imaginations back to the Galapagos archipelago in the eastern Pacific, where variations in the beaks of finches did so much to inform Darwin's ideas about evolution. 'Seeing this gradation and diversity of structure in one small, intimately related group of birds,' he wrote in *Origin of Species*, 'one might really fancy that from an original paucity of birds in this archipelago, one species had been taken and modified for different ends.' That *modification for different ends* is what is now going on in a very different chain of islands – the world's towns and cities. Urban areas are islands in the sense that the wildlife inside them is disconnected from other populations beyond the suburbs. Within the city, too, colonies are detached from each other by roads and railways so that they breed in isolation around particular blocks or in parks. Separate populations then do what they always do: *they evolve*. On 18 November 1878, an amateur lepidopterist and bug-hunter named Albert Farn sat down at his home in Dartford, Kent, and composed a letter to the world's most famous natural scientist. Farn was a man best known among his friends as an expert marksman who had once downed 176 snipe in as many shots, a champion of the billiard table and a notorious practical joker. His letter to Darwin, however, was written in all seriousness. Its subject was the variation in colour which he had observed in the annulet moth, *Charissa obscurata*, a species common throughout Europe. Its name, *obscurata*, meaning 'darkened' or 'obscured', is well-earned. As Farn noted in his letter, it is 'almost black on the New Forest peat; grey on limestone; almost white on the chalk near Lewes; and brown on clay, and on the red soil of Herefordshire'. He went on:

> Do these variations point to the 'survival of the fittest'? I think so.
>
> It was, therefore, with some surprise that I took specimens as dark as any of those in the New Forest on a chalk slope; and I have pondered for a solution. Can this be it?
>
> It is a curious fact, in connexion with these dark specimens, that for the last quarter of a century the chalk slope, on which they occur, has been swept by volumes of black smoke from some lime-kilns situated at the bottom: the herbage, although growing luxuriantly, is blackened by it.
>
> I am told, too, that the very light specimens are now much less common at Lewes than formerly, and that, for some few years, lime-kilns have been in use there.

The implication to Farn was obvious. What he believed he had seen was evolution in action, natural selection causing the moths in rapid time to match their colour to changing backgrounds. This would be confirmed in later studies of a different species, the peppered moth, *Biston betularia*, which famously darkened against the smoke and soot of the industrial revolution, only to lighten again when the air cleared. The sixty-nine-year-old Darwin's reaction to Farn's letter, however, was silence. Why did he ignore it? The Dutch evolutionary biologist Menno Schilthuizen suggests in *Darwin Comes to Town* that it was because of the apparent speed of change, which Darwin thought too fast to be believable. There is a hint of this in the *Origin*, where he writes: 'We see nothing of these slow changes in progress, until the hand of time has marked the long lapse of ages.' Farn apart, he had no reason at the time to think differently. Schilthuizen provides many examples of what has happened since, as more and more species have poured into the cities and helped to build urban ecosystems enriched not just by refugees from the lifeless fields but also by the many exotics which, whether by design or by accident, humans have ferried around the world.

Parakeets, for example, breed in Paris, Brussels, London and many other cities far from their Central American homeland. According to one legend, the London population owes its origin to a pair that arrived with Humphrey Bogart and Katharine Hepburn during the filming of *The African Queen* in 1951. Another insists that the 'Adam and Eve' pair was released by Jimi Hendrix in 1968. Recent research by Queen Mary University of London suggests a less glamorous explanation: that the flocks, now numbered in the tens of thousands, owe their origin to pets discarded by owners panicked by reports of potentially fatal 'parrot fever'.

Survival in the city demands very different skills from life in the countryside. Rapid take-off, for example, is vital for any bird that does not want to become roadkill or food for a cat. This calls for shorter, rounded wings rather than the long, pointed ones that generate high speeds in level flight. Scientists guess that this may explain why, on the evidence of stuffed specimens, starlings in New York's Central Park now have more rounded wings than their presumably less agile ancestors had in the 1890s. More contemporary studies of American cliff swallows show their wings shortening by an average of two millimetres per decade. The clinching evidence comes from roadkill. 'By the 2010s,' says Schilthuizen, 'the wings of dead birds by the roadside were about half a centimetre longer than those of live birds still happily flapping along.' In the case of urban lizards, the pressure was all the other way: to grow *longer* limbs to speed their escape along walls. Not all the adaptations are external, or even physiological. Urban diets scavenged from human leftovers require a different kind of feeding and digestive system than food in the forest. Blackbirds, for example, have developed shorter, blunter bills for tackling garden bird-feeders instead of probing into tree-bark. They also have shorter wings and legs, and longer intestines than their country cousins, though Schilthuizen points out that evolution is endlessly variable: wing- and leg-lengths vary from city to city. Urban songbirds also sing differently. Out in the countryside, it's the males with the deepest voices that get first pick of the females. Against the rumble of the city, however, a deep voice becomes inaudible so that the romantic leads now are all high-voiced, like tenors in an opera. They start earlier in the morning, too, when human interference is least. Another necessary adaptation is tolerance of humans. People in cities are less likely to be armed with guns or hounds, so birds have evolved to become less fearful. In the countryside, says Schilthuizen, a jackdaw will flee from any human who comes within thirty metres. In cities it is just eight metres. Jackdaws have been urbanised since at least the 1880s, more than a hundred years earlier than the great spotted woodpecker, but even since the 1970s the city woodpeckers have reduced their 'flight initiation distance' from twelve metres to eight. As Schilthuizen points out, this means that tolerance of humans evolves over time, and that the reduced fright zone, no less than the shortened wings and beaks, is genetic and not just individual learning. Which brings me back to my garden blackbird, whose 'flight initiation distance' is measurable in inches, and who sings at a seventy-five-year-old human as vigorously as he might to a desirable mate. That is not just lack of fear: it is *companionship*. And, as Schilthuizen suggests, it is perhaps a bird well on its way to becoming a whole new species, *Turdus merula* morphing by degrees into *Turdus urbanicus*.

Mammals, too, have made themselves at home in the city. They have done so in ways which, if achieved in a laboratory, would look like miracles of genetic manipulation. Once again Central Park provides the example. Discarded nuts and seeds, abundant in places where humans take their snacks, can develop mould which produces a carcinogen called aflatoxin. The Central Park mice reacted to this by developing a genetic modification that neutralises the poison and allows them to go on nibbling. They have also developed a gene to help neutralise the effects of an ultra-high-fat diet – 'another tell-tale sign', says Schilthuizen, 'that mice had evolved to manage typical Central Park foodstuffs'. He points also to bobcats in Hollywood, whose heavy consumption of poisoned rats caused an outbreak of mange. Rather than change their diet the bobcats copied the Central Park mice in becoming immune to the disease. Other species in other cities have similarly developed resistance to local pollutants and a keen eye for new opportunities. Researchers from St Andrews University discovered that birds in Mexico City were insulating their nests with cigarette butts. This was not just for the sake of warmth. The nicotine and other chemical residues worked as a natural pesticide that rid the birds of parasitic mites. Feeding habits, too, evolve to suit altered circumstances. The famous Japanese crows, lurking at traffic lights to crack nuts under cars, are the most celebrated example but there are many more. At Albi in southern France, catfish have learned to leap from the shallows and snatch pigeons bathing in the River Tam. Spiders are shifting their webs ever closer to electric lights that attract clouds of insects at night.

Attitudes to urban wildlife are, at best, ambivalent. Where a feral cat might anticipate a saucer of milk, a fox might expect a hail of stones. No species better exemplifies the irrationality of human attitudes. In December 2019 there was a furious outcry when a London lawyer clubbed to death a fox that had ensnared itself in netting outside his hen-house. Yet in the same city professional hunters insist they perform a public service by going out at night and shooting foxes in the head. It was one of these who complained to me about the 'misguided sentiment' of fox-lovers who put out food for them. It caused problems, he said, because the animals grew accustomed to human interactions and became less fearful. This, in his way of thinking, was 'a vicious circle'. Every important question about the nature and behaviour of urban foxes has received a scientifically validated answer, yet the myths are ineradicable. People really do believe that foxes hunt in packs, and that they are licking their lips outside infants' nurseries because old-fashioned dustbins have disappeared and they can't open wheelie-bins. It can't be argued that foxes never bite children – it's happened. But it's vanishingly rare, and almost always occurs when an animal feels threatened. As with child murder, there is a perverse logic at work. Incidences are too few to translate into a calculable risk, but it is their very rarity that grabs the headlines and creates an illusion of threat. The fact is that foxes are only slightly heavier than cats, and are solitary hunters that have evolved to eat mice. If you want to save children from being mauled by animals, then it's not foxes that should be culled. Dogs in Britain cause five thousand serious injuries a year. In the US it's a thousand a day. If they made the headlines that foxes do, then newspapers would have space for little else.

This is no time to be an elephant, or a rhinoceros, a lion or a tiger. It is not a good time to belong to any species that depends on space and liberty. The world is being twisted out of shape. Shrinking habitats, persecution and global heating are pulling and pushing species far from their historic homelands. Melting sea ice and warming waters are re-routing the migrations of birds and fish. Butterflies, birds and wild plants are being sucked northwards, with often dire consequences for long-established natives. Often these natives are human. In Arctic Russia, people were trapped in their homes by displaced polar bears maddened by hunger. In West Bengal, homeless elephants were pelted by frightened villagers with fire-crackers and flaming tar balls. More and more extreme weather events are threatening to extinguish whole species in bushfires and floods. Melting ice opened a channel from the North Atlantic to the northern Pacific that allowed a potentially fatal disease to jump from seals to sea otters. Man-made pollutants work their way up the food chain from insects to fish, birds and mammals, killing as they go. One dead whale in Indonesia was found to have a thousand pieces of plastic in its stomach.

After the foresters, farmers and urban planners come the guns. To be rare is to have a bounty on your head. To flaunt horns or tusks is folly. For many species in the hunters' sights, the only path ahead is the one already travelled by the aurochs, the bluebuck, the Madagascan dwarf hippopotamus, Steller's sea cow, the Galapagos giant rat, the desert bandicoot ... In 2019 alone some two dozen creatures were crossed off the list of living species, beginning on New Year's Day with the Hawaiian tree snail and ending on 23 December with one of the world's largest freshwater fishes, the Chinese paddlefish. There were local extinctions, or 'extirpations', too. Malaysia's last Sumatran rhinoceros died of cancer in November. Laos lost its last tiger. And still the scientists say we are only in the foothills of loss. Report after report hoists the same red flag. World wildlife populations have shrunk by sixty per cent during the lifetimes of anyone aged over fifty. Unless the world unites in preventive action, the torrent of vanishing insects, fish, amphibians, birds and mammals will turn into a flood in which humans, too, may drown. In 2020, researchers at Stanford University predicted that as many species would be lost during the next twenty years as in the whole of the twentieth century. Others have predicted the disappearance by the end of the current century of another thousand large species of bird and mammal.

The bigger the animal, the greater the threat. Elephants are doubly cursed in being both unmissable targets and bearers of treasure. The ivory trade has been illegal since 1989, but this has done little to hinder the poaching gangs that supply the booming markets in China and the Far East. Countless photographs of rotting carcasses and the enormity of the statistics – ninety per cent of African elephants lost in the last century; 700,000 killed in the 1980s alone – have induced revulsion around the world but had little effect on the trade. There was a brief respite after the Convention on International Trade in Endangered Species imposed the international trade ban, but the poachers fairly soon got back to business. With much of rural Africa more than two days' trek from the nearest police station, there was little to stop them. The market price of ivory multiplied tenfold between 1989 and 2014, since when, according to researchers at the University of Bristol Veterinary School, there has been a slow decline. It is impossible to say precisely how this has impacted on elephant deaths – counting carcasses in the wild is not an exact science – but the WWF believes that, regardless of any shift in price, the number over the last decade has steadily increased to an annual total of 20,000, or around fifty-five a day. The Bristol team puts it considerably higher, at 100 a day, but calculates the surviving population at 350,000 against the WWF's 415,000. It doesn't matter who is right. Gross up either of those numbers to a whole decade's worth, factor in the additional stresses of human conflict and lost or fragmented habitats, and you can see where the species is heading.

Rhinos wear their misfortune on their faces. In Roualeyn Gordon-Cumming's day rhino horn was valued only as a trophy. Now it is a commodity. Most of the specimens in European museums were collected in the late nineteenth or early twentieth centuries, and for each institution one was usually enough. For the traditional medicine trades of China and south-east Asia, one is never enough. There is a widespread misconception, for which Julian Huxley bears much of the responsibility, that rhinoceros horn is prized as an aphrodisiac. It is not. In fact this is the one benefit that seems not to have occurred to the ancient herbalists whose word in these matters gives quackery its kernel of faith. In most horned animals, the horn has a bony core within a sheath of keratin (the same stuff from which hair, hooves and fingernails are made). Rhinos are different. The horn is solid keratin. Powdered and dissolved in water, it is credited with magical properties sufficient to replace the entire stock of a western pharmacy (though if this is true, it would make as much sense to chew your fingernails or eat your haircut). Victims of this historic scam swallow it to rid themselves of fever, rheumatism, gout, typhoid, carbuncles, snakebite, headaches, nausea, hallucinations and daemonic possession. In Vietnam, where demand is rising fast, the list extends to hangovers and cancer. Apart from a flagging libido, the only things it seems unable to cure are the credulity of its purchasers and the cynicism of those who supply them. The numbers of rhinos killed in Africa rose steadily from 262 in 2008 to a peak of 1,349 in 2015, since when it has been gradually declining. Even so, rhinos are still dying at the rate of one every ten hours and many park rangers – some of the bravest men on the planet – have lost their lives to guerrilla bands armed with rocket launchers, AK-47s and NATO-standard Heckler and Koch G3 battle rifles. Every death is a loss; some are literally irreplaceable. On 19 March 2018, five years after I'd had the privilege of seeing him, the last surviving male northern white rhino died at the Ol Pejeta conservancy in Kenya.

Rhino hunting may be profitable but it is hard and dangerous work. At some time around the end of the first decade of this century, European criminals had a brainwave. The horns sent to museums by nineteenth-century adventurers were all still there, lightly guarded and worth a fortune. For hardened veterans of armed robbery, fraud, money-laundering and drug-trafficking, it was a no-brainer. From Sweden in the north to Spain in the south, Portugal in the west to Hungary in the east, natural history museums were targeted like stagecoaches in the Wild West. In a lunchtime attack on the Museum of Hunting and Nature in the Marais district of Paris, two men used what police described as a 'paralysing gas' to subdue guards and help them get away with the horn of a rare South African white rhinoceros. Teargas was used in a raid at the zoological museum in Liège, Belgium. On a Saturday morning at the Museum of Natural History at Gothenburg in Sweden, men armed with an electric saw smashed a glass case and lopped off the horn of a stuffed rhino. In March 2012 a British man was held by German police after what they described as an 'unbelievably audacious' raid in Offenburg, during which two people distracted museum staff while others climbed on a display case, took down a rhino head from the wall and smashed off its horn with a sledge-hammer. Ironies abounded.

A horn snatched from the Drusillas Animal Park, near Alfriston in Sussex, was part of an educational display about the illegal trade in rare animals. The items in the cabinet were all things that people were urged not to buy: coral, seashells, furs, turtle-shell, snake and crocodile skins as well as rhino horn. To avoid its becoming a criminal rather than educational resource, the entire display had to be removed. A deeper irony, given the purpose for which the contraband is sold, is that rhino horns were commonly preserved with arsenic. Do the patients who swallow them live long enough to register the shock?

How can Chinese traditional medicine survive in the age of organ transplants, antibiotics and DNA? The answer is in the name: it is *traditional*. A therapy dating back two thousand years is not easily shaken off. Despite the availability of modern scientific medicine, belief persists in the healing powers of tiger-bone, deer penises and the scales of pangolins. But death in the wild is not the only penalty for being in possession of saleable body-parts. The suffering in captivity of bears, permanently catheterised to drain bile from their gall-bladders, arguably is worse. The risk of all this to wildlife is even more pressing than it sounds. Traditional Chinese medicine is no more confined to its birthplace than the hot dog is to the United States. Practitioners are at work in more than one hundred and eighty countries, the retail end of a wholesale trade worth upwards of $60 billion a year. The threat is not just to individual animals unlucky enough to stray across a poacher's line of fire. It is to entire species.

Day by day, year by year, the world's newspapers report a mounting litany of loss. It is not all about elephants, rhinos and tigers. From micro-organisms upwards, huge bites are being taken out of the entire pyramid of life. Analysis of data published by the peer-reviewed journal *Biological Conservation* in early 2019 showed that the combined effects of pesticides, climate change and urbanisation now add up to a catastrophic threat to ecosystems worldwide. The mass of insects globally is falling by 2.5% a year, which means that, unless drastic action is taken to arrest the decline, they could all be gone by the end of the century. Kick away insects, and you kick away the foundations on which all other life-forms rest. Few people perhaps will mourn the fact that a quarter of all species of fly declined over the 2010s, but a 46% loss of bees, or 53% of butterflies? On farmed land in England between 2000 and 2009 the number of commonly seen butterfly species fell by 58%. Germany lost half its leafhoppers in the fifty years to 2010; the US has lost 3.5 million of the six million honeybee colonies that were recorded there in 1947. Yet again we drown in numbers too vast to visualise. What we *can* see, if only through noting their absence, is the loss of insectivorous birds and mammals. Spotted flycatchers in the UK have declined since 1967 by 93%. Across much of Europe, once-ubiquitous hedgehogs and bats are more rumour than reality. Britain has lost half its hedgehogs since the turn of the century. Elsewhere in the world, out of sight beyond the urban margins, darkness is beginning to descend on species after species, from puffins to sea cows, caribou to turtle doves, toads to vultures, sea bass, penguins, polar bears, tortoises, solenodons. The International Union for the Conservation of Nature Red List now classifies 37% of all known species as under threat of extinction, including 25% of mammals, 14% of birds, 41% of amphibians, 33% of reef corals, 30% of sharks and rays.

Against this tsunami of loss stands a thin green line of dissent, a torrent of fine words and a strange absence of political will, as if world leaders have either failed to notice the advancing juggernaut or been blinded in its headlights. In 2019 the sixteen-year-old climate activist Greta Thunberg became the youngest person ever to be named as *Time* magazine's person of the year. In her brief career as the world's most audible campaigning voice, she had inspired four million people to join a global climate strike, met the Pope and addressed world leaders at the UN. The novelist Margaret Atwood likened her to Joan of Arc. There were many others who would have liked to complete the analogy by burning her at the stake. Ageism and misogyny spurted like pus from a boil. Donald Trump, having himself been a nominee for the *Time* award, responded to his defeat by denouncing the choice as 'ridiculous'. Thunberg, he said, would better spend her time watching 'a good old-fashioned movie with a friend'. The US Treasury Secretary, Steve Mnuchin, described the award as 'a joke', and on Fox News the right-wing commentator Michael Knowles called her a 'mentally ill Swedish child'. Fox subsequently apologised for the 'disgraceful' remark, but middle-aged conservative commentators in America, Europe and the UK kept up their barrage of fire. Unable to counter her arguments, they focused less on her ideas than on her identity. How dare a teenage girl – a girl! – with Asperger's syndrome lecture adults about the kind of world she wanted to live in? They kept on even after Elizabeth Maruma Mrema, acting executive secretary of the UN Convention on Biological Diversity, gave them the obvious answer. Speaking on the eve of the Davos World Economic Forum in January 2020, she begged governments to join in concerted action to divert the ecological disintegration of the planet. 'Our children are asking what climate are they going to inherit from us if the planet they are seeing is polluted ... The children know exactly what they expect from their parents ... Whatever is negotiated today will affect our children more than us.' The fragility of humans' hold on their manufactured world then made itself devastatingly clear in the Covid-19 pandemic that sprang out of a Chinese animal market and by the beginning of 2021 had already consumed more than 1.8 million human lives. By the time these words appear in print it will be very many more. While Sweden's latter-day Joan of Arc did not burn, the world went on doing so – quite literally in Australia, where in early 2020 bushfires pushed native species to the edge of extinction and possibly beyond. But theology is fireproof, and the Trumpian theology dictated that climate change was a 'hoax', environmentalism was a trivial diversion from grown-up issues such as economic growth, and green politics was a childish reincarnation of old-fashioned 'End is Nigh' doom-mongering. Animals were fine in theory but they needed to keep their snouts out of the human trough.

This does not mean all hope is lost. Not quite. Once it is finally under-stood that there can be no fresh water or food without healthy ecosystems, and no healthy ecosystems without a survivable climate, then animal life, or as much of it as remains, will be an accidental beneficiary of human self-interest. But it sinks the world deeper and deeper into a stew of moral and ethical confusion in which few of us are wholly innocent. Our very existence costs lives. Ever since humans claimed sovereignty over every-thing that creeps, swims, flies or runs, 'managing' animals has meant killing them. The arguments for this are often tortuous. The European badger is a perfect example. In a continent that has largely rid itself of the top predators – wolves, bears and lynx – that historically maintained a rich and balanced ecology, mid-sized animals such as badger and fox now stand at the head of the forest food chain. This exposes them as enemies. Various reasons are given for the persecution of badgers. In the UK they were blamed for the spread of bovine tuberculosis and, with the blessing of the government between 2013 and 2020, at least 100,000 were slaughtered. After a scientific review in 2018 revealed that bad husbandry rather than badgers was the principal cause of disease, and that cows were being infected more by each other than by wildlife, the policy was due to be phased out from 2020 and the emphasis switched to vaccination. But it did not happen. Instead, the cull was extended to eleven new areas of England with 60,000 more animals scheduled to be killed. Nor is culling the only hazard. Badger-baiting has been illegal in Britain since 1835, but undercover filming and numerous prosecutions show that old ways die hard. Elsewhere in Europe the animals are given an even harder ride. Badger-baiting in France is as common as it was in the nineteenth century, and reportedly is popular with 'cruelty tourists' avoiding the risk of pros-ecution in the UK. The word 'tradition' is often heard in defence of such practices, as if they are entitled to the same protections as religious faiths or ancient monuments. In Germany, tradition allows hunters to kill tens of thousands of badgers every year for sport. Like the 'penitent butchers' of the early 1900s, the hunters justify killing one species as a means of protecting others. Badgers kill ground-nesting birds. Thus it follows that shooting badgers saves birds. The same logic is used to excuse the removal of eggs from predators' nests, and the shooting of crows.

The first hole in this argument is that the birds themselves then become targets for the shooters. The bigger hole has whiskers and answers to the name of Puss. It is impossible to know how many domestic and feral cats there are in the world, or to know how many birds each one kills, but a study funded by the US Fish and Wildlife Service in 2012 provided a vivid snapshot. Numbers of birds killed by cats in the continental US each year? Between 1.4 and 3.7 billion. Numbers of small mammals? Between 6.9 and 20.7 billion. Gross that up worldwide and the numbers would boggle the mind of an astrophysicist. Following the logic of the badger-hunters, the obvious answer would be to cull the cats. But when a regional council in New Zealand did indeed propose to ban domestic cats, the public outcry forced it to retreat like a vole from a tomcat. The double standards multiply when you switch continents and scale up to megafauna. In 2005, when Mozambique was struggling to rebuild and reunite itself after the long civil war that ended in 1992, I visited the ruined headquarters of the Gorongosa National Park. There in a bombed-out schoolroom I found two men squatting by a fire who turned out to be prisoners working off a fine they couldn't pay for poaching warthog. Their native tradition of hunting for the pot now carried the same label, *poaching*, and wore the same criminal sackcloth as killing for ivory or rhino horn. It is an image of conflicted priorities that returns every time I hear talk of wildlife crime. For better or worse, animals are killed or displaced for a reason, and conservation is not popular where humans feel their interests are secondary to the wildlife, or where conservationists behave with the violent incivility of a conquering army. Conservation cannot succeed without popular support, and people as well as animals need to feel the benefit.

Apart from Aboriginal subsistence hunting, the benefits that most people want to see are the survival of something that can still be called 'nature', and the avoidance of suffering. It is impossible to disagree with Peter Wohlleben, who argues in *The Inner Life of Animals* that 'suffering' must be taken to include the fear that animals feel when they are hunted and not just the pain of taking a bullet or being ripped apart by hounds. Being chased by humans, he says, is far more terrifying, and disruptive of natural behaviour, than being pursued by wolves. 'Contrast one four-legged hunter for every fifty square kilometres with about 10,000 two-legged hunters in the same space in Germany today.' He invites us to imagine what our own lives would be like if the situation were to be reversed and each square kilometre of Central Europe were home to two or three thousand lions. That, he says, 'roughly corresponds to the number of two-legged predators that confront hunted game in the area'. In a discomfiting echo of *Bambi*, he argues that fear of two-legged predators means animals will no longer graze open land in daylight, and that hunting is accelerating the migration of wildlife into cities. It is perhaps strange that the British protest so much more vociferously against hunting than the Germans do, with even drag-hunts bringing out the saboteurs. These are historic grievances that are not all about animal suffering. Foxhunting in England stirs the class warriors as well as those who campaign against cruelty.

A further division remains between those whose concern is for the suffering of individuals and those worried for entire species. The one issue over which they are united is trophy-hunting. For collectors of exotica, there is no more powerful a stimulus to the trigger finger than the rarity of the animal in their sights. By extension of this contorted logic, the most valuable specimen of all would be the very last survivor. Though trophy-hunting by its nature is international, it most often speaks with an American accent. The Humane Society of the United States describes it bluntly as 'an American problem'. High-rolling US trophy-hunters, it says, kill and import an average of 126,000 wildlife trophies a year. Those who can't afford Africa or Asia make do with home-grown bears, bobcats, mountain lions and wolves. It is almost always Americans whose behaviour provokes the deepest outrage. In July 2015 a Minnesota dentist called Walter Palmer stirred up a worldwide media storm by killing Cecil, a thirteen-year-old lion from the Hwange National Park in Zimbabwe who had been the subject of a long-term study by the University of Oxford. Fury was heightened not just by the fact of the killing, but by the manner of it. Ten or twelve hours elapsed from the moment Palmer first wounded the animal with a bow and arrow until a second shot finished it off. Anger was further stoked by the fact that Palmer, being in possession of a legal permit, was not charged with any crime. Two years later, in 2017, it was the turn of another US trophy-hunter, Hossein Golabchi, who posted online a photograph of himself with the body of a rare snow leopard slung across his shoulders. More than 100,000 people signed a petition demanding his prosecution before it was revealed that the photograph had been taken thirty years earlier and that, once again, no crime had been committed. In 2018 it was a thirty-eight-year-old Texan woman called Tess Talley who stepped into the spotlight after posting a video of herself killing a giraffe in South Africa. Again there was no legal repercussion and no repentance. In an interview with *CBS News* she declared that she was 'proud to hunt' and 'proud of that giraffe', from which she said she made decorative pillows and a gun-case, and which she had found 'delicious'. 'You do what you love to do. It's a joy,' she said. But it is a joy that few non-hunters understand. Why would anyone respond to the sight of a rare and beautiful animal by wanting to kill it, turn its body parts into furniture and hang its head on a wall? Why would they want to do this so desperately that they would pay £3,000 to get a shot at a giraffe (at the cheap end of the market because it's such an easy, cow-in-a-field target) and upwards of £20,000 for a lion? Opponents suggest that killing a big animal, like driving a fast car, is cover for a virility shortfall, inadequate men bigging themselves up. The hunters do themselves few favours in this respect by posing for their photographs in military-style camouflage. The counter-jibe is that the critics are armchair-bound ignoramuses who need to be educated in the realities of conservation. Killing animals is a service to local people. It stops rogue elephants and antelopes damaging crops and trees, and big cats raiding livestock. Trophy tourism also pumps money into needy local economies as well as satisfying a noble human impulse. Men have always tested themselves against animals bigger than themselves. It is an ancient imperative that is part of being human. On top of that, let it be remembered that industrialised meat production causes infinitely more suffering in the world than trophy-hunting does. Any non-vegetarian who criticises trophy-hunting therefore is a hypocrite.

None of these arguments survives exposure to daylight. The financial contribution made by hunting companies to conservation projects is tiny. Nor do they hugely benefit local economies. Data from the UN Food and Agriculture Organization and the International Council for Game and Wildlife Conservation show that their contribution to local communities in hunting areas amounts to no more than three per cent of their income. A study of eight African countries by Economists at Large in 2017 concluded that 'the current total economic contribution of trophy hunters from their hunting-related, and non-hunting related, tourism is about 0.03% of GDP'. Far more is earned by living animals attracting visitors armed with cameras. Hunters also seek out the best and most covetable trophies, not the rogue or redundant animals that are a nuisance to farmers. All the rest is clutching at straws. There is no arguable reason why the 'noble human impulse' to kill things should be valued above the nobler instinct to refrain from it, and the charge of hypocrisy against meat eaters rests on the morally unsustainable proposition that to condone *any* killing is to condone *all* killing. Neither can it be argued that the losses to wildlife populations are trivial. Figures from CITES show that 290,000 trophies from nearly three hundred protected species were exported between 2008 and 2017. The five most prolific exporters were South Africa, Canada, Mozambique, Namibia and Zimbabwe. The principal destination was the US, followed by South Africa, Singapore, Germany and Spain. It should not be forgotten, however, that the trophy-hunting pioneers and 'penitent butchers' of Africa and India were British, as are many of those now taking advantage of cheap air fares and packaged hunting holidays. Colonial rule casts a long shadow. Bizarrely, too, Britain is also a *destination* for trophy-hunters from America, Germany, Holland and China, lured by the rare Chinese water deer that have escaped from the Woburn Abbey deer park in Bedfordshire and fanned out through parts of East Anglia.

The frustration for conservationists and welfare groups is that international law has a yawning gap in it. Whereas CITES prohibits commercial trade in more than a thousand species of endangered animals and plants, the ban specifically exempts hunting trophies as 'non-commercial'. This is a fine distinction. Though the trophies themselves are generally not traded, the opportunities to shoot them most certainly are. In August 2019 a large group of European members of parliament and conservation groups wrote to CITES calling on it to 'treat the trade in hunting trophies in the same manner as it treats all other trade in wildlife'. They also demanded an end to so-called 'canned lion hunting', which each year permits thousands of mainly American trophy-hunters to shoot captive-bred lions fenced in at South African game ranches. Hope for these animals flickered briefly. In America, where the Humane Society of the United States had long campaigned against all forms of trophy-hunting, the US Fish and Wildlife Service moved in October 2016 to ban the import of trophies from canned lions. Then on 9 November of that same year came the election of President Donald J. Trump and the installation of an administration that saw defence of wildlife, along with most other forms of environmental protection, as obstacles to economic freedom. In March 2018 the Fish and Wildlife Service rescinded the bans on captive-bred lion trophies and elephant trophies from Zimbabwe and Zambia. Europe meanwhile still waits upon CITES.

The relationship of the law with animal rights and welfare organisations has been difficult in other ways too. Some groups in Britain have been infiltrated by undercover police officers and classified as extremists alongside Nazis and jihadists. A public inquiry in 2019 revealed that a policeman using a false identity had conducted deceitful sexual relationships with two different women while spying on animal rights groups. Others had done likewise. Thus it was not just activists who were appalled at being treated as enemies of the state. Women, too, were being abused by undercover policemen who, with supreme irony, were acting against people campaigning against the abuse of animals. Down through the ages came the ancient echo: women and animals coupled in the masculine mind as lower forms of life. If anyone thought this would have a dampening effect on protest, then they were as misguided in their thinking as in their methods. Two campaigning strands – climate protestors and rights activists – now united in common cause. Ninety-six years after the anti-slavery campaigner Elizabeth Heyrick began her campaign against Britain's largest meat market, Smithfield once again came under siege.

Nor was there any relaxation of the campaigns against other long-established targets: animal testing, *foie gras*, the fur and wool trades, wild animal circuses, bullfighting, rodeos, zoos, Japanese whaling, dolphin hunting, religious slaughter. New to the list was *kambo*, an ancient South American remedy recently adopted by western practitioners which relies on poison scraped from Amazonian giant monkey frogs. Pity the frogs; pity the patients. The benefit to the frog of its toxic secretions is that they dissuade predators from eating it. The supposed benefits to humans are much the same as those claimed for Chinese medicine. In this case the only malady it will not cure is tolerance of cruelty. The legs of live frogs are tied to sticks and stretched apart before the animals are subjected to stress – by exposure to flames or a blow to the head – to stimulate the flow of poison. The experience for the human patient is hardly less traumatic.

First, a burning stick is applied to raise blisters on the skin. Then the blisters are scraped away and the *kambo* dabbed on to the burned flesh, whence it speeds through the bloodstream looking for things to cure. The immediate effect is vomiting, which some patients welcome as a healing purge. After all that, they need to believe *something*. Like any other kind of investment, faith needs to show a return.

CHAPTER TWENTY-SEVEN

The Empty Sea

FAITH HAS NEVER BEEN THE ANIMALS' FRIEND. NO GOD EVER stands between an animal and its tormentors, or refuses a sacrifice. Religious slaughter is a force against which the welfare movement does not have a prayer. No one should suppose that the world's bloodiest ritual is a bullfight. Every five years at Bariyarpur in Nepal, the Hindu festival of Gadhimai is held in the belief that sacrificing animals to the goddess will save the people from evil and bring prosperity. Victims include goats, chickens and pigs but most are buffaloes, which worshippers slaughter with long-bladed knives. Animal charities reacted furiously in 2014 when a quarter of a million animals were killed in this way at what they called 'the world's bloodiest festival'. How could such carnage pass for religious observance? Relief came in the following year when the Indian Supreme Court ordered the government to stop the illegal shipment of live animals across the Indian-Nepalese border, and the festival itself was 'banned'. It made little difference. The faithful gathered, the festival duly went ahead in 2019 at the cost of 6,500 buffaloes.

In other traditions it is the slaughterhouse that draws the fire. Veterinary societies as well as charities regard the Islamic and Jewish methods of slaughter, in which the animals have their throats cut while fully conscious, as needlessly cruel. Leaders of the Jewish and Islamic communities on the other hand insist that their way is the *most* humane and respectful to the animal. In 2012 British newspapers reported in scandalised tones that a glut of religiously slaughtered halal meat had been passed off via burger bars, restaurants and supermarkets to the general public. The outcry was immediate. Slaughter without stunning is illegal in Britain and throughout the EU, though there is a derogation for religious communities to kill *for their own consumption*. Over-production of halal meat and dumping the surplus on the open market therefore was a crime.

It took a month of hard talking before I was allowed to visit a religious slaughterhouse – name and location to be withheld – and see the procedure for myself. The Qur'an is very clear on the point. 'You are forbidden carrion, blood and the flesh of swine', it says, 'also any flesh dedicated to any other than God. You are forbidden the flesh of strangled animals and those beaten or gored to death; of those killed by a fall or mangled by beasts of prey (unless you make it clean by giving the death stroke yourselves); also of animals sacrificed to idols.' It means in effect that the animal has to be alive at the moment of slaughter. This rules out the captive bolt, used to stun cattle in non-religious slaughterhouses, which pierces the animal's skull though doesn't kill it. For strict Islamic authorities it also rules out the electrical stunning of sheep and chickens. They believe the bolt or stun itself could kill, thus reducing the animal to 'carrion'. To dedicate the animals in the name of Allah, the slaughterman must recite a prayer over each one before severing the jugular vein, carotid artery and windpipe with a single stroke of his blade. All 'flowing blood' is then drained from the body. It is said that the animal itself hears the prayer and is soothed by it.

Both orthodox Jews and Muslims argue that ritual slaughter causes no distress. A cow will be unconscious within a few seconds and dead within half a minute. A sheep will die in twenty seconds. In all cases the animal will be unconscious before it feels anything. But veterinarians see things differently. Before it can have its throat cut, a cow first has to be immobilised, which means restraining it within a tight pen with hydraulic rams. Does this cause distress? Does the cut itself cause pain? How long does the animal take to die? To these the vets answer: Yes, Yes, and Too long. Loss of blood does not cause immediate loss of consciousness in every case. Researchers in New Zealand measured electrical activity in the brains of calves after their throats had been cut and recorded a distinct pain response. No such response occurred in animals that had been stunned. This was why slaughter without stunning was generally banned in Europe (and banned totally in Norway, Iceland, Switzerland and Sweden), and why vets wanted to see it ended everywhere. How does ritual slaughter look in practice? This is part of what I wrote at the time:

It is much like any other well-run slaughterhouse. Live animals are delivered; dead ones taken out. The floor is slippery with blood, and I have to pick my way around neatly-packed trays of recently-pumping hearts and lungs. In the yard are two huge tanks – one filling with blood, the other with the grassy mess that comes from ovine stomachs. The stomachs themselves are hanging on racks indoors, awaiting export. Other bits and pieces – heads, tails, feet, skins, glands, intestines – lie in their designated bins.

Now I am watching a nose-to-tail file of lambs, like commuters on an escalator, rising on a conveyor for their appointment with the knife. I calculate that their throats are cut at the rate of one every seven seconds. The average apparently is nine. The slaughterhouse stands on the edge of town in a valley surrounded by hills. Lorries deliver 3000 lambs a day, 15,000 a week. No metaphor was ever more apt than 'lambs to the slaughter'. Sheep are the ultimate herd animals. Contentment in a lamb is having another lamb to follow, a virtue which, at farm and slaughterhouse, converts them into self-loading cargo. Small wonder that religious leaders throughout history have been depicted as shepherds, and lambs as icons of innocence.

From the lorries they move into the covered lairage, where a sequence of pens leads stage by stage to the killing point. As each batch moves on, so the next one fills the space behind it, quiet and obedient as only lambs know how to be. Finally they reach a rotary pen divided like a revolving door into segments. This swivels so that each batch in turn aligns with a doorway, where stands the last shepherd they will see on earth. He steers the first one through, then stands back as the others jostle into line. Ahead of them waits a man with a knife.

I am on the other side of the doorway now, standing on a slatted floor above the lairage. It is a food production area, so I have had to put on a white overall, rubber boots, hair-net and beard snood. We wait while the slaughterman whets his knife. From behind me comes the sudden roar of machinery. 'Blood pump,' says my host, whom I shall call Hashim. All is now ready. Mute and unprotesting, the first three lambs come up from the pen. They are pinioned between the two rubber belts of a V-shaped conveyor that bears them smoothly upwards towards us. As the first one arrives, the conveyor stops like a checkout belt. Swish. The slaughterman is so fast, I hardly see what he does. The lamb's chin is tilted and in a micro-second the blade has done its work. Jugular vein, carotid artery, windpipe – all have been severed. No blood now flows to the brain, but flows instead from the neck. Immediately, soundlessly, the lamb slumps and becomes still. By law it has to lie untouched for 20 seconds while its life ebbs away. Then the belts start again, the dead lamb is hoisted by a hind leg on to a shackle and glides away on an overhead conveyor where, on its short journey to the processors, it will spill the 'flowing blood' that Islamic law insists must be removed. On average, says Hashim, it takes 90 seconds for a lamb to bleed out. As far as I can tell, it has been a swift and peaceful end. The collapse is immediate, and the animal doesn't move until the post-death convulsions kick in. You can look death literally in the eyes. As Hashim shows me, they are closed while the animal is unconscious but open again in death.

I watch two more lambs die like the first, but then the rhythm changes. The door now opens like a floodgate, and the lambs flow uncountably in a seamless river of wool. What follows is controversial, and central to any debate about halal. Another man now joins the crew. He holds a wand with a forked end squirting water, and it is he who steps forward as the next lamb reaches the top. The points of the fork are electrodes that bridge the animal's head; the water ensures conductivity. This is the electrical stunner that will render each lamb insensible before slaughter, and keep it insensible until it dies. It is how the system here normally works – the non-stun killings were a demonstration for my benefit – and with one minor exception it is exactly what happens in every other slaughterhouse that deals in lamb.

The exception is that the slaughterman mutters a prayer each time before he makes a cut. Hashim asks him to speak up. Like the cut itself, it is short and swift. *Bismillah, Allahu akbar* – in the name of God, God is great. Without the prayer, the meat cannot be halal; otherwise the method is exactly the same as you would see in any other slaughterhouse. The welfare of the animal and the quality of the meat are the same, which is why it is acceptable to supermarkets. Only a bigot would mind that three short words have been spoken over it, or believe that this constitutes, as one newspaper insisted, 'a cruel and barbarous way that causes unnecessary suffering to animals'.

Unless, that is, you believe *all* slaughter is cruel. Any method of slaughter is only as good as its worst practitioners, and conventional slaughterhouses can hardly boast a clean slate. Electric stunners are not perfect. Sometimes the electrodes may be incorrectly placed, or the wool too thick. Then the lamb receives a painful jolt but stays conscious and must be stunned again. This happened three times as I watched. Instead of collapsing, the animal struggled until the second shock quietened it. My guide told me this happened on average five to ten per cent of the time. It was partly with regret, and partly with relief, that I was allowed no opportunity to witness the slaughtering of cattle. There are horrific images on the internet of botched attempts. A frantic cow, half-severed head flopping over a partition, scrabbles like a newborn to stay on its feet. Another with its windpipe cut tries hopelessly to articulate its distress. Another falls and struggles to stand up again. But these are the work of incompetents; not the way it is supposed to be. All slaughterhouses of every kind are invisible to the public eye. None can guarantee that no animal ever suffers. No slaughterman has any aspiration of sainthood. Throughout the meat industry, in all its factions and facets, there are few places where an accusing finger might not point. To non-Muslims, a seventh-century prophet might not look like the best arbiter of twenty-first-century welfare. To Muslims, the obsession with non-stun slaughter looks like prejudice. For caring Muslims, Jews and heathens alike, every mouthful of meat requires a kind of faith.

Faith or despair? Every vision of the future rests on one or the other, hoping for the best or dreading the worst. In considering the natures of wild animals and their relationship to ourselves, few writers are more uplifting than Frans de Waal. But few are more clear-eyed. Reading him, you feel he wouldn't mind being reincarnated as a bonobo in the Congo or a chimpanzee in Tanzania, but absolutely not an orang-utan in Borneo. The world has not been kind to the old man of the forest. Orang-utans are not like foxes or pigeons, catfish, blackbirds, spiders or mice. Stripped of their historic environments they cannot just shuffle off into the city and adapt to new ways of living. Stripped of the forests, they are stripped of their lives. Confused juveniles cling to the last few saplings in a burned-down forest, while adults foraging in farmland are shot as pests. 'If I were born tomorrow as an orangutan,' says de Waal, 'and you were to offer me a choice between living in the jungles of Borneo or at one of the world's finest zoos, I would probably not choose Borneo.'

Few things within the conservation movement divide opinion more sharply than zoos. Many have campaigned for their abolition as vigorously as they campaigned against animals in circuses or birds in battery cages. They believe it is plainly cruel, and hence morally wrong, to shut a wild animal in a cage for no better reason than to display it to the public. But others argue that there *is* a better reason: the conservation, breeding and reintroduction into the wild of critically endangered species. The argument is more complicated than it sounds. Over the last few decades the balance between entertainment and education in zoos has decisively shifted. During my own childhood in the 1950s one of the unmissable delights of London Zoo was the chimpanzees' tea party, when chimps were dressed in human clothes and presented as living cartoons sitting around a table with cups, plates and teapots. If I were luckier still, I might be treated to a ride on an elephant or a camel. A dimmer memory is of riding in a cart pulled by a llama. With few exceptions, this fairground aspect of the 'zoo experience' is long gone and unmourned. The reasons for keeping wild animals in captivity are now very different.

Arabian oryx, European bison and Mauritius kestrel have all been returned to the wild through breeding programmes in zoos. As climate change, pollution, deforestation and urbanisation take ever-larger bites out of their habitats, zoos remain the best hope for many others. But here is a conundrum. Lost and degraded habitats are the reason animals become endangered, and there is no point returning them to those same environments unless they have been restored. Fiddling with the ecosystem seldom works, no matter how benign or malevolent the intentions of those who do the fiddling. Sacrificing forest for palm oil and beef is an environmental and ecological disaster, but so are misguided attempts at 'rewilding'. Ecologists learned a hard lesson on the vast Oostvaardersplassen conservation area, the 'Dutch Serengeti' established on land reclaimed from the sea east of Amsterdam in the Netherlands. Unchecked populations of grazing animals caused such an imbalance between the animals' needs and available food that in 2017 thousands of deer, wild horses and cattle either starved or had to be shot.

Once nature has lost its grip, it is not easily regained. In the most fragile and dwindling environments like the forests of Borneo, hope is turning to ash. Hence Frans de Waal's inner orang-utan's preference for the zoo, and hence another dilemma. What would be the justification for confining animals that have no prospect of ever returning to the wild? You might answer: a captive specimen is better than no specimen at all. But what of species that are *not* under threat in the wild? What, apart from making a public spectacle, is the point of keeping them? Well, say the zoo-keepers, the public spectacle *is* the point. What better way to celebrate the diversity of life, and to bend public opinion to the conservationist cause, than to give people the chance to see, hear and smell living creatures? Wildlife documentaries, though valuable in their way, are poor substitutes for live encounters. They have also been convicted of sentimentality, anthropomorphism and various kinds of fakery including captive animals masquerading as wild, mismatched soundtracks and, until very recently, turning a blind eye to environmental disaster.

A favourite mantra of politicians caught on the back foot is 'Don't let the perfect be the enemy of the good.' And that really is the nub of it. In a scarred world few things are perfect. There is sentiment and there is science. There is welfare and there is conservation. All point roughly in the same direction. The comfort of an individual animal and the survival of its species may demand different and contradictory solutions. Life in a zoo may be imperfect, but life in the wild is not all it's cracked up to be either. Easy answers are as rare as hairy-nosed wombats. All we can do is try.

Zoos may be the intensive care units of the natural world, but they are not the last hope. Since 1987 a group of enthusiasts in South Africa has been working to reinvent the quagga, an extinct sub-species of the plains zebra, through selective breeding. But this is one animal among thousands. The ultimate insurance against extinction is the gene bank. The Frozen Ark Project, begun at Nottingham University in 1996, aims to collect and freeze DNA samples from as many endangered animals as it can obtain. It was not intended to be an alternative to conservation in the wild, but rather as insurance in case conservation failed. Frozen Ark is now a consortium of some twenty-seven world-leading zoos, aquaria, museums and research institutions, spread across twelve countries. There is science but there is also faith. Faith that advances in molecular biology will mean in the 'not-too-distant future' that fallen species can be re-made from these frozen cells. At the last count they held 48,000 samples from 5,500 species. Multiple practical, ethical and moral issues stand between them and the day real animals troop out of the no-longer frozen ark. All the same problems remain. If an animal perished originally through habitat loss, then where would the de-extinted newborns live if not in zoos or aquaria?

Nowhere has simple faith taken more of a beating than at sea. Even the far-sighted George Perkins Marsh, while deploring 'man's ignorant disregard of the laws of nature' in the latter half of the nineteenth century, could see no reason to doubt the infinite plenitude of the deep. A fishless ocean was as impossible to imagine as an airless atmosphere. 'The inhabitants of the waters', he wrote, 'seem comparatively secure from human pursuit or interference by the inaccessibility of their retreats, and by our ignorance of their habits – a natural result of the difficulty of observing the ways of creatures living in a medium in which we cannot exist.' The only truth in this was the confession of ignorance. Who then could suppose that the seas would ever be emptied of cod or herring? Nature abhors a vacuum: thus it followed that waters would be replenished as fast as they were harvested. Too late, the folly of this optimistic assumption was revealed more than a hundred years later on the Grand Banks cod fishery off Newfoundland. When John Cabot first anchored there in 1497 the shoals were so dense you couldn't row a boat through them. For nearly five hundred years it seemed that the North Atlantic was indeed inexhaustible. By the mid-twentieth century so many giant factory trawlers were flocking there – from Britain, Germany, Spain, France, Portugal, Russia, even China and Japan – that the lit-up fleet at night looked like a floating city. Between 1960 and 1975 it siphoned off eight million tons of fish, peaking in 1968 at 800,000 tons in a single year: big fish, small fish, spawning females, anything that swam. In 1992 the fishery collapsed. The floating city would have had as much luck casting its nets across the Sahara. Other disasters had been piling up. North Sea herring collapsed in 1978 and mackerel in 1985. There were catastrophic declines in cod, sole, skate and bass. Seabird populations in Scotland crashed because there was nothing left for them to eat.

If lessons were learned, they were soon forgotten. The European Union's Common Fisheries Policy with its wasteful 'bycatches' and 'discards' drove scientists to despair. The scientists themselves were derided as ignorant busybodies who would do better to listen to those who really knew the seas: the fishermen themselves. And so the plunder continued. Rich nations went on sending their ships to poor nations' seas, wiping out entire local populations – birds, mammals, amphibians, fish – as they went. Whole marine ecosystems were sucked out. Anything too small or too unappetising for humans was ground down into fishmeal to feed pigs and farmed salmon, while the fish that depended on it starved. No cycle was ever more vicious. In February 1998 the University of British Columbia in Vancouver published an analysis of forty-five years' worth of world fishery statistics. What they showed was the exact speed at which seafood was sliding down the scale towards plankton. Scientists divide ecosystems into 'trophic levels'. Species at trophic level 1 are swallowed by those at level 2, which in turn are eaten by level 3, and so on all the way up to sharks. The statistics confirmed the suspicion that fishermen worldwide were working their way down through the food web, shifting their attention to ever lower trophic levels as the bigger species were exhausted. In place of cod and haddock they were forced to seek invertebrates and small plankton-grazers such as anchovy. As the quality of catches declines, so does volume. Although hauls of small fish initially increase when top-level predators are eliminated, they too eventually decline as the ecosystem is compromised and other low-level competitors move in to fill the gap. Overfishing in the Black Sea, for example, reduced the number of fisheries there from twenty-six to five, opening the way for nature to fill the vacuum with jellyfish. But still the warning words were snatched away like spume on an ocean breeze. In May 2019 a UN analysis of four-year-old data concluded that thirty-three per cent of marine fish stocks were being fished unsustainably, sixty per cent were being fished right up to the sustainable limit and just seven per cent were below the limit. The same report noted that more than a third of all marine mammals were in danger of extinction.

As I write, the future of marine fish stocks around Britain is a bitterly fought issue in the UK's trade negotiations with the European Union. The 'future' being fought over, however, has less to do with conserving the stocks than with the right to exploit them. In 2020 Britain's Marine Conservation Society launched a public appeal to help protect thirty species that had already fallen into the IUCN Red List of endangered species. These included Atlantic cod (classified as vulnerable), Atlantic bluefin tuna and halibut (endangered), common skate, European eel and sturgeon (critically endangered). Around the world it is not just the relentless pressure of hooks and trawls that threatens marine life. Warming and acidifying oceans, chemical pollution, seaborne plastics, disturbance by cruise ships, undersea mining, gas and oil extraction, salination plants and offshore windfarms all come at a cost. So where do, where *can*, we go from here?

Governments like to claim that the Marine Protected Areas, which now cover twenty-nine per cent of European territorial waters, work like terrestrial nature reserves. Thirty-six per cent of English waters are 'protected' in this way. But a better terrestrial analogy would be fields with their gates left open. The title of a paper in the *Science* journal in December 2018 told its own story: 'Elevated Trawling inside Protected Areas Undermines Conservation Outcomes in a Global Fishing Hot Spot'. The researchers had taken a hard look at industrial trawl fishing in and around 727 MPAs designated by the European Union. What they found was far from the marine paradise extolled by the politicians. Fifty-nine per cent of MPAs were commercially trawled. Fishing intensity within them was 1.4 times *higher* than it was in unprotected areas, and numbers of sensitive species such as shark, rays and skate were sixty-nine per cent *lower*. This 'widespread industrial exploitation of MPAs', the report concluded, 'undermines global biodiversity conservation targets' and intensifies rising concerns about 'growing human pressures on protected areas worldwide'.

At sea as on land, concerned scientists look in vain for leadership from their governments. Conservation charities now focus their attention on consumers. If you care about the environment, they say, then eat haddock, not cod; pollock, not squid. Always check with your fishmonger that the fish you buy is 'sustainably sourced'. But what fishmonger is going to say that it isn't? And how many people realistically are going to question the pedigree of their fish and chips, their *bourride*, *sole meunière* or *Pfannfisch*? Critics of the fishing industry are beginning to sound much like critics of industrial farming. If you *really* care about the environment, they say, don't eat fish at all.

Against both the anti-fishing and anti-meat lobbies stands a confederacy of competing interests, from religious and political dogma to superstition and the free market. Environmentalism is anathema to populist and right-wing politics. Economies must grow and stay healthy, at whatever cost to those who are trampled. These include many of those unlucky enough to belong to the wrong species. Animal suffering is locked into the market. For American trade negotiators it is an article of faith. The arguments about chlorine-washed chicken, hormone-fed beef and factory-farm antibiotics are passed off as concern for human health. Is this stuff fit for us to eat? The contented existence of many millions of overweight Americans is evidence that can be read either way. For free-market purists, any hindrance to trade is small-minded, parochial and protectionist. The protections their opponents have in mind, however, are not all about local markets and not even all about humans. Chemical treatments of American livestock are made necessary only by insanitary farming practices. Suffering animals have to be kept alive so that we can eat them and stay healthy. Except, of course, there is nothing at all healthy about relying on antibiotics to compensate for poor husbandry. If a malevolent scientist wanted to design a system for breeding antibiotic-resistant 'superbugs', then he could hardly do better than the factory farm. This is why the British National Health Service discourages the routine prescription of antibiotics for minor infections – an example yet to be followed by the world farming industry. Viruses no less than bacteria love densely packed indoor spaces with social distancing of zero. Pathogens in a factory farm are like matches in a gunpowder store. On chicken farms they explode with lethal force. Worse still, they change as they go into new forms that can jump species from animal to human, a process known as 'antigenic shift'. The global spread of H5N1 'bird flu' in 2005 originated in chicken farms. The 2009 H1N1 'swine flu' pandemic was nature's price for cheap pork. No one will have forgotten the most recent and most expensive species-hopper, the Covid-19 virus that hopped off a bat and found its way into a human at a live animal market in Wuhan. The result was a catastrophic loss of human life and the darkly comical irony of humanitarians hailing each new grim statistic as manna to their cause.

For those who campaign against cruelty the gains have been small. In 2018 the Greek government imposed a load restriction of a hundred kilograms, or a fifth of their own body weight, on donkeys on the holiday island of Santorini. Good news for three hundred of the world's two hundred million working animals, if rather less for obese holidaymakers who would have to struggle up the six hundred steps from the port to the town on their own. At the other end of the Mediterranean, the working lives of Spain's fighting bulls can be measured in minutes. For welfare charities in the age of Facebook and Twitter the nearest thing to good news here is an increasing degree of polarisation. The death or maiming of a matador will be mourned by some, but greeted on social media with rejoicing by others. Women may still throw their underwear at matadors, but the knickers now are likely to be of a larger size as the fans grow older. Bit by bit the young are turning away. Spain now has an entire political party, *Partido Animalista Contra el Maltrato Animal* (Animalist Party Against Animal Abuse) or Pacma, which is dedicated to animal rights and is fiercely opposed to the *corrida*. In Madrid, protestors come out in their tens of thousands to demand an end to what no one in Spain, not even those who cherish it as the lodestar of Spanish culture, dares to call a sport. Bullfighting special- ises in slow deaths and its own death will not be swift. But its life is slowly ebbing away. A national survey in 2016 revealed that only nineteen per cent of Spanish people aged between sixteen and sixty-five now take any interest in it, and sixty per cent of eighteen- to twenty-four-year-olds sup- port Pacma's campaign for a ban. In the general election of April 2019, only the byzantine complexities of the Spanish electoral system denied Pacma seats in Congress. It believes its time will come. The Covid-19 lockdown meanwhile added further pressure on the shuttered arenas, and even the *aficionados* have begun to lose heart. They complain that the bulls do not have the ferocity of old, and that the best fights now are across the border in France. But this is at best a maiming, not a kill. The *banderillas* may be stuck in, but old traditions die harder than bulls. In the end it may be apathy rather than anger that delivers the final thrust, a peculiar ignominy in a country that in 1947 observed three days of national mourning after the most famous matador of his day, Manolete, was fatally gored at Linares. But few boys now yearn for a suit of lights. Dreams are more likely to wear the colours of Barcelona or Real Madrid, and many would say *Olé* to that.

But apathy won't curb the free market, or restrain the political ideologues for whom global heating is a hoax and wildlife an irritating competitor for space and resources wanted by their biological superiors. It won't bring reform to industrial farming; won't bring an end to species-hopping viruses; won't stop ivory-poaching, whaling, cosmetic breeding, tail-docking, live animal exports, trophy-hunting, the breeding and shooting of canned lions, overfed pets, the destruction of habitat, the emptying of the seas, the melting ice … Won't save any doomed life or spare a single moment of suffering. Won't repair what is broken. Only determined and concerted action can do that; people and nations united in ways never before achieved in the history of civilisation. These are not all straightforward questions of good versus bad, wrong versus right. Few things are that simple. Good people eat or don't eat meat or fish. Good people write stories that grossly distort animal natures, or make wildlife documentaries that play soothing music over the death-spiral into which so many species are locked. Good people and bad campaign for an end to animal experiments. Good people and bad oppose them. Good people and bad do nothing.

Faith will not save us either. Across the globe, Muslims, Christians, Hindus, Jews and Buddhists engage daily in lethal warfare. Religiously inspired atrocities occur even in countries not otherwise engaged in war. Children are abducted; women abused; men shot, blown up and beheaded. In 2020, in supposedly civilised countries, black people suffered violent antipathy from resentful whites obdurately convinced of the racial superiority that their own actions so graphically denied. Nationalist movements grow from roots embedded in hatred: same is good, different is bad. Pythagoras built his argument upside down. Cruelty to fellow humans did not grow out of hostility to animals. Animals suffer because humans suffer. We persecute them as we persecute those within our own communities who worship differently, speak differently, are richer or poorer, or whose skin is darker or lighter than our own. If we cannot respect differences among ourselves, then how can we respect birds and fish? Religion, politics and commerce historically have been bad friends to animals, and the long catalogue of world conflicts stands as a bloody rebuke to those who make the glib association between ideology and morality. If we really want to understand our moral selves, then it is not to the gods that we should look. It is to those who swing above us in the trees.

Afterword

The hazard with any topical book is that a great deal can happen in the months between delivery of the manuscript and the production of bound copies. History takes no account of your last full stop.

The most influential organism in the world during the first few weeks after the text was completed in the late summer and early autumn of 2020 was nature's most unwelcome gift, the Covid-19 virus. But this did nothing to slow or divert the wonder and weirdness of our relationships with all other forms of non-human life. Good intentions were no guarantee of success. In Canada, researchers found that British Columbia's policy of culling wolves was failing in its purpose of saving the mountain caribou. The real culprits were loggers stripping their habitats. Destruction of habitat had also caused the 'functional extinction' of sharks, around twenty per cent of the world's coral reefs, and a seventy-six per cent decline in populations of migratory river fish since 1970. Nor was there any prospect of improvement. A paper in the journal *Science* calculated that the flow of plastic waste into the oceans was likely to triple over the next twenty years.

In Australia, bushfires stoked by rising global temperatures in 2019 and 2020 had killed nearly three billion animals – 'one of the worst wildlife disasters in history', in the words of WWF Australia's chief executive Dermot O'Gorman. As the coronavirus continued to rampage through Europe and America, an international report warned that the sole beneficiaries of the continued destruction of natural ecosystems were bats, rats and other species most likely to carry zoonotic diseases and cause pandemics. The International Tortoise Association also reported a 'huge problem' with rats attacking pet tortoises.

For most other species in their native habitats, the outlook was wretched. Locally in Britain, the first official 'Red List' of endangered species revealed that a quarter of its native wild mammals were at 'imminent risk of extinction'. The number of hedgehogs had halved in fifty years. Globally, the situation looked even worse. The WWF and Zoological Society of London's *Living Planet Report 2020* revealed that worldwide populations of wild mammals, birds, fish, reptiles and amphibians had shrunk by more than two-thirds since 1970. Unsurprisingly, the UN's *Global Biodiversity Outlook Report* revealed that not a single global target for the protection of wildlife habitats and ecosystems had been fulfilled.

Some fine words ensued. Sixty-four leaders from five continents, including France's Emmanuel Macron, Germany's Angela Merkel, New Zealand's Jacinda Ardern, Canada's Justin Trudeau and Britain's Boris Johnson signed a 'Leaders' Pledge for Nature', embracing a ten-point plan to tackle pollution, promote sustainable development and purge the oceans of plastic. But this was like an anti-crime pledge agreed by everyone except the criminals. The presidents of the United States, Brazil and China all refused to sign, and emissions of greenhouse gases continued to rise. A report by scientists from the universities of Leeds, Edinburgh and London concluded that the Earth had lost twenty-eight trillion tonnes of surface ice since 1994, thus greatly reducing the planet's ability to reflect solar radiation back into space.

There were some scraps of good news. Thanks to conservation and reintroduction, the population of Iberian lynx in Spain and Portugal had increased ninefold since 2002. Thanks to pressure from the European Union, France declared its intention to ban the trapping of wild birds on sticks smeared with glue. In Germany, the agriculture minister Julia Klöckner caused a furore and, inevitably, 'howls of protest' by promising a new *Hundeverordnung*, or Dogs Act, compelling dog owners to walk their pets twice a day for a total of at least one hour. There was good news of a sort for tigers, whose body parts were now in such short supply that they were being replaced in Asian traditional medicine by jaguar parts trafficked from Brazil.

Zoos around the world were a rich source for headline writers. At the Lincolnshire Wildlife Centre in England, a group of five grey parrots had to be separated in order to reduce the volume of obscene language. In Poland, Warsaw Zoo launched a pilot project to test the efficacy of cannabis oil in reducing elephants' stress levels, while at Bronx Zoo in New York a forty-nine-year-old Asian elephant named Happy was furrowing the brows of lawyers and philosophers as well as vets. How happy was

Happy? It could certainly be accepted that she was self-aware, since in 2005 she became the first elephant ever to pass Gordon Gallup's mirror test. So what might be her feelings about life in solitary confinement? The question she posed was profound. In 2018, lawyers acting for the Nonhuman Rights Project (NhRP), a campaign group describing itself as 'the only civil rights organization in the US working to achieve legal rights for members of species other than our own', filed a petition of *habeas corpus* demanding 'recognition of Happy's legal personhood and fundamental right to bodily liberty'. The Bronx Supreme Court agreed that Happy was 'an intelligent autonomous being who should be treated with respect and dignity', but dismissed the petition on the ground that 'animals are not persons entitled to rights and protections afforded by the writ of *habeas corpus*'. The serious point was that Happy is more than just a 'thing', or legal property, and that taking her from the wild was an infringement of her personal rights. A judgment on the NhRP's appeal against the court's judgment was expected in late 2020.

The assumption of human exceptionalism took a further knock when researchers in America discovered yet another parallel between humans and apes. Chimpanzees in old age do exactly as humans do, reducing their social contacts and relying on a smaller circle of well-established friends. Viewed in an evolutionary light, it might make more sense to say that humans in old age behave exactly as chimpanzees do. With supreme irony given the likely origins of Covid-19, we can also compare ourselves to bats. A study published in the journal *Behavioral Ecology* showed that wild vampire bats do exactly as Covid patients are told to do, isolating themselves when they are sick.

In Europe, a skirmish between vegans and the meat lobby ended with defeat for the carnivores when the European Parliament rejected their attempt to ban the use of terms such as 'veggie burger' and 'veggie sausage'. Even in Germany, a country unequalled for its love of sausage, veggie versions were pushing *Bratwurst* off the plate. A survey published in the journal *Foods* revealed that forty per cent of German people were reducing their consumption of meat. The livestock trade meanwhile seemed more to resemble the art market when a six-month-old ram called Double Diamond was sold in Lanark, Scotland, for a world record £367,500. More welcome market news came when the British government announced that it would not allow imports of chlorinated chicken or hormone-fed beef from the US.

Out in the wild, as ever, nature continued to astonish. An elderly pigeon called Pidge found its way back to its birthplace in New Zealand after an absence of twenty-four years. New Zealand was also the destination of a bar-tailed godwit which set a new non-stop flight record of 7,500 miles across the Pacific from Alaska. A rather less welcome airborne visitor was the giant 'murder hornet', so venomous that it can destroy entire honeybee colonies and cause renal failure in humans, which arrived to terrorise Washington State in the US. But it was another insect, the 'diabolical ironclad beetle', that presented the most serious challenge to credibility. Being stamped on or run over by a car was of no more concern to this tiny native of the American west coast than the fluttering of autumn leaves. Tests showed it could withstand loads of 39,000 times its own bodyweight, equivalent to an average human bearing the weight of 280 double-decker buses.

Acknowledgements

Where to begin? Throughout my working life I have been indebted to people who have shown me fresh ways of looking, and never more so than to those who – for the most part unknowingly – helped me shape this book. The idea of it came to me when reading Matt Cartmill's enthralling history of hunting, *A View to a Death in the Morning*, and James Serpell's magisterial history of pet-keeping, *In the Company of Animals*. This led me onward to Steven Mithen's *The Prehistory of the Mind* and Keith Thomas's *Man and the Natural World*, which I had ample time to absorb and which buoyed my spirits while recovering from illness. Thus informed, and with the encouragement of my agent Jonathan Pegg and editor Sam Carter, I took a deep breath and immersed myself in a reading list that refused to stop growing.

A reviewer of my previous book complained about the absence of footnotes. I am afraid I am going to disappoint him again. Instead of dotting the pages with references I have been careful throughout the text to make clear which authors or historical sources I am relying on. One or two of these deserve special mention. Menno Schilthuizen's *Darwin Comes to Town*, which explains how the drift of wildlife into cities is accelerating the pace of evolution, and Frans de Waal's *Are We Smart Enough to Know How Smart Animals Are?* and *Mama's Last Hug*, which demolish the barrier between human and animal intelligence, are eye-openers that should be read by anyone with even the smallest interest in the world around them.

I must thank also my old friend, the unsurpassable writer and photographer of African wildlife Brian Jackman, who generously provided many of the images, and Rida Vaquas, who researched and tracked down the rest. She also expertly translated the quoted passages from Felix Salten's *Bambi: A Forest Life*. A big thank-you also to my eagle-eyed copy-editor Kathleen McCully for steering me away from error.

As ever, I fail at the last hurdle, which is to find words enough to thank Caroline, to whom this work is dedicated. It is a simple fact that not a word of it would have been written without her. Every weekday for seven weeks she drove me thirty miles to hospital, and did so while still recovering from a serious illness of her own. With her support and encouragement, much of the early preparatory work was done in the radiotherapy suite of the Norfolk and Norwich Hospital, to which must go my final word of thanks. More than most when we ventured out to clap the carers during the Covid-19 outbreak in 2020, we had cause to be grateful.

Further Reading

The following titles were among the works consulted during the preparation of this book. A few of the earlier ones are available in later editions or in facsimile, and some are freely available online. Others may be available only in specialist libraries.

For background reading I recommend the works of Matt Cartmill, Steven Mithen, James Serpell and Keith Thomas. For sheer delight and astonishment, see Frans de Waal and Menno Schilthuizen.

Aesop: *Aesop's Fables* (620–564 BC)

Anon.: *Dives and Pauper* (fifteenth century)

Aristotle: *The History of Animals* (fourth century BC)

Aquinas, St Thomas: *Summa contra Gentiles* (1259–1265)

Augustine of Hippo: *City of God* (fifth century)

Bacon, Francis: *Of the Proficience and Advancement of Learning, Divine and Human* (1605); *Novum Organum* (1620)

Baratay, Eric, and Hardouin-Fugier, Elisabeth: *Zoo: A History of Zoological Gardens in the West* (2002)

Bartlett, Abraham Dee: *Bartlett's Life among Wild Beasts* (1900)

Beard, Mary: *SPQR* (2016)

Bekoff, Marc: 'Animal Emotions: Exploring Passionate Natures' (paper in *BioScience*, October 2000)

Bentham, Jeremy: *An Introduction to the Principles of Morals and Legislation* (1780)

Biswas, S. *et al.*: 'Current Knowledge on the Environmental Fate, Potential Impact, and Management of Growth-Promoting Steroids Used in the US Beef Cattle Industry' (paper in *Journal of Soil and Water Conservation,* July/August 2013)

Buck, Frank: *Bring 'em Back Alive* (1930); *Wild Cargo* (1932)

Buckland, William: *Reliquiae Diluvianae* (1823); *Bridgewater Treatise* (1836)

Byron (Lord), George Gordon, 6th Baron: *Don Juan, Canto XIII* (1823)

Carcopino, Jerome: *Daily Life in Ancient Rome* (1941)

Carson, Gerald: 'T.R. and the "Nature Fakers"' (article in *American Heritage* magazine, 1971)

Carson, Rachel: *Silent Spring* (1962)

Cartmill, Matt: *A View to a Death in the Morning: Hunting and Nature through History* (1993)

Clutton-Brock, Julia: *Domesticated Animals from Early Times* (Heinemann and British Museum, Natural History, 1981)

Cobbe, Frances Power: *Vivisection in America* (1890)

Cobbett, William: *Cottage Economy* (1821)

Daston, Lorraine and Mitman, Gregg (eds): *Thinking with Animals* (2005)

Darwin, Charles: *On the Origin of Species* (1859); *The Descent of Man, and Selection in Relation to Sex* (1871); *The Expression of the Emotions in Man and Animals* (1872)

Darwin, F. (ed.): *The Life and Letters of Charles Darwin* (1896)

Davies, Norman: *Europe: A History* (1996)

de Waal, Frans: *Are We Smart Enough to Know How Smart Animals Are?* (2016); *Mama's Last Hug* (2019)

Dobrenko, Evgeny: *Political Economy of Socialist Realism* (2007)

Flacelière, Robert: *Daily Life in Greece at the Time of Pericles* (1959; English translation 1965)

Fleury, Abbé Claude: *Les Moeurs des Israelites*, or *The Manners of the Ancient Israelites* (1661)

Food Climate Research Network: *Grazed and Confused* (report, 2017)

Friends of the Earth (various authors): *Why Women Will Save the Planet* (2015)

Gessner, Conrad: *Historiae animalium* (1551)

Girling, Richard: *The Hunt for the Golden Mole* (2014); *The Man Who Ate the Zoo* (2016)

Goodall, Jane: *My Friends the Wild Chimpanzees* (1967)

Gordon-Cumming, Roualeyn: *Five Years of a Hunter's Life in the Far Interior of South Africa* (1850)

Grandin, Temple: 'Evaluation of the Welfare of Cattle Housed in Outdoor Feedlot Pens' (paper in *Veterinary and Animal Science*, 2016)

Guerrini, Anita: *Experimenting with Humans and Animals: From Galen to Animal Rights* (2003)

Hagenbeck, Carl: *Beasts and Men* (1909)

Hall, Edith: *Introducing the Ancient Greeks* (2015); *Aristotle's Way* (2018)

Harrison, Ruth: *Animal Machines* (1964)

Hitler, Adolf: *Mein Kampf* (1925)

Hole, Christina: *Witchcraft in England* (1977)

Hume, David: *Essays Moral, Political, and Literary* (1882)

Huxley, Elspeth: *Peter Scott: Painter and Naturalist* (1993)

Huxley, Thomas Henry: *Has a Frog a Soul?* (1850)

Keegan, John: *A History of Warfare* (1993)

Kramer, Heinrich, and Sprenger, James: *Malleus Maleficarum* (1486)

Labarge, Margaret Wade: *A Baronial Household of the Thirteenth Century* (1965)

Lane Fox, Robin: *The Classical World* (2005)

Laurence, John: *A New System of Agriculture* (1726)

Leopold, Aldo: *A Sand County Almanac* (1949)

Lewis, C.S.: *The Problem of Pain* (1940)

Linnaeus, Carl: *Systema Naturae* (1735)

Locke, John: *Some Thoughts Concerning Education* (1693)

Lutts, Ralph H.: 'The Trouble with Bambi' (article in *Forest and Conservation History*, October 1992)

Lymbery, Philip, with Oakeshott, Isabel: *Farmageddon: The True Cost of Cheap Meat* (2014)

Marsh, George Perkins: *Man and Nature; or Physical Geography as Modified by Human Action* (1864)

McClintock, Inez, and McClintock, Marshall: *Toys in America* (1961)

Mill, John Stuart: *Nature and Utility of Religion* (1858)

Mithen, Steven: *The Prehistory of the Mind* (1996)

Mivart, St George: *The Common Frog* (1874)

More, Thomas: *Utopia* (1516)

Nietzsche, Friedrich: *Human, All Too Human: A Book for Free Spirits* (1878); *On the Genealogy of Morals* (1878)

Oldfield Howey, M.: *The Cat in Magic, Mythology, and Religion* (1955)

Osborn, Fairfield: *Our Plundered Planet* (1948)

Paley, William: *Natural Theology, or Evidences of the Existence and Attributes of the Deity Collected from the Appearances of Nature* (1802)

Pliny: *Natural History* (*Naturalis Historiae*, 77 AD)

Prideaux, Sue: *I am Dynamite: A Life of Friedrich Nietzsche* (2018)

Regan, Tom: *The Case for Animal Rights* (1983)

Romanes, George: *Animal Intelligence* (1878)

Roosevelt, Theodore: *African Game Trails* (1910)

Rousseau, Jean-Jacques: *Emile, or On Education* (1762)

Salten, Felix: *Bambi: A Forest Life* (1924)

Schilthuizen, Menno: *Darwin Comes to Town* (2018)

Schopenhauer, Arthur: *Parerga und Paralipomena* (1851)

Scott, Peter: *The Eye of the Wind* (1961)

Serpell, James: *In the Company of Animals* (1986)

Schwarzenbach, Alexis: *Saving the World's Wildlife: WWF – the First 50 Years* (2011)

Sharma, Vishnu: *The Panchatantra* (c.1200 BC–300 AD)

Shaw, George Bernard: *The Doctor's Dilemma* (1906); *Back to Methuselah: A Metabiological Pantateuch* (1921)

Shaw, Ian: *The Oxford History of Ancient Egypt* (2000)

Shelley, Percy Bysshe: *A Vindication of Natural Diet* (1813)

Singer, Peter: *Animal Liberation* (1975)

Slater, P.J.B.: *Essentials of Animal Behaviour* (1999)

Thomas, Keith: *Man and the Natural World* (1983)

Thorndike, Edward: *Animal Intelligence* (1898)

Topsell, Edward: *Topsell's Histories of Beasts* (1607–8, ed. Malcolm South, 1981)

Tryon, Thomas: *The Way to Health, Long Life and Happiness* (1683)

Ward, Geoffrey C.: *The West: An Illustrated History* (1996)

Washburn, Margaret: *The Animal Mind: A Textbook of Comparative Psychology* (1908, 1917)

Weiner, Douglas R.: *Models of Nature: Ecology, Conservation, and Cultural Revolution in Soviet Russia* (1988)

Weyler, Rex: *Greenpeace: How a Group of Ecologists, Journalists, and Visionaries Changed the World* (2004)

White, T.H. (trans.): *The Book of Beasts: Being a Translation from a Latin Bestiary of the Twelfth Century* (1954)

Wohlleben, Peter: *The Inner Life of Animals* (2016)

Worboys, Gordon; Strange, Julie-Marie; Pemberton, Neil: *The Invention of the Modern Dog* (2018)

Wrangham, Richard and Peterson, Dale: *Demonic Males: Apes and the Origins of Human Violence* (1997)

Wray, Britt: *Rise of the Necrofauna* (2017)

Zelko, Frank: 'Warriors of the Rainbow: the Birth of an Environmental Mythology' (online article at Environment & Society Portal, *Arcadia*, 2013)

Index

NOV 1 7 2021

WITHDRAWN